GHOSTS OF TRANSPARENCY — SHADOWS CAST AND SHADOWS CAST OUT

T0338925

APPLIED VIRTUALITY BOOK SERIES VOL. 13

GHOSTS OF TRANSPARENCY — SHADOWS CAST AND SHADOWS CAST OUT

MICHAEL R. DOYLE, SELENA SAVIĆ, VERA BÜHLMANN

BIRKHÄUSER
Basel

ASSIST. PROF. DR. MICHAEL R. DOYLE
Assistant professor at the Université Laval School of Architecture, Québec, Canada

DR. SELENA SAVIĆ
Researcher at the Institute for Experimental Design and Media, University of Applied Sciences
and Arts Northwestern Switzerland (FHNW), Basel, Switzerland

PROF. DR. VERA BÜHLMANN
Chair for Architecture Theory and Philosophy of Technics, Faculty of Architecture and Spatial
Planning, Vienna University of Technology (TU Vienna), Austria

SERIES EDITORS
PROF. DR. LUDGER HOVESTADT
Chair for Computer Aided Architectural Design (CAAD),
Institute for Technology in Architecture (ITA), Swiss Federal Institute of Technology (ETH),
Zurich, Switzerland

PROF. DR. VERA BÜHLMANN
Chair for Architecture Theory and Philosophy of Technics, Faculty of Architecture and Spatial
Planning, Vienna University of Technology (TU Vienna), Austria

ACQUISITIONS EDITOR: David Marold, Birkhäuser Verlag, A-Vienna
CONTENT AND PRODUCTION EDITOR: Angelika Gaal, Birkhäuser Verlag, A-Vienna
COPY EDITING AND PROOF READING: Michael R. Doyle, Selena Savić
LAYOUT AND COVER DESIGN: onlab, CH-Geneva, www.onlab.ch
TYPEFACE: Korpus, binnenland (www.binnenland.ch)
PRINTING AND BINDING: buch.one, D-Pliezhausen

The publisher and editor kindly wish to inform you that in some cases, despite efforts to do so, the
obtaining of copyright permissions and usage of excerpts of text is not always successful.

Library of Congress Control Number: 2019945977

Bibliographic information published by the German National Library
The German National Library lists this publication in the Deutsche Nationalbibliografie; detailed
bibliographic data are available on the Internet at http://dnb.dnb.de.

ISSN 2196-3118
ISBN 978-3-0356-1911-9
e-ISBN (PDF) 978-3-0356-1917-1 Open Access

© 2019 Birkhäuser Verlag GmbH, Basel
P.O. Box 44, 4009 Basel, Switzerland
Part of Walter de Gruyter GmbH, Berlin/Boston

9 8 7 6 5 4 3 2 1

www.birkhauser.com

TABLE OF CONTENTS

INTRODUCTION —GHOSTS OF TRANSPARENCY: SHADOWS CAST AND SHADOWS CAST OUT
MICHAEL R. DOYLE, SELENA SAVIĆ, VERA BÜHLMANN

I have heard articulate speech produced by sunlight! I have heard a ray of the sun laugh and cough and sing
I have been able to hear a shadow, and I have even perceived by ear the passage of a cloud across the sun's disc.
— Alexander Graham Bell (February 26, 1880).[1]

Code. Protocol. Channel. Data. Information. In everyday conversations, these words do not evoke images of buildings or of cities. And yet they have entered the common parlance of an architecture and urbanism looking to computation and quantum physics for inspiration. As the net is cast wider and other disciplines and fields are probed for concepts and theories, new words are gathered and circulated: Entropy. Negentropy. Isotropy. Anisotropy. Spectrum. Manifold. These words are appropriated and articulated into novel constellations of meaningfulness, as well as meaninglessness respectively.

At a certain point, communities form around particular words or groups of words, boundaries are drawn and territories with regard to

---

[1]   Alexander Graham Bell to Alexander Melville Bell, 'Letter from Alexander Graham Bell to Alexander Melville Bell', 26 February 1880 <http://hdl.loc.gov/loc.mss/magbell.00510307>.

worth and values are established. Faced with a jargon that has become sedimented, overused and corrupted, scholarship today tends to call for a new and adequate vocabulary for describing a novel common condition. We tend to disagree. With the abundance of words currently circulating in discussions around information and architecture, the challenge is not to supplement or supplant them with neologisms, but rather to engage with them anew, as something 'strange', unlikely, and even 'unknown'. In this edited volume, we want to *meet* with these words, not more and not less. The passage from the implicit to the explicit is not primarily an epistemological one, but, significantly, an architectonic one; and this means it can be not only a path that proceeds logically, and consequentially, but one that needs to cut angles, to proceed cunningly, in short: the passage from implicit to explicit is also always a literary one that draws from rhetorics, poetics, mechanics; it is one of construction, of plotting, of 'treatments', we could perhaps say, in the most general sense.

In the first book of *De Architectura*, the Roman architect Vitruvius writes that "architects who have aimed at acquiring manual skill (*fabrica*) without scholarship have never been able to reach a position of authority to correspond to their pains, while those who relied only upon theories (*ratiocinatio*) and scholarship were obviously hunting the shadow, not the substance."[2] To think of the shadow in this fashion suggests that *ratiocinatio*—skills in rendering intelligibility, rationalization—that remains disconnected from practical experience seeks hospitality in an immediate luminosity (an 'enlightening'), and will seek to protect it by hunting and eliminating shadows. *Fabrica*—manual skill or instrumentalization—that seeks no distancing from its workings takes place under a light that is unreasoned, whose source of luminance is taken for granted. In the case of the former, shadows are cast out; in that of the latter, shadows are simply cast. The training of the architect then lies in learning to invent how to treat a paradox[3] in the real but 'impossible' domain we want to call 'architectonic' here, a domain where shadow is constitutive and light can be related to only in diffractive and mediate manners.[4] Vitruvius's statement, which is historically so far from the present, seems to resonate with our contemporary thinking. If

---

2   Vitruvius, trans. by M. H. Morgan, *On Architecture*, Book 1, Chapter 1, trans. Morgan, (Cambridge, MA: Harvard University Press, 1914). Latin original: "[A]rchitecti qui sine litteris contenderant ut manibus essent exercitati, non potuerunt efficere ut haberent pro laboribus auctoritatem. Qui autem ratiocinationibus et litteris solis confisi fuerant, umbram non rem persecuti videntur. At qui utrumque perdidicerunt, uti omnibus armis ornati, citius cum auctoritate quod fuit propositum sunt adsecuti" (Vitruvius, trans. by A. Choisy, *De Architectura*, Book 1 Chapter 1, (Paris: Imprimerie-Librairie Lahure, 1909)).
3   Bernard Tschumi, 'The Architectural Paradox', in *Architecture and Disjunction*, Paperback ed., 5. print (Cambridge, Mass.: MIT Press, 1999) 218–28.
4   Vera Bühlmann, Felicity Colman, and Iris Van der Tuin, 'Introduction to New Materialist Genealogies: New Materialisms, Novel Mentalities, Quantum Literacy', *The Minnesota Review*, 2017, 47–58.

it is meaningful to speak of architectonics with regard to communication at all, then it must know how to consider and relate to the shadows that are being cast—and cast out.

Information and data are not synonyms: data (etymologically, the 'given') has to be treated, articulated, read or deciphered in such a way as to contain information. The sheer amount of data today tends to obscure this important difference between data and information: data is entropic, while information is where this entropy is negated; information is negentropic. An emerging political imperative of 'transparency' conflates the abundance of data with an increase in information. Unfortunately, the reverse is often the case: The more 'data' is rendered available and passed off as 'information' or 'knowledge', the more opaque the dealings with 'information' become. This is perhaps one of the greatest challenges we face with regard to becoming literate in the algorithmic and symbolization processes that organize data in our world today[5]—processes we refer to here as 'ghosts of transparency'.

What, you may ask, does this have to do with architecture and urbanism? Data and software are thought to reshape the city, while the word 'architecture' refers equally often to buildings and to the organization of computer software and hardware components. With this book, we want to cast a projective space that accommodates various *Auseinandersetzungen* (settings, or setting ups, articulated dispositions of grounds that are quarrelsome) with implicit and explicit mixtures of these two domains interpenetrating each other.

Contributions are, we could say, short enough to make a point, yet long enough to glimpse the great variety of 'scales' of abstractive contemplation that these points index. In architecture, like in many disciplines today, there is a proliferation of terms coming from information technology and mathematics: data, negentropy, spectrum, manifold, archive, communication, topology, digital, analogue. Our approach was not to seek 'experts' to define these words 'properly', nor to attempt an exhaustive overview of their uses across multiple disciplines. Nor do we claim that one new, consistent, vocabulary is necessary. The words that circulate in our discourses are themselves packets of energetic potential. In them, information channels energy, words and their usage do have an impact on our world today. We wanted to invite others to speak about these words as they begin to grow into a novel kind of 'force'—to *project*

---

5   Felicity Colman et al., *Ethics of Coding: A Report on the Algorithmic Condition [EoC]* (Brussels: European Commission, 2018) <https://cordis.europa.eu/project/rcn/207025_en.html>; *Coding as Literacy: Metalithikum IV*, ed. by Vera Bühlmann, Ludger Hovestadt, and Vahid Moosavi, Applied Virtuality Book Series (Basel, Switzerland: Birkhäuser, Part of Walter de Gruyter GmbH, Berlin, 2015); Antoinette Rouvroy, *'Of Data and Men': Fundamental Rights and Freedoms in a World of Big Data* (Strasbourg: Directorate General of Human Rights and Rule of Law (European Council), 11 January 2016), 37.

a corporeality for them that is carefully considered, rich in its articulation, overall generous and accommodating of more. To address them as somehow 'strange', as both luminous and shadowy. This is no gesture of embracing obscurantism, it is merely an expressed intent to know more, for instance, about the abstractions that went into the technique of handling codes, sourcing data, devising contracts and channels, the thinking that manifests in existing communication protocols (TCP/IP) and their standardization in the Open Systems Interconnected model (OSI), or in programming interfaces (APIs), the thinking that can be unlocked from the information-processing capacity of crystals, about the form of values, about virtuality, civility and civitas, code's publicness and privacy, about technique of handling spectrums, about mathematics as a technics of symbolization and an art of learning (mathesis). In indexing these terms, through the contributions of various scholars working more or less closely with them, we hope to familiarize ourselves with domains of abstraction in which they can be understood architectonically—as instruments in the service of a professional (objective) kind of *Können* (the German term for something akin to *being more or less* [rather than bound by an 'either/or'] *proficient in*, and *capable of*). An intellectual as well as embodied mastership in dealings with 'communicational contingency'. We ask our contributors and the reader to join us on this adventure.

The book begins with a contribution by Roberto Bottazzi (Bartlett School of Architecture), *Cryptoarchitecture: Notes on Machine Learning and Design*, which looks at cryptography as a technics of opacity with regard to computational techniques in architecture that tend to uncritically embrace transparency. Bottazzi asks how a cryptoarchitecture, one that goes beyond the biologically inspired top-down or bottom-up logics of parametricism or cellular automata, could employ ciphers in order to constantly rewrite the whole of the architectonic object. Such an approach would challenge the presumption that signs should have a stable relationship to meaning, or that syntax should be coupled with semantics.

Nikola Marinčić (ETH Zurich) presents the Self-Organizing Map (SOM) algorithm of Teuvo Kohonen as the key component in addressing communication as not merely 'social' but 'natural' in a more general sense. His chapter, *An Instrument for Communication: The Self-Organizing Model*, describes the workings of an instrument that would allow us to set into communication nearly any form of coded data, with neither needing to determine the nature of their relationships nor imposing a common language. Marinčić thereby offers a potential application of the SOM that differs from its common use as a clustering or analytical tool, to instead one that can partition spectra in ways that embrace contemporary mathematical conceptions of categorization (category theory) rather than classification (set theory).

In *Formal Creatures: Gilles Châtelet's Metaphors*, Ben Woodard (Leuphana University) examines how domains that would otherwise be seemingly unrelated can be bridged through metaphor. He invites us to see metaphor not as something merely hermeneutic or wedded to a Heideggerian *Dasein*, but rather as something material, that leaves traces. The metaphor can become energetic, conducting energies, encapsulating and transmitting forces. Their contents, however, are not always perfectly explicit but like Trojan horses, can carry something implicit as well.

Miro Roman's (ETH Zurich) contribution, *Voids, Brands, Characters and How to Deal with Lots*, takes the reader through a climatic, noisy mixture of millions of images scraped from the popular ArchDaily and Dezeen architecture and design blogs. Without interrogating their semantic content, he shows us both figuratively and algorithmically how he is able to navigate these 'visual mixtures,' introducing us to avatars and personas that are partially found, partially invented. Several of our contributors are experimenting with the SOM algorithm and Roman demonstrates how one may begin to project from the topological space to the geometrical in a playful and yet 'precisely crafted' manner.

Ambiguity and Information in the Context of "Natural Communication": An Obstacle-Oriented Galoisian Standpoint, by Elias Zafiris (University of Athens / University of Budapest) challenges commonsensical understandings of the simple and the complex. Rather than treat that which cannot easily be grasped as a problem to be solved, he invites us to see such a condition as an obstacle to be 'embraced', where *metaphora* can join in communication the domains whose connections cannot be exhaustively determined. Myths, narratives and mathematical theorems share more than one might think, Zafiris demonstrates, and he discusses these connections by examining the work of mathematician Galois and Hesiod's account of the birth of Aphrodite.

Elie Ayache (ITO 33) approaches the financial market as a world that is constantly written. In *From the Bit to the Pit: Poetics of the Financial Market*, he reminds us that the paradigm of communication based on the Markov chain relies on past instances in setting up probabilistic future states. In contrast, the financial market is not regressive, but forward-looking, based not on previously identified finite states but entities that emerge, carved out into discrete states, through market exchanges. By picking up on its implicit nature, Ayache provides an alternative view of money as a medium of contingency, one not lending to abstraction but rather to the fundamentally concrete.

In *The Art of Exaggeration*, Alexi Kukuljevic (University of Applied Arts, Vienna) reads closely Thomas Bernhard's 1986 novel, *Extinction*—a book whose main character seeks to write a novel capable of extinguishing its very subject. Picking up the book's references to Jacques Lacan, Kukuljevic examines the role of exaggeration in this endeavour of extinction, where a drive towards excess combines with over and understatement, allowing for substitutions, for absent presences and an art of exaggeration that challenges the act itself of writing more so than that which is written. How is one to write when that which is written must, in fact, be extinguished?

In *Architecture, an Artificial Intelligence*, Kristian Faschingeder (TU, Vienna) examines the autonomy of architectural representation and the architectural artefact enabled by the emergence of geometry in antiquity. A project like Le Corbusier's Saint-Pierre in Firminy operates, he says, as a "cosmic instrument," independent of the architect who died before it was built. Not only the plans, but also the building, act as "intelligent artefacts." The ruler, compass or framing square, function "like an artificial memory or an automaton." The turn from the plan to the elevation, made possible by the principle of homothesis as dramatized through the story of Thales's measurement of the Egyptian pyramids, permits, Faschingeder observes, a mathematical ruse, that turns the hierarchical plan, the view from above, to the point of any observer. Architecture, he continues, becomes "quasi-invisible" in the plan, whereas the elevation allows it to become representational. The difference in the gestures of the plan and elevation share a reference point that relies on an authority that is both intellectual but also situated in space. The autonomy of the tools of representation is not, he argues, to be suppressed, but rather transgressed, less towards the economical, than towards exuberance and excess.

Giorgios Tsagdis (University of Westminster) in his contribution, *The Aural: Heidegger and Fundamental Oto-cheiro-logy II*, reflects upon the importance of the ear, of hearing, with regard to thinking time via a notion of trace that is to "complicate and transform the metaphysical logic of concealment." By relating the *epochality* of time to the *mediality* provided by the ear, such that a self can "witness itself as a record," Tsagdis is interested in a notion of the trace that reaches beyond signification. The trace becomes a sign "which might or might not signify," establishing a "non-exclusive relation between two possibilities." The ear thereby delineates a field of mediality, it is maintained in this article, from which "the author is altogether elided." It is here that a particular im-possibility of asking about the meaning of a 'we' resides—a 'we' that manifests itself as the subject of an epoch. Self (*auto*) and ear (*oto*) are always asked together, this article argues.

In *Reflections of an Imaginary Object on a Silurian Lake*, Gregg Lambert (Syracuse University) picks up the French philosopher and psychoanalyst Jacques Lacan's question of whether, in the absence of an observing human subject, the reflection of an object mirrored in a lake still exists. Lacan's answer is affirmative because to him, the reflection on the lake manifests "the phenomenon of consciousness itself," even if, as Lambert points out, such consciousness, the recording of images, can be conducted '*automatically*,' even without the presence of a human ego. At stake in this article is an interest in what could be called 'objective time'.

This is important for Lambert in examining Quentin Meillassoux's concept of the arche-fossil. The arche-fossil posits an ancestrality that would be decoupled from the human witnessing of its trace, raising questions regarding the philosophical complexity that pertains to thinking 'time itself' in relation to its 'givenness,' as it manifests in the form of 'data'.

Jorge Orozco (ETH Zurich) works with the plenty 'of what a community circulates in communication,' to articulate and demonstrate models of communication where "the third party" is reduced "to a 'grain of sand'." In *Pentecost—A Model of Communication for 21st Century Architecture* he writes about his work with programmatically sourcing information circulated around different online communities. With his application, *The Swiss Architects and Elliot Alderson* he provides an objective and poly-scalar space in which different concepts can "talk to each other" as if without intermediaries. Picking up on Michel Serres' account of the parasite, Orozco is not trying to translate between languages so as to make people understand each other. He is interested in how circuits of information facilitate recognizing, without externally referential mediation, the rare from the norm, information from data, order from disorder, negentropy from entropy. The communication which he is interested in modelling is a kind of talk about architecture that needs no mediation by an interpreter, and that orients on no authoritative articulation of its relevant or irrelevant content.

Jonathan Powers (Concordia University), in *Between* Disegno *& Design Thinking*, looks at how drawing and designing are parts of a technical, intellectual and experiential practice. If the Renaissance term *disegno* is often translated into English as *drawing*, the two, Powers highlights, have important differences. Design produces artefacts that "point beyond themselves," which suggests a kinship to writing. The design process is pushed forward by an intellectual and imaginative process, not only by technical constraints. If Renaissance artisans saw drawing by the hand as a way to practise drawing in the mind, then *disegno* is also a form of cognition and a mental capacity that can be cultivated. Looking at the work of contemporary drawing reference for architects, D. K. Ching, Powers remarks a tendency to emphasize the visual aspect of drawing, whereas *disegno* is "communicative and conjectural, not strictly 'visual thinking'." Drawings stand in for what could be or might never be seen, becoming in part a substitute for experience. This brings drawing close to prototyping, opening up *disegno* to a broader contemporary conception of "design thinking" that may help initiate a larger conversation around the intellectual and technical skills developed by the act of designing.

In *Crystal of Things*, Poltak Pandjaitan (ETH Zurich) works from state-of-the-art knowledge on crystallography and foregrounds the increasing relevance of crystals for contemporary communication and information technologies. Crystals as emergent growing structures are interesting because, quite counter-intuitively perhaps, "they have specific properties that are otherwise not found as such in nature": you will never find highly arranged crystal lattices evenly spread in all directions, he explains. Real crystals always have "some defects in the lattice or impurities in the atomic composition." Of special interest to Pandjaitan are quasicrystals, which lack any pattern of symmetry. Their aperiodic structure "acts as a language and a code" he maintains, and they can only be described by a non-perspectival geometry of parallel projections: What he calls "the crystal code" is not apparent through central perspective, rather "it keeps the information under its noisy appearance." Pandajaitan discusses an example of his own work as an architect where the crystal is approached as an algebraic language that "never makes a statement, but only translates and communicates"—a work that illustrates how to him, "communication is not the linkage of two fixed states or positions, but the interlinking of possibilities."

"The only way to look at the sun is through a 'lunar' kind of translucency," Riccardo Villa (TU, Vienna) maintains in his contribution entitled *Architecture of the Diaphanous*. In order to think the contemporary as 'modern' we need to reserve what could be called 'a locus of moderation': We need to keep space and time from being considered as coinciding with each other. We need to 'bury' modernity as a tradition, he suggests, by devising a conception of the diaphanous architectonically: The diaphanous counts to him as a 'transparent medium' through which it is possible to theorize what he calls 'lunar translucency'. Villa's contribution makes suggestions of how to reactivate, to this end, key notions of optics (reflection), harmonics (canon) and metrics (ruler). He describes as an interplay between these a notion of spectrality that comes to act as an impersonal kind of agency proper to Averroes's notion of a material intellect. Along such lines, it is to be possible to invent an architecture in which the space of dwelling can be dispositioned such as to receive the reflection of its own picturesque (realistic) representation, while at the same time being capable of living up to the classical canons that inevitably inform such picturing.

"A clock is clearly a product of human synthesis; but could genetically modified bacteria be said to be a product of human synthesis?" Martyn Dade-Robertson (Newcastle University) asks in his article *The Designs of the Natural*. He picks up the current trend to see discourses on digital technology dominated, especially in architecture and design, by the discourses around synthetic biology. But the blurry distinction between things resulting from "nature's own agencies," and things designed entirely synthetically, is neither novel nor the most significant distinction for thinking about digital technology, he maintains. Rather, profiling the two against each other, in whichever attempt to keep them strictly apart, keeps us from focusing on what Dade-Robertson foregrounds as an interesting and under-theorized kind of 'self-synthesizing' that must count as natural as well as artificial: The scandalous thought is not so much that a modified bacteria might be considered the work of human synthesis, but rather that a clock may well be seen as being a result of "nature's own agencies." This article points attention to an unsuspected role of mimesis, the key practice at work in culture, present even in the most advanced biotechnological achievements of today's science, where we are "not creating life, only mimicking it."

Like many of the articles in this book, the contribution by Adam Nocek (Arizona State University) entitled *Mythic Noise: Architectures of Geological Communication* takes issue with the currently predominant positivist account of data. But it does so in a manner that maintains a certain proximity to the intellectual concerns within which positivism actually emerged, with Auguste Comte in the 19th century. It is in a retroactive fashion that Nocek folds back, what to Comte was progressing lines of science, upon themselves. Nocek exposes how a certain theory of transitive communication—communication that transmits messages and idealizes its own workings as transparent—is always already at work when we handle the kind of facticity that rests on an evidence given by data. He argues that such a paradigm is inappropriate for attending to geo-communication technology that attends to planetary systems at various different scales, as is at stake in contemporary earth science. He proposes a properly planetary point of view too, but one that is not totalizing, summing up, and committed to a global perspective. It is a view that recognizes that "the Earth has no face," and figures out how to address it locally, how to "feel the world differently," and "how to feel and think environments" with a precision—a finesse—that is not communicative; this, he proposes to call "a mytho-praxis of geomythology."

"There is no longer any need for the moral imperative of D. Hilbert ('we must know') to affirm that 'we will know'," Philippe Morel (ENSA Paris-Malaquais) maintains in his article *Photonic Communication*. He exposes a certain anthropocentrism in the science of photonics, which to him counts as "the physical science of light (photon) generation, detection, and manipulation through emission, transmission, modulation, signal processing, switching, amplification, and detection/sensing." Morel criticizes photonic science for taking too little distance from 'the desire for meaning'. Such pre-concern keeps science from recognizing conceptual and formal horizons that are opening up through photonic technology and that deserve, according to Morel, to be traced beyond questions of predictability and determinism. These novel horizons ought to provide for the semiotic action of what he calls "photonic communication." We can seek now a concrete apprehension of "the nature of the world as algorithmic," he urges. Acknowledging this novel manner of conceiving nature (as algorithmic) would foreground that in communication, all we ever do is 'interweaving algorithms' that are, for themselves, deterministic (by definition). The photonic communication Morel advocates here calls for a novel kind of storytelling, perhaps—a storytelling whose pre-concern is no longer narrative, but the copious scripting of a natural kind of realism.

In *Softness, Hardness: Contemplating Architectonic Circuits of Mediacy and Immediacy*, Michael R. Doyle (Laval University) reflects on the conceptions in architecture and urbanism of the 'soft' and the 'hard'. Their opposition, he observes, "appears to mirror that of the sciences and humanities and seems to fuel debates on the primacy of experience over reason, immediacy over mediacy." Thinking about Michel Serres' conception of the mutual implication of the soft and the hard, he proposes a fourfold setup of softness and hardness, examining how 'data' and 'information' can be understood 'massively' as constituted by softness and hardness. He asks what this means for the architectural project today, where a transparentism and explicitness seem to haunt both the analytical paradigm as well as the techniques of projection. Who is the architect to be, he asks, if not the servant of a logical system, the administrator of a semantic ontology? If architecture is "an inventive act of placing into communication that which otherwise would not resonate," then the gesture to explore is perhaps less one of building ontological systems than one of doping circuits of mediacy and immediacy.

The article by Gilles Dowek (ENS Paris-Saclay) collects excerpts from his book entitled *To Live, to Love, to Vote Online, and other Chronicles of the Digital*. In a surprising manner, Dowek speaks of a reality that is strangely familiar, yet novel, in which the digital challenges us, like the role of indexes in the legal constitution of our identities, or the thought patterns induced by writing customs. It has been largely forgotten today, over the habit of contemplating the relation between time and numbers as one of rational linearization and progressing serialization, that the numerical and the temporally cyclical have long already maintained interrelations. Dowek discusses key challenges raised by the digitalization through placing them in cyclical re-currencies in the fashion of colloquially told anecdotes drawn from a collectively shared cultural past. That the dominion of the numerical itself actually had earlier precedents before the rise of the computer is, perhaps, the healthy and sober 'news' of this kind of 'digital journalism' in which Dowek is so proficient, and gently informing.

"Concepts facilitate a kind of tourism," on a planet of resonating concepts, "where arguments cast shadows." With an interest in thinking about computability architectonically as well as architecture computationally, Selena Savić (FHNW, Basel) discusses the way local terminology informs distant domains of thinking. In *Travelling on Planets of Resonating Concepts*, she asks how might we identify and document the conditions for coming in and going out of discourses, move between disciplines, and establish this space as an *organized* space, and as a *public* space? She proposes to imagine a planet on which concepts, always coming from somewhere, resonate. A planet, in her thinking, refers to an architectonic articulation of abundant information on directionality of words, and also to a manner of thinking about architecture computationally. Picking up on Serres' discussion on message-bearing, she articulates a proposal for a 'tourist agency' on the planet of concepts that is able to suggest itineraries for different adventures, based on self-organized vectors of meaning and indexes of similarity. This is a way to be interested in concepts, and stay friendly to different discourses, without taking part in one particular community. Concepts always come from somewhere, her article appreciates, like the wind.

In *An Essay on the Glossomatic Process of Communicating Communications and other Words,* Jessica Foley (Maynooth University) presents a report from a conversation with "labyrinths and statues and architectural philosophers" at the ATTP Vienna. She takes the (plasticity of) language of telecommunications engineering as a point of departure, and works with words as choreographic objects, teasing meaning out of technical language. These glossomatic processes push and pull against the constraints of separating intellectual endeavours onto the scientific and humanistic, the creative and analytical. With her conversational experiments, including the one that she reports about, Foley introduces a notion of potentiality to be more precise with words, to create patterns of meaning.

Matt Cohen (University of Nebraska-Lincoln) in his essay *When Others Passing by Behold: Media Studies and Archives across Cultures* envisions a way of doing digital archives informed by non-textual, Indigenous archival practices. Preservation of knowledge would be a responsibility and ability of everyone *passing by*. If a digital archive is publicly available, then the sociality of the archive cannot be subsumed to the authority of right of access or contribution. Cohen puts the democracy of access in Western media against the sociality, repetition and responsibility of his particular case and discusses the Wampanoag memory media in order to articulate an electronic archive practice that would combine the benefits of the two.

Yasmine Abbas (Pennsylvania State University) talks about flows, mixing intentionally the fluidity of matter and information. *Fluid Spaces, Enchanted Forests* are spaces of contemporary magic, brought about by contemporary telecommunications. Building such spaces that accommodate magical moments requires spatial trickstery. She proposes designing for 'wayfounding': orienting and anchoring ourselves in the world by means of chance encounters, and by mastering techniques for composing climatic architecture with data, guiding the fluid arrangement of forms. Blurring the distinction between different materialities, Abbas puts focus on atmosphere, on forming conditions for communication and changing the properties of the milieu.

Darío Negueruela del Castillo (EPFL) approaches communication and architecture from an interest in the way the spatial dimension influences communicative process, through which sense-making is enacted in the city. In the essay *Space as Collective Affective Sense-Making Capacity*, he demonstrates how social collective spatial meaning is built on the substrate of socio-spatial practices. He proposes an understanding of space as a capacity, a potential enacted through our actions, but which influences our actions at the same time. Interested in affective enactment of meaning, Negueruela asserts that space is the resulting materiality of our co-presence, coexistence in it, while coincidentally being at the origin of our emotive and affective processes.

As if directing our minds to remain open, Anne-Francoise Schmid (MINES ParisTech) documents in her article entitled *A Few Protocol Sentences on: Non-Synthesis, the Voluminous Form of Ideas, Temporalities of Creation, Hypercompatibility* a veritable *wealth of ideas* regarding her quest for *generic* epistemologies. Schmid speaks of science as being silenced when without disciplines; she speaks of "objects produced by the present" and of "ideas as being in need of hospitality and accommodation by a notion of time" that is to be thought of as "thick, energetic and tempered"—a time for which memory appears to be "a dynamic hole"; it is as if anamnesis turns into something that needs to be facilitated by a kind of stubbornness that "can only be 'empirical'," at least if it is to conduct a novel sense of intimacy that "is collective." So (or also quite differently), the protocol sentences by Schmid invite us, each individually, to encounter and weave a tangle of threads that can, so she promises, lead us to a world depicted by a kind of writing that could be called 'generic'.

In her article *The Digital, a Continent? Anarchic Citizenship within the Object-Space of Cunning Reason*, Vera Bühlmann (TU Vienna) explores how a particularly "active and restless interplay of 'reasoning'" could be thought of as facilitating a civic domain of 'common places'. We need to alienate the digital from its Cartesian paradigm of a stasis that is to rest in a coordinated point of origin, she maintains, and instead recognize the digital as a versatile and logarithmic, projective and multi-scalar domain, where formality must count as mathematical *and* rhetorical, and hence as always inevitably *cosmetic (encrypted and contingent)*, rather than 'pure', 'simple' or 'immediate'. Cunning, like reasoning, works with clocked happenings, Bühlmann maintains; both involve objective and non-territorial 'time pieces' (reasoning and cunning are ultimately *gnomonic*) that not only quantify, measure and articulate, but also qualify, characterize and temper the 'chronicles' they render decipherable. The Digital as a Continent is imagined as a civic domain that is real and yet entirely 'unlikely', one to which no one is, originally, native. It is the territory of a reason that, counterintuitively, does not turn exclusive and scarce from being the object of rationalization, but rather grows the more it is being reasoned—in both its extent of territoriality, as well as its capacity. It is a cornucopian domain of copiousness and finesse, where perfection aims at reasoning and rationalizing nature—not in order to dominate it, but *in order to let it be.*

CRYPTO ARCHITECTURE: NOTES ON MACHINE LEARNING AND DESIGN
ROBERTO BOTTAZZI

I

ROBERTO BOTTAZZI is an architect, researcher, and educator based in London. He studied in Italy and Canada before moving to the UK where he is the director of the Master in Urban Design at the Bartlett, UCL. His research analyses the impact of digital technologies on architecture and urbanism. He is the author of *Digital Architecture beyond Computers: Fragments of a Cultural History of Computational Design* (Bloomsbury, 2018) and one of the editors of *Walking Cities: London* (Camberwell Press, 2017).

In his concluding remarks on the state of digital architecture, Antoine Picon[1] advocated a return to some forms of opacity in digital design, a discipline that in his view had wholeheartedly embraced transparency as an ethos and method. In aligning digital architecture with modernism, Picon saw digital design dangerously becoming a direct, transparent expression of its own working methods which did not need critical reflection to validate its status. This task might have appeared increasingly more urgent at the time giving the simultaneous diffusion of Big Data techniques for analysing massive datasets with its promise to re-shape all aspects of society from social media to financial markets.

Two years earlier, Chris Anderson had in fact provocatively announced that statistical analysis of massive datasets would have made theory redundant.[2] The article elevated Big Data to a new paradigm for scientific disciplines, a transformation that humanities were also quick to follow. Anderson's argument is a well-known one by now: The power of statistical analysis engendered by evermore powerful computers and algorithms would put an end to the scientific method as modern science had introduced it in the seventeenth century. Hence, the substitution of theory with statistical correlation. One the one hand, Anderson's argument has only strengthened over time as machine learning algorithms provide an effective method to deal with both even larger datasets and forms of cognition beyond human ones. On the other, the risk of this dual transformation is to uncritically embrace transparency as a conceptual model: In urban research, for instance, the promise is that by amassing data, parsing them through algorithms, one might generate entire designs bypassing any reference to historical or disciplinary concerns. In this scenario, only a greater, more complex theoretical and historical framework—rather than its abdication—would enable us to discuss the work. Casting aside such a *Semio-clast* attitude—as Paolo Fabbri puts it[3]—the argument proposed here is to open up such conversation to see the relation between data and design as a constant process of writing one into the other. The data deluge animating the urban environment is re-written into more or less tangible or permanent elements of the built environment: Similar to the mathematical term re-writing, a method for substituting (potentially even in a non-deterministic fashion) the sub-terms of a formula whilst maintaining mathematical identity, data can be engrained into design through a process of continuous substitution; a process that allows for invention and playfulness providing a

1   Picon, Antoine, *Digital Culture in Architecture: An Introduction for the Design Profession*, (Basel: Birkhäuser, 2010).
2   Anderson, C, 'The End of Theory: The Data Deluge Makes the Scientific Method Obsolete', (2008), available at: http://www.wired.come/2008/06/pb-theory/, [Accessed on August 20th, 2018].
3   Fabbri, P, *Lezione di Paolo Fabbri sulla crittografia*, available at: https://www.youtube.com/watch?v=b333yH9BgA4. [Accessed on October 8, 2018].

diaphanous filter to positivist approaches. Spatially this is a problem of distribution here controlled by machine-learning algorithms managing the interplay between patterns and randomness.

Similar conversations have unfolded in architecture drawing from philosophical or biological paradigms. However, more recently, digital architects have been looking more closely to the actual architecture of computation, to its intrinsic properties. Amongst these topics, cryptography has received little attention despite being a core concept of computation since its inception. Cryptography in fact plays with transparency and opacity, with obscurity and intelligibility. Its role in history has not only been connected with diplomacy and secrecy, but also with the playfulness arising from the creation of systems of signs with a special, highly unstable relationship to meaning. Digital computing also involves a continuous process of encryption and decryption which moves signs in and out of the realm of human legibility, bouncing them between the inhuman language of machines (based on binary code for digital computers) and comprehensible texts, images, sounds, etc. This has hardly been just a technical exercise as, since its first formal definition, it has been entangled in cultural and political conversations. Generally speaking, cryptographic operations divide into transposition and substitution. When designing with a deluge of data, the only practical approach is to move to a higher, more systemic level to manipulate abstract information. Designing with data becomes a problem of (spatial) distribution and substitution (transposition is a far less transferable technique); technical operations can be charged with intellectual intent moving the parallel between cryptography and design beyond the mere metaphor. This aligns with architecture on two different temporal frames. Architectural discourse has long speculated on the impossibility to regulate or even fix the relation between signs, meaning and interpretation giving rise to computational design methods also based on strong syntactic variations and weak semantic qualities. On a broader timeframe, cryptography alludes to logical techniques to venture into unknown numerical or (for architecture) spatial domains that might lie beyond human cognition. In architectural research, this echoes with the possibility to appreciate massive scales such as that of the planet, or confront temporalities both below and above our perceptive threshold (from climate change to high-frequency trading). Cryptography has a long history of dealing with these 'inhuman' domains characterized by a complex relation between patterns and randomness, and the 'alien' dimension of massive datasets.

Cryptography also involves cryptanalysis, the process of decoding signs. Since its emergence in the sixth century in Persia, cryptanalysis exhibits complex and highly relevant characteristics for this discussion: for instance, the use of statistical distribution to seek out correlations and substituting characters. The use of 'automatic' methods to relate signs to one another is not only still in use, but also holds the powerful idea that it is possible to manage signs without any prior knowledge of their meaning, as "messages without a code" paraphrasing Roland Barthes.[4] This is all the more relevant when we compare these proto-cryptographic techniques to Ramon Llull's system as presented in his *Ars* at the beginning of the fourteenth century. A device made of a series of concentric wheels generated combinations of letters that would then be decoded through a series of charts (proto-ciphers). Though the work of the Spanish philosopher derived from studies in mnemotechnics, he also confronted basic problems of cryptography such as the relation between syntax and semantics. However, the cultural and religious motivations inspiring his work prevented Llull from utilizing his wheels in what today we would call generatively: triplets and quadruples of letters randomly produced by spinning the wheels had to be discarded because, once decoded, they would give rise to sentences contradicting Llull's own metaphysics. In other words, the device produced an open system through recursion; such a complex syntax with its unprecedented amount of complexity had to be severely curtailed by a strict semantic system which only admitted a finite and predetermined number of solutions. The reward of such contradictory choice was the preservation of Llull's message. The relation between data—as invariant elements—and rule or, in modern parlance, algorithm—as a method to apprehend them—is crucial here as Llull's example already clearly shows how the two connect: The rule or set of rules we use to investigate affects what is returned. The renaissance would introduce important developments on the relation between cryptography and mnemonics. Whilst the latter only accepts a close relationship between signs and meaning, the former is actually interested in expanding the relation between the two—in fact, it wants to make it as broad and different as possible! By removing meaning from the equation, cryptographers could fully exploit the possibilities engendered by combinatorial logic, allowing for a much greater number of combinations, which eventually overcame the weaknesses of statistical frequency. The first polyalphabetic ciphers were introduced by Leon Battista Alberti and would be fully refined by Blaise de Vigenère in 1586.

The decoupling of meaning and syntax (now an algebraic problem) would give rise to modern cryptography and with it to a more complex notion of ciphers. Ciphers not only refer to the instrument invented by Alberti to encrypt and decrypt information, but also to their etymology indicating the key to resolving a mystery, injecting semantics into what only possessed syntactic integrity. The cipher tunes the two domains, it is not given, it must be invented, designed, it requires a great deal of artistry whilst being solidly resting on strict syntactic rules; it

4   Roland Barthes, 'Rhétorique de l'image', *Communications*, 4.1 (1964), 40–51 42).

captures elements of randomness, of an unknowable dimension through rational operations of combinatorial logic. These are also the basis of coding—albeit here still in its primitive purely numerical form. For this reason, the short passage at the end of Pico della Mirandola's *Heptatus* (1489) is of great relevance. In describing the origin of the world, Pico combines both individual letters and syllables to give rise to an open play of signifiers in search for meanings that could not be known in advance. Randomization (here understood as an 'extreme' form of combinatorial logic that can proliferate unbound) was an essential method to dislodge existing notions, to rationally venture into the unknown, the apparently irrational. As Umberto Eco[5] beautifully described it, this marks a clear difference with Llull's exercises whose reward is to free man from the laws of the cosmos, to set it as a mobile subject negotiating his position in the world, and to affirm a humanist project not as mere celebration of mankind but rather a more complex exploration in which man could grasp and potentially alter the very laws governing its existence. Combinatorial logic opened up to embrace and, in fact, seek out new wor(l)ds with an emphasis on learning and the unknown.

In 1913 Andrei Markov presented his analysis of Pushkin's stories. It was not a traditional piece of literary criticism, but rather a study purely based on the statistical distribution of letters neatly divided into vowels and consonants. In this work, randomness and cryptoanalysis conflated time opening up a method that is still largely used in social media and translation software. Markov inverted Llull's idea of treating letters as numbers and delivered statistical and algorithmic methods to compute and translate natural languages without the aid of prior knowledge of the text or even the language used in it. The emphasis moved from discrete elements (the individual letters making up the Pushkin's text) to the pure relations between the individual signs. Relations were treated purely statistically: patterns and randomness emerged in their own terms and were mined without the need to reduce the complexity of the text. For our argument this example shows the sheer power of re-writing and the artistry required to perform such operations. Markov overlooked semantics which consequently turned the original text into a cryptic message to unravel through the mathematization of language. By proceeding through pure counting, the whole of the text could be tackled (though, for practical reasons, Markov only parsed groups of 100 letters at the time) and through substitution a different image of its distribution emerges. Through a technical expedient, a different aspect of Pushkin's work can be charged with conceptual intentions.

---

5   Umberto Eco, *From the Tree to the Labyrinth: Historical Studies on the Sign and Interpretation* trans. by Anthony Oldcorn (Cambridge, Massachusetts: Harvard University Press, 2014), 414.

The power of statistics also extended to design disciplines as in the 1920s when Cornelis van Eesteren and Georges Pineau joined forces to produce a competition entry for the new traffic plan of Paris in which models for demographic analysis and statistical projection were used for both physical and social data. It was, however, the introduction of analytical tools in linguistics studies that was to have a deeper effect on architectural research. The work developed in Ulm, Germany, from the 1950s by Tomas Maldonado, Abraham Moles, and Max Bense employed analytical and 'scientific' methods to study the relation between signs and meaning in the physical environment. On the other side of the Atlantic, similar preoccupations were directing artists and, later on, architects towards more systematic studies on (computational) linguistics. Peter Eisenman deeply contributed to this conversation with his definition of conceptual architecture which builds on Chomsky's work on language as a computational, recursive system to take advantage of the instability between signs and interpretation as a means to charge architecture with greater conceptual depth.[6] The results of these experiments were captured in the famous series of ten houses produced at the time. The riddle-like nature of the spatial organization of the houses was attained through an intricate process of formal manipulations which only constitutes the most superficial correlations to examine here. More interesting was the creative, almost playful nature of the permutations explored through the design process based on a strict logical syntax to which corresponded an open, unstable semantics. This achieved a complex, alienating quality which Eisenman considered essential to the emergence of the conceptual spatial understanding. This element resonates with the exploratory, experimental nature of signs substitution also informing current design work on machine learning in which syntactic integrity is prioritized over semantic clarity. Eisenman's game was nevertheless hermetic, constrained by form as the sole set to play with.

Such historical considerations take a different meaning once we are confronted with the emergence of fully automated, data-driven architectures like contemporary factories and distribution centres. In buildings such as Amazon Fulfilment Centres, we literally experience spaces continuously encrypting and decrypting data, which bounce back and forth between machine language and intelligible signs. Here historical discussions on the relation between data, sign, and space take a new turn. Mnemonic techniques inherited from the classical tradition to provide a system to order space give way to algorithms no longer seeking to reduce complexity to attain an intelligible order; the dream of total transparency promised by computational treatment of data is radically complicated. In distribution centres, goods can be

6   Peter D. Eisenman, 'Notes on Conceptual Architecture: Towards a Definition', *Design Quarterly*, 1970, 1.

placed anywhere as they are trackable through radio-frequency devices (RFID), movement of workers is not based on visual clues; rather paths are calculated and communicated to robots (or humans) that will retrieve a particular good. It is a space of algorithms in which the physical experience, as ephemeral as it may be, results from the complex ecology of machines and codes circulating through it: a problem of distribution. Again, the scale of the information flowing in them can be planetary and highly granular as it conveys individual purchasing orders or desires. The problem of how to relate the abstract and the physical reoccurs and so does the question of what design might mean in such conditions.

The parallel with cryptographic issues provides an interesting frame of reference. Whilst the exploration on indexing of the 1970s still allows one to read the presence of the author, here space no longer carries clear indexical signs of the transformations it underwent. The complex process linking data to space makes the relation between the two 'nonproportional and electronic'.[7] Once this direct, one-to-one relation is lost, it is rather the notion of the cipher to link abstract to actual space in a way more rewarding than established categories of spatial analysis. Design here increasingly aligns with processes of encryption and decryption and re-writing in a rather direct fashion.

FIG 1
Chuanren Lin, Lei Wang, Qiuyang Zhang, Xi Meng. *Fluff*. Studies for a tower based on wind data. Master in Urban Design, The Bartlett, UCL, 2016. Tutors: Roberto Bottazzi, Kostas Grigoriadis.

7   N. Katherine Hayles, 'Virtual Bodies and Flickering Signifiers', *October*, 66 (1993), 69–91.

Such operations also exceed the models proposed by the coupling of biology and design or parametrics. Parametrics presupposes the identification of an ideal—no matter whether present or not—to seed out a whole series of instances all related by continuous variation. Re-writing and (more apt to spatial design) nesting allow for spatial and scalar inconsistencies; spatial articulation can take discontinuities whilst remaining logically coherent. It is no longer relying on ideals situated in a transcendental domain, but seeks pattern and randomness within its own bounds. The divergence from the biological model needs to be qualified further. It is not the emphasis on adaptation to be superseded here (on the contrary, as we shall see, this is still an important element), rather the particular way in which biological models and computational ones merged. This has mostly presupposed to move from the particular to the general: Cellular Automata describe simple conditions and rules which, once animated, can grow into complex formations. Datascapes are however given 'all at once', not as parts and they can only be treated at the very scale they exist as, at any given point, a database is always complete and self-referential (if well constructed). Cryptographic techniques offer a more compelling framework as they allow to re-write the whole by distributing ciphers through a given domain. This also provides a departure from some of the paradigms that have guided the discourse of digital architecture in recent decades as this approach can no longer be described as top-down or bottom-up, but rather as both. That is, scalar hierarchies are no longer able to account for the jumps, connections, correlations of relational approaches delivered through learning algorithms which rest on vast, highly granular datasets. These relations can be inferred or simply tested once the algorithm itself attempts some form of categorization (unsupervised learning). No longer bound by linear scalar approaches, these processes of encryption and decryption engender greater flexibility by moving indifferently between the granular and the planetary. The type of patterns returned by the algorithmic mining of large datasets (for instance, the type we can visualize with T-SNE algorithms) are no longer reducible to Euclidean or even topological spatial models of representations as they exhibit a unique level of granularity: Clustering of similar data can be punctual or extensive; a distribution of patterns not only no longer reducible to linear classifications, which also becomes the expression of the logic of digital computation. Though most databases used in urban design are relational, this is still a fundamentally static technology. In order to work within the constraints of digital computation, at any given moment in time a database must unambiguously determine the number of items in it and their individual value. If databases are dynamic, this can only be assumed to happen in a discrete fashion. How to relate the temporality of databases to design still remains an open question requiring more experimentation. However, it is already clear that large datasets allow to operate on spatial qualities that exceed that of pure formal manipulations.

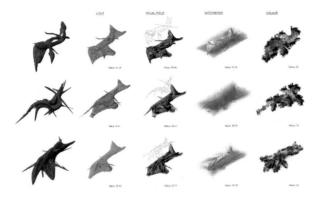

FIG 2
Anna Kampani,
Apostolopoulos
Apostolos, Caitling
Brock. *Perceptive
Datascapes.*
Diagrams showing
formal transforma-
tions based Machine
Learning algorithms
evaluating visual
permeability. Master
in Urban Design,
The Bartlett, UCL,
2018. Tutors:
Roberto Bottazzi,
Tasos Varoudis.

What is at stake in this work is a different form of spatial and informational distribution that could straddle opacity and transparency, jumping beyond formal coherence whilst having a robust logical basis. As
complex ideas and technics increasingly penetrate design, so does the
need to widen the range of fields and timeframes to avoid quick, 'transparent' alignments of data and design.

FIG 3
Chuanren Lin, Lei
Wang, Qiuyang
Zhang, Xi Meng.
Fluff. Studies for
a tower based on
wind data. Master in
Urban Design, The
Bartlett, UCL, 2016.

AN INSTRUMENT FOR COMMUNICATION: THE SELF-ORGANIZING MODEL
NIKOLA MARINČIĆ

II

NIKOLA MARINČIĆ is an architect, computer programmer and a musician, working as a postdoctoral researcher at the chair for Computer-Aided Architectural Design at ETH Zurich. He earned a PhD with a medal of distinction from the ETH, with a thesis entitled *Towards communication in CAAD: Spectral Characterization and Modelling with Conjugate Symbolic Domains* in 2017. In 2009 he graduated as an architect from the Faculty of Architecture in Belgrade, and in 2011 completed a Master of Advanced Studies programme in Architecture and Information at ETH Zurich. In 2012–13 he was a guest researcher at the Future Cities Laboratory, interdisciplinary research programme of the Singapore ETH Centre for Global Environmental Sustainability. In 2019, Birkhäuser published his PhD thesis as a part of their Applied Virtuality book series.

The following text is an excerpt from the doctoral thesis entitled *Towards Communication in CAAD: Spectral Characterization and Modelling with Conjugate Symbolic Domains* defended at ETH Zurich in 2017 and awarded with ETH's medal of distinction. The thesis investigates computational models in architecture, a topic usually studied in the field of Computer-Aided Architectural Design (CAAD). Its motivation comes from the author's ever-growing concern with the field's lack of self-reflection and interest to orientate and position itself within the larger context of mathematical and computational modelling. This brings about a general hypothesis that this lack of interest to explore outside of one's field of expertise (often introduced with disciplinarization of computation within a field) might be preventing the field of CAAD from broadening its research domain towards directions that have been successfully explored for a long time in information technology and science. Finally, to show that such a seemingly non-pragmatic effort has an actual research potential, the thesis committed itself to challenge the existing computational models in architecture with contemporary modelling approaches, characteristic for quantum physics, in which computation is regarded from the perspective of *communication* between different domains of a problem. The challenge was actualized in the last part of the work by introducing a new communication-inspired model and applying it in an architectural experiment.

The work engages with an unusually extensive body of knowledge with the aim of providing additional angles to its principal research domain: computational models in architecture. This body of knowledge involves early analytic philosophy, computability and probability theory, formal logic, quantum physics, abstract algebra, computer-aided design, computer graphics, glossematics, machine learning and architecture. However, the reason for such a comprehensive approach and perhaps radical gesture is not to claim any expertise nor mastery over the aforementioned fields of knowledge. To the contrary, it is a matter of methodology, aiming to operate in a more architectural manner, without losing the necessary rigour and consistency required of an academic work.

The first part of the work begins in the 19th century, delves into the body of thinking from which computation emerged and traces two general attitudes towards mathematical modelling, which will each eventually lead to different interpretations of computation. The first one, described as the *logicist tradition*, saw the potential of formal, mechanized reasoning in the possibility of constructing the absolute foundation of mathematics, its means of explanation and proof. The second one, the *algebraist tradition*, regarded formalization within a larger scope of model-theoretical procedures, characterized by creatively applying abstraction towards a certain goal. The second attitude proved to be a fertile ground for the redefinition of both mathematics and science, thus paving a way

GHOSTS OF TRANSPARENCY

for contemporary physics and information technology. On the basis of the two traditions, this dissertation identified a discrepancy between the computational models in architecture, following the first tradition, and those commonly used in information technology, following the second.

The Internet revolution, initiated by the development of search engines and social media, is recognized as indicative of the changing role of computers, from 'computing machinery' towards the generic infrastructure for communication. In this respect, three contemporary models of communication, proponents of the algebraic tradition, are presented in detail in the second part of the work. As a result, the *self-organizing model* is introduced as the concrete implementation of the ideas appropriated from communication models. This model is described in the following pages.

SELF-ORGANIZING MAP

In a 1976 paper, neurobiologist David Willshaw and physicist Christoph von der Malsburg made a hypothesis that the relation between two laminar structures[1] in the brain is characterized by topographical, system-to-system, rather than cell-to-cell mapping.[2] Their model was based on a microscopic mechanism that utilized concepts of neural excitation, inhibition and self-organization.[3] Inspired by the ideas from neurobiology and neural computation, Finnish physicist and engineer, Teuvo Kohonen generalized the idea of Willshaw and Malsburg in his 1982 paper, *Self-organized formation of topologically correct feature maps*. He stratified his model in two domains and showed that the logic of self-organization is "readily generalizable to mechanisms other than neural."[4] To complement the theory, he introduced the self-organizing map algorithm (SOM) aiming to address the question of "how symbolic representations for concepts could be formed automatically."[5] His initial discovery was that structure-preserving mapping can be automatically established between input signals in the event space and a topological network responding to those signals.[6] Steinbuch's cybernetic notion of a learning matrix (Lernmatrix) inspired Kohonen to define the response layer of his model as a memory matrix.[7]

1   D. J. Willshaw, and C. V. D. Malsburg, 'How Patterned Neural Connections Can Be Set Up by Self-Organization', *Proceedings of the Royal Society B*, 194, no. 1117 (November 12, 1976): 431–45, (433). Sheets of brain cells, namely pre- and postsynaptic.
2   Ibid., 442.
3   Ibid., 433.
4   Teuvo Kohonen, 'Self-Organized Formation of Topologically Correct Feature Maps', *Biological Cybernetics*, 43, no. 1 (1982): 59–69, (59).
5   Ibid., 59.
6   Ibid., 59.
7   "Another early construct which was introduced for the explanation of brain functions and implementation of artificial intelligence is the Learning Matrix due to Steinbuch. It is a system of crossing signal lines, with an adaptive connection at each crossing." Teuvo Kohonen, *Self-Organization and Associative Memory*, 2nd ed. Springer Series in Information Sciences, eds. T. Huang and M. Schroeder, vol 8 (Berlin: Springer, 2012). 74.

FIG I
Kohonen's illustra-
tion of a system
which implements
an ordered mapping.

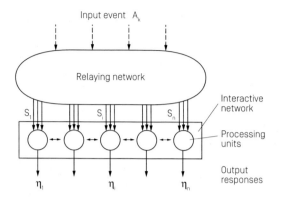

SOM AS A REPRESENTATION

Kohonen showed that different network topologies could be implemented as a response layer of his model.[8] The topology of a two-dimensional lattice revealed some advantages in this respect: It yielded good
results, allowed for easy visualization[9], and complied with the idea of
brain maps.[10] The output domain of Kohonen's algorithm was named
a *map*, and the algorithm the *self-organizing map*.[11] The naming also
implied that the communication between different domains was in fact
a *mapping*. The two-dimensional representation of the self-organizing
map algorithm influenced its interpretation in the artificial intelligence
circles.[12] In the mid 1990s, the availability, memory and speed of computers increased enough to accommodate for the high computational
cost of the algorithm. Researchers attained the means to conduct more
experiments and demonstrated novel capabilities of the algorithm,
many of which were completely unrelated to visualization and analysis.[13] Thirty years later, Kohonen acknowledges a surprisingly wide
variety of applications and modifications of the algorithm and tries to

8   Teuvo Kohonen, 'Essentials of the Self-Organizing Map', Neural Networks, 37 (January
     2013): 52–65 (55–56)
9   " ... the 2-D grid allows rough visual presentation and interpretation of the clusters."
     Vesanto and Alhoniemi, "Clustering of the Self-Organizing Map," 599.
10   "It is believed that many other kinds of maps exist in the hippocampus or other parts
     of the brain system." Kohonen, *Self-Organization and Associative Memory*, 121; ... for
     example *tonotopic maps* in auditory cortex of the brain, Ibid., 120.
11   "The earliest SOM models, tending to replicate the detailed neural-network struc-
     tures, were intended for the description and explanation of the creation of brain maps."
     Kohonen, "Essentials of the Self-Organizing Map," 55.
12   Elaborated in the next sub-chapter.
13   Such as: Guilherme Barreto and A. Araújo, 'Identification and Control of Dynamical
     Systems using the Self-Organizing Map', *IEEE Transactions on Neural Networks*, 15,
     no. 5 (September 1, 2004): 1244–59, and Guilherme Barreto and L. Souza, 'Adaptive
     Fitering with the Self-Organizing Map: A Performance Comparison', *Neural Networks*,
     19, no. 6 (July 2006): 785–98.

create a consensus by describing the algorithm as simply an "automatic data-analysis method."[14]

VISUALIZATION AND CLUSTERING

Unlike in abstract algebra where the term *map* captures functionality[15] in terms of functors, in the context of Kohonen's two-dimensional network topology, the term has a topographic connotation. It implies a graphic representation, which is to be visually perceived and then interpreted. Figure 2 can serve as an example: it shows the cartographical representation of Wikipedia's word frequency mapped onto a low-dimensional landscape.

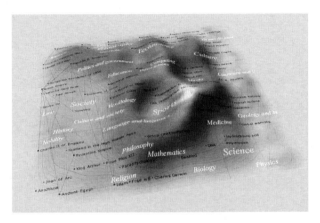

FIG 2
A typical representation of a self-organizing map as a visualization method based on Wikipedia featured article data.

In 1993, Alfred Ultsch, one of the leading researchers on the topic, introduced his unified distance matrix (U-matrix) as a technique utilizing the SOM's response layer as a basis for clustering.[16] In Ultsch's paper, however, Kohonen's initial fascination with automatic concept formation is absent. The algorithm is explained simply as a tool for mapping between spaces of different dimensionality with the promise of visualizing the low-dimensional target space.[17] In a 1996 paper, Kohonen seemed to agree with this interpretation and affirmed that the strongest features of his algorithm

---

14 Kohonen, "Essentials of the Self-Organizing Map," 52.
15 Zalamea, Fernando, trans. by Z. L. Fraser, *Synthetic Philosophy of Contemporary Mathematics* (Windsor Quarry: Urbanomic, 2012), 245.
16 Ultsch, Alfred, 'U*-Matrix: A Tool to Visualize Clusters in High Dimensional Data', published online 2003, available at: https://pdfs.semanticscholar.org/1d9d/ ba44f2d237ee9d8f0388299afbcc0e581621.pdf. And Ultsch, Alfred, 'Clustering with SO: U*C', *Proceedings of the WSOM 05, 5th Workshop on Self-Organizing Maps*, 75–82. Ultsch has created two more algorithms which improved the clustering on top of the SOM, namely U*-matrix and U*C-matrix.
17 "Through a learning process, this neural network creates a mapping from a N-dimensional space to a two-dimensional plane of units (neurons)." Ultsch, Alfred, 'Self-Organizing Neural Networks for Visualisation and Classification', in *Information and Classification*, eds. Oppitz, Lausen and Klar (Berlin: Springer, 1993): 307–13 (307).

were visualization and data analysis.[18] In a similar manner, Vesanto concurred that the algorithm has shown itself valuable in many applications, but most prominently in visualizing high-dimensional spaces.[19] In one of his early papers, he made an overview of different visualization methods.[20] A year later, Vesanto employed a k-means algorithm on top of the SOM response layer and concluded that in many cases SOM clustering yields better results than other clustering techniques.[21] However, he found this to be a fortunate side-effect of the SOM's powerful visualization abilities.

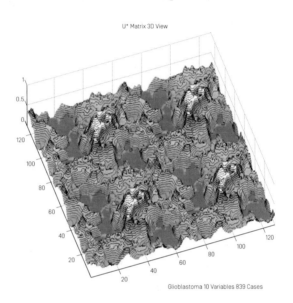

FIG 3
Example of Ultsch's
U*Matrix of the
'Glio' data set.

18 "Accordingly, the most important applications of the SOM are in the visualization of high-dimensional systems and processes and discovery of categories and abstractions from raw data. The latter operation is called the exploratory data analysis or *data mining*." Kohonen, Teuvo, et al., 'Engineering Applications of the Self-Organizing Map', *Proceedings of the IEEE*, 84, no. 10 (October 10, 1996): 1358–83 (1358).
19 "Visualization of complex multidimensional data is indeed one of the main application areas of the SOM." Juha Vesanto, 'SOM-Based Data Visualization Methods', *Intelligent Data Analysis*, 3, no. 2 (January 1, 1999): 111–26 (112).
20 Ibid., 115–24.
21 "In [16], partitive methods (i.e., a small SOM) greatly outperformed hierarchical methods in clustering imperfect data." Vesanto and Alhoniemi, 'Clustering of the Self-Organizing Map', 588.
"Another benefit is noise reduction. The prototypes are local averages of the data and, therefore, less sensitive to random variations than the original data." Ibid., 588.
"The experiments indicated that clustering the SOM instead of directly clustering the data is computationally effective approach." Ibid., 599.

GHOSTS OF TRANSPARENCY

In order to reach a better understanding of the capabilities of self-organizing maps, work by other researchers focused on the applications of the algorithm reaching beyond mere analysis and representation,[22] including nonlinear time series prediction, function approximation, control of dynamical systems[23], nonlinear adaptive filtering[24], data exploration (in industry, finance, natural sciences, and linguistics), digital signal processing/transmission[25], and nonparametric encoding for high-dimensional spatiotemporal dynamics.[26] In his doctoral thesis on pre-specific modelling, Moosavi provided a rich list of indexes around the SOM algorithm.[27]

SELF-ORGANIZING MODEL

If the dominant theoretical interpretations of the algorithm are correlated to the diversity of its applications indexed by Moosavi, there appears to be an unsettling discrepancy between the platitude of interpretations and the actual demonstrated capacity. How can a tool for visualization or an automatic data-analysis method be so successfully used for function-approximation, control of dynamical systems, or prediction of time-series? The important hypothesis of this work is that the insistence on the terms *map* and *mapping* to describe Kohonen's algorithm reduces it to a visualization and analytical tool, hence obscuring the actual capacity demonstrated in applications. Such interpretations systematically neglect higher-level architectonics on top of which the algorithm is conceived, thus, in our opinion, invoke erroneous theoretical consequences. The ambition of this work, motivated by the work of Hovestadt, Bühlmann, Moosavi, Wassermann, Zafiris, and Hjelmslev[28], is to propose an alternative

---

22 "... However, most of this methods do not use the representational power of the SOM to build the prediction models." Barreto and Araújo, "Identification and Control of Dynamical Systems Using the Self-Organizing Map," 1257.

23 Barreto and Araújo show that "the SOM can be successfully used to approximate dynamical input-output mappings, with minor modifications in the original algorithm." Ibid., 1244.

24 For example: identification and equalization of communication channels, Barreto and Souza, "Adaptive Filtering with the Self-Organizing Map: a Performance Comparison," 787.

25 Kohonen, 'Essentials of the Self-Organizing Map', 52.

26 Vahid Moosavi, 'Computing with Contextual Numbers', *ArXiv* abs/1408.0889 (August 5, 2014).

27 Vahid Moosavi, 'Pre-Specific Modeling: Computational Machines in a Coexistence with Concrete Universals and Data Streams', in *Metalithikum IV, Coding as Literacy*, ed. by Vera Bühlmann, Ludger Hovestadt, and Vahid Moosavi (Vienna: Birkhäuser, 2015), 132–66 (71).

28 see Birkhäuser's Applied Virtuality Book Series edited by Hovestadt and Bühlmann; replace with: Elias Zafiris, *Natural Communication: A Functorial Approach*. Applied Virtuality Book Series, edited by Ludger Hovestadt and Vera Bühlmann. (Basel: Birkhäuser, forthcoming). Moosavi, 'Pre-specific Modeling'; *The Putnam Program: Language & Brains, Machines and Minds* accessible at: https://theputnamprogram. wordpress.com.

theoretical interpretation of the self-organizing map from a more abstract mathematical perspective. The hypothesis is that the very architectonics inherent to the algorithm, not only its specific implementations, makes it unique among the computational frameworks. Such interpretation should provide an adequate account for its seemingly extraordinary capacities.

REASON AND COEXISTENCE

The idea of a system is not new, but its usual interpretation within the computer science circles is usually credited to Norbert Wiener. This is not very surprising as computer science "directly applies the concepts of cybernetics to the control of devices and the analysis of information," such as cellular automation, decision support, robotics and simulation.[29] Cybernetics had a crucial influence on artificial intelligence, computer modelling and artificial neural networks, under which the SOM is usually classified.[30] Hovestadt argues how the cybernetic notion of a system is conceived upon the notions of *reason* and *causality* (in a Newtonian sense), which makes it incompatible with today's body of thinking conceived upon the invention of electricity and the development of quantum physics.[31] Notions of reason and a cause are also constituents of the scientific method. In his prolegomena, Hjelmslev described the role of these notions in defining the limits of scientific knowledge:

> Science always seeks to comprehend objects as consequences of a reason or as effects of a cause. But if the object can be resolved only into objects that may all indifferently be said to be consequences or effects of all or none, a continued scientific analysis becomes fruitless.[32]

The book, *Coding as Literacy*,[33] appearing in Birkhäuser's *Applied Virtuality Book Series*, discussed the potential of Self-Organizing Maps as a model[34] from the perspective of computational literacy. In the chapter on elements of digital architecture, Hovestadt takes a quantum perspective to invert the customary interpretation of the SOM as a map. He gave an example of the self-organized map of Zurich where

29 Wikipedia, *Cybernetics*, last modified August 30, 2017, 17:55, https://en.wikipedia.org/wiki/Cybernetics.

30 Wikipedia, *Cybernetics*.

31 As an overview of Hovestadt's position on the topic see: Ludger Hovestadt, 'Elements of Digital Architecture', in *Metalithikum IV, Coding as Literacy*, ed. by Vera Bühlmann, Ludger Hovestadt, and Vahid Moosavi (Vienna: Birkhäuser, 2015), 28–114. And Ludger Hovestadt, 'Cultivating the Generic: A Mathematically Inspired Pathway for Architects', in *EigenArchitecture: Computability as Literacy*, ed. by Ludger Hovestadt and Vera Bühlmann (Vienna: Ambra Verlag, 2014), 7–67.

32 Louis Hjelmslev, *Prolegomena to a Theory of Language*, trans. F. J. Whitfield (Wisconsin: The University of Wisconsin Press, 1963), 84.

33 Vera Bühlmann, Ludger Hovestadt, and Vahid Moosavi, eds., *Coding as Literacy: Metalithikum IV*, Applied Virtuality Book Series (Basel: Birkhäuser, 2015).

34 "The self-organizing map articulates the logical form of chronological elements in probability values … Therefore, we suggest that we should not talk about a self-organizing map but a self-organizing model." Hovestadt, 'Elements of Digital Architecture', 108.

"the constellation of elements changes according to the analytical/chronological position of the observer."[35] In his doctoral thesis, Moosavi further investigated the notion of coexistence in the context of urban data streams and showed the scope of applicability of data-driven models.[36] Inspired by the ideas of Wassermann[37], Hovestadt and Bühlmann, this work reinterprets self-organizing maps by identifying the role of the algorithm within a more general, *self-organizing model*. This model abandons the idea of systematicity based on reasoning and facilitates the notion of *coexistence* in the world of data.

KOHONEN'S ALGORITHM AS A KEY

If we put the emphasis on the implementation of Kohonen's algorithm, we can acknowledge the existence of two data structures resembling different structural domains.[38] Kohonen's input layer is implemented as an n-dimensional list of m-dimensional vectors, where n and m are positive integers. The response layer (or map[39]) is implemented as a two-dimensional array (the common encoding of a graph/matrix) of m-dimensional vectors, where the dimensionality m of the input layer vectors, matches the dimensionality of the response-layer vectors.[40] Kohonen's crucial discovery demonstrated by the algorithm is that the input signal alone is sufficient to enforce self-organization in the response layer, but only if the response layer has a specific architecture and implements a local feedback mechanism.[41] The response layer (map) should then be interpreted by acknowledging that the mechanism imposed on the set of input vectors forces unlabelled classes to emerge in the response layer, with the effect that the topological distances within the response layer resemble similarities between the classes. The interesting discovery is that the schema of Kohonen's algorithm can be accurately represented by means of a key of the same anatomy as Zafiris's motivic key. Here, the input and output layers could be interpreted as different domains, and mapping and interpretation as adjoint communication bridges.

35 Ibid., 109.
36 If we assume "… each of the prototypical forms in the trained SOM metaphorically as a word or a letter in a language, a trained SOM in coexistence with data can be interpreted as a pre-specific dictionary of the target phenomena." Moosavi, 'Pre-Specific Modeling,' 73.
37 See: *The Putnam Program*.
38 "This principle is a generalization of the formation of direct topographic projections between two laminar structures known as retinotectal mapping." Kohonen, 'Self-Organized Formation of Topologically Correct Feature Maps', 59.
39 … also known as lattice in case of 2-dimensional response-layer.
40 Ibid., 61
41 Ibid., 59.

FIG 4
SOM algorithm rep-
resented in a form of
Zafiris's motivic key

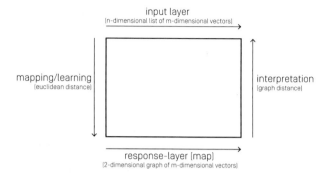

On the level of technical implementation, the elements of this schema appear to be too specific if compared with the Zafiris's motivic key. However, this is an important first step towards building a more abstract perspective. As a next step, I will demonstrate that successful SOM applications are in fact taking advantage of inverting or reinventing one or more elements of key defined as such.

MODIFICATIONS OF THE INPUT LAYER

In their paper *Neural methods for non-standard data*, Hammer and Jain explored the possibilities of different structures serving as an input layer of the algorithm. Instead of vectors, they explored the possibility of utilizing strings, sequences, trees, graphs or functions.[42] In his paper *Computing with contextual numbers* Moosavi created a two-level input layer structure by replacing the original layer with a one-dimensional self-organizing map, acting as a non-parametric encoder.[43] These approaches are very powerful as they allow much greater freedom in the constitution of the encoding.

MODIFICATIONS OF THE RESPONSE LAYER

The work of Alfred Ultsch involves many experiments on the output layer of the self-organizing map. To minimize the learning error, he explored different network topologies in the response layer, for example hexagonal and rectangular grids.[44] U-matrix, U*-matrix and U*C-matrix algorithms directly exploited the response layer of the SOM. They handled the response layer, its distances and densities, as an input for clustering. Algorithms like neural gas and growing neural gas, replaced the two-dimensional lattice with a flexible and adaptive response layer.

42 Barbara Hammer and B. Jain, 'Neural Methods for Non-Standard Data', *ESANN 2004 Proceedings*, 281–292, Bruges, Belgium (2004), 289.
43 Moosavi, 'Computing with Contextual Numbers', 13.
44 Alfred Ultsch and L. Hermann, 'The Architecture of Emergent Self-Organizing Maps to Reduce Projection Errors', *Proceedings of the European Symposium on Artificial Neural Networks (ESANN)*, 1–16, Bruges, Belgium (2005), 2.

Such a response layer could subsume any topology as it dynamically adapted itself to the variability of the input signals.[45]

MODIFICATIONS OF THE MAPPING/LEARNING

The generative topographic mapping algorithm (GTM) was a counterpart to the SOM, which tried to overcome its limitations by rethinking the *mapping* between the domains. For that purpose, it uses a "constrained mixture of Gaussians whose parameters can be optimized using the EM (expectation-maximization) algorithm."[46]

MODIFICATIONS OF THE INTERPRETATION

Without attempting any interpretation of the results of SOM training, Barreto and Souza utilized the nodes of the response layer as the reference inventory for prediction by using the k-nearest neighbours algorithm.[47] The vector, whose missing value (dimension) was to be predicted was first introduced into the response layer and compared to those of its vectors without the missing value. The influence of every node was calculated according to their relative distance and the missing value interpolated. For the control of dynamical systems, Barreto and Araújo established a feedback loop between the input and response layer, thus enforcing the dynamic control of a system.[48]

COEXISTENCE KEY

The intention behind presenting these applications was to demonstrate that the modification or replacement of the particular elements of SOM architecture need not change the form of the key used to describe its architecture. In this regard, what differentiates SOM from other machine learning algorithms lies in its structural properties. Hjelmslev's differentiation between variants and invariants can help us to understand why this might be the case. His conception and terminology support the argument that all the presented modifications of the original algorithm are in fact *variants* by the virtue of placing a specific algorithmic procedure to a specific position

45 Bernd Fritzke, 'A Growing Neural Gas Network Learns Topologies', *Advances in Neural Information Processing Systems*, 7 (1995), 625–32 (626).
46 "... lack of a theoretical basis for choosing learning rate parameter schedules and neighbourhood parameters to ensure topographic ordering, the absence of any general proofs of convergence, and the fact that the model does not define a probability density." Christopher Bishop, M. Svensén and C. Williams, 'GTM: The Generative Topological Mapping', *Neural Computation*, 10, no. 1 (January 1998), 215–34 (216).
47 Guilherme Barreto, João C. M. Mota, Luis G. M. Souza, and Rewbenio A. Frota, 'Nonstationary Time Series Prediction Using Local Models Based on Competitive Neural Networks', in *Innovations in Applied Artificial Intelligence*, ed. by Bob Orchard, Chunsheng Yang, and Moonis Ali (Berlin, Heidelberg: Springer Berlin Heidelberg, 2004), 1146–55 (1146).
48 Barreto and Araújo, 'Identification and Control of Dynamical Systems Using the Self-Organizing Map', 1245.

within the key. Consequently, the *invariant* property of the self-organizing model is reflected in the position of an element within the key, and is defined relationally in respect to other elements. This in an indicator that there is more to the SOM than just an algorithm. It is a computational framework resting upon a mathematical contract established by the motivic key and its invariant anatomy. We can define such a key as a *coexistence key* and such a framework as the *self-organizing model*. The coexistence key maintains a contract established upon mathematical symmetries, while the self-organizing model furnishes its elements with computational procedures.

FIG 5
Coexistence key of
the self-organizing
model.

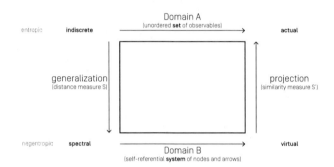

In the manner of Zafiris's motivic key, the coexistence key stratifies the self-organizing model in two levels, as shown on Figure 5. The domain *A* is defined as an unordered set of observables, and domain *B* as a self-referential system[49] of objects and arrows. According to Kohonen, the input signal alone is sufficient to enforce self-organization in the response layer, if the response layer has a 'specific architecture' and implements a local feedback mechanism.[50] The proposed stratification gives new insights to Kohonen's requirement. If we are interested in what would be the invariant property of Kohonen's 'specific architecture'—concerning we have acknowledged that many different structures could successfully serve as the response layer—an answer comes from the category theory. A domain which allows to be self-organized must be self-referential. As we have seen with growing neural gas algorithm, any topological structure allows for self-organization as long as every node has a reference to itself and to all the other nodes.[51] At a computational colloquy held at the CAAD chair, Hovestadt presented a series of experiments on the coexistence between data and the wide range of self-referential topological structures, ranging from linear chains to multiple graphs. To represent

---

49   The notion of the system is taken from Hjelmslev, meaning premised system. Hjelmslev, *Prolegomena to a Theory of Language*, 16.
50   Kohonen, 'Self-Organized Formation of Topologically Correct Feature Maps', 59.
51   Ibid., 60, fig. 2.

GHOSTS OF TRANSPARENCY

the model, I suggest using the category theory instead of graph theory, as it is better suited for representing its structural properties.

Metaphorically speaking, domains A and B can be regarded as different 'natures' of things.[52] From the perspective of Hjelmslev's glossematics, an obstacle or a problem observed in the domain A would be a specific purport formation (substance), apparent to us by the virtue of its content-form encatalysed within the same domain. By introducing another domain, we are seeking to find a new purport formation within the domain B describing the same obstacle or a problem by the virtue of a different content-form.

In order to establish coexistence between the domains A and B, the model uses encoding and decoding bridges. For the encoding bridge, the self-organizing model requires a generalization procedure that can produce a partition spectrum from an indiscrete, unordered set of observables. The self-organizing map algorithm provides that functionality. In the process of self-organization, the pockets of negentropy emerge from the entropic data set resulting with a partition spectrum.[53] Once the spectrum is obtained, the obstacle or a problem is represented by means of a new cipher (a category) within the spectral domain B. Let us assume that in the domain B there exists a procedure allowing to bypass the obstacle, or solve the problem. In order to interpret what was resolved in the spectral domain B, the self-organizing model uses a decoding bridge. The decoding bridge requires a projection procedure that utilizes virtual distinctions from the partition spectrum to distribute the original set of observables (encoded as the unordered set) into a category of sets corresponding to actual distinctions. The actual distinctions give the interpretation to the solution/obstacle within the original domain.

FORM AND SUBSTANCE: ENCODING THE BLACK BOX

According to Zafiris, the notion of data assumes a geometrical encoding. Hjelmslev sees data as a *content-substance*—formed purport encatalysed by means of the content-form.[54] This suggests that the encoding principle itself is a *form*. In a chapter from *A Thousand Plateaus*, Gilles Deleuze has multiplied this elementary gesture until he stratified "the whole earth" and beyond, by means of coding and territorialization.[55] This gesture introduces a very important modelling question: What is the role of a form

---

52 This is in the sense that physical laws that apply in the quantum scale, seem to be completely different from those that apply in the macroscopic scale, and according to that they could be considered as different "natures" of things.

53 Resolution of this spectrum is directly proportional to the number of nodes (objects) that were selected to constitute the network, and its number can be larger or smaller than the number of elements in the initial set of observables.

54 Hjelmslev, *Prolegomena to a Theory of Language*, 54.

55 Gilles Deleuze and F. Guattari, '10,000 B.C.: The Geology of Morals; Who Does the Earth Think It Is?', in *A Thousand Plateaus*, trans. B. Massumi (London: Bloomsbury Academic, 2004), 44–82 (45–48).

in the context of a stratified model? Zafiris gives an example of applying his model to quantum physics, where the motivic key enables communication between two physical levels: atomic and microscopic. On an atomic level, no technical means are sufficient to locate an electron and its interactions. Thus, the whole domain can be thought of as a black box. On a microscopic level, physicists observe interference patterns and think of them as a reflection of unknown events happening on the atomic level. For Zafiris, modelling consists of establishing a pair of functors from the observational universe to the microscopic universe and back.[56] In this way, we can regard these two levels as functives, one of which is giving form to another. In this way, a form is given to something that cannot be observed.

This perspective must be investigated from the standpoint of the coexistence key. By applying the same gesture, we can consider the domain A of the coexistence key as a 'black box' characterized by a set of observables. We can assume that the observables describe some meaningful process, but the semantics is not explicitly present in the observables. Starting from the domain A, the application of the generalization bridge will establish a partition spectrum. The resulting spectrum is constructed in another cipher, and at the same time juxtaposed with our original set of observables (a black box). The new cipher of domain B, known as a *category*, comes with a greater operative and symbolic potential than the cipher of the original domain (set).

However, we are still missing the process of formalization. In order to give form to the domain B, the system of objects and arrows must be composed in such a way that it resembles relations between the observables in the domain A. The role of the generalization bridge is to give form to the domain A within the domain B. In the same way, we can see the projection bridge as responsible for obtaining semantics in the domain A according to the form of the domain B. By doing so, the projection bridge closes the path and establishes coexistence between levels A and B.

PROCEDURAL CATALYSIS OF SYNCRETISMS

In order to formally define the process of formalization, Hjelmslev introduced the term catalysis. The term implies that "form is encatalyzed to substance and language encatalyzed to the text."[57] If we apply the concept of catalysis to the self-organizing model, instead of saying that the domain B gives form to the domain A, we can say that the self-organization procedure encatalyzes the form of the category to the set of observables. If the first criterion that makes self-organization possible is self-reference, the second criterion would be the possibility of

56 Zafiris, *Natural Communication*.
57 Hjelmslev, *Prolegomena to a Theory of Language*, 96.

information exchange between the nodes of the system. Such property, Kohonen calls a local feedback.[58] In the self-organization procedure, objects within the system are pushed/pulled towards each other as they exchange information. The mechanism which enforces this behaviour in the SOM algorithm is known as the distance function.[59] This function provides a metrical criterion of similarity. By applying the concept of catalysis, we can say that the distance function locally encatalyzes the form to the set of affected observables. Influenced by the distance function, nodes receiving the local feedback begin to share the same-expression form. This is especially visible between two directly connected nodes of the system.

Such behaviour corresponds very well to the Hjelmslev's definition of syncretism.[60] It is a category established upon the suspended mutation which he called overlapping.[61] Therefore, we can regard the distance function as the form which is encatalyzed locally to the set of observables and establishes overlapping between the nodes within the system. In other words, the nodes are organized in such a way that they will be 'pushed' to share the same expression-form according to the applied distance function. Hjelmslev uses the notion of syncretism to define the term concept:

> concept—a syncretism between things (namely, the things that the concept subsumes).[62]

According to the definition, and by the virtue of the distance function, we can define the population of nodes that exhibit overlapping, a *concept*. This can be illustrated with an example of an experiment that the author conduced in 2012. Here, the self-organizing map algorithm was used to explore design possibilities of a generic parametric model. The model consisted of six parameters that defined the shape and colour of a single geometric figure. This figure was replicated in one thousand instances with random parameter values and the SOM algorithm was used to organize them into a two-dimensional lattice. As Figure 6 shows, the outlined collection gathers locally similar shapes, but as we 'zoom out' and start to consider the population of shapes, we can notice the difference between shapes belonging to different collections. From the standpoint of expression-form, each two neighbours within a single collection are overlapping. However, if we select two shapes belonging to different collections, they are most likely not overlapping. Those that overlap, can be said to establish a category defined by the overlapping. Thus, their collection, as the one marked on the image, can be regarded as the concept.

58 Kohonen, 'Self-Organized Formation of Topologically Correct Feature Maps', 59.
59 Kohonen, 'Essentials of the Self-Organizing Map', 53.
60 " ... the category that is established by an overlapping we call (in both planes of a language) a syncretism." Hjelmslev, *Prolegomena to a Theory of Language*, 88.
61 Ibid., 88.
62 Ibid., 93.

FIG 6
Interpretation of
Hjelmslev's notion
of a concept within a
partition spectrum.

From the perspective of glossematics, the relational property of the model that enforces that each individual shape locally reflects the arrangement of all the others, we can call a *connotator*. Therefore, in the previous example, each individual shape is considered to be the connotator of the category it belongs to.

EXPERIMENT

In the last part of the doctoral thesis, the self-organizing model is applied in an architectural experiment. Its aim is to address the question of how similarity between spaces in architecture could be accounted for within a paradigm of communication. The hypothesis is that the question of similarity cannot be adequately posed within the established computational models in architecture, due to their reliance on a pre-given notion of space in which the architectural representations are submerged. Being able to speak about the similarity of spaces requires addressing the problem outside of the given space of representation, finding or constructing another level of representation of the same phenomena, where the question can be posed and answered once the coexistence between two levels is established. By applying the self-organizing model, the author attempts to show that this is indeed possible. The experiment was defined as following:

The objects of modelling in this experiment are floor plans. After addressing the questions of conventions of floor plan representation, its scale, format, and availability in terms of data, the decision had been made to operate on raster images of floor plans.

The 2009 book typologie+[63] contained 189 floor plans that satisfied the requirements of the experiment and that were digitally scanned, cropped in high resolution at the same scale and stored in raster format. The plans' computational ambiguities were resolved in the data pre-processing stage, namely representation of walls' interior as empty space bounded by lines, and deciding how the plans should be oriented (Figure 7).

63   Ebner, Peter, Eva Herrmann, Roman Höllbacher, Markus Kuntscher, and Ulrike Wietzorrek. *typologie+: Innovativer Wohnungsbau* (Basel: Birkhäuser, 2009).

FIG 7
The final data
set after the
pre-processing stage.

At this stage, it was possible to think of the collection of floor plans as *an abstract object* characterized by the dataset of raster images. The codes and ciphers found at this level (graphical and symbolic elements and their conventions) are familiar to every architect, but do not provide an adequate basis for the comparison of floor plans. The aim is to establish a completely new level, where the same abstract object can be represented, but in entirely different terms. The codes and ciphers on this new level are expected to provide a more adequate basis for comparison. For this reason, the choice was made to construct the new level on a symbolic basis. The first and most important step towards this goal is the creation of communication bridges.

The modelling begins by partitioning this object in order to obtain the partition spectrum. The partition of each individual floor plan into parts is accomplished by dividing the image in such a way, that the collection of equal size parts covers the image entirely, with a variable amount of overlapping between the parts.

When the partition procedure was applied to all 188 floor plan images with a desired overlapping, and after applying a rotation transformation group to each part, the abstract floor plan object was represented as a collection of 573,488 image parts. Figure 8 shows around 23,000 image parts extracted from it.

FIG 8
23,393 floor plan
parts on a single
image

What follows is an application of the translation and mirroring invariance bridge that translates each floor plan part into a histogram of frequencies representing the lengths of stretches of black pixels (obstacles) registered in scanning each part in horizontal and vertical direction line by line. This procedure helped to bypass a complicated problem of how to appropriately choose the position of each individual cut.

In the next stage, the generalization bridge of the self-organizing model is applied to the collection of elements (each now represented as a list of 20 characteristic frequencies) which yields a partition spectrum. Kohonen's self-organizing map algorithm serves as the implementation of this generalization bridge. The first level of the self-organizing model was defined as an unordered set of observables represented by the collection of floor plan parts represented as 20-dimensional frequency vectors. The generalization procedure connects this level to another level—a category—represented by a self-referential system of objects and arrows, with objects have the same dimensionality, but different connections.

By applying partition and generalization procedures of the self-organizing model to a large number of floor plan images, a finite collection of elementary geometric expressions was extracted, and a symbol attached to each instance (Figure 9).

FIG 9
10,000 randomly
chosen floor plan
parts extracted from
the initial data set
and clustered into
100 sets of actual
distinctions.

This collection of symbols is regarded as the alphabet and any floor plan created by the same conventions, can thereby be defined on this symbolic basis. Finally, each floor plan is represented as a chain of probabilities, based upon its individual alphabetic expression of a written language, and its values used to compute similarities between plans. The Figure 10 shows the space of floorplan similarities, where the similarity of any two plans A and B taken from the original data set can be expressed by the topological distance between their respective cells.

FIG 10
Topological distance
between the cells as
the measure of floor
plan similarity.

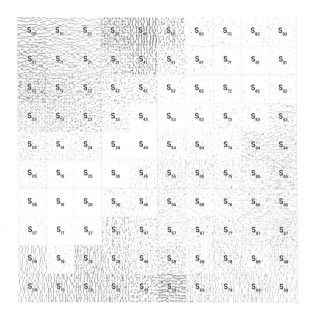

EPILOGUE

The experiment attempted to set the self-organizing model in motion by implementing it in an architectural context. It was demonstrated how a contemporary concept of communication could be applied to architectural modelling. Despite the real benefits of the symbolic representation applied to floor plans, this latter may prove to be insufficient in future research. This would miss the point of the experiment. Its object might be specific, but its aim is not: to present a novel perspective on how the concept of similarity could be derived from an object and in an object's own terms, and, furthermore, how we can computationally encode such an idea by learning from seemingly very different fields such as quantum physics, not the most obvious research context for architecture. One of the promises of communication models such as the self-organizing model is that they allow us to overcome the limiting assumptions of set theory about the constitution of the very modelling. Objects we are trying to model need no longer be sharply defined or have clear boundaries in order for us to encode them computationally. They may be hard, but also soft, or any state in between. This is due to their fluid identity which oscillates as we change the ratio between the information and symmetry we are willing to extract or maintain in each modelling scenario. As a consequence, communication models allow us to take modelling seriously and rigorously, as it is expected in a scientific context, while drastically extending the amount of contingency of what can be articulated in favour of old necessities.

FORMAL CREATURES: GILLES CHÂTELET'S METAPHORS
BEN WOODARD

III

BEN WOODARD is a postdoctoral researcher at the Institute for Philosophy and Art Theory (IPK) at Leuphana University in Lüneburg, Germany. His research focuses on the relationship between naturalism and idealism, especially during the long 19th Century. He has published two monographs *Slime Dynamics: Generation, Mutation, and the Creep of Life* (Zero, 2012) and *On an Ungrounded Earth: Towards a New Geophilosophy* (Punctum, 2013). His book *Schelling's Naturalism: Motion, Space and the Volition of Thought* was published in 2019 by Edinburgh University Press. He has also published numerous articles on weird and science fiction. He is a co-founder of P.S., a philosophy collective at the Performing Arts Forum in St. Erme, France.

My aim is to explicate Gilles Châtelet's use of metaphor as a philosophical tool. Rather than analysing the philosophical use of metaphor broadly (which in itself would require volumes), I wish to specifically examine how Châtelet sees metaphor as a type of *formal creature* that is related to both the gesture and the diagram. While Châtelet expresses the movement of the gesture, to the diagram, to the sign, as a rigidification of formal expression of the conceptual act, the function or role of the metaphor is one of uncertain accompaniment in such a process. This is not to reduce metaphor to its usual life as mere rhetorical firework, but instead to understand metaphor as a necessary parasite of the conceptual through its formal phase-changes. In other words, the metaphor is caught between a conceptual place-holder and a vehicle for speculation in which an uncertain concept or practice is injected into already existing ideas, fields, and sciences, in order to take advantage of the surrounding landscape without becoming lost within it. As a secondary goal, outlining Châtelet's understanding of metaphor will serve to instructively complicate his association with Gilles Deleuze.

BREAKING THE GREY

It's a question of seeking confrontation and of crying Down with grey! Down with the Neutral! Long live Anger! Long Live the Red! We should never forget that grey neutralizes intensities by mixing together all the colours that are already given. Style is not a polite way of thinking: no style, no thinking! Style is a discipline of breaking language out of itself, a martial art of metaphor. The haranguing tone of the pamphlet is a working on language, and style is an entirely integral part of thought qua thought experiment. The effectiveness of the philosophical concept is fuelled by a work of torsion of material language on itself. It's a matter of capturing and organizing the forces that could break through and tear apart 'straight-talking' and 'promoting quality culture.' Note also that, in order to break through, one must understand the Hegelian-Marxist helix not as a routine movement within History, but as a corkscrew that leverages a torsion of natural language.[1]

In *A Martial Art of Metaphor* Châtelet is nearly immolated by his own rhetorical excesses as he launches invectives against the neo-liberalization of philosophical thought. Working in the mode of his barbed text

---

1   Gilles Châtelet, *A Martial Art of Metaphor: Two Interviews with Gilles Châtelet*, trans. R. Mackay, M. Hare and S. Huitre (Windsor Quarry: Urbanomic, 2017), Available Online at https://www.urbanomic.com/document/gilles-chatelet-mental-ecology/

To Live and Think Like Pigs, Châtelet nevertheless maintains a strong connection to his earlier work regarding the relation of style to thought.[2] Even in this political moment we see the connection between thought experiment and style, which is captured in the scientific conceptual use of metaphor. This is further advanced in the example of torsion, and of the corkscrew, which Châtelet argues comes about through the understanding of the relation between mechanics, electricity, and diagrammatic thinking flowing from Schelling, to Faraday, to Hamilton, to Maxwell. We will discuss this below. For now, what is important is to try and understand the immanent to evental shift that occurs in the most abstracted region of expression, that of space itself.

Any detailed inspection of a landscape or of a domain of knowledge presupposes a survey, and the horizon is what endows caution with some style. If this survey were reduced merely to prescribing a 'horizontal' reading and a 'vertical' reading; it would lead only to a fixed stratification. The survey induces an axis of distribution of the mobilities that reactivate knowledge: The strata become a field, whose exploration implies a norm of virtual grasp of the statements. This norm never offers itself up placidly for analysis and always evades anyone who would seek it 'on the near or far side' of the horizon that controls it. Its withdrawal is always painful and is paid for by a 'metaphorical' dislocation of the field or by its reduction to significant networks subordinated to a code. The implicit pressure of the horizon is like the scar of a gesture ...[3]

Metaphors are thus not a free play of meaning despite their dramatic presentation in *To Live and Think Like Pigs.* Metaphors are transports whose trespasses across the fields of meaning leave marks (scars) every time the field is realigned, or a space is navigated. There is no easy or carefree investigation—even the horizon which would seem given to us issues a pressure, a weight. It is important to keep in mind that Châtelet does not wish to keep metaphor in purely linguistic dress. Metaphors capture, but imperfectly and violently, the trajectories of the ideas and concepts mucking about. Thus, Châtelet's metaphor about metaphor being a form of martial art must not be read in a generally Heideggerian manner—that language is the prison house of being, that only language can break language. Châtelet's attitude towards Heidegger's philosophical trajectory makes clear the lack of any potential affinity.

Châtelet writes in *Autour du vrai-faux rapport d'Éric Alliez: De l'impossibilité de la phénoménologie* that Heideggerians embrace a kind of para-phenomenology, and that the followers of such pseudo-theological

---

2   Gilles Châtelet, *To Live and Think Like Pigs. The Incitement of Envy and Boredom in Market Democracies,* trans. R. Mackay (Windsor Quarry: Urbanomic x Sequence Press, 2014).
3   Gilles Châtelet, *Figuring Space: Philosophy, Mathematics, and Physics* (London: Springer, 1999), 54.

radicality are all aboard a ghost train, "screaming in concert" that no one can understand "the spoils of the Great Heideggerian quivering" before "the angel of the event." Furthermore, these para- or negatively-theological passengers "have a sort of obsession with legerdemain: constructing an X, which would have all the determinations of X but which is not X as such. They believe they can get drunk on the nectar dispensed by Chance and Event while they only desperately mimic the pursuit of the absolute *epoche*."[4]

It should be clear that Châtelet is not telling us that language gives us the lock-pick to being, only that the relation of expression (which is also importantly mathematical, gestural, and diagrammatic) to thought is one that often produces an overhang, an excess which allows thought to test itself against itself. Again, not in terms of finding the meaningfulness of being, but of the proper way to symbolize the actions of thought that cut effectively into the chaos of the world (and not reveal any proper way of being in the world). These cuts, as expressions of thought, can be solidified—while they begin as intuitions they quickly bloom into gestures, then curl up into diagrams, before eventually becoming signs. But these expressions are meant to mangle and rewrite the understanding of the human, to bend space and redraw the interiority of the notion of self.[5]

The very un-Heideggerian quality of such a claim should not be too hard to follow: The matheme, the diagram, the topological tracing of abstract space, is effectively a technique of the self that has just as much, or more power, as discovering the limits of the human as any hermeneutics tangled up with *Dasein*.[6]

KNOTS OF THE HORIZON, TURNS OF THE SCREW

Knot theory thus evokes gestures which are classical for it, but completely new in the domain where it is imported as 'notation'. Thus certain *a priori* not very suggestive complicated formulae of tensor calculus can be condensed in a fulgurating way and launch new calculations. This upsets the very notion of indexation which becomes *bi-dimensional* in the freeing itself from the successive: It is very much a victory of the

4   Gilles Châtelet, 'Autour du vrai-faux rapport d'Éric Alliez: "De l'impossibilité de la phénoménologie"', in *Multitudes*, accessible at: http://www.multitudes.net/autour-du-vrai-faux-rapport-d-eric/
5   Châtelet discusses this via Foucault and the notion of convexity as a technology of the self in 'Autour du vrai-faux rapport d'Eric Alliez'
6   Here Châtelet unexpectedly functions as a makeshift bridge between Frege and the post-Kantian tradition's interest in mathematics, whether it be Schelling's algebraic topology, Maimon's calculus of magnitudes, or Hegel's pre-paraconsistent logic. Frege's artificial or technical languages suggest a breaking with common language in order to explain the productivity of concepts that are neither strictly found nor made from scratch. For more on this, see Hare and Woodard, 'Anti-Eureka', in *Glass Bead 2*, Logic Gates, 2017, accessible at: http://www.glass-bead.org/article/anti-eureka/

hand that comments on itself, the indexation no longer being delivered by an external 'set', but by a process of deformation and modification of diagrams. This confronts us with a remarkable situation: Theorems of mathematics make it possible to support the notation for this same mathematics. We propose to analyse in detail this *revenge* of the hand which no longer content to drone out x1, x2, then x3 etc., as prescribed by linear successivity, but can play on all the routes permitted by the (interlacing) tracery. The notation *contaminates* to some extent the calculations, in order to create a new context like literary metaphor.[7]

Châtelet's invocation of the gesture appears to waver between poetic and pragmatic, yet this is hard to separate from our generally received notion of gestures as expressive additives to oration. Yet the gesture, which is something of a conceptual egg for metaphor (put metaphorically!), has an important function for Châtelet as a local articulation of abstract space. Again, this can appear too much a flight of fancy, or it can simply designate a 'working space' between the discrete and the continuous, between the quantitatively measured and the qualitatively constructed. This is not to divorce these actions, but merely emphasize that Châtelet is drawing the space where both physical objects and thought experiments take place.

While pulling from Schelling's notion of abstract space as a nest of forces and polarities, Châtelet emphasizes that metaphors function as 'allusive devices' particularly in scientific and mathematical thought experiments during the early 19th century. In particular, Châtelet explores how electrodynamics required the muscle of metaphorical creatures in order to advance concepts and configurations of forces which were not adequately expressible in then-contemporary ways. For instance, the treatment of electrodynamics in Châtelet's narrative moves from being presented as a geometrical peculiarity, to an anti-mechanistic fluid, to finally an updated celestial 'mechanics' made of particles and forces. Across these transitions, the metaphor allows a nascent theory to inhabit other established worlds (electricity as a fluid, electricity as a force) in such a manner that it is advanced, but never absorbed by, its host.

Thus, for Châtelet, neither a straightforwardly progressive nor a revolutionary model is satisfactory for describing the movements of science. To say, for instance, that the treatment of electric current as akin to the behaviour of fluid dynamics was simply a mistake would itself be an error in judgement since that metaphorical treatment of electricity as fluid fed into the attempt to contain it, i.e., in the construction of the first chemical batteries. Châtelet builds off Schelling's spatial

---

7   Gilles Châtelet, 'Interlacing the singularity, the diagram, and the metaphor', ed. Charles Alunni, in *Virtual Mathematics: The Logic of Difference*, ed. Simon Duffy (Bolton: Clinamen Press, 2006), 36.

observation that while magnetism should be understood in terms of length, electricity should be understood in terms of width. Not only does this lead to eventually articulating the electrical field, it also means that width could no longer be understood as simply an external measurement upon a given chunk of physical material. While length seems to be the active adventure of a point, a trajectory which we can project ourselves into the horizon (aware of the scarring mentioned above) width takes on an altogether different understanding with the electric field since these fields return to their origin point, to zero. However, the 'o' of the electrical field is not a motionless starting point as it is with 'you are here' and the horizon, it is a point between two different trajectories which are not straight or towards anything other than itself.

As Châtelet points out, electric thinking opens up the notion of a *non-neutral zero* since a negative charge is active, albeit in a different way. The association of the electric with a fluid makes sense given the fact that the understanding of the mechanical at the time could not account for fields of energy, for two different kinds of forces emanating from one point (the closest analogy being that of the polarization of a magnet). As he writes, "Electrical positivity is not that of accumulation, but that of current that loops the around opened by separation [...] The metaphor of the positive and negative 'fluids' had attempted to counter the 'self-evidence' of the solid and manipulable units of mechanics."[8] Chemical difference (the ions of different elements) when bridged by a transmitting fluid (salt water or many other mediums) produces a looping flow of energy. Thus a battery becomes a capture of a loop of current that, when given a release or an outlet, becomes a power source.

As Schelling was aware, as Châtelet notes, there was a temptation to explain the polarities of a battery with the polarities of the magnet, i.e., equating the positive with the north and the negative with the south.[9] But Faraday's and other investigations into the physical body of the magnetic and the chemical body of the battery demonstrated that electromagnetism provided thought with a motion that explained the emergence of bodies themselves. Instead of bodies in motion, electrodynamics and its relation to magnetism starts to give us an idea of space that can issue bodies out of forces.[10]

These lines of force "are neither 'real' wires nor illustrations of knowledge already deposited in an encyclopedia; they lead the exploration of a field which is neither exactly in Nature nor exactly in Understanding."[11] Furthermore, and as Maxwell realized, it is a space of force that allows one to see the interaction of the lines as interlacing and

---

8   Châtelet, *Figuring Space*, 154.
9   Ibid., 160.
10   Ibid., 165–166.
11   Châtelet, *Figuring Space*. 167.

as knots in order to understand bodies as both the result and the per-turber of a cosmos of forces. With the metaphor of the screw, of a flick of the wrist (as gesture), one can understand how an axial motion can seem to affect or penetrate space itself, i.e., rational movement is translated into a direction through the metaphor of the gear wheel or the corkscrew. Thus, Châtelet argues that metaphors of Maxwell function as a Trojan horse in order to breach the fortress of the mechanical imaginary.[12]

One could easily forget this entire chemical path in viewing an en-tity such as a black hole as merely a cosmic corkscrew or whirlpool. Yet without the knowledge gained from the electric, to the chemical, to the electro dynamic, a black hole would certainly not be black, or time-slowing, or ravenous. Furthermore, it explains, for better or for worse, why much of contemporary physics can gain so much explanatory (at least mathemati-cally) traction in following Châtelet's secularization of the invisible through the making of knots in the vibratory fabric of space. Or, diagrammatically, it is not such a long journey from lines of force to quantum strings.

CONCLUSION

It may be that the above use of metaphor can be deemed trivial. I hope, however, that it at least demonstrates a valiant effort to demonstrate an alliance between two supposedly divided halves of the world: the quantitative and the qualitative. While Châtelet is often discussed as a follower of Deleuze, and is dismissed too quickly as much by Alain Badiou as others, Châtelet's emphasis on metaphor as well as his at-titude towards mathematics carves out an important space between Deleuze and Badiou, and suggests that the mathematical and the vital are not so violently at odds with one another.

In his 1968 lectures on Kant and the Synthesis of Time, Deleuze and Châtelet engage in a brief exchange regarding the role of mathe-matical construction in relation to time. Deleuze invites Châtelet to say something about the mathematical treatment of time in antiquity vis-à-vis Kant's modern concept of time as synthesis. Importantly, where Deleuze and Châtelet disagree is in regard to the link between measure and parameter. Châtelet insists that the two are different:

> The parameter is not a result. A number, for the Greeks, is sim-ply a measure, here the measure of time is possible because ... in mathematics parameter has no definition, it's simply a notion. Time become parameter is no longer a result, it becomes an ini-tial given. A parameter is what is given, what varies.

12   Ibid., 180.

Deleuze responds:

> I think that it amounts to exactly the same thing: to say that time
> ceases to be a number or that time ceases to measure something
> and thus is subordinated to what it measures, and that time be-
> comes a parameter, time is related to a problem of constitution.
> When I said that time un-curves itself, becomes a straight line ...
> There is something equivalent in this modern conception of time
> where it is at the same time that an empty form of parametric
> time appears and a complementarity with something which
> makes a function, whether it is the caesura in the tragedy, or else
> the cut in mathematical instrumentation. I am just a bit bothered
> by the key role that Gilles Châtelet gives to Plotinus.[13]

In essence, Châtelet argues that the difference between the Greek's
notion of time as eternity, on the one hand, and a measure of cyclical
change on the other, is not radically different from Kant's treatment of
space as a necessary (*a priori*) condition for the possibility of experience
connected to inner sense. This bothers Deleuze because he thinks one
of Kant's great accomplishments is the freeing of time from eternity
and becoming a tool of the subject, a constructive aspect of experiential
synthesis. Yet it seems that Châtelet wants to be more careful when it
comes to construction—a line of measure is not an abstract line which,
on the one hand, one could argue is somewhat supported by Kant's use
of magnitudes as the basis for the inner sense's intensity and thus arithmetic. Both measurable and metaphorical captures of intensity produc-
tively soften the stitches binding experience to subjectivity.

This in the end may be the difference which Châtelet's metaphors reveal in all their romantic recklessness—that while Châtelet
can support Schelling's dictum that being (as nature) precedes thinking,
Deleuze's final turn to Fichte betrays the opposite tendency.

13   Gilles Deleuze, 'Lecture on Kant: Synthesis and Time', Available online at http://deleu-
     zelectures.blogspot.de/2007/02/on-kant.html

VOIDS, BRANDS, CHARACTERS, AND HOW TO DEAL WITH LOTS

IV

MIRO ROMAN

MIRO ROMAN is an architect and a scholar. His main focus is at the overlap of information technologies and architectural articulations. Miro holds a Master of Advanced Studies degree in Computer Aided Architectural Design from ETH Zurich, and a PHD in Architecture from ETH Zurich (2019). Since 2004 he is collaborating with Luka Vlahović on project romanvlahovic. From 2013 to 2015 he was a part of the Future Cities Laboratory, interdisciplinary research programme of the Singapore ETH Centre for Global Environmental Sustainability (SEC). Currently he is a postdoctoral researcher at the Chair of CAAD at ETH Zürich.

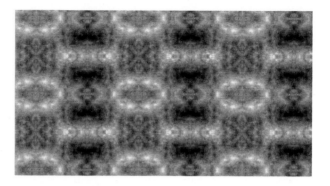

AMBIENCE

Branding, mediating, curating, measuring, communicating, coding. Information, data, lists, indexes, pixels. This story deals with a lot, with a lot of lots. By diluting common sense, it tries to play with meanings. While escaping from one understanding of nature, it participates in many traditions. Like lots do with their numerous etymological meanings. A lot can be anything from dice to straw, but also a chip of wood with a name inscribed on it used to determine someone's share. A lot is that which falls to a person by lot. A plot of land which is given by fate, God, destiny or a game of chance. With its rich meanings a lot becomes an intriguing triangle: a lottery, a group, a collection.[1] An encoding, a chance, and a great many. This is how I will try to think about big data and a big plenty. My mask is that of an architect. This text is neither scientific, nor artistic. It is architectural in always being a part of both traditions. Yet, it is architectural in another manner. Most of its elements are already around, ready to be found if one can acknowledge them. This story, like architecture, is about bringing elements, parts and things in relation. To be more precise, it is about articulating constellations with an ever-increasing number of parts: architecture, blogs, images, information, indexes... How does an architect in a world of a lot behave?

The ambience: aliens, mutants, migrants, cyborgs, avatars. Neither mortal nor immortal, neither of heaven nor of earth. Always part of streams, merging and mingling among themselves and others, with objects and collectives. Belonging to distinct natures, but still communicating. No one is pure; all are always mixtures of many kinds of creatures, of multiple worlds, of reality and fiction, of various media, of particular concepts, restless and unsystematic... Always on the move, making noise, complementing each other, enriching capacities, and producing different constellations. This is what makes it interesting, but

[1] Douglas Harper, 'Lot (n.)', Online Etymology Dictionary, 2017 <https://www.etymon-line. com/word/lot> [accessed 2 April 2017].

impossible to understand. If one looks around, there are more and more mixtures, but the more you focus, the harder you'll see. No classes, no labels, no boxes; just clouds and crystals.

Some avatars live in the cloud, on the 'Google planet'; they hang out among other avatars and aliens. Social media is their means of transportation, the manner in which they render their faces at a certain moment, in a specific locality. Yes, avatars have many faces, and they tell a lot of stories. Branding is their way of expression, Bitcoin is their currency and the way of making contracts. However we look, they influence the world. They give the real many faces. They are not realistic but a part of any specific reality; they are independent and dependent, a subject and an object, a collective. Internet, web, information, avatars—this is an immediate virtuality, with fast and direct channels to the actual and back. The virtual becomes the actual, reality and the model become one and the same. Avatars are us, modalities mix, becoming more and more complex, entangled, and less distinguishable.

This text celebrates a play of architectural avatars. It wants to articulate their faces from a lot, encode their mood as characters of weather, and write brands with their flavours. But there is no clear separation: Faces with their expressions create atmospheres, and atmosphere is a part of the weather filled with smells and odours.

ARTICULATING FACES

VOID AS AN INGREDIENT
Ours is a world of a lot, filled with creatures of varied, and ever-changing conceptions of nature. Avatars change their faces, and fashion themselves in the form they prefer. Their faces appear from a lot, disappear and reappear as brands, or blends of different characters which are in themselves encodings of lots. Brands, Characters, Lots; they can change their places, they fluctuate, while dancing around a void—a symbolic limbo between actual and virtual. Better to say: A dance, a sound—with, within and around the void. A void is being filled more and more, yet it appears empty. Its content is encrypted, and the information contained invisible. It is full and empty at the same time, depending on the cypher. These are void-elements—algebraic and complex in their appearance, inhabiting different temporalities, acting as clouds, rendered in spectrums and rainbows. In their formation, they follow the tradition of Lucretius: "[...] what we term void exists as an ingredient in things,"[2] while being monadic: "Now where there are no parts, neither extension, nor shape, nor divisibility is possible."[3] Elements

---

2   Titus Lucretius Carus, *On the Nature of Things*, trans. by Martin Ferguson Smith (Indianapolis: Hackett Publishing Company, Inc., 2001), 967.
3   Strickland, Lloyd, *Leibniz's Monadology: A New Translation and Guide*, 1. edition (Edinburgh: Edinburgh University Press, 2014), 14.

without shape, a void with capacities. Void elements with an empty centre contain an empty container. They can symbolize anything, that which has no name: X. X is a spectrum, a void with qualities and quantities, translatable, following many laws at the same time. It is a question of encoding and performance. Is this information?

DANCING AROUND VOIDS

DANCE 1 - LOTS ENCODED IN CHARACTERS

A void as an ingredient, filled elements without form, an emptiness with qualities and quantities. A void on which projections are projected to merge with other projections. These mixed projections can be imagined as characters that are encodings of a lot. Emperor in Barthes' Tokyo can be thought of as one of those characters. "The city I am talking about (Tokyo) offers this precious paradox: it does possess a centre, but this centre is empty. The entire city turns around a site both forbidden and indifferent, a residence concealed beneath foliage, protected by moats, inhabited by an emperor who is never seen, which is to say, literally, by no one knows who."[4] All power resides in an empty centre, encoded in characters of emperor, power, tradition, institution, society, hierarchy ... Cyphers start to perform a beautiful dance, visible only if one has the key. Otherwise one is left with a generic city and an empty centre.

DANCE 2 - CHARACTERS WRITING BRANDS

On the one hand, characters encode a lot; on the other, characters write and constitute brands. Claude Lévi-Strauss in his *Structural Study of Myth* tells a similar story. His character is a mythical hero, a Greek god, an avatar, Oedipus. A character who is so empty that he can be loaded with new meanings repeatedly for more than two thousand years. It is an empty consistent centre which is always in motion. "On the other hand, it cannot be too strongly emphasized that all available variants should be taken into account. If Freudian comments on the Oedipus complex are a part of the Oedipus myth, then questions such as whether Cushing's version of the Zuni origin myth should be retained or discarded become irrelevant. There is no one true version of which all the others are but copies or distortions. Every version belongs to the myth."[5] His avatars and characters resemble a specific alphabet or a framework of a particular thinking. It is a tradition without origin and history, a myth without sense, an ever-changing structure, a traditional structurability.

4   Roland Barthes, *Empire of Signs*, trans. by Richard Howard (New York: Hill and Wang, 1983), 30.
5   Claude Lévi-Strauss, 'The Structural Study of Myth', *The Journal of American Folklore*, 68.270 (1955), 428 <https://doi.org/10.2307/536768>.

Or to put it in different terms: Fashion as an expression of the void. Every season a new collection, consisting of different episodes, mixed genders, changing vectors. Always consistent, never explicit, articulating the same brand in different manners. Imagine a scenario:

Take a readymade concept or an artefact. Float in-between fashion and art, mix avatars and brands, Marxism and luxury. Make them dance around an empty centre. This void is articulated as a lifestyle. Cherish and emphasize contradictions. Make it public and visible, collect 'likes'. No explicit description is needed:

- Indexes: DHL, Anne Imhof, Faust, Balenciaga, Vetements, Demna Gvasalia, Ikea, Eliza Douglas, Golden Lion ...
- Package: body, performer, control, power, glass, subject, exist, dog, room, create, capitalism, consumption, image, form, hand ...[6]

Indexes perform a sophisticated branding, a relaxed dance of flavours symmetrical to both art and fashion shows. A lot is in the background: an ecology of videos, images, PR, stories, capital, abundance, decadence, information, lifestyles ... This beautiful fiction animates specific articulations into a play around a void.

A SPECIFIC NOISE: ARCHITECTURE

This is neither a subjective nor an objective process. It is a 'quasi-' subject, object and collective.[7] A point of return to architecture. A quasi-subject needs an interest to constitute an axis and an empty centre in the entropic field. It is a generic plain of particular interest—a plain of architecture—with empty axis orthogonal to it, an avatar. Here the revolution happens. Avatars are revolving on top of the generic plain: famous architects, beautiful buildings, architectural blogs, magazines, books, manifestos, images, videos ... different styles, approaches, drawings, thinking, schools, traditions ... cities, big, small, clean, screaming, silent, efficient, sustainable, green, adventurous, smart, stupid ... These are projections, new projects of the informational age. Virtual and actual at the same time. The beauty of it is that one can never explicate what it is all about. It is a position without a fixed point, a void, an attitude, both architectural and universal. There is no clear strategy; it is instead an interplay of surfing, learning, and training in a vertigo. A new ability to deal with any media as information in a world of a lot. This is what architectural brands are doing: They are navigating the clouds.

---

6 Anne Imhof, 'German Pavilion 2017', *Faust*, 2017 <http://www.deutscher-pavillon.org/>.
7 See Michel Serres, *The Parasite*, trans. by Lawrence R. Schehr (Baltimore: Johns Hopkins University Press, 1982).

FIG 2
A Specific Noise:
Architecture

The void, the generic plane, the entropic state, all common scenarios of dissolution. From Pritzker to Google, from books to the magazine, to online magazine, to social media, finally dissolved with Google, where everything is connected to everything: A flatland. What if one inverts this story and looks at this process as parallel encapsulations that enrich each other in infinite self-referential loops? This is what the digital brings to the table: "[...] not the end of history, but an intensifying and multiplying of histories."[8] Time is not flowing linearly any more: It is percolating, it's circular, it's a spiral; past, future and present are mixing; pre, post, neo, retro, futuristic, bio, techno; it's a question of taste and choice. It is digital and immediate. Time is the weather. Porn and drama mix in a new kind of public space, around a novel literacy of a quantum city. But not all is so new. Twentieth-century architectural masters were and are actively dealing with a lot. As a response, or other to early modernist tradition of Mies's "Less is more,"[9] star architects reply:

Less is a bore,[10] I am a whore,[11] More and more, more is more,[12] Yes is more![13]

The twentieth century deals and plays with complexity, contradictions, junk, genericness, capital, brands and much more. 'More' becomes an

8   Sam Jacob, 'Faster, but Slower', *Log*, 29. Fall (2013), 145–52 (150).
9   Quote by Ludwig Mies van der Rohe, 1947 (borrowed from Robert Browning poem 'Andrea del Sarto' published in 1855)
10 Robert Venturi, *Complexity and Contradiction in Architecture, The Museum of Modern Art Papers on Architecture*, 2nd ed. (New York: Museum of Modern Art; distributed by New York Graphic Society, 1977).
11 Quote by Philip Johnson, 1982.
12 Rem Koolhaas, 'Junkspace', *Obsolescence*, 100. Spring (2002), 175–90.
13 Bjarke Ingels, *Yes Is More: An Archicomic on Architectural Evolution* (Copenhagen: Bjarke Ingels Group, 2009).

explication of a global condition. Architects are engaging with a lot, producing a spectrum of architectural clichés, each one with its own maxim, each in its own way. How to step out of this competition, and not add just another slogan, but still consider the spectrum? Avatars, bots, Google, cryptocurrencies, social media ... all play the game. They scan everything, relate everything to everything, make traces and trouble. They are always transmitting, not as individuals, but as multiplying and proliferating identities. The digital brings ever more to the table. It is a different world.

FANTASY

I want to play with information—store, deal, emit and receive. I want to scan ten years of online architectural publishing in one afternoon, and imagine all the different weathers and atmospheres it can produce. I want to encrypt and decrypt ... To open the crypt and move the bones of saints to another space—in other words, to translate. A crypt and a translation are spaces where information merges with materiality, where virtual and physical relate in an explicit way. It is a place where one can play with many tastes of architecture. It is a way of writing poems in a language which is not natural. Coding as literacy.[14]

ENCODING WEATHER

PLAYING WITH CLOUDS

Two familiar clouds, two different curations of contemporary architectural cosmos: ArchDaily[15] and Dezeen.[16] Both strong architectural identities—ones most liked in the network. Yet there are multiple clouds, many blogs, various consistencies, with different atmospheres and ecologies. In the digital, they mix and produce always more. The fantasy comes from mixtures. The weather changes fast. Here, focus is on the two, on their relations, behaviour, and the atmospheres they create. This, of course, is a question of preference and choice among many possible constellations.

ArchDaily and Dezeen are clouds with directionalities, without borders, but of many intensities. They bundle times, and encapsulate spaces. Indexes fill the surrounding air. It is a matter of articulation. When perceived as clouds, these curated databases gain informational abilities. With indexing, different streams appear: Texts, images, architects, drawings, times, cities ... Encoding renders specific streams to spectrums: weather, clouds, flows; not to explicate, but to open

14 'Introduction – Coding as Literacy', in *Coding as Literacy: Metalithikum IV*, ed. by Vera Bühlmann, Ludger Hovestadt, and Vahid Moosavi (Basel: Birkhäuser, 2015), 12–22.
15 See https://www.archdaily.com
16 See https://www.dezeen.com

communication channels. The focus now goes to the stream of images: houses, sketches, floor plans, lamps, colours, homes, pixels, smells … Current speed 30,000 images per year, per blog, and getting faster and richer. Weather forecast in architecture: storms, summers, beautiful springs, tornados … Many atmospheres at the same time. How to play with them? Instagram, smartphones, cameras, Flickr, Pinterest, Twitter … collect, curate, mediate, measure … a turbulent space of flows and currents … a characterization of stunning atmospheres …

DIGITAL ATMOSPHERE

How does one behave in a cloud? Weather does not follow laws, not in our time at least. Its codes and manners of behaviour are not a part of the common. Digital weather is a part of an informational planet whose atmosphere is a blend of clouds, fumes, sounds and smells. It is being articulated in a quantum city[17], via a new kind of literacy. Clouds and the web are a novel and different kind of space in which public, private and sacred are interwoven and fused in not-so-obvious mixtures. It is a digital agora with extraordinary atmospheres. This climate is not only reserved for big clouds like Google, Facebook, Amazon. There are many clouds and different weathers. Anyone is welcome. What if one starts playing with the atmospheres?

Scan everything, take snapshots. As an avatar in a cloud, one behaves like a search engine. Yes, it's possible, and very palpable. And suddenly one is dealing with hundreds of thousands of informational objects, without being afraid of them. One possible way to explore this is to dive right into it; personal filtering, searching, crawling, articulating. Use machine learning. Write a poem, or code a couple of them. Make sense of what the weather is like. Compose your own cloud by playing with data—play with information. Forecast a weather forecast; take snapshots, and browse the public form of online publishing; take a walk in the cloud. The first steps, the first poem. It is not too complicated: One only needs to write a crawler, a bot, a small program and collect. Here is a poem that collects all the images from ArchDaily. Ten lines for ten years. A powerful poem:

17   See Ludger Hovestadt, Vera Bühlmann, Diana Alvarez, Miro Roman, and Sebastian Michael, *A Quantum City*. Vol. 10. Applied Virtuality Book Series (Basel: Birkhäuser, 2015).

FIG 3
Poem for ArchDaily

```
ADpages[page_] := Module[{source, pos, links},
  source = Import[page, "Source"];
  pos = StringPosition[source, "<span itemprop='url'>" -- Shortest[__] -- "</span>"];
  links = "http://" <> StringDrop[StringDrop[StringTake[source, #], 28], -7] & /@ pos]

ADimages[link_] :=
 Module[{source, strings, image, imagelink, images, imagelinks, pos, dateY, name},
  source = ToString@Import[link, "Source"];
  pos = StringPosition[source, "<li class=\"theDate\">" -- Shortest[__] -- "</li>"];
  dateY = StringTake[StringDrop[StringTake[source, pos], -5], -4];
  strings =
   Flatten[
    DeleteDuplicates[StringCases[StringSplit[ToString[source]],
      "data-src='https://images.adsttc.com/media/images/" -- __ -- ".jpg"]] /. {} -> Nothing];
  strings = StringDrop[strings[[#]], 10] & /@ Range[Length[strings]];

  If[Length[strings] > 2, {
    strings = Delete[strings, {{-1}}];
    If[Length[strings] > 12, {strings = Take[strings, 12], Flatten[strings]}];
    {image = Import[#, "Graphics"], name = StringJoin[{dateY, "_", StringTake[#, -10]}], #} & /@
     strings
    }, (Print["article does not have enough images"])]]

input = "http://www.archdaily.com/page/"; startpage = 1; stoppage = 1;
pagelinks = input -- ToString[#] & /@ Range[startpage, stoppage];
links = Flatten[ADpages[#] & /@ pagelinks]
article = 2; imgAD = ADimages[links[[article]]][[1]];
ImageResize[imgAD[[#, 1]], 300] & /@ Range[Length[imgAD]]
```

One can simply scan the cloud. This poem is able to take 10 years of
publishing from ArchDaily in one evening. Another poem, another online magazine, another topic, a different search. In this case it is Dezeen.
Together these two online clouds provide a noisy nebula of half a million
images. One is participating in a new weather. But how to look at this
huge cloud? How to see half a million images and get a feel for them?

ENCRYPTING FICTIONS

Clouds are playing an informational play: ArchDaily and Dezeen acquire
new identities and atmospheres—many of them. They are translated into
numbers, and informationally encoded. These clouds become vectors of
various directions and distinct moods. They participate in many weathers.
They are curated, mediated, and measured in many manners. But how to
measure a cloud? What is the unit of Dezeen? One needs to articulate the
instrument and the unit. This is not a universal measuring device with a
basic unit; the instrument is not scientific. It should be something different,
closer to a musical instrument. Every setup produces another atmosphere.
It is a subjective meter of matter in a certain manner. This does not mean
one should leave and forget the seven unifying units. This is yet another
way of how to think of measure. It complements the first one. Matter and
meaning, nature and culture, what and how, are being co-constituted. Barad
suggests: "Measurements are world-making: matter and meaning do not
preexist, but rather are co-constituted via measurement intra-actions."[18]

18 Karen Barad, 'What Is the Measure of Nothingness? Infinity, Virtuality, Justice = Was
    Ist Das Maß Des Nichts?: Unendlichkeit, Virtualität', Gerechtigkeit, *100 Notes – 100
    Thoughts / 100 Notizen – 100 Gedanken*, 99 (Ostfildern: Hatje Cantz, 2012), 6.

Yes, measurements are world-making, but the world makes the measurement as well. Basic units are in harmony, derived from the base and later from each other, but what the base is is not unambiguous any more. Clouds celebrate these contradictions, without having an explicit a priori base unit. It is a different perspective. What if it is not about measuring but about encrypting and decrypting? What if it is about making profiles of weather and mixing of clouds? Then this is another game. One is not seeking for specific properties and measuring them, but trying to develop a communication channel through which one can articulate profiles of different encodings. Electricity performs this all the time—it is energy, it is matter and it is information, a wave and a particle, depending on how one wants to have it. Different co-constitutions in their contradiction are enriching the space of possibilities. Paradoxes dope fantasy. There is no unit of image, yet images are profiling blogs from many perspectives simultaneously. This is a search for the most general and abstract ingredients in a given situation. An image becomes a constitutive part of a letter of an alphabet that articulates a blog, a void element. One is encoding frequencies to look at the clouds. These are frequencies of whatever our probes can reach. They depend on the mood of the moment. A spectrality of imageness:

- colours (most frequent RGB values)
  {{0.819608, 0.827451, 0.764706}, {0.827451, 0.835294, 0.768627}, {0.854902, 0.854902, 0.772549}, {0.886275, 0.878431, 0.788235} ...},
- edges (frequency of edges in an image)
  {0., 0.00494277, 0.000260146, 0., 0., 0.201093, 0.153226, 0., 0.0293965, 0.182622, 0.248959, 0.0176899, 0.213059, 0.203434, 0.187825 ...},
- waves (a transformation of an image to frequency domain - encoding it into sine and cosine components)
  {38.4397 + 6.54782*10^-17i, -0.0350414 + 3.12362i, 1.34676 + 1.04524i, 0.703196 - 0.90463i, -0.0595718 - 0.736424i, -0.259281 - 0.236514 i ...}.
- image recognition, ratings ...

This is open. Encodings don't have a fixed form—they are code dependent. There are infinite ways of how one can encode an image. Code is beyond subjective and objective. It is a literacy. Each encoding opens a different spectrum of possible decodings. These encryptions don't define what an image is, but provide a ground for specific context and its articulations. The measurement becomes a part of the encoding process. It becomes a cypher open to many articulations. This opens a communication channel - cryptography, measurement, and communication are interwoven in a delicate way. One image, one vector, a mist. Many images, a matrix, a cloud. Clouds of images constitute a weather of a blog.

Weathers mix and produce new weathers, virtual mutants, their families and offspring. The roots are infinite and fluid. The medium is not fixed. Encryption and indexing define the resolution. Images, texts, sounds, ratings ... Here is one. The informational encoding of Dezeen. Each row is the encoding of a different image, each column is a spectral view to a specific index (e.g., Pixel):

2006_barnaby-bar_1_.jpg	0.	0.006	0.0816	0.	0.	0.	0.	0.1228	0.	0.	0.0584	0.0608	0.1108	0.166	0.0868
2006_barnaby-bar_4_.jpg	0.	0.052	0.0112	0.	0.0188	0.0152	0.0572	0.0392	0.01	0.	0.0412	0.0412	0.134	0.0736	0.
2006_bodo-sperle_1_.jpg	0.2432	0.1808	0.1984	0.2172	0.1844	0.142	0.1332	0.1592	0.1312	0.1456	0.1468	0.116	0.1932	0.1156	0.1344
2006_bodo-sperle_4_.jpg	0.04	0.038	0.2496	0.2568	0.2648	0.046	0.056	0.2516	0.2736	0.2664	0.104	0.0652	0.2432	0.2944	0.2636
2006_dezeen-love_2_.jpg	0.	0.0292	0.0768	0.0772	0.03	0.072	0.118	0.0476	0.0888	0.1656	0.06	0.166	0.0684	0.0584	0.0512
2006_dezeen-love_5_.jpg	0.0032	0.0832	0.144	0.0536	0.0052	0.1328	0.0988	0.0804	0.0776	0.066	0.036	0.016	0.0724	0.1932	0.13
2006_droog-and-b_2_.jpg	0.1296	0.0544	0.0928	0.1812	0.118	0.022	0.1324	0.1012	0.0348	0.1016	0.0388	0.0416	0.0932	0.0724	0.0158
2006_droog-and-b_5_.jpg	0.	0.0028	0.1168	0.0024	0.	0.	0.1132	0.3836	0.0996	0.	0.	0.0124	0.2286	0.0112	0.
2006_joris-laarm_2_.jpg	0.0644	0.1476	0.1036	0.1252	0.0572	0.1476	0.1044	0.1752	0.1576	0.1404	0.1576	0.052	0.0736	0.1348	0.1792
2006_klein-dytha_2_.jpg	0.0356	0.01	0.	0.	0.	0.1604	0.0832	0.008	0.0212	0.0332	0.2128	0.114	0.1344	0.1356	0.142
2006_klein-dytha_5_.jpg	0.1556	0.0548	0.0528	0.0304	0.16	0.1764	0.1216	0.162	0.0204	0.0716	0.1368	0.1376	0.1664	0.114	0.014
2006_marcel-wand_2_.jpg	0.	0.	0.	0.	0.	0.0128	0.2368	0.298	0.2628	0.0252	0.0152	0.3052	0.348	0.2884	0.0288
2006_more-from-m_3_.jpg	0.0204	0.	0.0356	0.	0.	0.006	0.0764	0.0996	0.	0.	0.	0.144	0.1536	0.0536	0.
2006_more-from-m_6_.jpg	0.0488	0.1252	0.0968	0.0512	0.	0.0788	0.1924	0.108	0.0468	0.	0.0512	0.176	0.0892	0.0588	0.
2006_morphosis-s_3_.jpg	0.	0.	0.	0.0656	0.	0.0596	0.048	0.0272	0.074	0.0436	0.1716	0.1716	0.2312	0.0952	0.202
2006_moss-presen_2_.jpg	0.0164	0.02	0.0188	0.0164	0.0052	0.026	0.024	0.0028	0.0212	0.0208	0.	0.0388	0.0556	0.0552	0.0944
2006_new-swarovs_1_.jpg	0.	0.	0.	0.	0.	0.0712	0.1288	0.1052	0.0196	0.	0.1712	0.2672	0.2588	0.1424	0.1424
2006_new-swarovs_4_.jpg	0.	0.	0.0196	0.0196	0.03	0.0716	0.2556	0.3564	0.3628	0.3476	0.2836	0.344	0.3724	0.3716	0.1848
2006_wanders-see_1_.jpg	0.	0.	0.	0.	0.	0.178	0.124	0.136	0.1012	0.0676	0.204	0.2036	0.252	0.1478	0.1236
2006_wokmedia-sh_2_.jpg	0.	0.034	0.0204	0.	0.0244	0.	0.0248	0.02	0.0084	0.0464	0.	0.02	0.0428	0.0612	0.07
2006_wonderwalls_3_.jpg	0.	0.0288	0.0036	0.0784	0.	0.	0.02	0.0048	0.0972	0.	0.	0.0532	0.1416	0.1316	0.
2006_yves-behar-_3_.jpg	0.1136	0.0756	0.0604	0.112	0.1748	0.0812	0.0644	0.0116	0.248	0.0788	0.3328	0.2448	0.0216	0.2584	0.0496
2006_yves-behar-_6_.jpg	0.3348	0.0916	0.07	0.1064	0.1012	0.326	0.	0.	0.	0.1048	0.3028	0.0004	0.	0.0228	0.1844
2006_zbox-by-zah_1_.jpg	0.0432	0.0112	0.	0.	0.	0.022	0.0408	0.0128	0.0424	0.0348	0.026	0.0532	0.042	0.104	0.0224
2007_100-11th-av_1_.jpg	0.212	0.072	0.0524	0.1448	0.096	0.1684	0.096	0.0868	0.1632	0.086	0.184	0.1124	0.0856	0.1748	0.1112
2007_100-11th-av_4_.jpg	0.0616	0.2348	0.3268	0.0404	0.0136	0.046	0.2572	0.308	0.068	0.0132	0.0316	0.2264	0.3004	0.0372	0.
2007_100-design-_1_.jpg	0.0872	0.0536	0.0788	0.0728	0.0492	0.0588	0.0648	0.0768	0.0688	0.0588	0.074	0.0784	0.074	0.0576	0.0736
2007_100-design-_4_.jpg	0.0348	0.0412	0.0488	0.0152	0.004	0.1064	0.0984	0.1168	0.0968	0.0888	0.0896	0.0628	0.1052	0.0752	0.0036
2007_11-by-estab_3_.jpg	0.0464	0.0284	0.11	0.1108	0.096	0.0788	0.0372	0.0736	0.0044	0.08	0.082	0.0628	0.0688	0.0792	0.0588
2007_12-blocks-p_3_.jpg	0.0484	0.0872	0.0616	0.0788	0.0636	0.0132	0.1124	0.0836	0.	0.0824	0.	0.0112	0.0192	0.0168	0.068

FIG 4
Informational Encoding of Dezeen

The cloud is different now. More familiar, but less intuitive. One is suddenly playing with millions of images. Just another poem.

WEATHER IN ARCHITECTURE

The weather is changing. ArchDaily and Dezeen are the clouds. Their atmospheres and stories, mixtures and distillations, are both a matter of information, instrument and the player. Various moods come from the same cloud. They change like the weather. The way I look and what I am looking at constitutes my articulation. Jumping between contextualities constitutes an indexical cloud. Elements start to remember. A generic, informational materiality of data is articulated in an infinity of ways, never as good or bad, always in changing spectrums of many consistencies and beauties. Sophistication and branding become a part of this spectral constitution.

Here they are. Beautiful artificial articulations composed out of millions of images. Governed by poems, images gather. A specific poem, an algorithm: A Self-Organizing Map.[19] Similar images group together. Similar images like each other. Similar according to my encoding. That is all: informational materiality of images and many encodings. Now decrypt, decode, decipher, and render:

19 Teuvo Kohonen, 'Self-Organized Formation of Topologically Correct Feature Maps', *Biological Cybernetics*, 43.1 (1982), 59–69 <https://doi.org/10.1007/BF00337288>.

Weather in architecture, an architectural mutant of ArchDaily and Dezeen, an artistic cloud, ten years of architecture, an impression, a face, a rendering, different resolutions, many consistencies, various temporalities. A mixed matter of rendering, articulation, and data;

#WeatherInArchitecture
#TimeInArchitecture
#TimeIsTheWeather

FIG 5
A Cloud of
Architecture

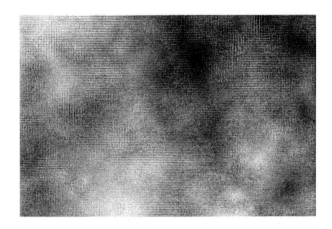

Another weather, a different interest, various renderings:

Split the mutant[20], mix in many directions, split times, bundle them back, render each character individually[21], by year[22], check the entropy. Scan fast: What kind of photographs do they use; what kind of composition do they make, colours, objects, energy, flavours, moods, entropy...? What is in fashion today, or ten years ago?[23] Just by writing short poems. Working with millions.

WRITING BLENDS

QUEST FOR FLAVOURS
Images, photographs, distinct compositions, beautiful colours, objects, peculiar tastes... odours of the weather. Can this be a way to search for flavours, to articulate aromas, to compose spectrums and menus? An instrument is needed. Maybe the strings of this instrument are expressions of personal blends, informational masks, and avatars. While

20   See http://romanvlahovic.com/img/archdaily/10yearsOfArchDaily.html
21   See http://romanvlahovic.com/img/dezeen/10yearsOfDezeen.html
22   See http://romanvlahovic.com/bigpictures/de_yearlyPostcards_2000.gif
23   See http://romanvlahovic.com/bigpictures/ad_yearlyPostcards_2000.gif

playing, sounds and harmonies mix into a weather composed of many flavours and distinct bouquets. Each tasting is a peculiar sensation: Never the same flavour, but an ever-changing notion of taste. Every time, its development is tuned in a slightly different fashion. The flavours, more abundant than before, concentrate into a new harmony, a blend. It is an art of combining elements, a search for constellations of concepts, consistencies and aromas inside an architectural mutant without having a clear notion of what those elements are. A question of taste: very personal, but consistent. Consistency is in the spectrum. Let's taste a few encodings. The today's menu features:

The textured objects, light in weight, like stones that fly: These are the molecules in which every element is celebrated—I have some sympathy for that—it's like a good whisky, blended, a beautiful intoxication:

FIG 6
Flavour I
Textured Objects

Quite inverse to lonely solids heavily placed in the white abstract space. Explicit and strong in their taste. A yes or no situation. I don't like it: It is like Schweppes—works only in cocktails. But on the other hand, I like cocktails:

FIG 7
Flavour 2
Lonely Solids

Or the new chic look—soft shadows, always interior, the floor and ceiling are merging to celebrate a specific materiality of an object—an unknown delicacy—fast as fashion:

FIG 8
Flavour 3
New Chic

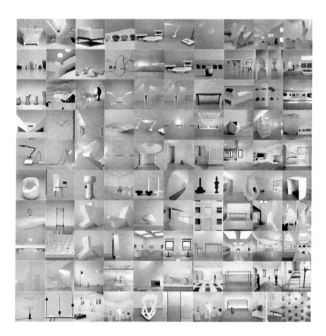

Or the patterns. Oh, I like patterns and matrices! They can become anything; they are abstract enough, but always with an odour:

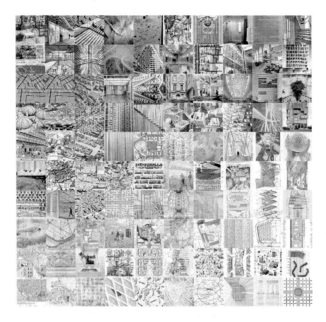

FIG 9
Flavour 4
Patterns

And the buildings, let's not forget buildings. The distilled crystals. But which
ones, the vertical ones or horizontal, simple or complex, for gods or for people?

FIG 10
Flavour 5
Distilled Crystals

I like a bit more the horizontal ones, inhabited by gods. That's just my taste, maybe with a bit of green garnish ... yes, a generic setup, a huge potential:

FIG 11
Flavour 6
Green Garnish

This can go on forever, from sparse smells to condensed flavours. An aftertaste is still present. I think I am onto something. That's my taste condensed and projected back onto the cloud. Each flavour is as consistent and infinite as an independent Instagram account. A spice route composed of many cells, each one containing another table full of flavours. Some known, some unknown. Yes, one is composing with unfamiliar flavours. There is no need to explicitly predefine what a flavour, object, texture, house, drawing or an image is. That is the beauty of information, a virtual full flavour. Brands and blends are dancing around the void.

THAT WHICH BLOWS

My consistency, my many brands. An environment of fluctuating interferences. Colourful objects, flavourless photographs. Trends in settings, aromas, drawings, motives, fashion ... Bazaars, data banks, markets ... Not fearing a lot. Playing, observing, collecting fast. Making artificial flavours. Blends are being distilled from a lot. Taste is a digital filter, a vector in a particular context. It changes as the context changes, but stays intimate, particular, or deliberate. It is an adventure, a game, an articulation, an explosion and a condensation of flavours. Behaving like social media and search engines. Mixing streams are encapsulating the

GHOSTS OF TRANSPARENCY

world; a storm of letters and numbers; an inverse of Google, Facebook, Instagram. An ability to articulate multiple avatars. A dance around an empty axis of lifestyles at any particular moment in life. A fantastic occasion of articulating in millions.

This is the taste of my day, my flavour, my filter; a cocktail out of patterns and drawings, horizontal buildings with green garnish ... that's all. This is what I like. It is my empty centre for today. I also like other streams and objects; I can have many avatars. That's why the centre is empty—it is not explicit. I can project whatever I like. I never say why I like something, only what I like. Images are passing through. It is working: I am getting a mask. It is not perfect, but I can always tune it in another way. A taste is developing. Flavours are not directed towards an ideal blend, but towards the ever-changing conceptions of taste, constantly refining their own role. Anyway, it is my taste of the day. My projection on ArchDaily and Dezeen. A hybrid. Tomorrow is a new day, a new mask, a new identity, a new brand. I can have many of them. Every day is different. The void is never fixed. Many flavours, various masks. Brands become expressions dancing around the void. They are symbolic and algebraic; figures, fugues, faces, masks, atoms, elements, characters, avatars, indexes. It is a play with flavours on a cloudy day.

FIG 12
Blend of the Day

AMBIGUITY AND INFORMATION IN THE CONTEXT OF 'NATURAL COMMUNICATION': AN OBSTACLE-ORIENTED GALOISIAN STANDPOINT

ELIAS ZAFIRIS

V

ELIAS ZAFIRIS holds an M.Sc. (Distinction) in Quantum Fields and Fundamental Forces and a Ph.D. in Theoretical and Mathematical Physics, both from Imperial College at the University of London. He has published papers on category-theoretic methods in quantum physics and complex systems theories, modern differential geometry and topology, and many other topics in the foundations of physics and mathematics. He is also the author of two books on these subjects. He is a research professor in theoretical and mathematical physics at the Institute of Mathematics at the University of Athens and is currently a visiting professor in the Department of Logic, Eötvös Loránd University in Budapest.

The present essay arose out of the curiosity to delve deeper into the nature of obstacles or obstructions that prevent a single, uniform, and linear approach to dealing with systems, entities or, more generally, beings, and their communication. The current motivation comes from a certain degree of dissatisfaction with the overflow of scientific production on what is called 'science of complexity' and the qualification of what accounts as 'information of complex systems' based exclusively on specific 'target-oriented approaches'.

The thread of this amphiboly starts from questioning what is considered to be 'complex' in contradistinction to what is considered to be 'simple.' Usually these terms are implicitly pre-loaded with an ontological meaning, which essentially identifies complexity with certain aggregations of elementary sharply distinguishable constituents developing emergent properties that are behaviourally observed under specific interactions or conditions. This approach is assumed to be valid irrespectively of scale, depending on what is axiomatically baptized as an elementary constituent, so that certain statistical patterns can be applied upon them targeting the simulation of their behaviour. A natural set of questions in this setting is the following: What makes an entity a constituent, how can an entity be characterized as elementary, and most important, how can an entity be sharply distinguishable?

The afterthought of these considerations is that the epithet 'complex' emanates from the contradistinction to what is called 'simple', where what is 'simple' is identified with the 'axiomatic elementary' in the context of the vast majority of these 'target-oriented approaches'.

Notwithstanding these scientific tendencies of the present, this is not actually the way that humankind came to terms with complexity. The targets were not predefined, but rather always emerged out of necessity to cope with obstacles in communication of every particular sort. In this respect, the meaning of complexity is altered dramatically if theorized from an 'obstacle-oriented' standpoint instead of a 'target-oriented' one. More precisely, the ability to locate obstacles or obstructions forcing a deviation from some condition of inertiality becomes the primordial task. The localization of an obstacle necessitates a process of metaphora around this obstacle, i.e. a temporal flow around it through another level of hypostasis. The metaphora is effective if the flow is communicative, i.e. if it establishes bidirectional bridges connecting these two levels. In this sense, an 'obstacle-oriented' approach is not directly a 'problem-solving' approach, but an indirectly 'problem-embracing' one. The different levels are not in any relation of hypotaxis of one to another, but only in relation of parataxis, and what really matters is the connectivity in the passage from one level to another in a bidirectional way via the bridges. Most significantly, connectivity does not pre-suppose sharply distinguishable entities, but is deformation invariant given the localization of an obstacle. This is quite intuitive to conceive, since otherwise it would defeat the purpose of metaphora in relation to communication.

In this state of affairs, if the history of humankind is viewed from the standpoint of the 'obstacle-oriented approach' to complexity, pertaining to locating and embracing obstructions of any particular type, a naturally arising problematics refers to delineating the most persistent and covariant forms of this stance. The character of temporal persistence and covariance is meant to serve as a criterion for the 'ousia ontos ousa' of history. Surprisingly enough, this criterion filters out only two kinds of entities, namely myths and theorems. At a first encounter with this provocative claim, there seems to be a contradiction, but this is only apparent, caused mainly from a certain type of pre-occupation with 'target-oriented' methods instead of 'obstacle-oriented ones'. Indeed, both myths and theorems become noematic if they are obstacle-embracing: They are actually different types of metaphora in relation to communication. Myths and narratives constitute an embodied symbolic process of metaphora around a localized obstacle. Mathematical theorems constitute an abstract symbolic process of metaphora around a localized obstacle. Although mythos and logos deceptively seem to occupy opposite sides of the linear spectrum forced by 'analytic reason', they are, in fact, antipodally inter-related and topologically glued together in the projective geometric rooting of this linear spectrum, centred around the notion of an obstacle.

In order to articulate this claim, we will consider the dual pair of concepts consisting of ambiguity and information in relation to communication. On the side of the myth, we will scrutinize the narrative referring to the genesis of Goddess Aphrodite according to Hesiod's Theogony. On the side of the logos, we will scrutinize the theorem referring to the genesis of the roots of a polynomial equation by radicals according to Galois' Theory. The remarkable conclusion is that in both cases information emerges as 'anadyomene' from another level of hypostasis, being in communication with the level where the initial obstruction is located via bidirectional bridges. Before embarking on this task, it is instructive to include a basic familiarization with the model of 'natural communication', which constitutes the 'nuts and bolts' of the 'obstacle-oriented approach' to complexity.

THE MODEL OF 'NATURAL COMMUNICATION'

The main initial motivation behind the set-up of the model of 'natural communication' has been the transcendence of the current, 'target-oriented' complexity paradigm into a new one, envisioning and implementing an architectonics of communication, encapsulating the concepts of category theory, sheaf theory, and quantum mechanics. The primal realization is that an architectonics of relations based on communication is ultimately necessitated in all cases, where direct accessibility to sharply distinguishable domains of objects and their behaviour is not feasible due to obstacles or obstructions of any particular type. In these domains, objects are intrinsically shaped according to foamy or cloudy patterns, and they are characterized by topological plasticity, emergent properties and generically probabilistic attributes. The application of pre-specific, readily-tailored design ontologies to these domains, based on the notion of sharply-distinguishable elementary constituency, not only distorts the architectonics of their non-trivial connectivity patterns, but limits and restricts, even inadvertently, their potential computational capacities.

The basic idea to address and utilize the architectonic modelling of these domains is the following: Instead of analysing not-directly-accessible domains in terms of set-based elements and their hypothetical absolute relations, adjoin to them other adequately-understood or directly-accessible domains, which can provide pointers and open up communication channels with the former ones. The process of adjoining should not be ad hoc and should not depend on artificial choices, meaning that it should be qualified as structurally-respecting, at least, locally or partially. This refers to the 'naturality requirement' of the model, a term which is exemplified in the context of category theory. Technically, this adjunction process is described in terms of a pair of adjoint functors between the involved categorical domains.

In practice, the process of adjoining a controllable domain to another one, initially not directly accessible, or obstacle-laden categorical domain, amounts to viewing these domains as different categorical levels in a stratified universe of discourse, which are bi-directionally connected by means of opposite-oriented bridges. The architectonics of communication targets precisely the conception and explicit construction of these bridges, once suitable probing domains have been structurally delineated for adjunction to the directly inaccessible domain. The bridge directed to the controllable domain plays the role of an encoding bridge, whereas its inverse plays the role of a decoding bridge. These connecting bridges affect the communication between the involved domains, in the sense that they naturally establish universal bidirectional communication channels through which a schema of metaphora is accomplished, based on the notion of an 'obstacle-encircling' temporal flow. Topologically thinking, the initially inaccessible categorical domain is resolved cyclically by a process of unfolding with respect to the probing domain that has been adjoined to it. In this manner, the invariants emerging by the process of unfolding depict the invariant characteristics of the reciprocal communication flow between these domains. Consequently, the complexity of the not-directly-accessible, or obstacle-laden, domain is not specified constitutionally on the basis of a pre-assumed or axiomatic elementary ontology, but relationally and functorially, in terms of the invariants emerging in the bidirectional communication flow established with some appropriate probing domain. From an algebraic viewpoint, these invariants can be qualified in terms of structural group-type ciphers for the symbolic encryption/decryption of the induced flow.

In a nutshell, the obstacle-embracing schema of metaphora giving rise to this cyclic flow, called 'logical conjugation', is conceptually based on a legitimate logical manoeuvre through a controllable or a directly accessible domain that is adjoined naturally to an obstacle-laden domain, furnishing markers or pointers or gauges of specifying the latter indirectly through bidirectional communication bridges. The logical conjugation method should be thought of operationally in terms of a 'motivic key' that bears the capacity to unlock harmonically the complexity of the inaccessible domain depending on the nature and type of the obstacle. The creative art of the 'obstacle-oriented approach' in the context of the model of 'natural communication' consists in the innovation of motivic keys suited to the nature and type of an encountered obstacle. A motivic key always gives rise to a partition spectrum of the obstacle-laden domain. Each cell of this spectrum is characterized completely by the pair of encoding/decoding bridges utilized for communicating an aspect of the directly inaccessible domain with respect to the probing domain.

For all practical purposes, the model of 'natural communication' can be implemented algorithmically as follows: We consider a problem in the context of a domain whose object and relations are directly inaccessible. It is instructive to think of this domain as a particular level in a broad 'universe of discourse', which can engulf other possible levels as well. First, we move out of the context of the problem, formulated at the level of the inaccessible domain, by adjoining to it another controllable domain, assuming existence within the same universe. In order to accomplish this, we have to set up an encoding bridge from the level of the inaccessible domain to the level of the accessible domain. Once we have succeeded to set up this bridge, we are able to mirror the initial problem at the level of the controllable domain, where we have the means to solve it effectively. The process is completed by setting up an inverse decoding bridge from the level of the controllable domain to the level of the inaccessible one.

In this way, the solution established at the controllable domain can be lifted at the initial context of the problem, and thus the problem is resolved in the context of its initial formulation. The reciprocal encoding and decoding bridges constitute the means of a novel architectonics of communication. This architectonics gives rise to a schema of metaphora that resolves an inaccessible domain by a communicative bidirectional and cyclic process of embracing the obstacle causing the direct inaccessibility. It has to be stressed that the schema of metaphora can be iterated by the involvement of more than one controllable domains adjoined jointly to the inaccessible domain. The skeleton of this algorithmic procedure of resolving inaccessible domains via motivic keys remains invariant under the adjunctions of deeper levels, and most importantly, always gives rise to a partition spectrum of the inaccessible domain, whose cells are indexed by the respective pairs of encoding/decoding bridges. Conclusively, the spectral resolution conducted by setting up a motivic key to an inaccessible domain for embracing the type of obstacle it is laden with constitutes the essence of logical conjugation, whence the communicating domains, represented by levels connected by the encoding/decoding bridges, are called conjugate domains.

THE GALOISIAN CONCEPTION OF AMBIGUITY AND INFORMATION

Galois' memoir is entitled *On the conditions for the solvability of equations by radicals*. In this work he manages to resolve completely the problem of algebraic solvability of polynomial equations, i.e. equations of the form $p(x) = 0$. In particular, he demonstrated that a general formula for the roots of a fifth (or any higher) degree polynomial equation does not exist by utilizing only the usual algebraic operations of addition, subtraction, multiplication, division, and applying radicals, i.e. roots of nth degree.

The first novelty of Galois' method consists in the introduction of the group concept, which he devised as a structure G to encode the permutations of the roots of a polynomial $p(x)$ in $F[x]$, which map each root onto a conjugate of it, where F is a field, called the ground field of coefficients. The second novelty of Galois' method consists in employing the structure of the above group G together and in relation to the structure of its invariant subgroups under conjugation, i.e. its self-conjugate or normal subgroups. The underlying reason is that the notion of structural divisibility of a Galois group becomes possible only with respect to its normal subgroups. The third novelty of Galois' method consists in the notion of group solvability. The triumph of Galois' theory is based on the theorem that a polynomial equation is solvable by radicals if and only if the corresponding Galois group of the equation is solvable. A solvable group is a group whose derived series terminates at the trivial subgroup in finitely many steps. Intuitively, the derived series is set up by stratification into group levels together with a descending staircase among these strata formed by identifying each subgroup in the descending series with a normal subgroup of the previous one such that the induced factor group is Abelian.

In this state of affairs, the Galois group G corresponding to a polynomial p(x) in F[x], where F is the ground field, can be thought of as a non-numerical, but structural measure of complexity of this polynomial. In turn, the iterative process involved in setting up the derived series of G, by means of normal subgroups, can be thought of as a process of complexity reduction until the trivial subgroup of G is eventually reached. It is important in this frame of thinking to clarify what we mean by a structural measure of complexity as this is encoded in the Galois group of a polynomial p(x) in F[x]. The general notion of a group is associated with a criterion of symmetry under its action. What is the implicated notion of symmetry in this case, and how can it be associated with a measure of complexity?

The answer comes from noticing that the Galois group G, being the group of permutations of the roots of a polynomial p(x) in F[x], which maps each root onto a conjugate of it, actually encodes these F-transformations of the roots of p(x) that cannot be distinguished from the resolution capacity afforded by the ground field F. In other words, the Galois group G of p(x) is an ambiguity group with respect to F, and this ambiguity structure amounts to a measure of complexity of p(x) in relation to the spectral resolving means afforded by F. Henceforth, the symmetry encapsulated by the Galois group G of p(x) in relation to F can be reduced only by possible successive symmetry breakings until the total symmetry constituting the structural measure of F-complexity is completely reduced.

Reciprocally, the annihilation of the ambiguity encoded in the Galois group G of p(x) in relation to F—at the level of groups—is decoded by a gradual process of successive field extensions of the ground field—at the 'obstacle-laden' level of fields—to be thought of as an unfolding process of F to larger or more refined fields that increase the resolution capacity afforded by the ground field itself, until eventually all roots can become spectrally distinguishable. More precisely, given a polynomial p(x) in F[x], of degree n, it can be shown that there exists a minimal extension of F, called the splitting field Fp of p(x), in which all n roots of p(x) can be distinguished. The splitting field Fp of p(x), constitutes in this way the smallest total field extension of the ground field F over which the polynomial p(x) splits or decomposes into linear factors. Spectral distinguishability of the roots of p(x) constitutes the pre-condition for qualifying each of these roots as a bearer of information, by means of an actual spectral distinction in the context of the splitting field Fp of p(x).

In this manner, ambiguity—as a group-theoretic measure of complexity—, and information—as a spectral measure of actual distinctions—, form a Galoisian complementary pair, whence the level of groups and the level of fields constitute conjugate domains. The descending series of ambiguity groups starting from the Galois group until the trivial group is eventually reached, represents all the successive stages of symmetry breaking, i.e. all the successive stages of complexity or ambiguity reduction with respect to the ground field until all the roots of $p(x) = 0$ become spectrally distinguishable in the inversely proportional ascending series of field extensions from the ground field to the splitting field of $p(x)$. Therefore, information in Galois' theory emerges via a cyclic metaphorical process from the 'obstacle-laden' level of fields to the level of groups and back in the form of 'anadyomene' through the foam of spectral ambiguity, embracing eventually the roots-obstacles.

THE MYTH OF APHRODITE ANADYOMENE REVISITED

Following the narrative of Hesiod's Theogony, the genesis of Goddess Aphrodite took place in an extraordinary manner. She emerged in the form of a fully-grown female figure rising out of the sea foam (aphros). Her name Aphrodite, or Aphrogeneia, according to Hesiod, originates from the fact that she grew and formed amid the sea foam. The epithet 'anadyomene' uncovers the metaphor process of Aphrodite's genesis. This is a process of circulation between the Heavenly level (Uranus), and the Earthly level (Gaia), which is meant to embrace the obstacle of heterogeneous, chimerical and intrinsically incongruent constituency of these two levels. The initiator of this obstacle-embracing communicative process is the Titan Chronos, who stands for the personification of Time as a unitary circular flow bridging reciprocally these two levels into a germinal syzygy. According to the myth, Chronos forced the transposition of the sperm of Uranus into the sea water, and out of this syzygy a white foam spread around the locus of germination in the sea from the immortal flesh. In this 'ambiguity foam' there started to grow the maiden Aphrodite virtualized, to emerge eventually as a fully grown in-formed spectral figure by inverse transposition to the level of Gods, completing in this way the temporal circulatory metaphorical process of anadyomene initiated by Chronos. It is important to highlight that the two levels of the myth are not hierarchically ordered, meaning that there is no relation of hypotaxis or subordination of one level to the other. On the contrary, the two levels exist autonomously in parataxis and only the unitary circular flow of Chronos binds them in communication through reciprocal bridges. The bridge from the Heavenly to the Earthly level is the germination bridge, whereas the reciprocal, or conceptually inverse one, is the virtual growth bridge. The latter is characterized as virtual because the growth of the figure to emerge as Aphrodite is always surrounded by the sea foam, and thus, the growing figure is indistinguishable and inseparable from the foam. This is crucial for conceiving both the symmetry implicated by the circular unitary flow-action of Chronos and the emergence of Aphrodite as a fully grown in-formed figure only after gradually breaking the symmetry of this inter-level communicative flow, and thus, separated by the sea foam and distinguished or discerned spectrally from it at the level of Gods.

FROM THE BIT TO THE PIT: POETICS OF THE FINANCIAL MARKET
ELIE AYACHE

VI

ELIE AYACHE was born in Lebanon in 1966. Trained as an engineer at L'Ecole Polytechnique of Paris, he pursued a career of option market-maker on the floor of MATIF (1987–1990) and LIFFE (1990–1995). He then turned to the philosophy of probability (DEA at la Sorbonne) and to the technology of derivative pricing, and co-founded ITO 33, a financial software company, in 1999. Today, ITO 33 is the leading specialist in the pricing of convertible bonds, in the equity-to-credit problem, and more generally in the calibration and recalibration of volatility surfaces. Ayache has published numerous articles on the philosophy of contingent claims. He is the author of *The Blank Swan: The End of Probability* (2010), and of *The Medium of Contingency: An Inverse View of the Market* (2015).

When pondering the question of present-day communication and whether the deluge of data might end up obscuring information, it is difficult to content oneself with part of the universe and not to consider the total communication system that the whole universe is. Philosophers of quantum computation like Seth Lloyd equate the universe with a gigantic quantum computer, in which scripts keep being generated at random, eventually constituting stable physical systems and autonomous life forms.[1] Markus Gabriel teaches us, on the other hand, that the world is a bigger entity than the universe. The universe is the collection of all physical systems produced by quantum code, with a perfect duality between object and property, physical system and physical law, whereas the world is the collection of all things imaginable. There is the physical world or universe, of course; but there is, additionally, the world of dreams, the world of literature, the world of man, etc., and perhaps even the world of communication.

The universe exists, while the world doesn't, according to Gabriel.[2] The collection of all things cannot exist. Speaking of the world is usually the indication of a shift in discourse, from physical to metaphysical. One typically speaks of the end of the world, not of the end of the universe, and in the typical limiting movement that worries us, in which the excess of information becomes equivalent to its lack, or density becomes equivalent to the void, or total memory becomes equivalent to a blank; it is the world that becomes implicitly our object of discourse—a *metaphysical system* rather than a physical one.

We claim that the financial market is of the same category as the world and is also a metaphysical system, not a physical one. Probably for this reason, it gets no mention in the computational renderings of the universe, such as Seth Lloyd's. Yet we wonder: Can't the market be considered a consequence of the randomness that is produced by the universe, similarly to physical systems? The market exists, after all. Can't it also be considered a script, perhaps even an unavoidable one, obtained by the computational universe? Or does the world of man have necessarily to get involved in its making? Should books and poems be considered the result of the computational universe too?

Perhaps the necessity of emergence of the market within the computational universe is due to the possibility of annihilation of any script and of the failure of communication—a possibility that necessarily exists. Indeed, the condition of possibility of communication, or its material medium, is at the same time the condition of its impossibility, in case this medium is annihilated. And it suddenly strikes us that the entire analysis of the universe as a prodigious quantum computer might

1   Seth Lloyd, *Programming the Universe: A Quantum Computer Scientist Takes on the Cosmos* (New York: Alfred A. Knopf, a division of Random House, 2006).
2   Markus Gabriel, *Why the World Doesn't Exist* (Cambridge and Walden: Polity Press, 2015).

be based on a notion of randomness and of its communication channel that ignores writing and its (indispensable) other face, which is the necessary possibility of annihilation of the written record.[3]

Thus, it ignores the *exchange* of written records, which is the other face of their material nature. To anticipate our discourse of the market, the reason financial contracts are materially exchanged between individuals, and priced solely in this fashion instead of being valued by an algorithm, is that they can be annihilated or defaulted. The market exists and is not programmable, the market is not redundant, because of the necessary intervention of the world (and of the end of the world) in the universe.

The computational vision of the universe can only comprehend the financial market as one among other data-producing systems. Nobody sees the market as a means of communication with something totally different, with the end of the communication, for instance. This is because nobody wants to antagonize the very archaeology of thought that produces the computational vision; nobody wants a criticism of the notion of *state* (computational or otherwise).

Can it reasonably be argued that the financial market presents itself in the universe because of the forgotten criticism and that if one were to supplement an analysis like Seth Lloyd's, which is great for saying what the universe is in effect, with the clause of failure of communication, or with the channel that communicates with the event and with the end of the world, then this revolutionary medium which communicates with the incommunicable would be the market (or its generalized notion)? We fear this new category might elude any positive analysis. For, instead of speaking of information and of communicational content, we speak of systems that lie in no computational state—of systems that lie in a total absence of state, which is a state of total preparation for writing and for communication with the event.

What good would writing be, indeed, if not to communicate with the event? What good would thinking be—all the invisible things that one keeps pushing in a corner of the world—if it were all reducible to code, and positively transmissible by the channel of communication?

ABYSS OF THE CONCRETE WORLD

The bit, or the basic unit of information, is a random variable X that switches between 0 and 1. It is communicable because the variable X

---

3   Not to mention the converse situation, in which the written record survives the death of the two communicating parties and literally breaks free from the initial context of communication. This is not an accident, according to Derrida, but the very definition of writing, which therefore can never be reduced to a *means* of communication. On the contrary, it signals the failure of communication qua transmission of meaning or intention. See Jacques Derrida, 'Signature, Event, Context', in *Margins of Philosophy*, trans. by A. Bass (Chicago: Chicago University Press, 1985).

is *real* (in a sense we shall define shortly) and measurable. It is the answer to a question; it is an output. As a matter of fact, it is a function of something very strange that abstract probability theory recognizes as the 'sample ω'.

Indeed, the random variable X is a mapping between an abstract space, the 'universe' or 'sample space W' which is meant to remain unanalyzed, and a set which will be subject to mathematical analysis, typically the set of real numbers:

$$\Omega \to \mathbb{R}$$
$$\omega \mapsto X(\omega)$$

Ironically, the sample ω is the index of the *concrete* situation or *concrete* case, of that which has concretely to happen in the world—call it the random draw—in order that the random variable may admit a value. The sample ω isn't a variable; it is something else. A 'variable' represents the lowest level in mathematical analysis; and rightly so, probability theory reserves that term to X and not to ω.

The Markov system is the paradigm of communication systems and the important notion of *state* of that system is in truth derived and not primitive. It is the consequence of two characteristic properties of Markov chains: first, that singletons of values of the random variable are measurable and can enter in the definition of conditional probability; second, that the past and the future are independent, conditionally on the present state that has just been defined. This enables the definition of the *probability of transition* between states, which is therefore a derived notion too. Communication, state and transition between states are thus indissolubly linked, but they all derive, as we will see, from something infrastructural and more fundamental—literally, the incommunicable.

Indeed, the basic unit of information, 0 or 1, or the bit, is not the deepest level of information. It doesn't get to the bottom of things. It is not the 'absolute' information because it is the state of a random variable, therefore the reflection of a point of view. It presupposes a context or a preliminary choice of the algebra of events (or possibilities), which is always relative. One has to edit the absolute concrete in order to produce the real. Information is *real*; it is definitional of the level of reality, in our construction, because it is the answer to a well-posed question. As real, however, information is underlain by the concrete sample ω, by that which has *absolutely concretely happened* in order to make the value 0 or 1 appear.

Let us add, parenthetically, that probability should be the first arithmetic and the first science of numbers, the one tying them up with the concrete world and with 'what has concretely happened'. Nothing happens in analysis, by contrast. Thus, the truly fundamental 'variable' should be the one that indexes the concrete world and is rooted in it; it should be the concrete sample ω, which is not a variable in the sense of analysis. In any deconstruction enterprise, one should first tackle this infrastructure. The conditions of impossibility of communication are part of the concrete world that is presupposed by the screen of reality and by the editing of the real, that is to say, by abstraction.

Yet, the sample ω cannot be measured. We cannot measure what has absolutely concretely happened. There is no communicable information contained in this, no question that would map the states of a random variable and would admit of an answer. This literally communicates with the incommunicable, with the abyss of information that *matter* constitutes in any case.

Why this word, *matter*? Why is matter an abyss of information? Because the event that would bring communication and the whole world to an end belongs to no previously established algebra of events. It escapes any context, any frame of reference, and for this reason it is absolute like matter. It 'carries with it a force of breaking with its context'.[4] On the other hand, ω, or the concrete sample of abstract probability theory, is the first sign of irruption of matter into the formalism, or of thought thinking matter, and for this reason it is abysmal.

One should not confuse mass and matter. The semblance of infinity that contemporary mass media produce should not be equated with the infinity of the abyss in which the random sample ω is thrown. Indeed, we deal with intensity, in the latter case, not with extensity and quantity; we deal with the unmeasurable mass of that which has *absolutely concretely happened*.

The concrete world is not just an accessory, in abstract probability theory. Our first impression is that the concrete detail is supplemental and concerns only the contingent world. However, detailing the colour of the dice or the colour of the sky above it is only an image and an illustration. What really counts in the concrete world is that the descent in its abyss should be indefinite, that is to say, infinite. That 'it' happens, without further specification, is in itself an abysmal notion. The logic of randomness claims this infinity, because it claims repetition. If it were not for the concrete world and for the indefinite level at which the line of abstraction is drawn (which just underlines the infinite play between thought and matter), there wouldn't be the notion of independence and repetition, which is fundamental for randomness.

RANDOMNESS AND THE EVENT

Anyone who throws the dice once throws it an infinity of times. This is because the dice is *there*, concretely. This intensive infinity is only the

---

4 Jacques Derrida, 'Signature, Event, Context', in *Margins of Philosophy*, Alan Bass trans. (Chicago: Chicago University Press, 1985).

expression of the stroke of the matter of the dice, as it gets inscribed in thought. The strong law of large numbers, or the convergence of the frequency of appearance of a particular face when throwing the dice until the end, is only the indication of localized matter. Given the bottomless pit and the bottomless question of what has absolutely concretely happened, given that everything that will have ever happened in the history of the universe could be virtually recounted as a single sample that the world has drawn from the urn, once and for all, this fall is in reality always suspended, the line of abstraction is always drawn at some level of the concrete abyss, and a point of view is always adopted.

A local physical object is thus carved out of the world, and *this automatically entails that the object has multiple faces and that multiple samples can produce the same face.* This brings about repetition, therefore randomness in the ordinary sense and convergence of the frequency. Now that we have suspended the fall and broken the 'once and for all', we can only repeat. For otherwise, we are never done with the first sample, never done answering the question of what has absolutely concretely happened.

Ultimately, the traditional logic of randomness exhausts history by the notion of density and totality, by a sample space that is supposed to contain all that has ever been the case from the beginning until the end of times. In its ontology, the event of a meteorite falling and killing the players who are throwing the dice is not a radically emergent event. Surely enough, it wasn't imaginable or perhaps even conceivable beforehand; it wasn't part of the game of dice and its algebra of measurable events; it belonged completely outside the context of the game. However, according to the totalizing logic of sample space, the case that brought it about has always been part of the big urn that the world is drawing its samples from.

The event becomes conceivable after it appears. Just as the face of the die never happened as such, but something concrete happened instead, the sample ω, and made the face of the die appear, just so, something happens now, making the meteorite appear, yet has always been an element of sample space. Now that the falling meteorite has become a conceivable event, the algebra of events is recalibrated and further refined (we advance the filtration by one step) and a new 'face' is added to the die. It is as if we were suddenly able to look more closely into the detail of the concrete situation and the meteorite was only a previously indiscernible detail.

Another name for this twisted metaphysics is the *backward narrative*. The backward narrative is an attempt to bring history to an end, as it implies that the end has always been at the beginning. A liberating alternative would be to 'stop' history by the void and not by density, or equivalently by the absolute capacity, by claiming that what has 'absolutely concretely happened' is that everything, anything, *can happen*.

It is characteristic of communicable information (of its algebra, of its filtration) that one be able to regress in the abyss, at each iteration, and say: 'This is the way things must have happened from the beginning; this is what my algebra of events must have always been, from the beginning.' An alternative way of placing oneself at once in the infinity of 'what has already happened,' a progressive and not a regressive way, consists in saying that *it hasn't yet happened*. Intensity, not extensity. The infinite intensity is such, in this case, that one writes effectively after the event, before it. Although the event doesn't exist yet, although it is absolute difference (all the more absolute as we don't know what the event is different from), we have to establish contact with it and communicate with it, in a single stroke.

To this end, we must consider a transformation of probability that tests the limits of the logic of randomness and takes up the total set of cases, or universe W, to transform it into a *world*. This transformation will produce the financial market and will throw the abyss forward. We won't be reconstructing the universe, anymore, in an ever-regressive fashion, but finally meeting with the world. This amounts to saying that the reality of the market will replace the 'reality' of abstract probability theory (its algebra of events) and will be, from now on, in contact and in continuity with the absolute concrete. We won't be tumbling down the abyss of the absolute concrete anymore, in search for its absolute detail, because it will be projected before us at once, for all times.

MONEY

Communication by the market, as medium of contingency, is communication with the infinity of the concrete situation, an intensive and not extensive infinity. It is not a set whose elements can increase or decrease in number, and not even a variable that can run over a total.

The financial market is usually confused with the deluge of statistical data. This is because the argument from the derivatives has been overlooked, a qualitative and not a quantitative argument, as we shall see, which issues from the operation of *conceptualization* and not of abstraction. Indeed, we shall interpret the successive writing of derivatives and their successive re-immersion in the trading pit as a succession of degrees of *conceptualization* that will never rise above the immanence of the exchange and will always reaffirm the trading pit as only concrete, not as successive levels of abstraction of that concrete. The distinction we make between conceptualization and abstraction is thus fundamental. But first, a word about money.

The argument against the state and possibility, or against communication and probabilistic transitions, should stem from the local and not the global, from what's hidden under our very feet. Jean-Yves Girard, whose *Le Fantôme de la transparence* (or ghost of transparency) was certainly an inspiration to the title of the present volume, is right to speak of the implicit, in the particular instance, and particularly so of money.[5] Money is implicit, he writes, because "it represents everything, or rather, anything." From which I speculate that it corresponds to the intensity of the abyss; that it 'communicates' with the incommunicable and not with the extensive collection of data or the extensity of information. The concrete sample ω was invariably implicit too, under the surface of measurable things. "Thought belongs to the domain of the implicit," writes Girard, "while the explicit limits itself to verification." So the fascinating question becomes: What would be the alternative, to both the world and communication if the abyss of money became the only concrete?

The alternative to the abstraction of probability theory is the conceptualization of the trading pit. This is our thesis. There is infinity in money because money is at the same time its own ground and own abyss. It lends itself to speculative bubbles and to market crashes *at the same time,* and not in alternation. The pit presents us with the vision of its interior because of this spontaneous infinity. This vision from the inside (consisting in riding the channel of money instead of measuring values and verifying information from the outside) is the one, in our view, that requires conceptualization instead of abstraction.

At play is the implicit character of money. When money, which applies to anything, is applied to itself, it becomes the only end of the world, and the trading pit closes itself on us. We no longer buy the stock to acquire a value (that of the issuing company) but only to purchase the future price movement of the trading stock. We then can only make money or lose money. The stock price can only go up or go down. There are no other measurable events in this world. And this is not an abstraction over a concrete sample that might be infinitely richer in the point of unmeasurable detail. This is simply money.

People buy the stock because its price could go up, and its price goes up because people buy it. Or they sell it because its price could go down, and its price goes down because people sell it. Money is in itself the primary abstraction and then it becomes the only concrete. It screens off any other concrete. There Aren't even two events in this world (the price going up or down). There is only money, which becomes more fundamental than randomness and perhaps even time.

As soon as the stock exchange (or the trading pit) is given, randomness is given. The infrastructure of sample space is no longer needed. Once the free exchange is accepted, speculation, or the market looking at itself reflexively, becomes the only ground, a constantly moving ground.

---

5   Jean-Yves Girard, *Le Fantôme de la transparence* (Paris: Éditions Allia, 2016). All quotes are my translation.

The movement of the stock price becomes the only commodity and precisely derivatives (a.k.a. contingent claims) are written, which pay off if certain price paths are realized. And now the implicit character of money plays the crucial role. It is such that the payoff those derivatives return when they expire is made of the same money as the one that is made or lost in the process of trading their underlying stock. This, after the Nobel-prize winning discovery by Black, Scholes and Merton (BSM) in 1973,[6] allows derivatives to be replicated by a self-financing dynamic trading strategy involving the underlying stock, and hence it allows them to be re-immersed, in their turn, in the same market and in the same trading pit. This invariable reversion of the overlying to the underlying, of the derivative (no matter how complex) to the basic trading floor, is the *implicit definition of the market*, in our view.[7] The money in which one would be tempted to value the derivatives externally as lotteries is, once again, of the same nature as the one in which they are traded and admit a price.

Money doesn't have two faces, 0 and 1. Money is not a coin we flip or a die we cast. Money is the concrete world become liquid. The entire abyss slips itself inside money and now constitutes a ground on which we stand in order to project the entire concrete world in the opposite direction. That money should have no other meaning but to be made or lost, that money itself could become worthless and should have the end of the world as its other face (that is to say, no other face at all); that this should be the *implicit definition* of money is what enables us to replace the explicit state, 0 or 1, by the single self-financing trading strategy and by the single face of money.

THE TRADING PIT

Trading is not a matter of drawing a sample from the urn. Trading *means* randomness. By the efficient market hypothesis, the stock price cannot but be volatile. If asked what the meaning of the market is, what the *concept* of the market is, we should answer: volatility. We may not know what the value of anything is, because there is only price and price is volatile, but now we know volatility. Volatility becomes the *value* of the market. Thus, it is the very *concept* of the trading pit of the underlying stock (volatility), and not its abstraction, that BSM have transformed into the value of the derivative written on that underlying, a value soon to join the trading pit again and to become price again.

6 Fisher Black and Myron Scholes, The pricing of options and corporate liabilities, *The Journal of Political Economy*, 81(3), May—June 1973, 637–654.
7 Elie Ayache, *The Medium of Contingency: An Inverse View of the Market* (Basingstoke and New York: Palgrave Macmillan, 2015).

What is there to abstract, anyway? Remember that money and trading are the only concrete, and that there is no deeper, underlying concrete. Remember that the trading pit is the only world. So it cannot be abstraction that we are achieving here, no longer a cut, but a conceptualization of the whole thing. This is an alternative schema of thought altogether. We are thrown in the abyss of trading from the beginning and BSM show us, via Brownian volatility and the self-financing dynamic trading strategy, that the contingent payoff is the result of conceptualization of the trading of the underlying stock, rather than its mere probabilistic abstraction as a random process. In the concept of trading a stock, there is *both* the randomness of its price *and* the variability of the size we are holding. This newly synthesized contingent payoff can then only become a materially written contingent claim and be traded in its turn. This is the crux of the matter.

When money and trading are the only ground, a thing can be conceived, that is to say, carved out of the concrete world, only if it is *exchanged*. This is the different order of time and matter we are dealing with. There is always infinity in the way thought joins itself with matter then separates itself from it. One infinity results in the usual view of randomness and of the concrete situation, and another results in the exchange. One is backward, the other is forward.

One really has to understand how different the two masses are from each other, and how exclusive of each other. Something in the archaeology of thought places the abyss of the concrete situation on one side, and the same thing makes it so that one possible transmutation of the mass is the abyss of the exchange. In one case, the realm of abstraction generates random variables and values of random variables, or the vision from outside. In the other case, the single face of money (identity between the ground and the abyss or between the speculative bubble and the market crash) generates contingent claims and prices, or the vision from inside in which the event is already an integral part.

By contrast with the infinite but regressive descent in the abyss of the concrete situation, writing, or the immersion in the trading pit, is infinite and progressive. To give oneself a total and pre-existing sample space, over which only to draw the line of abstraction, is what causes the finite character of this regressive infinity: an infinity that is not spontaneous. The culprit is thus the schema of abstraction, or the traditional logic of randomness. It causes the recalibration of the algebra of events always to take place as a backward narrative, while denying, every time, that it has gone backwards in this fashion. It causes thought constantly to be hiding from itself and not being in sync with itself.

Money goes forwards, by contrast. By the implicit definition of the market and of money, the prices of all derivatives are all given at once, despite the seemingly sequential order in which those derivatives are written and traded. As prices, they vary from any probabilistic

GHOSTS OF TRANSPARENCY

valuation, before they even move. The recalibration process of the algebra of events, which was always stopped at a finite level and always restarted in total denial of the previous stage, is now spontaneously unfolded, going forward. Time is no longer absorbed by the abyss. It liberates itself into historical time.

There is no communicable information in the market, because any piece of information, any level of reality and of abstraction that one reaches in order to communicate is at once translated into the exchange. Any stage of abstraction that would allow an algorithm to create its reality and its referents can be concretely written as the payoff of a contingent claim, and the latter, precisely because of matter and of the first affliction which is, in the present instance, that anything written is traded at once, can only be united with the first (and only) level of reality, the reality of trading.

Strangely enough, this homogeneity (or hegemony) of price is the reason why some thinkers have lost any interest in the market and have considered it, from the beginning, as just a shapeless mass of transactions, or simply chaos. They did not perceive the richness in the back and forth movement of trading and writing. Trading a stock is the same as writing a derivative on that stock, is the same as trading the derivative, is the same as writing a derivative on the derivative, is the same as trading the second derivative in turn, etc. In a single stroke, the infinity of the abyss of the concrete world is handed back from the other end, never to be totalized again in a universe of cases.

This singularity of the market, which enables it to communicate directly with the singularity of the event, makes it foreign to any notion of progressive unveiling of information. For this reason, the alternative metaphor is, to my eyes, that of the blank that is filled by the single stroke of writing and by the single poem. The end of the world can only be communicated by writing. Under no circumstance does a poem or a book communicate information.

Thus style is the opposite of information. Books and poems communicate the former, not the latter. Another meaning of style is stylus, or the sharp and pointed instrument with which to impress matter and engrave it. One speaks of an *amount* of information or of a *filtration* indexed by time. Information is metrical—either volumetric, or chronologic—whereas the book is intense and possesses only writing style. It may have the volume of an entire world and may communicate with the end of the world; it nevertheless constitutes a single stroke. *In Search of Lost Time* is a single directed stroke; it is not a collection of words. For this reason, one cannot subtract a single word from it.

THE ART OF EXAGGERATION
ALEXI KUKULJEVIC

VII

ALEXI KUKULJEVIC is an artist and a philosopher based in Vienna. He is the author of *Liquidation World: On the Art of Living Absently*, published by MIT Press. His work has been exhibited internationally at venues such as the Palais de Tokyo, Paris and the ICA, Philadelphia. He is a teaching assistant in the Department for Art Theory at the University of Applied Arts in Vienna. His most recent solo exhibition was entitled BIRDWAR, at Åplus in Berlin. He is currently working on a book entitled, *Like Hell It Is.*

Everyone has heard the story of the man of Picardy for whom, on the scaffold, they presented a wench, offering (as our justice sometimes allows) to save his life if he would marry her. He, having looked at her for a while and noticed that she was lame, said: "Tie up, tie up! She limps." — Montaigne[1]

Franz-Joseph Murau, the central character of Thomas Bernhard's last published novel, *Extinction* [*Auslöschung*], is more than a figure who tends towards exaggeration: he is an exaggeration artist [*Übertreibungskünstler*]. Like the man of Picardy who chooses death over a limping wench, Murau puts a "fanatical faith in exaggeration." As he himself puts it: He has *Übertreibungsfanatismus.*[2]

The man of Picardy is a fool. And wise counsel when confronted with a forced choice, advises the path of least resistance. If it is going to be one's money or one's life, let it be one's money, so that both are not lost. It is better to lose the least. And this, of course, is the motto of good bureaucrats, precisely those who Lacan suggests are the ones who will truly "set things off" by following orders, rules, and regulations, "mechanically, down the chain of command, with human wills bent, abolished, overcome, in a task that ceases to have any meaning." He adds: "That task will be the elimination of an incalculable waste that reveals its constant and final dimension for man."[3] The human being—this maker of footsteps that become for the artist holes in the ground—ends up filling them with his or her own refuse. Yet, if reduced to the calculus of its conservation, whose end, Lacan tells us, is the elimination of all waste, the human being ends up at a loss without being a *true* loser. The man from Picardy is indeed a true loser. He gains something in losing that which cannot be won. He gains his very loss.

Murau is like the man from Picardy, and, like Lacan, has no fondness for bureaucrats:

> For the last century, the whole of Europe has let itself be tyrannized by three-ring binders, and the tyranny is increasingly oppressive. Soon the whole of Europe will be not only tyrannized but destroyed by them ... Every German book written in this century is a product of this tyranny. German literature has been tyrannized and almost destroyed by three-ring binders, I said. And this present-day literature, produced under this tyranny,

1   Michel de Montaigne, 'That the taste for good and evil depends on large part of the opinion we have of them', in *The Complete Essays of Montaigne*, trans. Donald M. Frame (Stanford: Stanford University Press, 1948), 34.

2   Thomas Bernhard, *Extinction*, trans. David McLintock (New York: Vintage International, 1995), 307. I have also referenced the German edition: *Auslöschung: Ein Zerfall* (Frankfurt am Main: Suhrkamp Verlag, 1986), 611.

3   Jacques Lacan, *Seminar VII: The Ethics of Psychoanalysis, 1959–1960*, ed. Jacques-Alain Miller and trans. Dennis Porter (New York: W. W. Norton & Company, 1992), 233.

GHOSTS OF TRANSPARENCY

is naturally the most pathetic there has ever been. No other age has seen such a helpless, pathetic literature, a ludicrous desktop literature dictated by three-ring binders. All we have now is a petit bourgeois bureaucratic literature ... For at least a hundred years we've had nothing but what I would call binder literature, lower-middle-class bureaucratic writing, and the masters of this literature are Musil and Thomas Mann, to say nothing of the others. The one exception is, of course, Kafka, who actually was a bureaucrat, though he didn't write bureaucratic works, but none of the other writers could write anything else. Kafka, the bureaucrat, was the only one who produced not bureaucratic literature but great literature.[4]

For Murau, just as for Lacan, the bureaucrat is the quintessential figure who wants nothing more than to keep to his place, and who does everything in his power to hold that *thing* at bay which could threaten it. The bureaucrat knows that the *thing* [*das Ding*] is not-good, making it perhaps great, but most certainly evil. By simply toeing the line the bureaucrat sees no evil, hears no evil, and avoids at all costs being laid "open to the awful humiliation of failure."[5] Fearing the exposure of the monstrous *thing* within, the bureaucrat hands himself over to the task of good management.

The literary man for Murau opposes himself to the bureaucrat. Yet, in fearing to appear bureaucratic one reproduces its form. It is as if Musil and Mann, for all their ambition, were not ambitious enough. Too eager to protect the literary, by striving to write *good* literature, they become its *executors* and thus its peddlers. They produce a literature that is good, that is correct, but is not great. They do not risk Kafka's exceptionality, according to Murau, which lies in not trying to be something he is not. He is a bureaucrat and thereby can produce non-bureaucratic literature. He can thus produce the *thing* he is not. He can give it an adequate form. By exaggerating the bureaucratic, he produces literature that is not good, but great. By not shying away from what is not literary, i.e. the bureaucratic, by not separating literature from whom he, in fact, is, i.e. a bureaucrat, he does not simply reproduce himself, which is to say, the world to which he belongs. This is perhaps why, for all their gifts, Musil and Mann, for Murau, reproduce the world's petit bourgeois mentality. Unlike the man from Picardy, they make the correct choice. They do not take the art of exaggeration to a ridiculous extreme.

For Murau, exaggeration is not simply *an* art, as Thomas de Quincy proposed, for example, to speak of murder as one of the fine arts. Rather, the art of exaggeration [*Übertreibungskunst*] is the

---

4   *Extinction*, 305–306; *Auslöschung*, 607–608.
5   *Extinction*, 308; *Auslöschung*, 611.

quintessence of *great* art and thus art as such: "The painter who doesn't exaggerate is a poor painter, the musician who doesn't exaggerate is a poor musician, and the writer who doesn't exaggerate is a poor writer ... Exaggeration is the secret of great art, I said, and of great philosophy. The art of exaggeration is in fact the secret of all mental endeavour [*Geistesgeheimnis*]."[6] Exaggeration as art [*Kunst*] is the secret of *Geist*. One can imagine Bernhard suggesting that *Geist* drives, but *ist kein Streber*.[7] Ambition is not a striving after greatness; it is a matter of biting off more than one can chew.

Great art is conceived as the effect and evidence of an excessive drive [*Trieb*], an overdrive [the most literal rendering of *Übertreibung*] that makes art and the artist tend either toward over- or under-statement: "With some, of course, the art of exaggeration consists in *understating* everything [*alles zu* unter*treiben*], in which case we have to say that they exaggerate understatement [*übertreibt die Untertreibung*], that exaggerated understatement is their particular version of the art of exaggeration [*macht die übertriebene Untertreibung so zu seiner Übertreibungskunst*]."[8] Art is driven to exaggerate. In exaggeration, the drive's excess becomes manifest. Even when absent, the presence of this absence must be excessive. Exaggeration is always too much or too little, over- or under-stated, and it is through this excess that the drive becomes legible.

The legibility of the drive lies in its partiality, its excessive attention to detail. Exaggeration always concerns details: certain things missing or grotesquely amplified. Exaggeration confuses the object exaggerated either with the presence or absence of a detail. And, when pushed to an extreme, a substitution takes place in which the detail takes the place of the object. Partiality reigns and the whole is subordinate to an imperious part. In one of his many diatribes against photography, commenting on a photo he happened to take of sisters that forever imprinted the image of their mocking face on his mind, he writes:

> I once told Gambetti that when I spoke of my sisters I was speaking not of my sisters as such but only of their mocking faces, captured by chance in this photograph ... I have often tried to rid myself of their mocking faces, to transform them into faces that don't mock, but I've never succeeded. I have no sisters, I told myself, only their mocking faces. There's no Caecilia and no Amalia, only two mocking faces, frozen forever in this hideous picture ...

6   *Extinction*, 307–308; *Auslöschung*, 612.
7   A *Streber* is what one might call a try-hard. See Thomas Bernhard, 'Leute, die ein Gespräch führen wollen, sind mir verdächtig' in *Der Wahrheit auf der Spur: Reden, Leserbriefe, Interviews*, Feuilletons, ed. Wolfram Bayer, Raimund Fellinger, and Martin Huber (Frankfurt am Main: Suhrkamp, 2011), 246–247.
8   *Extinction*, 307–308; *Auslöschung*, 612.

Just think of the photo of Einstein sticking his tongue out. I can no longer visualize Einstein without his tongue sticking out, Gambetti, I said. I can't think of Einstein without seeing his tongue, that cunning, malignant tongue, stuck out at the whole world, indeed the whole universe. And I can only see Churchill with his lower lip distrustfully thrust forward.[9]

The reduction of Churchill to his lower lip, Einstein to his malignant tongue, and his sisters to their mocking faces is a metonymic operation in which a part is substituted for the whole. The *Übertreibungskünstler* has certain mania for metonymic substitution: "We're often led to exaggerate, I said later, to such an extent that we take our exaggeration to be the only logical fact, with the result that we don't perceive the real facts [*eigentliche Tatsachen*] at all, only the monstrous exaggeration [*nur die maßlos in der Höhe getriebene Übertreibung*]."[10] Driven beyond all measure, exaggeration positions the subject outside propriety. Exaggeration drives a property of something beyond the place to which it has been assigned by a proper measure. Without measure [*maßlos*] the object no longer belongs to itself; a part no longer belongs to the whole. The exaggerated feature monopolizing the whole becomes a ridiculous *thing*, something improper. The transformation of the object through exaggeration detaches the subject who exaggerates from its *reality*. No longer seeing Churchill but Churchill through the lens of his protruding lip, the grip that his power holds loosens, becoming the play thing of the drive that works him over, making him a subject that is not whole. Whether undercut through restraint (understated) or excessively present (overstated), compelled beyond (*Über-*) or below (*Unter-*), art is driven by *impropriety*. Its risk is thus utter and complete ridiculousness [*Lächerlichkeit*].

All of Bernhard's figures are doubtless given to exaggeration, wearing the excess of their preference for the negative on an impeccably tailored sleeve. And no one is endeared to the grim stylist without a strong taste for his refinement for the overstated. However, Murau is the only figure, that I can recall, that regularly has the ridiculousness of his overstatements returned to him in the form of laughter. I am not referring to the laughter of the reader, but that of Murau's pupil Gambetti who frequently bursts into his characteristic laughter, his so-called "*Gambettilachen*", or that of his friend, Maria, the only other figure alongside Kafka that constitutes for Murau an exception to the tyranny of the three-ring binder. She refers to him jokingly as an "expert in extinction" for "doing violence against philosophy [*sich an der Philosophie vergreiffen*], of sinning against spirit [*sich am Geist*

---

9   *Extinction*, 120–122; *Auslöschung*, 240–245.
10 *Extinction*, 307; *Auslöschung*, 610–611.

Versündigenden]."[11] He is her "extinction expert" and it is this joke that he takes in earnest that becomes not only the title, but the essential operation of his account. "I was her *extinction expert* [*ihr* Auslöscher]," she said: "whatever I set down on paper was automatically extinguished [*was ich zu Papier bringe, ist* das Ausgelöschte]."[12]

Extinction [*Auslöschung*] becomes the key operator of his method of exaggeration. Both the name of his account and its operation, the work of extinction will serve the function of nullifying the "whole complex of his origins":

> It's not enough to make notes about something that's important to us, perhaps more important than anything else, I said, namely the whole complex of our origins [*unseren ganzen Herkunftscomplex*]. We must produce a substantial account, not to say a long account, of what we emerged from, what we are made of, and what has *determined our being* [*unsere Existenz* geprägt] for as long as we've lived. We may recoil from it for years, we may shrink from such an almost superhuman enterprise [*übermenschlichen Anstrengung*], but ultimately we have to set about it and bring it to a conclusion ... I'll call my account *Extinction*, I had told Gambetti, because in it I intend to extinct everything: everything I record will be extincted [*alles, das ich in diesem Bericht aufschreibe, wird ausgelöscht*]. My whole family and their life and times will be extincted; Wolfsegg will be extincted ..."[13]

Extinction is an outrageous book: outrageously ambitious and more to the point, outrageous in its failure. As Murau puts it to Gambetti: "But I can't abolish [*abschaffen*] my family just because I want to."[14] The endeavour and its impossibility assumes a comical monstrosity in light of its beginning, which is occasioned by Murau's receipt of a telegram from his sisters informing him that both his parents and his brother have been killed in an accident: *Eltern und Johannes tödlich verunglückt. Caecilia, Amalia.* The dark comedy of the novel consists in the fact that Murau who has been struggling and failing to write the account which will extinguish his family, struggling and failing to escape them, to will them out of existence, through a stroke of *bad* luck, gets what he wished for. The obstacle to beginning has been resolved. Their present absence makes it possible to begin *Auslöschung.*

The account now takes as its task the *Auslöschung* of *their absent presence,* their all too symbolic grip on his being, his *Existenz.* Having become the sole inheritor and executor of the Wolfsegg Estate, their absent presence has become suddenly all too real. Only through the exaggeration

11 *Extinction*, 273; *Auslöschung*, 541.
12 Ibid., 273; Ibid., 541.
13 *Extinction*, 100–101 (translation modified); *Auslöschung*, 200.
14 *Extinction*, 8; *Auslöschung*, 17.

of the inordinate symbolic place that Wolfsegg holds over his psychic life does he transform the tragic into the comic, does he consign it and his family to the place of their absence. Thus, in response to Gambetti who accuses him of being "a typical Austrian pessimist [*Schwarzmaler*]," and a "*maßlosen Übertreiber*" Murau responds that his exaggerations are in truth "monstrous *under*statements [*maßlosen* Unter*treibungen*]."[15] This is indeed Bernhard's general approach: to ruthlessly understate the over-stated, to treat exaggeration not as an exception but the rule. Something becomes some *thing* it is not—not through becoming its opposite—but by understating what it in fact is: a matter of complete and utter indifference, cosmically insignificant, but of absolute significance for the subject caught in its grip. For Murau, understating overstatement is the correct response to the horror he inherits. Paired down to essentials, the novel in effect treats a singular mind's tortuous effort to be done with the horrors of inheritance. He overstates its overwhelming presence in order to mark its underlying absence: The over-stated is thus under-stated.

If exaggeration is Murau's manner of sinning against spirit [*Geist*], it is perhaps because he pits *Auslöschung* against *Aufhebung*. "I've thrown away more manuscripts than I've kept, I thought, and those that I've kept I can't bear to look at [*Ich habe mehr Manuskripte weg-geworfen, als aufgehoben, dachte ich, die aufgehobenen darf ich nicht mehr anschauen*]."[16] If *Aufhebung* elevates what it nonetheless cancels, preserving the negated form of the *aufgehoben*, *Auslöschung* destitutes, consigns to oblivion, what is *ausgelöscht*. If philosophy is a matter of *begreifen*, grasping through conceptualization, Murau's writing is a *vergreifen*, a mishandling of the concept. Hegel is conspicuously absent from the philosophical pantheon that Murau often cites. Descartes, Pascal, Kant, Schopenhauer, Kierkegaard, Nietzsche, even Heidegger is mentioned (albeit dismissively), but Hegel is peculiarly absent, casting his grey shadow over the movement of Murau's thought. *Aufhebung* defines the movement of *Geist's* success, the capacity of thought to determine retrospectively the conditions of its own emergence. For all its failures, its false starts, and misdirection, it is not *essentially* a failure. Its stupidity is not fundamental. It has a *sens*, meaning and direction. *Geist's* dialectical movement is not the discourse of a fool.

However, only a fool sets out to write a book with only a title in mind: "The only thing I have fixed in my head, I had said to Gambetti, is the title, *Extinction*, for the sole purpose of my account will be to ex-tinct what it describes [*in ihm Beschriebene auszulöschen*] ..."[17] And: "*Extinction*, I thought, but to be honest I still had only a vague notion of

15 *Extinction*, 62; *Auslöschung*, 123–124.
16 *Extinction*, 272; *Auslöschung*, 541
17 *Extinction*, 99 (translation modified); *Auslöschung*, 199.

the form the work should take, though I had thought about it for years."[18] This may indeed be an exaggeration, but to take it in earnest serves to position whatever is written down, "whatever is brought to Paper," as Maria formulates it, in the *essential* void of its content, "the notorious gaping void," the mute obstacle constituted by its fundamental lack of sense.

An annihilating machine: Whatever enters into its operation will be *ausgelöscht*, it will be brought to not. By relentlessly exaggerating the negative relation he has to the object of his account, he positions the object within the space of its own absence, as the thing it is not. Although the operation, *Auslöschung*, feigns reflexivity, the object included in its operation, the *ausgelöscht*, is in the empty place marked by its present absence. *Auslöschung* establishes the present absence of the 'object' through the logic of exaggeration that substitutes the *thing it is not* for the *what* that it is. *Auslöschung*, i.e. extinction as a process of extincting the extincted, exaggerates the failure to comprehend, taking the lack of understanding to a ridiculous extreme, by reducing the significance of *what* is said to the mere act of saying it. By repeating what is said, the stress shifts from the meaning to the *formal* manner of its saying:

> We say something that seems quite clear at the time, then a moment later we don't know what it was, I told Gambetti. I've just said something about Montaigne, but now, two or three seconds later, I don't know what it was. We ought to be able to say something and then record it in our minds [*zu protokollieren in unserem Kopf*], I said, but we can't. I've no idea why I spoke of Montaigne just now, and, of course, I've even less of an idea *what* I said. We imagine we reached a stage where we've become a thinking machine [*eine Denkmaschine*], but we can't rely on its thinking. This machine works unremittingly against the mind [*Kopf*], I said. It generates thoughts, but we don't know where they come from, why they were conceived, or what they relate to. The fact is that this nonstop thinking machine overtaxes us. The mind is overburdened but has no escape, as it's inevitably linked up to the machine for the rest of our lives. Until we die. You say Montaigne, Gambetti, but right now I don't know what that means, any more than I know what Schopenhauer means. You might just as well say *buttercup*: I wouldn't know what that meant either.[19]

No matter what we say, we are saying it. And if we say it, in order to retain what we say, for the mind to record it, it must be said again, it must be repeated, perhaps with some variation, but regardless it will

---

18 *Extinction*, 309; *Auslöschung*, 615.
19 *Extinction*, 79 (translation modified); *Auslöschung*, 157–158.

nevertheless be different. What I say, when I repeat it, *will have been* spoken and this pits the thinking machine against the mind. We ought to be able to say something and record it, to pass from the I to the me, we ought, as Lacan's "birdbrain" would have it, say: "But still, all the same, I am me!"[20] Yet, as soon as the mind is inscribed by the thinking machine, by language, the I is spoken. The I speaks, but *it will have been spoken*, and the I can do nothing other than speak *it*. And it is truly exhausting.

It makes the I say things, and as Murau notes, what it generates does not make sense. The thinking machine generates an infernal racket, a "frightful chaos" that the mind tries to follow, to make sense of, but fails. The mind [*Kopf*] depends upon the thinking machine for its thoughts, but this overburdens it, exhausts it: I say, but *it* was said, because "I" was said, but *who* then said it!? Such a question makes the head hurt, the mind stumble in the direction of answers that promise *nothing*. In passing from *I* to *it*, the I that says something is always saying nothing in addition to whatever was said. This surplus of absence, the place of nothing, when exaggerated threatens all meaning with indifference. All sense becomes the mere surrogate of the nothing it drags along with what it says. *What* one says is interrupted by the act of saying it. Whether one speaks of Montaigne, Schopenhauer, or a buttercup, they do not serve the interests of the mind that seeks to grasp them by saying what it thought it said. In these moments, when the nothing that says (the act of saying) overwhelms *whatever* it was that was said, one "taps" one's head and finds that that it is "entirely void."

The most that one can do is attempt to grasp the manner in which *what is* is mishandled [*Vergreifen*] in its recording, producing an account of or a report on the mind's failing. This is what Murau does with *Extinction*. The book comprises the failure to write the book. *Extinction* fails successfully.

The book can then write its own failure by making an object (a book) of the subject's failure to write. To make the act of writing, not *what* is written, into the object of concern. This is the genius of Bernhard's subtle device that makes his novel into a frame for the representation of Murau's account. Sharing the same title as Murau's book, Bernhard is nonetheless careful to offset his novel, adding a subtitle, "*Ein Zerfall*" [A Collapse] (unfortunately left out in the English edition) and the epigram from Montaigne: "I feel death ever pinching me by the throat, or pulling me by the back." He also intervenes decisively at the beginning and the end of Murau's account in order to situate it as written and not spoken. In the opening sentence, we read: "On the twenty-ninth, having returned from Wolfsegg, I met my pupil Gambetti

20 Jacques Lacan, *Seminar III: The Psychoses, 1955–1956*, ed. Jacques-Alain Miller and trans. Russell Grigg (New York: W. W. Norton & Company, 1993), 289.

on the Pincio to discuss arrangements for the lessons he was to receive in May, writes Murau, Franz-Joseph ..." Bernhard, or the narrator's, decision to write the name as if being written down upon a report or a legal document, introduces an exaggerated level of formality: the empty formality one encounters for example when filling out a form. This narrator does not reappear until the final page: "From Rome, where I now am again and where I have written this *Extinction*, and where I will remain, writes Murau (born in Wolfsegg 1934, died in Rome 1983) ..." It is here that we learn that the account that Murau has been insistently referring to as a book to be written, no matter how difficult the writing will be, has been written. This makes Murau's account that we have read a book that *will have been* written. Yet, the account that we read is not strictly speaking Murau's account, but its facsimile that is positioned by the third person that informs that Murau *writes*. This difference is striking in the last line of the novel, since Murau tells us "I have written this Extinction" and the third person tells us that he *writes* this "I have written." In other words, the novel's formal narratological device reproduces the problem that Murau discusses between the mind and the thinking machine. What Murau writes will have been written. This positions the I of Murau that is always addressed to an other (*Gambetti hatte gesagt*, etc.) in relation to a third that makes Murau's first-person account into an object that is being recorded or transcribed as "Murau writes." Murau's I is thus ineradicably, because structurally, exterior to itself. And this is achieved through the exaggeration of interiority. The first person is inscribed within the third person, within the impersonal. Its interiority is a device, an artifice, because he is writing it down.

If we take seriously Murau's claim that whatever he writes down is extincted [*ausgelöscht*], we are observing his extinction [*Auslöschung*]. What we read is not just Murau's *Extinction*, but *Murau's extinction*. We thus do not just read *Auslöschung*, but *ein Zerfall*. His account and thus his "I" is presented to us by a third person whose presence is understated. An exaggerated stress on interiority is positioned by an understated exteriority; the "I" is positioned by an understated "it." This gap between under- and over-statement is stressed by the jarring tension between the present and past tense that concludes the novel: the impossibility of Murau "writing" *Auslöschung* in the present tense and being already dead: "writes Murau (born in Wolfsegg 1934, died in Rome 1983)." His life is excised from a writing which presents a subject, an I in the process of its *Selbstauslöschung*, in the very place of his absence.

> When I take Wolfsegg and my family apart, when I dissect, annihilate and extinct them, I am actually taking myself apart, dissecting, annihilating, and extincting myself. I have to admit that this idea of self-dissection and self-extinction appeals to me, I told Gambetti. I'll spend my life dissecting and extinguishing

myself, Gambetti, and if I'm not mistaken I'll succeed in this self-dissection and self-extinction. I actually do nothing but dissect and extinguish myself. When I wake up in the morning the first thing I think of is setting about my work of dissection and extinction with a will.[21]

This is a fool's endeavour, for only a fool chooses nothing, like the man from Picardy, giving the gift of death. His account begins with such a gift and ends with such a gift, deciding to give "Wolfsegg, just as it stood, with *everything belonging to it*, as an unconditional gift to the Jewish community in Vienna." When he dies, he dies happy, he dies lucid, because he is an *Übertreibungskünstler*. He has effectively *extincted* the horrors of inheritance, ensuring that its world and its malignancy shall not be reproduced in and by him. Like the man from Picardy, he chooses a happy death over a miserable life.

To explain anything properly we have to exaggerate. Only exaggeration can make things clear. Even the risk of being branded as fools ceases to worry us as we get older. In later years there's nothing better than to be declared a fool. The greatest happiness I know, Gambetti, is that of the aging fool who is free to indulge his foolishness. Given the chance, we should proclaim ourselves fools by the age of forty at the latest and capitalize on our foolishness. It's foolishness that makes us happy, I said.[22]

—Written in my 40th year.

21 *Extinction*, 147 (translation modified); *Auslöschung*, 296.
22 *Extinction*, 65; *Auslöschung*, 128–129.

ARCHITECTURE, AN ARTIFICIAL INTELLIGENCE

VIII

KRISTIAN FASCHINGEDER

KRISTIAN FASCHINGEDER teaches at the Department of Architecture Theory and Philosophy of Technics (Technical University Vienna), the New Design University St. Pölten, and the FH-Campus Vienna. In 2008–2010 he was a research assistant to the Chair of Design, Theory and History of Modern Architecture at the Bauhaus University Weimar, where he also received his PhD in 2011. In 2011–2013 he curated the permanent science centre exhibition Sonnenwelt in Großschönau in Lower Austria. Numerous publications in architectural and theory journals. He has practised in Austrian and international architecture offices.

In the foreword to his sixth book, Vitruvius tells the story of the pre-Socratic philosopher Aristippus of Cyrene, who was shipwrecked off the desert island of Rhodes and driven ashore. Though he didn't know where he was, he soon realized that this place had to be inhabited by humans: Geometric figures were drawn in the sand—unmistakably the traces of civilized people. Equipped with this knowledge, Aristippus set off for Rhodes to rush straight into the gymnasium, where he took part in the philosophical debates.[1] Daniele Barbaro, Venetian architect and above all translator and commentator of Vitruvius, later remarked on this story, that figures like those on the beach were rather the indisputable signs of higher thought. A footprint would have signified a human, but a triangle signified a mind.[2]

ONCE AGAIN

Ulysse runs ashore. Not a long time before Christ, but many years into the future. Not on a foreign coast, but on an alien planet: The protagonist *Ulysse Mérou* has been shipwrecked on the planet of the apes. The apes consider humans as we usually consider animals—some may possess intelligence but are not endowed with the faculty of reason. Ulysse is captured and locked in a cage, awaiting scientific research. Many long weeks pass by until Ulysse finds a way to convince Zira, one of the research apes of his faculty of reasoning: "Why hadn't I used this simple means before? Mustering my school-day memories, I drew the geometric figure illustrating the theorem Pythagoras." Now, the dam is broken:

> Now it was she who appeared eager to establish contact. I gave thanks to Pythagoras and went a little further on the geometric track. On one side of the notebook I drew, the best I could, the three conic sections with their axes and focal points—an ellipse, a parabola and a hyperbola. Then I drew a circular cone on the opposite page. I remember here that the intersection of such a body by a plane produces one of the three conic sections, following to the angle of the cut. Now I demonstrated how an ellipse is created and pointed out the corresponding curve in my first drawing. The she-ape was amazed. She snatched the notebook out of my hands, drew a cone with another cutting plane and pointed to the hyperbola with her long finger. I was so moved that tears came to my eyes and I clasped Zira's hands.[3]

Ulysse, the French spaceman of the future, has succeeded. Not by some usual means of communication, not by learning a language, and not by

---

1   Vitruvius, *The Ten Books on Architecture*, trans. by M. H Morgan (Cambridge: Harvard University Press, 1914), 167.

2   Werner Oechslin, 'Geometry and Line. Vitruvian Science and Architectural Drawing', *Daidalos*, 1 (1981), 20–35 (20–35, 27–28).

3   Pierre Boulle, *La Planète des singes* (Paris: Presses Pocket, 1990), 88f (my translation); significantly, this form of communication does not occur in the movie.

              GHOSTS OF TRANSPARENCY

conveying a culturally conventional meaning,[4] which might be stored in the immemorial memory of mankind, but definitely not in that of the apes. Rather, it was the mediation of geometric, abstract structures, a basis not of *ours*, but of *the* laws of nature. They do not come about through the agreement of like-minded people; rather, they are objective in a genuine sense. They always work; their truth content is *demonstrable*. Thus, even here, where nature and culture meet under inverted relations (ape: nature; man: culture), they remain the pivotal point of a communication that is, first of all, one thing: a form of translation.

That's interesting. When Barbaro, through Aristippus, deduces the presence of mind from the geometric figures in the sand, and Zira, the ape, deduces, from a conic section, the presence of mind in Ulysse, then it cannot actually be that of mankind alone. Man is not present at the drawn figure on the coast of Rhodes; neither a certain explanation nor the presence of humans is necessary. The figures and drawings act by themselves. Plans in architecture are no different. They enable the transfer of ideas from the planners to those who realize the construction. The presence of the architect is not required. Even if there are pragmatic reasons for this—anyone who can read plans should at least know what is meant by the drawings. The church of Saint-Pierre in Firminy by Le Corbusier, for example, whose construction began in 1970, was not completed until forty-one years after the death of the architect, according to his plans. These also draw a simple geometric figure: The interior is formed by a square base that tapers upwards into a circle (initially at least). Daylight enters through light boxes and through a series of well-placed openings that relate to the constellation of Orion (by the way, that's where Ulysse went). The light boxes are designed so that on certain holidays, such as Good Friday and Easter Sunday, the altar is lit by the sun. The architecture here is a cosmic instrument that precisely measures the high holidays.

However, not every form of precision is necessary *in order to be precise*. The frontispiece by Michael Burghers certainly gets one thing wrong: What distinguishes geometric drawings is that they do not necessarily have to be drawn precisely in order to be correct. They do not need fixed quantities and numbers, but often deal with relations.[5] Plato's *Menon* contains a demonstrative passage in which an uneducated servant reconstructs the diagonal of the square by 'remembering' it under the guidance of Socrates:[6]

---

4 Cf. the divergent approach of Ekkehard Drach, 'Architektur und Geometrie: zur Historizität formaler Ordnungssysteme' (Bielefeld: Transcript, 2012), 7f. For Drach, 'Architecture and inevitably the architectural form cannot be arbitrary, they are conventionally determined' (my translation). However, there are aspects that determine form that are not cultural, meaningful conventions, but structural in nature.

5 In the sense of proportions or relations. Ideally, geometric constructions only require a triangle and a compass.

6 Michel Serres, *Les origines de la géométrie: tiers livre des fondations* (Paris: Flammarion, 2011). Plato calls this recollection 'anamnesis'.

In conversation with his pupil Meno, Socrates calls a young servant and draws a square in the sand. First, he makes sure that the boy knows that doubling one side of the square doubles its area, and if the other side too is doubled, the initial area quadruples. The boy also understands that doubling this square, of which a side length of two feet is assumed, results in an area of eight feet. However, the boy cannot answer the question of how large the edge length of the square must be in order to result in a square twice as large with a total area of eight feet. First, he tries it with a length of four feet: That gives an area of sixteen. Then he assumes a length of three feet: That makes an area of nine. Socrates demands of him a measure, the servant gives a quantity.[7] Socrates now restates his questions: The boy should no longer start from the sides of the square, but from its diagonals. Now he understands how to get a square with the area of eight feet: One multiplies those triangles, which result from the diagonal division of the square. A triangle forms half of the square. But if you put four such triangles together, you get double the area: eight feet. The servant was limited in his thinking by calculating in whole numbers and by the arithmetic of multiplication tables which produce only natural numbers. It was only by thinking in geometric terms—and thus switching from quantitative to qualitative terms—that he was able to answer Socrates's question correctly. In the algebra of the Pythagoreans, only whole or rational numbers existed, but not the triangle with its irrational, therefore innumerable hypotenuse.[8]

FIG 1
The philosopher Aristippos goes ashore on the island of Rhodes and deduces the presence of people from the geometric figures drawn in the sand.

7   Ibid., 283.
8   Ibid., 279, 283, 285.

GHOSTS OF TRANSPARENCY

Aristippus is not the only one rushing from geometry to philosophy. Another, again a Frenchman, refers like no other to the implications of the dialogue in the Menon and to the evidence it contains. "There is no demonstration before the Greeks," says Michel Serres, none "before the apagogical proof, before geometry, before the irrational. [...] If you prefer not to make calculations, then show! This is an origin sentence."[9] For Serres, the area makes things—lengths—visible, which the calculation could not capture. The proof (and the apagogical proof) demonstrates that numbers make things impossible that the surface makes possible as a matter of course. Another method to which Serres refers is used by Thales of Miletus to determine the height of the pyramids—without climbing or even touching the sacred tomb of the pharaoh. Instead, he uses a mediator, a stick, whose shadow at a certain moment of the day is as long as the stick itself. Measuring the shadow of the pyramid at the same time, he can tell how high it is. Of course, ancient Egypt could calculate the height of their pyramids, but Thales demonstrates the geometric similarity between the stick and the pyramid; between a length that is known and one that has to be found out. They're homothetic, because they have a common point of agreement (the sun), which in this case allows a translation from one object to another. Thales thus measures the relationship between the lengths of the shadows and at the same time invents the *homothetia*, and thus also the scaling and the scale. Serres designates both the side of the square from which Meno's servant proceeds in his calculations and the staff used by Thales as a *gnomon*. The term actually refers to the rod that casts the shadow on sundials from which the time of day can be read. Originally however—and for a very long time—this rod was used to determine the geographical latitude of a place, the northern direction, the equinoxes, the solstices and the ecliptic; it was not primarily a clock but an astronomical instrument.

In any case, Serres uses the term to designate tools that can be used to perform measurements within certain limits—whole numbers in the case of a servant whose *gnomon* is the side of the square; and a certain position of the sun at Thales, whose gnomon is the rod. This list could be extended at will. Examples by Serres himself are the 'gnomonic numbers' of Theon of Smyrna, or the Pascal triangle. Both are mathematical methods that are used to determine ongoing numbers. Euclid, in turn, calls in his *Elements* an L-shaped figure a gnomon,[10] and by this means the geometric abstraction of the right-angled carpenter's

9   Serres, *Les origines de la géométrie*, 281; translation from the English edition: Michel Serres, *Geometry: The Third Book of Foundations*, trans. by Randolph Burks (London: Bloomsbury Academic, 2017), 171.
10 See Euclid, *Stoicheia (Euclid's Elements)*, Book II, *Explanations* accessible at: https:// archive.org/details/euclidisoperaomno1eucluoft/page/n6

angle of the same name. Called équerre in French, the relationship to the square (*carré*) and the sundial (*cadran*) is still present. Thus, instruments that originally drew the stations of the sun in the sand become tools that serve to depict abstract, geometric figures: The simple carpenter's square is replaced in geometry by the construction tools of the compass and ruler. The latter comes from the Latin term *regula* from *rectus*, the straight line, and at the same time also designates a rule.[11] And the latter is what it's about, because with objects like these certain rules are set that allow or even dictate procedures. How should one define the gnomon differently, asks Serres, than as the law of a series? "The *gnomon* is defined as a law of construction, as the rule of a sequence or its engendering. An automatic rule, functioning all by itself."[12] As a consequence, it only offers a limited set of possibilities. The servant calculates in his head, thinks in tables and remembers the multiplication tables. For Socrates and his school, this traditional tabular knowledge amounts to ignorance. Socrates, the philosopher who says he does not know, helps the servant to remember another knowledge and thus to free himself from his stencil-like tools of thought by leading him step by step, systematically and methodically, to the new, abstract world of geometry. A different thinking, a different knowledge; after Ulysse, the servant is the second person liberated by geometry.

The gnomon, Serres says, "functions all by itself, without any human intervention," like an artificial memory or an automaton.[13] "The gnomon is thus intelligent in the literal sense of the word, since he puts together situations selected from thousands of others, and thus discerns and understands."[14] An artificial intelligence: "Artificial intelligence doesn't date from yesterday," Serres emphasizes. "From the origin of science, there have existed things or states of affairs that the history of our languages has attributed to mental activities, as if these artefacts—plumb line, ruler or compass, framing square—passed for subjects of thought."[15] For Serres there is therefore not only the recognizing subject, but also the intelligent artefact. His artificial intelligence stands for him independently next to what we commonly call intelligence when it is conceived as an ability that, at least until recently, was ascribed to man exclusively:

> To name three automatisms by an identical name—that of the stake raised towards the sun, that of the framing square or the lateral band that's added or subtracted, and that of the operation

11 Serres, *Les origines de la géométrie*, 262.
12 Ibid., 263; English translation: Serres, *Geometry*, 163.
13 Ibid., 239; English translation Serres, *Geometry*, 133.
14 Serres, *Les origines de la géométrie*, 246; My translation. For an alternate translation, see Serres, *Geometry*, 140.
15 Ibid., 264; My translation. For an alternate translation, see Serres, *Geometry*, 155.

whose iteration constructs series of numbers—leads us to artificial intelligence. We see their avatars in these three states: first as thing, post or axis—a speculative tool—then as a ruler, that will at leisure reproduce straight lines, angles, ideal polygons, which are extracted from this rule, or better still abstracted from it, and finally as a formal operation on numbers; an automatic rule, an algorithm.[16]

So Serres identifies things—artefacts, rules, and mathematical tools—that think with, for, and beside us. It might be surprising that Serres finds this artificial intelligence not only in the algorithm-based technology of our days, but already in the ancient and simple artefacts whose sediments can be detected in our language, and whose traces lead to epistemology and philosophy. The undeniable signs of higher thinking that Daniele Barbaro recognizes in the figures Aristippus encounters on the beach of Rhodes are perhaps not only those of man. Man-made—they are: But things that act on their own, like automatons. Originated and developed at a certain time, through a local culture, they attain a universal claim. Our own thinking would not get far without them.

RATIONALIZATION ACCORDING TO PLAN

The Greeks were famous for their skill and resourcefulness. Serres notes that they invented a trick of the mind, the 'ruse-mathematics' [*mathématique-ruse*]: "They gave us systems and schemata that were so different from each other that, taking the Greeks at their word, we arranged them along a linear evolution."[17] As an example, Serres cites two different political orders by means of which the historian Jean-Pierre Vernant traces the revolutionary changes in Greek culture. The forerunner is the strictly hierarchical organization of the archaic world, vertically organized and pyramid-shaped, with the ruler at the head. Innovative are the Greeks who organize themselves horizontally: They line up in a circle, and those who want to speak to the group stand in the middle, surrounded by their listeners. The hierarchy flattens out, with which the Greeks realized their famous *isonomy*, the democratic equality of rights. But it is not only society that organizes itself in a circular fashion; the same geometric figure also structures a new worldview: one that is no longer mythical and religious, but rational and geometric. The cosmos is organized similar to society, thereby losing its original, gradual structure: In the old order the gods are above, mortals in the middle, demons and other infernal beings below. In the new geometric order, the cosmos

---

16 Ibid., 263; My translation. For an alternate translation, see Serres, *Geometry*, 153f.
17 Serres, *Les origines de la géométrie*, 127; My translation. For an alternate translation, see Serres, *Geometry*, 49.

loses its composition;[18] it becomes a place that has neither floor nor ceiling, neither cellar nor attic, and thus loses its "fascinating quality as a phenomenological habitat."[19] Instead, indifference now prevails on the basis of equivalence through symmetry.

But it's not as clear-cut as Vernant claims, Serres replies. If one sees the archaic as elevation, and the Greek as plan view, the two schemata become connected to each other. It is the same model, equally symmetrical and organized according to the same plan. The only difference then is the mode of projection, which is rotated by a quarter. It is true that the Greeks disclose in the Agora those matters that concern the city, which suggests a desecration and rationalization of political life. The discussions of the Agora are based on the circular assembly, with a speaker in the centre and listeners on the periphery. At the end of his presentation, the speaker leaves the centre and moves to the edge, while a new speaker moves from the edge to the centre. Due to this symmetry and interchangeability, all are equal. The archaic city, on the other hand, is organized hierarchically, with the king at the head, who dominates the ruling class, which in turn dominates the submissive people. However, even in Greek society this equality only applies to the aristocracy. It is superior to the rest of the city; it forms a closed circle, and thus excludes all others: The height reverts into distance, which basically remains the same, regardless of whether it is vertically or horizontally oriented. What counts is the relationship to the centre, to the pole or the axis. The relationship of forces, formerly embodied by dominance, height and severity, is transformed into the concept of relationship, from the reference to the point of reference, as in a geometric representation. The hierarchy also remains in rational thinking, but there it becomes transparent and invisible, says Serres. In the moment we think rationally, we turn toward a centre, a reference system, an *arché*.[20] "The essential thing for the whole affair [...], remains the law of projective transformation, that quarter turn that makes one believe in democracy."[21]

The big difference between the archaic and Greek conceptions is not due to the principle of organization, but to the observer's point of view. There is a difference whether you look at something in the elevation or in the plan view. Both depict the same, but nobody sees, according to Serres, neither the world nor society as if they were looking at it from above. This position is above the king, it is that of the mind. In this way, things can be viewed from outside the world; now the universe can be thought of outside it. Already the practice of this drawing proves the

18   Note: This refers to the world view of Anaximander.
19   Serres, *Les origines de la géométrie*, 120; My translation. For an alternate translation, see Serres, *Geometry*, 43.
20   Ibid., 123, 124f, 137.
21   Ibid., 126; My translation. For an alternate translation, see Serres, *Geometry*, 48.

existence of another world. The Greeks invent in this way—and Serres sees this as the biggest cut—theory, a stage of vision—*theoros* means 'spectator'. They invent representation. From this vantage point, the world can be seen as a spectacle, as a theatre. "The Greeks' production is projection. And the optimization of a projecting site: the flyover from on high or from outside the world."[22]

MENON, WITHOUT SOCRATES

It took a detour to get back to the plans of the architecture, in which much of what has been mentioned before can be found: The projection, the observation from above, which leads Le Corbusier to remark that everything starts from the plan view: "le plan est le générateur," he says in 1923 in *Vers une Architecture*.[23] And perhaps architecture used the potential that the Greeks had discovered early on only so much later. While an architect such as Étienne-Louis Boullée—whom Le Corbusier admired—situates the educating effect of his *architecture des ombres and architecture ensevelie* (ink drawing is for him the appropriate way of depicting the monumental effect of light and shadow for his cenotaph for Newton [1784]) in the elevation, the power of architecture is later relocated into the ground plan, which is decomposed and analysed as diagrams; not least by protagonists such as Rudolf Wittkower, Bill Hillier and Michel Foucault. The comprehensible, visible and symbolic effect of a representative architecture is transferred into the sober, ornamentless ground plan, objectified and thus made quasi invisible. Although August Schmarsow considered architecture as 'space designer'—*Raumgestalterin*—and characterized the history of architecture as the "history of the sentiment of space," in which a "history of worldviews" was displayed,[24] and the concept of architecture as an actual spatial art has persisted since, there has always been a clear conceptual separation between plan view and elevation. The representative character of architecture is manifest in the elevation, the organizational one in the ground plan. And while the difference between archaic and Greek worldviews is based on a simple twist, from the outline to the ground plan, in architecture the connection between these two forms of representation is still an absolute rarity until the 15th century.[25]

22 Serres, *Les origines de la géométrie*, 127f; My translation. For an alternate translation, see Serres, *Geometry*, 48f.
23 My translation from the original: "Le plan est le générateur. Sans plan, il y a désordre, arbitraire. Le plan porte en lui l'essence de la sensation." Le Corbusier, *Vers une architecture* (Paris: G. Crès, 1925), 8.
24 see Fritz Neumeyer, *Quellentexte zur Architekturtheorie* (Munich: Prestel, 2002), 333.
25 see J Sakarovitch, *Epures d'architecture: de la coupe des pierres à la géométrie descriptive XVIᵉ-XIXᵉ siècles* (Basel: Birkhäuser, 1998), 45.

That's remarkable. Throughout the Middle Ages, a system of pro-portions was sufficient to infer the object from the ground plan. Such a system required a very codified architecture whose proportions were extraordinarily repetitive. This was made possible by squaring, a system of doubling the area of the square (by means of the diagonal, of course), which, however, can only be proven in Gothic architecture at the end of the 15th century (although Villard de Honnecourt was taking steps in this direction already in the 13th century).[26] The architects of the Middle Ages could not cope well with leaps in scale. New projects were often copying an existing project, whose floor plan was then often simply enlarged. The list of cathedrals that collapsed during construction is long. They were closely observed during construction and, in the event of some deforma-tion, reinforced as needed. One finds here a constant of medieval build-ing practice: a purely empirical, step-by-step procedure of algorithmic thought, based on traditions as an almost artificial memory, but, on the other hand, always in search of new technical solutions.[27] But without the-ory, without abstraction and without planning—in the sense of a forward concept, into the future—it is hardly possible to ask the right questions.

Once it has been understood that a great deal can be achieved with the abstraction of geometry, it becomes more obvious to transcend the existing limitations. By combining the two schemata of ground plan and outline into a coherent system of planning, a new form of geometric rep-resentation could emerge: "First I draw a rectangular square of any size on the surface to be painted; I assume that it is an open window through which I look at what is to be painted here," Alberti describes his construc-tion of perspective space.[28] This new space immediately serves another purpose: not planning, but above all the social role of architecture. For Alberti, the perspective is the prerequisite to provide for an action—an istoria—su luogo, its frame, space and place. It should not just be a neutral container, but already possess dramaturgical qualities. The perspectival construction is the necessary prerequisite for an event to unfold there.

At the same time, certain objects are excluded with this mode of representation. Hubert Damisch notices that such a perspective shall have only *knowledge* of those things it can set within its order: things which occupy a place and whose contour can be defined by a line. The first modern perspective, which its inventor Brunelleschi used with the help of his *tavoletta* (a small panel), is a theoretical demonstration: It shows that the vanishing point coincides with the point of view.[29] Brunelleschi

26 Sakarovitch, 41.
27 J.-M Savignat, *Dessin et architecture du Moyen Age au XVIIIe siècle* (Paris: Ecole na-tionale supérieure des beaux-arts, 1983), 30.
28 Leon Battista Alberti, *Über die Malkunst = Della pittura*, trans. by Oskar Bätschmann and Sandra Gianfreda (Darmstadt: WBG, 2013), 93.
29 see Hubert Damisch, *Théorie du nuage: pour une historie de la peinture.* (Paris: Éditions du Seuil, 1972), 157, 170.

will not *depict* heaven but *show* it by means of a mirror. A clear limitation of the construction to its possibilities; for what the mirror *shows* is what the geometric means cannot cover. The sky occupies no place, it has no measure; and as far as clouds are concerned, they do not allow for fixed contours, nor for their forms to be examined with regard to their surfaces. The cloud belongs to the 'bodies without surface', as Leonardo will write later, bodies that have neither a precise form nor extremities and whose boundaries penetrate each other. Clouds cannot be captured by the method of perspective, but Leonardo will nonetheless deal with them: To get closer to nature, and to combine in the painting quantities with qualities.[30]

First the clouds, then architecture: As Robin Evans writes, the classic building was axially-symmetric.[31] An ideal centre line represented as much the plane of symmetry as the plane of the most advantageous section, which does not just lead through a cavity (because it makes little sense otherwise), but also runs through the apex of a vault. This line then corresponds to the development axis of the building, which manifests on the main façade through a centred entrance. For a sufficient representation of such a building, three drawings are sufficient: Floor plan, outline and section. However, Hans Scharoun almost failed with these given means: the Berlin Philharmonie (completed in 1963) does not have a main façade; it is neither rectangular nor symmetrical, nor does it have a central axis. It was mostly designed through models and sketches. The usual drawings were supplemented by large-scale sections that cover the entire building at close intervals in order to gain a reliable overview and control of the project. Although the two published sections through the auditorium provide a fair description of the interior, they are insufficient to describe the geometry of its bevelled and curved surfaces more precisely. For the execution, the traditional cut was compressed to such an extent, that in fact a profile was created with which the building was cut into thin slices. Perhaps this was a short-sighted approach, less tied to experience than the classic cut, and anything but economic. Nor was it suitable for describing the geometric properties of the outer skin.[32] Nevertheless, this building embodies a fundamental virtue of architecture: It is not conformity to the available means that distinguishes it, not appropriateness, but rather exuberance and excess; the transgression of what Serres calls the gnomon. This Architecture went ahead of its plans.

30 Ibid., 218, footnote 4; "And just as music and geometry take into account the relationships of constant magnitudes, and arithmetic the relationships of unsteady ones, so painting subjects all constant magnitudes to contemplation, and in addition the qualities of relationships, of shadows and lights, and of distances, in their perspective." After: Leonardo Da Vinci, *Traktat von der Malerei*, trans. by Heinrich Ludwig and Marie Herzfeld (Jena, 1909), 32.
31 Robin Evans, *The Projective Cast: Architecture and Its Three Geometries* (London: MIT Press, 1995), 119ff.
32 Ibid., 120.

THE AURAL: HEIDEGGER AND FUNDAMENTAL OTO-CHEIRO-LOGY II

GEORGIOS TSAGDIS

GEORGIOS TSAGDIS is a Fellow at the Westminster Law and Theory Lab. He has taught at the universities of Greenwich, Surrey, the UCL, the London School of Philosophy and other institutions. His work operates across theoretical and disciplinary intersections drawing on 20th century, Contemporary and Ancient Greek Philosophy. His *Archeology of Nothing*, an investigation of the origin and destiny of occidental ontology, is revised for publication. His current project thematises the function of the negative in the ontology of matter from Plato to New Materialisms. In other recent research, he explores various themes in the historic encounters of philosophy and nature, from the figure of the animal in the Platonic corpus to post-humanism and parasitism. He has written on the question of love with reference to theological, political and feminist discourses. His essays have been published in various book collections and international journals, among which *Parallax* and *Philosophy Today*. Since 2014 he has been organizing the *Seminar of Neoplatonic Studies*, a London intercollegiate study and research group, hosted at the Warburg Institute.

> Hearing even constitutes the primary and
> authentic openness of Da-sein for
> its ownmost possibility of being[1]
>
> —Heidegger, *Being and Time*

The ear. Certainly, the hand and the ear. The distances and spaces, the fields they demarcate; this is the question at hand, at the heart of *mediality*. At the same time, the hand and the ear designate the figural limits of *epochality*, the emergence of time, no less than the time of emergence, all that is decisive in the *kairos* that sets into motion an era. And as perhaps we seem to be drifting away from the era of the writing hand, an era with only an ear for itself—or rather as this era seems to be drifting away from us—we, who ask on the meaning of this 'we', unavoidably also ask on the meaning of the ear. Self (*auto*) and ear (*oto*) are asked together.

THE SELF AND THE EAR

The question persists: Why *this* question? To muster the self and the ear in the intensity of this proximity, more than a claim to a distorted homophony and the augury of an epochal closure is needed. We begin to discover the necessity of this proximity in Heidegger's epigraph. In order to open up and remain open in its ownmost possibility, the possibility of being that most properly belongs to *itself*, in order that is to *be*—the verb moving here beyond the copula—*itself* (*auto*), Da-sein must be able to hear; this untranslatable existence must develop an ear (*oto*) for hearing. For certainly, not every ear hears. We hear more closely, longer:

> Hearing is constitutive for discourse. And just as linguistic utterance is based on discourse, acoustic perception is based on hearing. Listening to … is the existential being-open of Da-sein as *being-with for the other*. Hearing even constitutes the primary and authentic openness of Da-sein for its ownmost possibility of being, as in hearing *the voice of the friend* whom every Da-sein carries with it. Da-sein hears because it understands.[2]

Discourse and the other, *for* if not *from* the other. Openness towards oneself as being-with. Hearing as understanding. The voice of the friend. The Heideggerian fragment mobilizes more than the whole apparatus of *Being and Time*, in what it calls to be understood. It proposes an intricate constellation of notions, which seem arranged along a hierarchy of orders of primordiality, while folding at the same time this hierarchy upon itself.

1   Martin Heidegger, *Being and Time*, trans. Joan Stambaugh (Albany: SUNY Press, 1996) § 34, 153.
2   Ibid., 153. My emphasis.

Heidegger writes: "The existential-ontological foundation of language is discourse [*Rede*]."[3] And then: "Discourse is existentially equiprimordial with attunement and understanding."[4] The translation of Rede into discourse is sufficiently perplexing; those who hear the German, understand the word as conversation and speech in their pre-differentiated unity. Logos is here dialogue rather than dialectic; and it finds itself on par with understanding. Yet, Heidegger adds: "Hearing and keeping silent are possibilities belonging to discoursing speech [*redenden Sprechen*],"[5] while as we already know: "Hearing is constitutive for discourse."[6] And then: "Discourse and hearing are grounded in understanding."[7] Collecting the utterances under a principle of transitivity, hearing appears as a constitutive possibility of *Rede*, which like the latter is grounded in, despite being equiprimordial with, understanding.

These tensions—constitution and possibility, ground and equality, the ontological before and after, no less than synchronicity—should not be understood as slips or contradictions, but undoubtedly through the logic of the supplement, in the opening between description and declaration. Hearing is grounded in understanding, which nonetheless it supplements—for without hearing there is no understanding. Indeed, hearing [*hören*] as the most generic term is refracted into hearkening [*horchen*], that is, a hearing that understands,[8] and listening [*zuhören*], which accompanies as a before and an after the intelligibility of articulated discourse.

The logic of the supplement is redoubled within *hearing*, for not only—thinking for a moment against Heidegger—is the genus of hearing ontologically supported by its most profound species—namely, harkening—but in all this, *silence* with its various modulations, presents a specific complication at the heart of hearing and in turn of discourse and understanding altogether. Heidegger: "As a *mode of discourse*, reticence [*Verschwiegenheit*] articulates the intelligibility of Da-sein so primordially that it gives rise to a genuine potentiality for hearing and to a being-with-one-another that is transparent."[9] One mode of discourse offers the potentiality of another. Equality and synchronicity do not preclude conditioning. A certain modulation of the mode of hearing makes the latter, indeed its most profound mode, possible. Silence as reticence potentialities hearkening, that is, understanding in hearing: "in talking with one another the person who is silent can 'let something be understood'."[10]

3   Ibid., 150.
4   Heidegger, *Being and Time*, 150.
5   Ibid., 151.
6   Ibid., 153.
7   Heidegger, *Being and Time*, 154.
8   Ibid., 153.
9   Ibid., 154. My emphasis.
10 Heidegger, *Being and Time*, 154.

Yet, at the same time, silence is conditioned upon *Rede* and understanding: "Authentic silence is possible only in genuine discourse." And: "he who never says anything is also unable to keep silent at a given moment." [11] Finally, although there is no understanding without hearing, and no proper hearing without silence, we also hear that "Da-sein hears *because* it understands." In this cascade of supplements, the attuned ear and understanding converge.

Similarly, the hand converges with thought:

And only when man speaks, does he think—not the other way around, as metaphysics still believes. Every motion of the hand in every of its works carries itself through the element of thinking, every bearing of the hand bears itself in that element. All the work of the hand is rooted in thinking. Therefore, thinking itself is man's simplest, and for that reason hardest, handiwork [*Handwerk*], if it would be accomplished at its proper time. [12]

One thinks because one speaks, one hears because one understands. These propositions, in the various possibilities of their mutual folds (one speaks because one understands, one thinks because one hears, and so on), demarcate a series of imperfectly aligned sequences, sequences which do not run parallel—a series of supplements and intersections. The hand appears in *What is Called Thinking?* as the figure that articulates speech *and* thought, while nothing seems to collect in *Being and Time* hearing *and* understanding. The present essay proposes the ear (Greek *ous*) as the figure of this collection—it might no less have been the mouth (Latin *os*), since ear and mouth are aligned on the side of 'discoursing speech', [13] hand and eye on the side of writing, understood in a limited sense from within this polarity. If the hand in Heidegger, as in the passage above, appears to cut across this alignment, reaching out towards speech, it is because writing receives even here its significance from speech—language is primordially *Rede*—and yet *the hand thinks*, thought is the simplest and hardest, the most essential handiwork.

In sum, a strange ear. Just like the hand, it must be thought as severed, incorporeal and singular. Unlike the hand, however, it is unspoken, unarticulated, absent, since Heidegger nowhere thematizes the ear, preferring to speak instead of *hearing* (underwriting at the outset

---

11   Ibid., 154.
12   Martin Heidegger, *What is Called Thinking?*, trans. Fred D. Wieck and Glenn J. Gray (New York: Harper & Row, 1968), 16–17. The German in brackets is my inclusion.
13   The exposition of the inextricable alignment of orality and aurality, must necessarily remain incomplete without turning to *Being and Time*, § 29, where the *Stimmung* supplants the *Stimme* in conveying 'Being in its *Da*'. Here, Agamben's iteration of Novalis's understanding of *Stimmung* as the 'acoustics of the soul', will have to serve as an indication in the place of such exposition. Giorgio Agamben, *Language and Death, The Place of Negativity*, trans. Karen E. Pinkus with Michael Hardt (Minneapolis, University of Minnesota Press, 1991), 55–56.

aural incorporeality). This ear we think with and against Heidegger, in order to think its folds, beyond the helix and the antihelix; what calls to be understood is the way in which the ear constitutes the supplement of understanding, upon which it is in turn constituted. Albeit far from conclusive, the analysis of this supplementation must now give way to an examination of the way in which the absent body of the ear allows for the constitution of the space of existence.

Heidegger opens the section on discourse and language by means of a fissure, or rather an opening up of Dasein, foregrounding the *being* of the *there* [Da]: "The fundamental existentials which constitute the being of the there [*das Sein des Da*], the disclosedness of being-in-the-world, are attunement and understanding."[14] The being of the there, which designates the being *of* the world as a being *in* the world, is constituted by what in turn the supplement of the ear constitutes. Although Dasein is not a subject, being barely a *self*, it is surely itself, fulfilling its ownmost possibility insofar as its being is an issue for itself, insofar as it hearkens. Accordingly, the there of being opens up the space of the self, by constituting the being of the there as a certain soundscape, a certain field of sonority. The ear supplements the self by delineating its horizon, that is, the field of *mediality*.

MEDIALITY AS PHILOTELEGRAMOPHONY

The field of mediality comprises the material and immaterial structures and dynamic processes that support all mediation. In being-with, the field of mediality constitutes the hyphen, the passage from Being to the with—already underway, always incomplete. The effort of this passage, its precarity and fragility we call communication. Communication determines the folds of the ear.

In this indeterminate determination, communication folds the ear upon itself as well as upon attunement and understanding. One comes here across the other. In discovering its ownmost possibility, Dasein discovers the other. Indeed, the text warrants, perhaps even necessitates, the inverse movement, which Heidegger would relinquish unto Levinas: Dasein arrives at itself only through hearing, which is always the hearing of the other, as other. Through the effort of communication Dasein discovers *itself as an other*.

No less is understanding at the outset an understanding-with: "*Mitda-sein* is essentially already manifest in attunement-with and understanding-with."[15] One understands either with *das Man*, the Heideggerian *hoi polloi*, thereby failing in truth to understand, or with the friend—Heidegger never says: the lover. It is in the distance of a

14 Heidegger, *Being and Time*, § 34, 150.
15 Ibid., 152.

stellar friendship that the sharing of communication must be sought. A friendless Da-sein, if such an existence were possible, would be an existence unable to recover truth in communication.

In order to carry on, it is important to tarry here. Da-sein *carries* the voice of the friend. For Fynsk this carrying is constant and silent: "in its silence, the voice of the friend speaks to Dasein of its death."[16] Death is never far for Heidegger; it is undoubtedly at the heart of these reflections. But the identification of the voice of the friend with the voice of death merits a slower pace. Carrying here designates the *imperative* of the 'with'. Insofar as being is being-with, one must carry the other. The words of Celan, which were to leave an indelible mark on late Derrida, resound here differently:

Die Welt ist fort, ich muss dich tragen.[17]

The death of the other, each time the unique end of the world; the end of the world, each time the death of the unique other. Dasein carries not only its own death but at the same time the death of the other; it carries the community of death. The voice of the friend speaks in silence when the friend is absent, temporarily, somehow always permanently. A familiar *phonē* arrives from an inscrutable distance. This spectral telephony is always *with* oneself—Heidegger writes here *bei sich*, rather than *mit*. We are reminded that *bei-sich-sein* designates in Hegel the absolute concept, the spirit "that has made its way to both inside and outside."[18] Although the Hegelian nexus exceeds the present horizon, the passage between interiority and exteriority is decisive.

The voice always bespeaks an interiority, even where interiority has lost all sense, as in the case of the voice of God. The voice is living spirit, life itself of the ghost in the machine. At the same time the voice is exteriorization, its reaches delimit the field of sonority and thereby the horizon of communication. The voice refracts the unity of spirit, marks the passage of an inside to an outside:

For before any appliance bearing the name 'telephone' in modern times, the telephonic *technē* is at work within the voice, multiplying the writing of voices without any instruments, as Mallarme would say, a mental telephony, which, inscribing remoteness, distance, différance, and spacing [*espacement*] in the *phonē*, at the same time institutes, forbids, and interferes with the so-called monologue.[19]

16   Christopher Fynsk, *Heidegger: Thought and Historicity* (London: Cornell University Press, 1993), 43.
17   From the collection *Atemwende*. "The world is gone, I must carry you." See Michael Hamburger, *Poems of Paul Celan* (New York: Persea Books, 1988), 267.
18   David Farrell Krell, Phantoms of the Other, Four Generations of Derrida's Geschlecht (Albany: SUNY, 2015), 108.
19   Jacques Derrida, 'Ulysses Gramophone, Hear Say Yes in Joyce', trans. Tina Kendall and Shari Benstock, in *Acts of Literature*, ed. Derek Attridge (London: Routledge, 1992), 271–272.

Voice, which is always the voice of the other, interrupts monologue. This interruption is the first death, as the voice loses the plenitude of life sustained within interiority, the absolute proximity of the voice. This necessary loss, recuperated through countless effects, proceeds upon a law of spacing that measures the distance from the point zero of interiority. The formula is here catalytic: "Existentially expressed, being-with-one-another has the character of *distantiality* [*Abständigkeit*]."[20]

On the one hand, in Heidegger's understanding, one distances oneself from the 'they' that distances itself in turn, setting into motion an incessant struggle of egotism, if not narcissism, against the mass imperative of the erasure of all distance. Dasein constantly reinstates its distance, sustained by the phobia of a relapse into the levelling of average uniformity. Being-with is here the impersonal abyss whence one constantly strives to escape. On the other hand, one always carries the voice of the friend as the distance within; a benevolent distance and an ideal proximity. Here, being-with discovers the harmony of *distantiality*, the law of spacing supporting the uniqueness of Dasein. Carrying the other, carrying the distance-within, Dasein discovers its ownmost possibility, it arrives, however fleetingly, at its absolute self-proximity. In a contrary motion, the Dasein attempts to produce a distance from the plural other (the 'they'), by hearkening to the distance-within, which the Dasein receives from the singular other (the friend). In this motion the Dasein escapes the vortex of absolute proximity of the other, to arrive at the absolute proximity of itself as an other.

The ear supplements, making good the foredoomed motion. The voice of the friend no less than the voice of Being is at once too far and too near. The ear folds this impossible distance upon itself in a communion of the far and the near:

> Therefore, if 'Being is farther than all beings and is yet nearer to man than every being', if 'Being is the nearest', then one must be able to say that Being is what is near to man, and that man is what is near to Being. The near is the proper; the proper is the nearest (*prope*, *proprius*). *Man is the proper of what right near to him whispers in his ear*; Being is the proper of man, such is the truth that speaks, such is the proposition which gives the there of the truth of Being and the truth of man.[21]

All the same, the proper of proximity reaches man as the remotest. Dasein is left with two possibilities: either to accept the necessary law of spacing at the heart of the voice, and thus allow the self-inscription of this telephony of friendship. Accordingly, by welcoming this *grammē* inside, to discover the exteriority of the interior, of the ownmost, to

20   Heidegger, *Being and Time*, § 27, 118.
21   Jacques Derrida, 'The Ends of Man', in *Margins of Philosophy*, trans. Alan Bass (Chicago: The University of Chicago Press, 1986), 133

witness itself as a record, perhaps even a trace of this philotelegramophony. Or, in order to resist this monstrosity of language, to strive to maintain the living voice, which speaks always of death, in the life of one's existence. In that sense, to carry the other amounts to an interdiction against recording his voice, against witnessing and bearing witness to it as a voice of distance, and by the same token, the voice of an other. To carry the voice of the other in absolute self-proximity, is thus to *incorporate* the other in the living presence of the self. The absent corporeality of the ear echoes in the labour of carrying the living body of the voice of the other, a sonic incorporation.

The latter response traverses the history of metaphysics, from Plato through Hegel to Heidegger and beyond. The earlier infects it from the beginning and outlines the limits of its closure—as such the limits of an epoch and the *kairos* of its abandonment. It outlines the operation of oto-cheiro-logy as auto-kairo-logy.

FINAL TRANSMISSION

We experience the becoming-manifest of the trace. As such we experience a profound tension. Levinas, who was among the first to sense this epochal tension and thus among the first to thematize the trace, understands it, at the outset, through the phenomenological logic of concealment: "the signifyingness of a trace consists in signifying without making appear," its exceptionality consisting "in that it signifies outside of every intention of signalling."[22] A sign, which signifies without intention and without even appearing, the trace complicates and transforms the logic of concealment.

The epochal tension consists in forcing into appearance what has hitherto been the most recalcitrant and had in its elusiveness both supported and undermined a history of metaphysical figurations that comprise much more than the history of philosophy. Science and literature advance and bear testimony—retaining the traces—of the struggle towards the arrival at this epochal tension. Kittler marks Rilke's decisive contribution:

> Rilke draws conclusions more radical than all scientific boldness. Before him, nobody had ever suggested to decode a trace that nobody had encoded and that encoded nothing.
> Ever since the invention of the phonograph, there has been writing without a subject. It is no longer necessary to assign an author to every trace, not even God.[23]

22   Emmanuel Levinas, 'The Trace of the Other', trans. Alphonso Lingis, in *Deconstruction in Context, Literature and Philosophy*, ed. Mark C. Taylor (Chicago: The University of Chicago Press, 1986), 356.
23   Friedrich A. Kittler, *Gramophone, Film Typewriter*, trans. Geoffrey Winthrop-Young and Michael Wutz (Stanford: Stanford University Press, 1999), 44.

Not only is the interiority of the author abolished, but the author is altogether elided. With the same stroke, or rather the same inscription, the trace reaches beyond signification. The trace becomes a sign which might or might not signify, establishing a non-exclusive relation between the two possibilities. The ear still hearkens the record of these traces, balancing over the abyss of the two possibilities.

REFLECTIONS OF AN IMAGINARY OBJECT ON A SILURIAN LAKE

X

GREGG LAMBERT

GREGG LAMBERT is Dean's Professor of Humanities at Syracuse University, New York, where he currently teaches in the Department of Philosophy. He is the author of numerous works in contemporary philosophy and critical theory. In the 1990s, he studied with Lyotard at the University of California, Irvine, and later co-edited (with Victor E. Taylor) a three-volume collection on Lyotard's philosophy published by Routledge Press (U.K.) in 2005.

Recently, I have been reading Lucretius's great poem *De rerum natura*. At the same time, I have been reflecting on my own coming death. Of course, these two activities naturally go together, since Lucretius himself wrote the poem, basically, as an argument concerning why we should not fear death, or rather, why the fear of death is the cause of the greatest amount of suffering and illusions in life, especially the illusion of a god. According to Lucretius, fear of death is a projection of terrors experienced in life, of pain that only a living (intact) mind can feel. Being completely devoid of sensation and thought, a dead person cannot miss being alive. Therefore, as a consoling gesture, Lucretius also puts forward the 'symmetry argument' against the fear of death. In it, he says that people who fear the prospect of eternal non-existence after death should think back to the eternity of non-existence before their birth, which didn't cause them much suffering.

Upon further reflection, it suddenly occurred to me that this may be one way of understanding what is partly a psychological motive for the 'problem of ancestrality' in the recent argument by Quentin Meillassoux. It has been little more than ten years ago that he first put us on the track of the arche-fossil as a 'hidden path' that will lead a temporality prior to consciousness and of life itself, in order 'to get rid of ourselves', which is to say, to get rid of the necessity of the subject entirely as the true cause of all our suffering, a suffering that has grown to encompass the earth, if not the universe. I thought to myself: might this not be a contemporary version of Lucretian materialism that admonishes us to reflect on the eternity of non-existence before the advent of our species?

No doubt, Meillassoux would not disagree that the material universe he describes bears some implicit kinship with the Lucretian universe, the contemplation of which, in a certain sense, was also fashioned as a manner of 'getting rid of ourselves' (i.e. getting rid of the Subject, albeit in Lucretius is a much more poetical fashion than merely discoursing "about a past in which both humanity and life are absent").[1] Nevertheless, he would surely object to any implicit 'subjectivist' account of his motive: the fear of death, *the absence of the Ego*. Here, in reformulating Meillassoux's speculative hypothesis, I am substituting the 'Ego' as the position of reflective (or thetic) consciousness that is declared to be 'absent' in the grasping of the ancestral realm. No doubt, at this point he would accuse me of importing a foreign and, moreover, blatantly psychoanalytic concept into the analysis, which threatens to spoil the purely objective illusion of the ancestral realm.

Nevertheless, I do think there has been a great deal of unnecessary confusion lately between the subject and the ego around the place

---

1   Quentin Meillassoux, *After Finitude: An Essay on the Necessity of Contingency*, trans. by Ray Brassier, Pbk. ed (London: Continuum, 2009), 27.

GHOSTS OF TRANSPARENCY

of consciousness, since psychoanalysis has shown that it is precisely that the function of a subject occurs in the absence of consciousness of the Ego. From a rigorous psychoanalytic perspective, it is the reality of the symbolic order that has effectively reduced the necessity of consciousness, which is why the consciousness is not altogether absent, but according to Lacan's famous formulation, 'decentered' in relation to the world of symbolic calculation. For example, in the case of mathematical symbols, or algebraic calculations, which is to say the order of machines that function without the need of anything like empirical or individual consciousness, this has something to do with the production of an absence necessary for the machines to function on their own, as *automata*.

To illustrate this, let me turn to a similar (if not identical) speculative hypothesis that Lacan employed very early on to demonstrate a similar claim that Meillassoux will make fifty years later with the example of the arche-fossil; although, he will draw very different conclusions concerning the significance of the phenomena of consciousness as such. "Suppose all men to have disappeared from the world," he begins, then immediately adds the following rejoinder, speaking mostly to the philosophers who are in attendance: "I say men on account of the high value which men attribute to consciousness."[2] Moreover, "let us take it to the point where all living beings have disappeared and there are only waterfalls and springs left—lightning and thunder too." It is at this point, in the splendour of this post-Anthropocene world, as you might have suspected, Lacan posits the existence of an object mirrored in a lake—"once again, we are dealing with a mirror"—and asks: "The image in the mirror, the image in the lake, do they still exist?"[3]

Of course, they do! he immediately exclaims, since the rays that return to the mirror cause us to locate in a purely virtual space an object that supposedly exists in reality; however, the real object is not the object you see in reality. *Voila!* "So here we have the phenomenon of consciousness as such."[4] Therefore, let us also recognize that the order of the mirror has evolved into the order of the machine at the high point of our civilization, so that we can imagine instruments sufficiently complicated enough to go on recording images in the lake despite the fact that all living beings have disappeared. So, according to what Lacan identifies as "a purely materialist definition" (recalling at this point the material universe of Lucretius as well), this is also a phenomenon of consciousness as such, though phenomena might not be the right word

---

2 Jacques Lacan, *Seminar II: The Ego in Freud's Theory and in the Technique of Psychoanalysis, 1954–1955*, The Seminar of Jacques Lacan, bk. 2, trans. S. Tomaselli (Cambridge: Cambridge University Press, 1988), 48.
3 Ibid., 48.
4 Ibid., 46.

since it won't have been perceived by any ego-like experience, or "any kind of ego or consciousness, the ego being absent at the time."[5]

Here we might get a glimpse of a certain 'correlation' with Meillassoux's example of the arche-fossil. According to Meillassoux's speculative hypothesis, the arche-fossil functions exactly like an object in a mirror, or like a reflection of a mountain upon a Silurian lake, since it contains or presents an image of an entity that is in-itself, given that there is no ego posited to apprehend its image. This is presented as the entire paradox of ancestralism: 'how can a being manifest being's anteriority to manifestation?' Of course, this question already presupposes that what we call manifestation occurs in the shadow of the presence of an Ego, a Subject, whatever you want to call the being anterior to manifestness as such. In other words, as Meillassoux asks:

> How are we to think the meaning of a discourse which construes the relation to the world—that of thinking and/or living—as a fact inscribed in a temporality within which this relation is just one event among others, inscribed in an order of succession in which it is merely a stage, rather than an origin? How is science able to think such statements, what and in what sense can we eventually ascribe truth to them?[6]

Reflecting on this last question, it occurs to me that before you can gain access to the ancestral realm, you must find some way to cause the present world to disappear, which in the above passage is accomplished by appealing to the existence of real numbers on a line of quantitative duration, on the basis of which we can have little machines called thermonuclear clocks that function without the shadow of any ego-like experience. Nevertheless as the mathematician Julien Pacotte has observed, "any measure bears within its own principle a kind of vicious circle."[7] For example, contemporary science is in a position to precisely determine—albeit in the form of revisable empirical hypotheses—the dates of the formation of the fossils of creatures living prior to the emergence of the first hominoids, the genre of life between different extinction events, the date of the accretion of the earth, the date of the formation of stars, and even the 'age' of the universe in approximate real numbers. "For what is at stake here," Meillassoux posits, "is the nature of scientific discourse, and more particularly of what characterizes this discourse—i.e. its mathematical form."[8] Thus, "we shall therefore maintain the following: all those aspects of the object that can be formulated in mathematical terms can be meaningfully conceived as properties of the object in itself."[9]

---

5   Ibid., 47.
6   Meillassoux, *After Finitude*, 10.
7   Pacotte, *La physique théorique nouvelle*, (Paris: Gauthier-Villars et Cie, 1921), 99.
8   Meillassoux, *After Finitude*, 26
9   Ibid., 3.

Nevertheless, in response to the above claim, we could easily propose from the perspective of a machinic universe, such as a posthumous perspective of a race of machines, as in a science fiction, that the basic paradox of what Meillassoux calls 'correlationism' is still present; although, it is simply displaced onto the universe of machines, or more accurately, the continual progress of a theoretical mathematics at a quantum level of measurement. Secondly, recently the astrophysicist Adam Frank and NASA's Goddard Institute director Gavin Schmidt addressed a number of misconceptions about studying the past. One of the first things they discuss is the fossil record. We've all seen the remains of ancient creatures on display, but these specimens represent only a tiny sliver of life on Earth. "Organisms only fossilize under very specific conditions. An extinct species could have numbered in the millions, and maybe none of them fossilized."[10]

Returning to Meillassoux's own description, although ancestrality is a temporal notion, "its definition does not invoke distance in time, but rather anteriority in time." This is why the arche-fossil does not merely refer to an un-witnessed occurrence, but to what he calls a non-given occurrence—"ancestral reality does not refer to occurrences which a lacunary givenness cannot apprehend [like the inverse side of a cube], but to occurrences which are not contemporaneous with any givenness, whether lacunary or not [thus, negating any extrapolation or geometrical calculation as well]." At one point in the argument, moreover, Meillassoux strips the arche-fossil of extension as well, as if its being has been reduced to the purely punctiform event of facticity, that is, to a date or a pure number. Since it has been stripped a priori of all secondary qualities—those that would arrive precipitously in correlation to a subject—the arche-fossil has neither any relation to a 'life-world' (as phenomenologists like to say after Husserl), nor even to any ancestral present, and thus no form of self affection, *no symbol of its own genesis*, since it is reduced to simple qualities; that is to say, "all those aspects of the object that can give rise to a mathematical thought and thus can be meaningfully turned into properties of the thing not only as it is with me, but also as it is without me."[11]

Concerning Meillassoux's claim, therefore, one question that would concern us is whether the manifestation of the primordial time of anteriority would even be possible as "[...] a deeper level of temporality, with which what came before the relation-to-the-world is itself

10 Ryan Witwam, 'Silurian Hypothesis: What If Humans Aren't the First Civilization on Earth?' Accessed on April 19, 2018 at 1:01 pm https://www.extremetech.com/extreme/267855-silurian-hypothesis-what-if-humans-arent-the-first-civilization-on-earth

11 Meillassoux, *After Finitude*, 123.

but a modality of that relation-to-the-world."[12] But what is this deeper temporality? Under what form of 'manifestness' does it appear (and for whom)? Certainly not the arche-fossil itself, which is denied all extension and thus could not even be qualified as a phenomenon, but merely the trace of a non-existent object of consciousness. And, finally, why 'deeper'? Does this not simply mean more 'significant', 'eventful', 'meaningful' for the subject of the statement, that is to say, the subject of speculative realism for whom the pure and simple 'fact' of the anteriority of the arche-fossil is a singular and 'critically potent' event for all philosophical speculation afterwards. In other words, in the temporality announced by the major statement of speculative realism, we can find a strict grammatical correlation drawn between subject and object, but the temporality of this correlation does not refer to the past for its ancestral significance (which is simply a 'before'), but rather to the future that is manifested as the statement's own singular, eventful, and critical potency in the contemporary time of philosophy.

12   Ibid., 123.

GHOSTS OF TRANSPARENCY

PENTECOST — A MODEL OF COMMUNICATION FOR 21ST CENTURY ARCHITECTURE
JORGE OROZCO

XI

JORGE OROZCO is a postdoctoral researcher and lecturer based in the CAAD group at the ETH Zurich's Department of Architecture, from which he obtained his Dr. sc. degree. He is interested in the world of architecture online and the machine intelligence that operates it. Jorge writes and codes on the novel abilities and the corresponding stabilities that this interplay presents to the tradition of architecture. Jorge was a guest researcher at the Future Cities Laboratory in Singapore. He holds a Master in Advanced Architecture degree with specialization in Digital Tectonics from IAAC, Barcelona, and a Master in Advanced Studies degree from ETH Zurich. He graduated from the UMSNH's Faculty of Architecture, Mexico.

Books, articles, interviews; journals, magazines, newsletters; competitions, projects, buildings; floor plans, models and maps. Online communities cover the world of architecture. The members of these communities uninterruptedly talk to each other from all around the world, in different languages, and from many positions. Regardless of quantities, the applications that engender them make communication easy, so that within the whole, all members are found in places for understanding and comfort: They share common languages and interests. Without these intermediaries, a community exists in the noise, with no third party between them, no assurance that what is received is what is sent, plus or minus themselves. This prominent performance is possible due to the developers' novel instrumentality and understanding of what an online community is and what it circulates: information.

This article argues for models of communication having the capacity to deal with today's world of architecture, all of it, personally and vividly. It addresses the role of the intermediary in an online community by exploring the scenarios that open up if we 'get rid' of it and source and symbolize for ourselves the data that a community circulates. On these grounds, we see in the day of Pentecost a promising model of communication that reduces the third party to a 'grain of sand', as it is a model without intermediaries and with the capacity to celebrate and embrace what a community that is interested in architecture circulates, whatever it is, further suggesting new imaginings to the philosophy of architecture.

ON MODELS OF COMMUNICATION: HERMES, LEIBNIZ, SHANNON, THE HOLY GHOST, FACEBOOK AND THE PARASITES

Can a network without the constraints of mediation be constructed where objects can be in relation to one another without a third interpreter? Philosopher Michel Serres presents the model of Pentecost as a possible answer.

In his book *The Parasite*, Serres[1] presents a philosophy for a natural economy based on parasitic relations between all things of the world, regardless of established ontologies or categories—i.e. regardless of being objects that 'belong' to science, religion, history, society. With a Pentecostal model of communication, Serres reduces the third—the parasite, the interpreter, the mediator—to a minimum, and presents the new abilities that 'liberated' parties gain.

To discuss the capacities of such a model of communication, Serres places this latter next to another two models—those of Leibniz and Hermes—that sequentially replaced each other, touching on their abilities and limits.

---

1   See Michel Serres, *The Parasite*, trans. L. R. Schehr (Baltimore: The Johns Hopkins University Press, 1982 [1980]).

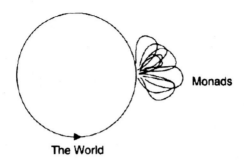

FIG 1
Monads and The
World. Gilles
Deleuze, 1993

Monads

The World

A model of communication introduced by Leibniz explains the nature of the substance present in all the things of the universe—the monads. A monad is "a simple substance which enters into compounds, 'simple' meaning without parts."[2] They have no extension or shape and are indivisible. These atomic elements aggregate into things; they interconnect, crisscross; they talk to each other, so every monad expresses all the others and mirrors the universe. But even in this 'all connected' condition, every element relates to the rest through a unique intermediary, so that "the influence of one monad over another is merely ideal: It can have its effect only through the intervention of God."[3]

An image of this model's network is centred. Talks go from the plural towards the singular, from local to global, and God is in the centre. It renders, for Leibniz, a perfect assemblage where sources and destination are predetermined and the noise between them is at its minimum.

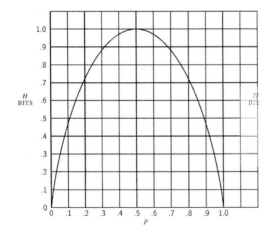

FIG 2
Entropy in the case
of two possibilities
with probabilities
p and $1-p$. Claude
Shannon, 1948.

2 See Lloyd Strickland, *Leibniz's Monadology* (Edinburgh: Edinburgh University Press, 2014 [1714]), 14.
3 Ibid., 24.

Leibniz's model of communication resonates with Claude Shannon's,[4] for whom a talk happens only when the noise that may have been added to the message at the moment of transmission is reduced to zero; when a channel between a monad and God is pure. His goal was to calculate the correct sequence, the optimum, between source and destination. The problem was formulated as the exact reproduction of a message sent from one point at another point, given an established source, code and medium. For Shannon, the source encodes and sends a message; the destination receives and decodes it. The limits of Leibniz's model lie in the ability to talk on behalf of, or distanced from, a unique intermediary. Politics is at the limits of this model, and Hermes is at the beginning of politics.

FIG 3
Sebastiano Ricci,
*Mercury, Herse and
Aglauros*, 1720–1734,
oil on canvas,
88.5 × 58.8 cm,
Manchester
Art Gallery, UK

Another model of communication can be attributed to Hermes. Hermes, son of Zeus, was more than a messenger between gods and humans, because he acted on his father's behalf. In the *Iliad*,[5] when Hector's dead body is not given the proper rites, the gods urge Hermes to steal the body from its captor, Achilles. This, however, was not Zeus's way. Instead, he sends Hermes to guide Priam to Achilles in order to do politics on Hector's body. Hermes is the intermediary between two protagonists, between two distanced centres capable of influencing the behaviour of the rest.

4   Claude Shannon, 'A Mathematical Theory of Communication', Bell Systems Technical Journal, 27 (1948), 623–656.
5   See Homer, *The Iliad*, trans. Robert Fagles, Penguin Classics (New York: Penguin Books, 1991). (Vol. 20), 588–614.

Hermes is at any crossroads and exchange. He holds the unique position between two parties: "He produces, alone, a relation among an incongruous mixture of subjects and practices and an incongruous set of objects and merchandise,"[6] rendering a many-one-many network, where the received message is what is sent, plus or minus Hermes.

Such a model resonates with the applications that today engender communities online, like Facebook. Facebook designs the way in which users talk to each other online, giving them little to no say about how they want to act—the 'home' button points to a space to talk about anything, the 'your-face' button points to a space to talk about you; 'here' are some friendly people to talk to. From two billion active users, each one lives in a comfortable and familiar space, where the unpleasant goes away with one click. The applications that engender these communities carry the messages, listening, recording, operating and creating new values from them.[7] The limits of this model lie in its ability to listen to and operate upon what the community is saying—Hermes performs as long as there are messages to pass on.

But what happens if a speaker is heard as is? Can the many be connected to the many, without an intermediate?

FIG 4
El Greco, *Pentecost*,
c. 1596, oil on canvas,
275 × 127 cm,
Museo del Prado,
Madrid, Spain

6   See Serres, *The Parasite*, 42.
7   Instagram is a good example, it was bought by Facebook in 2012 for approximately 1 billion USD [en.wikipedia.org/wiki/Instagram (accessed 23.8.2017)] when the company was thirteen computer scientists (See Jaron Lanier, *Who Owns the Future?* (London: Penguin Books, 2014)).

On the day of Pentecost,[8] the apostles and company gathered to celebrate God, their common exchanger. They did not share a common tongue, as they came from many lands. Fire came, and a sudden sound filled the whole room 'as of a rushing mighty wind', and they began to speak in other tongues and were able to communicate without a translator. It was fire, something outside themselves, that brought this new ability.

The relations between the people gathered that day were many-many, without a third in between. The image of such a network is de-centered, with neither crossroads nor interceptors, neither many gods nor one God: A challenging self-regulation.

If we look for a contemporary scenario where any speaker speaks in his own language and every hearer understands in his own, regardless of the language and location, we can say that Google Translate is a prominent example as it translates between over a hundred natural languages instantly. This ability is implemented in a number of online applications, like the mobile app that takes a photo of a restaurant's menu, recognizes its characters and language, and translates the food items to a desired language. Or in applications like Skype that offer real-time voice and text translation on phone calls. Even when these applications present new capacities to communicate, however, the abilities that we argue for go beyond an explicit understanding of what happened on the day of Pentecost, beyond linguistic translations. We are arguing for the ability to recognize, locally and without mediation, the sound from the noise—the rare from the norm, order from disorder, negentropy from entropy, information from data—that may be circulating in an online community.

FIG 5
The Economist,
cover, May 2017.

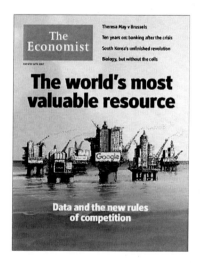

8   As told in the Holy Bible's book of Acts.

Interestingly enough, online communities show us ways to put together applications like those we argue follow Hermes. MOOC (Massive Open Online Courses) like Udacity, offer courses to learn programming languages, to specialize in libraries used by prominent developers, and to be proficient in the cutting-edge instrumentality—i.e. machine intelligence—used by 'world-changing' companies. The only requirement: access to a computer and an Internet connection.

The focus of these MOOCs is to promote the development of applications able to engender big communities that can be the intermediary for big circulations—whatever they may be about—as these are the primal source of new economic and political values.[9]

Our interest is to explore, within the same scenario and from an architect's position, a hypothetical turn from Hermes-like to Pentecost-like models of communication online, as such a turn promises to embrace the abundance of information circulating in communities personally and as a whole, opening up spaces that were not available before, and bringing new capacities and imaginations to the philosophy of architecture.

The question is, what would this model look like from the position of an architect?

ON 20TH CENTURY ARCHITECTURE:
EISENMAN, TSCHUMI, LIBESKIND AND LYNCH

In architecture, we can think of a Pentecostal model of communication when we have the ability to talk about architecture without an interpreter and beyond an authoritative articulation. In today's global condition, where all theories, projects, manifestos, images, regulations, software, interviews, floor plans, profiles, tutorials, competitions, doors, windows, elements, lectures and documentaries are available online, such a model of communication aims to engender architectural talks by celebrating the abundance of information that online communities emit, receive, store and process.[10]

Our contemporaries have already formulated similar questions. Peter Eisenman, for example, sees in 'text' a strategy to liberate a building from an authoritative 'reading', i.e. from a correct relationship between the building and what it signifies.[11] Something like: We don't

9 Facebook has 2 billion monthly active users [en.wikipedia.org/wiki/Facebook (accessed 23.8)] and their data is claimed to be used significantly for political purposes, as seen in "Ich habe nur gezeigt, dass es die Bombe gibt. —Der Psychologe Michal Kosinski hat eine Methode entwickelt, um Menschen anhand ihres Verhaltens auf Facebook minutiös zu analysieren. Und verhalf so Donald Trump mit zum Sieg." [www.dasmagazin. ch/2016/12/03/ich-habe-nur-gezeigt-dass-es-die-bombe-gibt (accessed 23.8.2017)].

10 See Michel Serres, 'Information and Thinking', Society for European Philosophy and Forum for European Philosophy Annual Conference, *Philosophy After Nature*, Utrecht, September 3, 2014.

11 See Peter Eisenmann, 'Architecture as Second Langauge—The Texts of Between', in P. Eisenmann, *Eisenmann Inside Out*, (New Haven: Yale University Press, 2004 [1998]).

see the same thing when we look at the same building, and it is fine. Celebrating the information that a building emits.

Eisenman finds the multivalency of text—the impossibility of a single unique reading—liberating, even when, for him, an architecture of texts is 'unnatural' due to architecture's temporal and spatial specificity and presence. By dislocating architecture with texts of 'between'—between the building's origin and its authorial value, and the 'thick' object—Eisenman aims to free a building from its specificity.

To do so, he looks at what happens in films, where these dislocations are natural. "Film is the *sine qua non* of a dislocated place and time because it always has at least two times and two places: the actual time and place of watching, and the narrative time and place."[12] As an example, he analyses David Lynch's Blue Velvet from the late 1980s which narrates a story from the early 1950s, but includes strong elements from the late 1950s and 1960s. Showing that the linear temporal structure of the film is dislocated, and suggesting that the consistency of the film, the mastership of the narrative, is beyond a specific time and space—beyond its 'thickness'.

Eisenman recognizes the violence that this presents to a building—to all its former articulations—because if he celebrates the ability of a building to speak about anything, its origins appear without control, its foundations are set in motion, truth multiplies, doubt is introduced, authorship is questioned, and centralities vanish. In other words, the old values introduced by an authority, the well-established stabilities, stop working.

12   Ibid., 228.

His solution is to formalize the abundance of information that a building may emit through a production process, introducing machinelike diagrams as generative devices,[13] which make material, specific and taxonomic the building's dislocations. Furthermore, these diagrams claim to be the architect's device to unveil the building's interiority by placing, layer by layer, an accessible history of a 'thick' object.

This position is actually shared by other contemporaries. Bernard Tschumi introduces drawings that propose to transcribe an architectural representation of reality, with the explicit purpose of transcribing things normally removed from conventional architectural representation, as a way to access the object's origin.[14] Daniel Libeskind, similarly, talks about machines that propose a fundamental recollection and retrieval of architecture, which, once they are in motion, can facilitate interpretation of architecture's history, program or poetics.[15]

In these terms, a Pentecostal model of communication aims to keep a building's abundance of information 'alive'—to talk instead of to define, as opposed to Eisenman and Co.—and to find new stabilities with neither an authority nor a taxonomy but from the circulation of information.

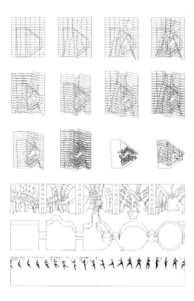

FIG 7
Diagram of Church of the year 2000. Peter Eisenman, 1996.

FIG 8
Transcribing reality to architecture. Bernard Tschumi, 1981.

FIG 9
One of the three machines from Three Lessons in Architecture—The machines installation. Studio Libeskind, 1985.

13 See Peter Eisenmann, *Diagram Diaries* (New York: Universe Publishing, 1999).
14 See Bernard Tschumi, *The Manhattan Transcripts* (London: Academy Editions, 1994 [1981]).
15 See Daniel Libeskind, 'Three Lessons in Architecture: The Machines', 1985, accessible at: www.libeskind.com/work/cranbrook-machines (accessed 23.8.2017).

Elsewhere, I have presented three applications that celebrate models of communication without intermediaries.[16] They address different on-line communities—e.g. Tumblr, Wikimedia Commons, Wikia, World-architects—and give the users new abilities to deal with the information they circulate, decoupled from those given by the engendering application.

One of these applications sources text from different online communities and creates an objective and scalable space for two different living concepts to talk to one another. One is the voice of today's Swiss architecture and the other of a person, Eliot Alderson—a character from the TV series Mr. Robot.

Swiss-architects.com is a community that celebrates architecture built in Switzerland today. Over 600 Swiss offices are profiled there with a selection of their projects. They offer descriptive texts, philosophy, awards, numbers, images and, occasionally, floor plans. Around these, profiles of manufacturers, lists of jobs, agenda and news. If an office has a building site in Switzerland today, its profile is most probably featured in this community. Swiss-architects is part of the world-architects network, curated and membership-based.[17]

FIG 10
A sourced quote in German translated to English by Yandex Translate API.

"Die einfache Sache ist schwer. Das Projekt ist dann gelungen, wenn alle Anstrengungen nicht mehr spürbar sind und sich Leichtigkeit einstellt."

– zech architektur

#translate #graph

♥ ⟳ ❤

7 months ago

"The simple thing is difficult. The project is then managed, if all your efforts are noticeable and lightness sets in."

– zech architektur via translate.yandex.com

#translate #graph

♥ ⟳ ❤

7 months ago

16 See Jorge Orozco, *Indexical Architecture. Prominent Positions, Applications and the Web*, doctoral dissertation, ETH Zurich, Switzerland, 2017.
17 See www.world-architects.com/en/pages/about (accessed 15.07.2017)

Wikia.com[18] and magicalquote.com are two communities that celebrate TV series and their characters. On Wikia, each TV series has its own subdomain and, even when they are organized differently, most have a reserved place for their characters and episodes. Characters are extensively characterized by their background, significance, physical appearance, personality and even some external references. The community is open and adopts the Wikipedia model, in which members can create and edit entries following predefined directions and standards. Magicalquote.com, on the other hand, is a blog that collects quotes from movies, series, books and authors. Since 2013, it has put together a database representative of the popular tastes. If the show has an Emmy associated with it, its characters are most likely featured there. The blog is openly accessible but the creation or editing of entries is limited to the community members.

In a first movement, this application sources from the communities' servers (a) the profiles and projects of every architectural office featured on swiss-architects.com—i.e. all text and images—and (b) all that is written about Elliot Alderson on Wikia[19] and Magicalquote.[20]

To source a community is necessarily to profile it and to put together a custom web bot, which requests and parses documents programmatically. It typically starts with a seed address, requests the document at that address, stores locally the response and looks for the hyperlinks in it—the text or image that links to another document with one click. This simple process is performed iteratively.

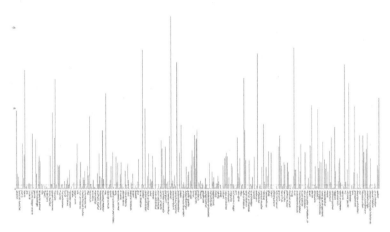

FIG 11
Bar chart showing the number of unique words for 431 offices.

18   Wikia, Inc. describes itself as the largest entertainment fan site in the world with more than 385,000 fan communities and a global audience of over 175 million monthly uniques. See www.wikia.com/about (accessed 15.07.2017)
19   www.mrrobot.wikia.com/wiki/Elliot_Alderson (accessed 15.07.2017)
20   www.magicalquote.com/character/elliot/ (accessed 15.07.2017)

The corpus of architects comprises 640 profiles, each one talking about itself and its projects. Some offices have a lot to say, as much as 10,000 unique words, and others not more than a couple sentences. Furthermore, not all the text is in English, so this application translates them from German using Yandex Translate API.[21] On Elliot, the corpus is over 3,000 unique words, a combination of his quotes and what other people write about him.

Text is what constitutes the corpora. It is the ground of comparison for the two different concepts to talk. How do we know now what they are both talking about?

The application has the combined vocabulary of the Swiss offices and Elliot. What follows is to model both for similarities and differences to emerge. The starting point is to know which office says what by a bag-of-words (BoW) model.[22] Imagine a matrix where the rows are the offices and the columns the words in the vocabulary—3,344 words by 431 offices—and is filled with ones and zeros, very scattered. The next step is to transform this model into a term frequency-inverse document frequency (tf-idf) model, so that, instead of ones and zeros, the matrix is of numbers between 0 and 1 that reflect how important a word in a document is.

One ability gained at this point is that the user can construct an idea of what the offices may be talking about—whether rooms, land, or the stars—with a vocabulary that is completely defined by them, not by the application or the user. What the application can do with it next is fantastic: Just by multiplying and adding, it can construct topics[23] (in this example, 200) to which each office can be directly related. Each topic is a little bit of this word plus a little bit of that word, minus the other word. For example, topic number 7 is constructed by 0.265 of the word 'school', plus 0.254 of the word 'competition' plus 0.210 of 'price' and so on.

Let us imagine the matrix again. It used to be of 3,344 dimensions (columns) by 431 observations (rows), with a lot of zeros and very few numbers from 0 to 1. Now the matrix is 200 dimensions (where each dimension is one topic) by 431 observations (where each observation is one office). The matrix is full of numbers from -1 to 1 now, because each office talks about each topic, but in different quantities.

The similarities and differences between offices are in this matrix. But we cannot see them, of course, amidst the 86,200 numbers: We need the application to do it for us.

21   See www.tech.yandex.com/translate/ (accessed 15.07.2017)
22   See Wikipedia's entry on this model at en.wikipedia.org/wiki/Bag-of-words_model (accessed 26.09.2018)
23   See Wikipedia's entry on Latent Semantic Analysis at en.wikipedia.org/wiki/Latent_semantic_analysis (accessed 26.09.2018)

"be
building
house
new
space
residential
area
room
floor
design
construction
location
have
project
build
…"

swiss-architects' words

#topics

"be
have
person
not
see
do
make
just
know
take
other
social
world
maybe
work
much
even
think
…"

elliot's words

#topics

7 months ago

"be, project, design, …
competition, price, plan, …
house, family, villa, …
house, price, bern, …
bern, have, center, …
building, price, competition, …
project, design, ag, …
school, casa, henz, …
building, architecture, ch, …
space, have, architecture, …
detach, extension, basel, …
architecture, biel, school, …
architect, extension, school, …
…"

swiss-architects' topics

#topics

7 months ago

"be, not, make, …
bug, something, look, …
question, isn't, evil, …
attention, easier, much, …
secret, hack, person, …
always, other, devil, …
friend, devil, hacker, …
hacker, control, look, …
mask, face, then, …
face, vulnerability, then, …
part, top, mask, …
paranoia, attention, isn't, …
avoid, friend, change, …
…"

elliot's topics

#topics

7 months ago

FIG 12
Vocabularies of
swiss-architects and
Elliot, respectively.

FIG 13
Learned topics of
swiss-architects and
Elliot, respectively.

FIG 14
Scatter plot of three
different models:
BoW, tf-idf and top-
ics. Each one show-
ing the 431 offices.

FIGURE 15
Detail showing
the same office:
'schwarz-schwarz',
in three different
neighbourhoods.

In a third movement, the application learns to find patterns in the matrix, reducing 200 dimensions to two, while keeping its topological distances. This process is called non-linear dimensionality reduction and is

implemented with the python library scikit-learn.[24] It is repeated with the other two models already put together—BOW and tf-idf. Figure N shows the three different models of the same speech, offices talking to each other and positioning themselves on a plane according to their topics of conversation. The closer they are, the more they converse. Now that a common plane is constructed, we can see where Elliot places himself.

FIG 16
Elliot Alderson
and his four closest
neighbouring offices.

"Elliot. Just a tech."

"The architecture is always also a social project."

"Our goal is to create innovative architecture that respects both the needs of the people, as well as the local context."

"Through the combination of architecture, consulting, research and teaching, we are using our Knowledge to always be one step ahead."

"If you want to build according to everyone's advice, gets a house, the crooked city."

Finally, this application constructs a common plane for offices to talk to each other. They all relate to the same vocabulary but use it differently, so their talks are not the same. It now looks at Elliot's talk and compares it with that of the Swiss offices. Once Elliot is on the plane, distances to offices can be measured. It turns out that Elliot is not an alien. Figure P shows four close offices to him. They talk about society, the needs of people, and the city as a political concept. And if we know Elliot, we could say that it is not that strange, as he is a hacker who actively tries to break down the system through its digital infrastructure. At the same time, though, we cannot be sure, since there is no definition of Elliot to evaluate the offices against, suggesting that the evaluation of their talk at the level of sympathy.

Both corpora can always accommodate more text, changing their positions on the plane of comparison. The offices and Eliot are thought of as animated concepts, which are kept alive and can continue to talk about architecture.

ON 21ST CENTURY ARCHITECTURE: THE ARCHITECT

On the day of Pentecost, after the astonishment of those present by their new abilities, the future of the Church was discussed. "What shall we do?" they asked, and arguments started to be articulated, reasons were constructed, answers were found, and decisions were taken by those present, not by fire. This distinction of abilities resonates with our

24   See scikit-learn.org (accessed 12.12.2017)

application. Our application listens and reads, like the fire; us, we talk and write, like the community members. We address the world of architecture online with personal and vivid applications, in its vastness, diversity, and speed. And it is us who ask questions, construct arguments, address concepts or make decisions on architecture, not the application. What does not resonate, though, is that on the day of Pentecost the fire was given, as it came to them as a surprise and performed 'as is', no questions asked. It was natural. Our application, on the other hand, is constructed and discussed. Do we like what it is doing, do we sympathize with the results? These answers stay open and change, making our application a political object. The promise that a Pentecostal-like model of communication presents to the architect is to step out into the world of paradoxes from a rich and stable position, and talk and write, as the rest is with the machines.

BETWEEN DISEGNO   XII
& DESIGN THINKING
JONATHAN POWERS

JONATHAN POWERS is the academic director at the Thomas More Institute in Montreal. He champions the liberal arts and humanities against the rising darkness. He avers that creativity, architecture, and followership rank among the most interesting and important liberal arts. He has put bread on the table by teaching, winning innovation competitions, coding real-estate spreadsheets, serving civilly, waiting tables, editing resumes, and so on. He works every day (to varying degrees of success) on sharpening his listening skills, his curiosity, and his humility.

The phrase *design thinking* has in recent years risen to prominence in business parlance, where it means a "proven and repeatable problem-solving protocol that any business or profession can employ to achieve extraordinary results."[1] Vague promises of "extraordinary results" for employing a simple "protocol" accessible to "any business or profession" would seem to belong more to the domains of charlatanism and late-night infomercials than to serious thinking or craft. Yet homologous characterizations of design thinking are current in many mainstream publications—even in the pages of the *Harvard Business Review*.[2] Can design thinking (or indeed *any* kind of thinking) really be as simple and effective as promised? Whatever the prestige of its promulgators, I expect that this oversimplification of design thinking would meet with a certain coolness (if not outright contempt) from most professional designers and architects, who have typically undertaken years of strenuous study and training in a broad palette of knowledge and skills.[3] If a foolproof, rinse-and-repeat method could guarantee fruitful design processes and desirable design results for anyone and everyone, there would be no need to train designers. A glance at any design curriculum, however, suggests that advanced practitioners hold that mastering the intricacies of design demands supple intelligence, broad competence, and intense diligence. And even if anyone and everyone can design at some level, skill and experience make a marked difference. On the other hand, I suspect that most architects and designers would be pleased to have the public—from which the overwhelming preponderance of clients emerge—possess a first-order sense that what designers do is comprehensible, versatile, and effective. (And I would contend that design thinking does indeed possess these traits.) A basically honest and positive oversimplification of design thinking, in other words, would seem desirable not only for designers, but also for those who stand to benefit from the value that design thinking can add to products, processes, and—why not just say it—all human endeavours. The modest philological analysis that follows does not aim either to debunk or defend any particular oversimplification of design thinking, but rather to suggest

1   Fast Company Staff, 'Design Thinking ... What is That?', *FastCompany* https://www.fastcompany.com/919258/design-thinking-what, [accessed 12 December 2017]

2   Brown, Tim. 'Design Thinking', *Harvard Business Review*, 2008, <https://hbr.org/2008/06/design-thinking>

3   I presume that the reader will grant without serious reservations the reciprocal relevance of design and architecture, though with the possible caveat that architecture be recognized not as the privileged center of design practice, but rather as one "design discipline" among many. See Rodgers, Paul A., and Craig Bremner, 'The Concept of the Design Discipline', *Dialectic* 1.1 (2016): 19–38. <http://dx.doi.org/10.3998/dialectic.14932326.0001.104>

GHOSTS OF TRANSPARENCY

that the basic concept of design thinking is both robust enough to support oversimplification and important enough to deserve the broader audience that oversimplification affords.

BETWEEN *DESIGN* AND *DRAWING*

The English word *design*—as well as all of its cognates in other modern European languages—draws its principal meanings from the Italian word *disegno*, which in turn descends from the Latin verb *designare*, which means "to mark out," "to indicate," or quite simply, "to designate." Historically speaking, the Italian word *disegno* becomes interesting for our purposes in the 14th and 15th centuries, when in the artisanal workshops in Florence it came to refer to an ensemble of practices by which a plan or intention for an artefact was generated, elaborated, and communicated. The most distinctive of these practices were—and still are—the construction of models and the making of drawings. Indeed, the latter of these practices remains the principal meaning of the word *disegno*, which is why the most common translation of *disegno* into modern English is simply "drawing." There are, of course, significant differences between the meanings of *disegno* and *drawing*. (For reasons on concision I will focus on English here, though other modern European languages have metabolized the meanings of *disegno* in ways that preserve the most important ambiguities and tensions present in the 15th century Italian word.[4]) I would like to highlight three of these differences.

First, the most basic and dispositive of difference between *disegnare* and *drawing* is that fact that the former is a semantic verb, while *to draw* is a manual verb. To feel how trenchant this difference is, we might imagine coming upon a draughtsman working at his table. We ask him, "What are you doing?" And he replies, without the slightest irony, "Designating." Such an answer would capture a large part of what a Renaissance artist and his clients would have meant by the word "*disegno*." The bedrock sense of *design* is not *technical*—in the sense of knowing how to make things—but rather *communicative*. At the

---

4 Modern Italian, for example, naturally preserves almost all of the ambiguousness of the 15th century meaning—manual and semantic senses are thoroughly conflated. Modern German possesses *das Design*, but it is a thin noun reflecting a narrow slice of the modern English word; yet the German verb *zeichnen* ("to draw") is a straightforwardly semantic verb, originally meaning "to symbolize" or "to show"—and the German verb *entwurfen* ("to design") traces its ancestry back to terms meaning "to cast (throw)" and "to warp." The modern French verb *dessiner* means principally "to draw," with the more semantic senses of *disegno* now subsumed under more rationalistic verbs like *concevoir* ("to conceive") and *élaborer* ("to elaborate"). The French noun *projet* and the English noun *project*—both descended from ancestors meaning "to throw" and thereby aligning with *entwurfen*—can both stand in for the English noun *design*. In most modern European languages, the overall pattern of semantic alliances and antimonies among the meanings compassed by *disegno* exhibits remarkable consistency.

same time, *design* remains ineluctably and thoroughly factural: Design is about *making* (crafting, ordering, assembling) artefacts that signify (point beyond themselves). In the word *disegno*, the manual act of making marks on a surface and the semantic act of using one thing to indicate another are thoroughly conflated, but with priority given to the semantic senses and uses. The closest analogue to *disegno*, in terms of its role in its semantic ecosystem, thus turns out to be *writing*, for both practices refer to the making of material traces that point beyond themselves.

A second difference between *disegno* and *drawing* is that the former's essentially semantic character gives it a much broader compass than marks on a surface. In 15th century Italy, the noun *disegno* was often used to refer to a drawing, but it might also refer to a model. The phrasal noun *disegno di legno proportionate*, for example, meant not a scale drawing in wood, but "a scaled wooden model." Even a model large enough to enter bodily—such as Filippo Brunelleschi's (1377–1446) demonstration model for the dome of the Florence Cathedral—could be termed a *disegno*. This breadth of scope derives from the fact that *designo* entailed an essentially semantic activity rather than a strictly technical one. While we may presume that Brunelleschi constructed his model principally in order to demonstrate or communicate an idea, this does not mean that his model did not directly address technical and factural issues. I am arguing here that technical issues have always been unembarrassed subordinates in design, yielding precedence to questions of intention and communication, because it is manifestly *intentions*—and not technical challenges—that propel design processes forward. Anyone who has actually engaged in designing something understands something of the difficulties involved in holding together the evolving intentions that motivate a design process and the series of partial draughts that culminate in the final product. This basic tension between motivating intentions and technical constraints has always characterized our understanding of design. Contemporary thinking along precisely these lines has even led to the suggestion that *rhetoric* (which would include not only speech-making, but also conversation and verbal composition in general) be classed as a "design art."[5] We would, I submit, readily accept that verbal products (reports, narratives, meeting minutes, etc.) can often effectively articulate and elaborate important aspects of designs, just as drawings and models do.

A third difference between *disegno* and *drawing* is that the former refers to a form of cognition as well as to a mechanical or manual activity. *Disegno* entails the making of artefacts, and so it is undoubtedly a craft (*techne*) or technical activity in many important aspects.

5   See David S. Kaufer, and Brian S. Butler, *Rhetoric and the Arts of Design* (Mahwah, N.J.: L. Erlbaum Associates, 1996), 28ff.

But because the products of *disegno* self-consciously aim to articulate, communicate, and inform human intentions, *disegno* must also mean a specific and quite subtle form of cognition. Renaissance artisans self-consciously spoke of *disegno nella mente*—"drawing in the mind"—as a high-level skill related to but distinguishable from drawing with one's hand. The basic link between the two is that manual *disengo* and mental *disegno* were understood to activate and educate the same form of cognition. The apprentice first learns how to draw with his hand, but the practice of this manual skill demands that he exercise his mental capacity to *designate*—to hypothesize, elaborate, and conjecture. Becoming skilled at *disegno* means becoming skilled at imagining and evaluating the counterfactual possibilities inherent in the subjects of one's *disegni*. At bottom, *disegno* comprises a complex of skills that are intimately (and often awkwardly) entangled with the basic human capacities of forethought and communication. *Disegno* entails, in short, the co-crafting of artefacts and the intentions that motivate their production. Since the making of artefacts and the shaping of intentions occur in parallel, what is at stake in a design process is not only the final product, but also the characteristic mode of cognition—"design thinking"—that actuates such a process, and which improves with practice and reflection.

DESIGN AS A PRACTICE

The amphibious nature of Renaissance *disegno*—simultaneously manual craft and form of cognition—exhibits a remarkable historical persistence. A simple juxtaposition of quotations will serve to indicate the robustness and coherence of *design thinking* as a basic concept. First, a pair of quotations pulled from the two writers who may be said, respectively, to have opened and closed the epoch that established the basic meaning of *disegno* that we have inherited. Cennino Cennini's so-called *Il libro dell'arte* (after 1396) is accepted as the earliest craft manual of the Renaissance. In it, Cennini asks, "Do you know what will happen to you, practising drawing [*il disegnare*] with a pen? You will become expert, practised, and capable of much *disegno* within your head."[6] Practise with a pen leads to skill drawing in your head. One hundred and fifty years later, Giorgio Vasari's *Lives of the Most Excellent Painters, Sculptors, and Architects* (1568) effectively closes and catalogues the Renaissance as an artistic revolution. Based on his research, Vasari recommends to aspiring artists that "the best thing is to draw men and women from the nude and thus fix in the memory by constant exercise the muscles of the

6   Cennino d'Andrea Cennini, *Il libro dell'arte: o, Trattato della pittura*, originally composed a. 1396., rpt. eds. Gaetano and Carlo Milanesi (Firenze: Felice Le Monnier, 1859), 9 = ch. XIII. My translation.

torso, back, legs, arms, and knees, with the bones underneath. Then one may be sure that through much study attitudes in any position can be drawn by help of the imagination without one's having the living forms in view."[7] Attentive practice drawing human nudes will result in an analytical understanding of the specific geometry of the human body, which will underwrite a synthetic capacity of the imagination to compose human figures in the mind. The years separating these observations changed nothing of the basic sense, with the exception of nominating the imagination as the specific mental faculty educated by the practice of manual *disegno*. (I will return to the imagination in a moment.)

To this characteristically Renaissance attitude toward *disegno* I would like to compare a remark made by Francis D. K. Ching, one our own epoch's recognized masters of drawing. The following text, which concerns the value of drawing as a catalyst to creative thinking, is drawn from the preface of one of Ching's books. In fact, the quote is posted on Amazon.com's website as the book's summary blurb. Such positioning tells us that this passage represents uncontroversial received wisdom about the value of drawing as an artistic practice. Ching asserts that:

> [d]rawing cannot be detached from seeing and thinking about the fundamental nature of the subject matter being represented. The knowledge and understanding gained through drawing from life directly enhances our ability to draw from the imagination. Just as thought can be put into words, ideas can be made visible in a drawing to promote visual thinking and further stimulate the imagination. Once what is seen or imagined is made visible in a drawing, the image takes on a life of its own and communicates graphically.[8]

True to the original artisanal notion of *disegno*, Ching represents drawing as a semantic act—analogous to writing—that grapples with the "fundamental nature" of matters, renders "ideas" visible, and operates communicatively. Also like his predecessors, Ching presents drawing as a *practice*. Every act of drawing interacts with the artist's thinking about what she's drawing; and further, practising drawing on an ongoing basis enhances the practitioner's overall aptitude for thinking about ideas in general (insofar as they can be drawn). We are nowadays accustomed to defining design in terms of its material products. And there is, of course, nothing wrong with thinking about design along craft lines—which is to say, in terms of technics. But design is *also* a

---

7   Giorgio Vasari, *Vasari on Technique*, trans. by L. S. Maclehose, revised edition (New York: Dover, 1960), 210, quoted in van den Akker, Paul, "'Out of Disegno Invention is Born' – Drawing a Convincing Figure in Renaissance Italian Art," *Argumentation* 7, 1 (1993): 63. <https://doi.org/10.1007/BF00735042>
8   Francis D. K. Ching, *Drawing: A Creative Process* (New York, NY: John Wiley & Sons, 1989), quoted in https://www.amazon.com/Drawing-Creative-Francis-D-Ching/dp/047128968X.

practice, by which I mean simply that the designer herself changes—as a designer specifically and as a thinker generally—as a result of her practice. Since there must be designers in order for there to be designs, we may assert—invoking the traditional Aristotelian distinction—that the fact that design is a practice (or *praxis*) is at least as important as the fact that design comprises crafts (or *technai*). A final point of continuity, to which I will return presently, is the nomination of the *imagination* as the proper psychological locus of design thinking.

IMAGINATION AND DESIGN KNOWLEDGE

One noteworthy difference between our Renaissance authors and Ching is that the latter characterizes the thinking catalysed by drawing as *visual*. But this, I would suggest, is a potential pitfall. The association in our thinking between design and vision depends primarily upon our lexical habit of using visual metaphors and cognate terms to qualify the kind of cognition that underwrites design practice. *Disegno*—and so, I would argue, contemporary design thinking—activates and educates essentially communicative and conjectural thinking, not strictly "visual thinking." As we saw above, words and objects (the latter of which may be chosen for haptic rather than visual reasons) may be metabolized into design processes as easily as pictures are. For a variety of reasons, we habitually formulate our verbal accounts of the characteristic powers of conjectural thinking by means of an analogy to the characteristic powers of sight—favouring words such as "foresight," "visionary," "prospect," "point of view," and so on. Although pictures are visible, they need not represent anything that the drawer actually sees or has seen—or even that anyone could ever see, even in principle. Design thinking, when used in a conjectural or speculative mode, has the power to make absent things seem present, at least to some extent. We can think and even, in a limited form, experience objects, places, and events that do not exist or are not present. When the artisans of the Renaissance set out to explain how an artisan thinks while he works, they had to adapt general psychological terms to explain the specific character of artisanal cognition. In classical thought broadly, the primary role of the imagination was to effect the transposition of sensory impressions into mental ideas or concepts. It was therefore directly connected to memory, and had the paradoxical power of making absent things seem present.[9] Renaissance artisans thus nominated the imagination as the proper faculty of *disegno*.

---

9   On the imagination in classical thought generally, see Murray Wright Bundy, *The Theory of Imagination in Classical and Mediaeval Thought*, University of Illinois Studies in Language and Literature, 12, vols. 2–3 (Urbana: University of Illinois Press, 1927) and Gerard Watson, *Phantasia in Classical Thought* (Galway: Galway University Press, 1988).

As the psychological site of *disegno*, the imagination became much more than just a mental photo album that collected the diaphanous afterimages of perception; it became a partially effective substitute for experience. Just as literature has the power to teach us moral lessons because it helps us to imagine undergoing the experiences described in a narrative, so design thinking has the power to coordinate productive activity because pictures (in the mind, on paper, on screens) can underwrite our imaging not only what it might be like to use objects, inhabit places, experience events, but also how we might actually make such things. We might then usefully conceive *design thinking* as something like a disciplined practice of the imagination that can, under certain conditions, substitute for experience. Thus the knowledge produced by what we call design processes—what Michael Jemtrud and Keith Ragsdale have called "fabricative knowledge"—is neither theoretical nor technical, but essentially *experiential*.[10] Where theoretical knowledge clarifies the world and technical knowledge helps achieve our goals, experiential knowledge enriches our awareness of what is actually happening to us, around us, and as a result of our actions. If the knowledge that design processes produce is indeed experiential, prototyping (by which I mean the serial production of models or draughts that are self-consciously partial) then appears as a method for disciplining the vagaries of experiential learning. Prototyping—which is perhaps design technique par excellence—aims to produce a kind of incrementally specified experience. We lay out a broad and vague intention, produce a drawing or draught or model, then adjust the intention and produce another drawing, draught, or model, inching toward a completed product. To put it differently, we could say that prototyping intensifies the educative effects of fabricative experience by deliberately focusing it into a preselected channel. We deploy drawings, draughts, and models with the intention of gaining new knowledge—often quite specific—about our intentions, the final result, and the choreography that will be required to materialize it. We may speculate that Brunelleschi built a scale model of the dome of Santa Maria del Fiore not only to communicate his intentions for the structure, but also to prototype his ingenious herringbone coursing, which allowed the dome to be built without the scaffolding that was typically required at the time when constructing domes.

I have argued that, notwithstanding some important and interesting discontinuities, there are impressively strong continuities between the semantic ecosystem that nourished the Renaissance notion of *disegno* and the one that nourishes the contemporary concept

10   Michael Jemtrud and Keith Ragsdale, "Three Little Shacks: An Inquiry in Technics, Tool-making, and Invention," in *Rethinking Comprehensive Design: Speculative Counterculture*, ed. by. Ning Gu et al. (Hong Kong: Association for Computer-Aided Architectural Design Research in Asia, 2014), 883–92.

of *design thinking*. I would suggest that the current rise in the prominence of design thinking is underpinned in part by the fact that it may be usefully oversimplified in order to afford an entry into the subject for non-specialists. The strong linkages between our inherited concept of design and the philosophically robust notions of practice, imagination, and experience provide useful indications as to how any discussion of design thinking might be fruitfully deepened.

CRYSTAL OF THINGS   XIII
POLTAK PANDJAITAN

POLTAK PANDJAITAN finished his Ph.D. in September 2019 at the Chair of Computer Aided Architectural Design (Prof. Ludger Hovestadt) at the ETH ITA Zurich. His research project *Architectonics of Crystal Space: Mediating and Joining of Spatialities* addressed the question of how to implement and translate spatial concepts in crystal topologies. In 2016 he worked as a project architect for Christian Kerez, for the Incidental Space installation in the Swiss Pavilion at the 15th La Biennale di Architettura Venezia 2016. He worked as an architect at Gramazio Kohler Architects in 2014 and received the TISCHE scholarship from the Federal Chancellery of the Republic of Austria for Arts and Culture in the same year. From 2012 to 2013, he worked as a project architect in Vienna. He studied Architecture at the University of Technology Vienna, where he graduated his Architectural Studies with honours with the diploma thesis *Das verborgene System* in 2011.

Crystals and their specific characteristics dictate the literal pulse in life from the time when quartz crystals were used as oscillating clocks in quartz watches and revolutionized mechanical driven ones. Crystals actually have had a more significant influence on people's daily lives, since the beginning of the information age. The main focus is not the healing effects of brightly coloured berg crystals, but crystals in the form of crystalline semiconductors. Computers, tablets, smart phones, digital cameras, even the Internet, and all the other things that make communication so much easier these days are all dependent on semiconductor technology.[1]

Semiconductors are the built-in transistors, diodes and microchips that led to the information age and contributed to the mobile revolution. These semiconducting materials made it possible to integrate a large number of transistors into a single silicon chip and to place them in a small, universal computer, called smart electronic devices, which we use every day for all our communications and connectivity. Even the basic principle of the semiconductor itself embodies this communication, but on the level of elementary particles. Silicon, which we know in form of silica as sand or in pure composition as quartz crystals, plays an important role for semiconductors.[2]

COMPOSITION

Crystals as emergent growing structures are interesting, because they have specific properties that are otherwise not found as such in nature. A crystal, despite being so small, is an individual by itself with completely equal properties to those of the large crystal. It is a complete structure, but only to the extent of its internal structure and its external regular form. Its size, however, is not definite: It can always continue to grow as it finds the prerequisites and without changing its nature. In a crystal, the atoms or molecules are arranged in a periodic structure. Each cell is surrounded by neighbouring cells that form an identical pattern. Crystallography is often associated with the study of ideal crystals, where every atom is embedded in a perfectly repeating and ordered structure. But under realistic conditions, you will never find this highly arranged crystal lattice, evenly spread in all directions. Real crystals are configurations of structurabilities, always have some defects in the lattice or impurities in the atomic composition.

1   Michel Serres, 'Gnomon: The Beginnings of Geometry in Greece', in *A History of Scientific Thought: Elements of a History of Science*, ed. by Michel Serres (Oxford; Cambridge, Mass: Blackwell, 1995), 73–123.
2   Ludger Hovestadt, Vera Bühlmann, and Sebastian Michael, *Genius Planet. Energy Scarcity to Energy Abundance: A Radical Pathway for Creative Professionals and Environmental Active Amateurs*, Applied Virtuality Book Series, 11 (Basel: Birkhäuser, 2017).

In 1982, the world of crystallographic science was confounded by the discovery of a crystal that, although it had a regular structure, was nevertheless globally non-periodic—that is, each cell is surrounded by a different pattern. In terms of crystallography, such a structure possesses a long-range orientational order, but no translational symmetry. Just like a 'typical' crystal, these quasicrystals still render sharp diffraction points, but the pattern does not show any crystallographic symmetry. The classical crystallographic restriction theorem indicates that all crystalline structures must have periodically repeating patterns and can only possess two, three, four, and six-fold rotational symmetries.[3] A quasicrystal is thereby defined as a structure that has a non-periodic ordering and that lacks translational symmetry.[4]

INTERVAL

The approach to the geometry of crystals or even quasicrystals does not go along with the idea to treat geometry as an accumulation of elements in space. Geometry as a measurement of space is only applied to the projection of the crystal's algebraic origin. Basic shapes of geometry, such as the triangle, the square and even the beginning of crystallographic thinking, with the platonic solids as definitions of vertices in space, are already renderings of a specific kind. The vertices have been determined in the Euclidean space and do not inherit the information of the abstract as such.

Different from Euclid and his predecessors, to see the open triangle and the resulting diagonal as an enclosed space, the triangle can also be represented as the half of a square with equal legs, or in general as a parallelogram in two-dimensional space. With that in mind, they would probably have treated the nature of the triangle in the vector space. All the incorporated basic ideas, such as the point as a null vector, the segment as a multiplication of a vector with a scalar, the diagonal as the addition of the vectors, the angle of the segments by creating their scalar product and even the aperiodic Fibonacci chain by vector projection with the dot product of vectors with an irrational slope, is embedded in the algebraic nature of the vector space:

> The metric diagonal was historically lived as a drama of the irrational and certain death for pure thought: We can think it as what could have been the first step of a higher rationality than Euclid's, so much more profound that the former pure becomes mixed, impure, poorly analysed. So the drama changes camps: the Greek miracle becomes bad luck or a logical error; the idea

3   Walter Steurer and Sofia Deloudi, *Crystallography of Quasicrystals: Concepts, Methods and Structures*, Springer Series in Materials Science, 126 (Heidelberg: Springer, 2009).
4   Marjorie Senechal, *Quasicrystals and Geometry* (Cambridge: Cambridge University Press, 1995).

of vector space forces me to forget an entire history, seen from then on as a blindness of clear thought.[5]

The set of all possible unit vectors has the form of a circle in two dimensions, the shape of a spherical surface in three dimensions and the form of a general sphere in higher dimensions. The sum, the linear combination, of the vectors of the formed circle and the sphere are linear dependent and cancel each other out, which results in a zero vector: $a_1v_1 + a_2v_2 + ... + a_nv_n = 0$. The complete crystal space is thereby at the same moment the non-existence of it, in which the zero vector, 0, is also an element of the vector space: $\sum_{j \in J} a_j v_j = 0$

The n-dimensional vector space is the algebraic encapsulation of any crystal system: $e_1 = (1, 0, ..., 0)$, $e_2 = (0, 1, 0, ..., 0)$ to $e_n = (0, 0, ..., 0, 1)$. The coordinate vectors $(e_1, e_2, ..., e_n)$ build the basis and are represented as a sequence of scalars, which are the components of the vectors. It is a finite or infinite set B of vectors b_i, which spans the whole space and is linear independent. Any linear combination of the basis multiplied by scalars an can express any vector and by that it envelopes the entire space: $v = a_1 b_{i1} + a_2 b_{i2} + ... + a_n b_{in}$. Linear independence means that each vector is unique and none of the vectors is a result of a combination of the others.

The crystal structure is embedded in the sequence of scalars. Perfect crystals, which are built on a regular periodic structure, are classified by their Bravais lattice. They are groups of the seven possible lattice systems (translational groups) in crystallography: $R = n_1 a_1 + n_2 a_2 + n_3 a_3$. The definition of crystals is based on primitive vectors that span the lattice. With integers ni and linear independent vectors ai, in case of three-dimensional crystals, i has the value 1, 2 and 3. The vectors and their unit scalar define the specific crystal system. Since perfect crystals have a regular structure and consist of unit cells placed next to each other, the underlying sequence of scalars is simple and repetitive. In case of any non-periodic crystal and combinations of multiple crystal systems, the sequence becomes more complex and significant. The pattern acts as a code, which in the widest sense resembles a language.[6]

The code is only an abstraction, which acts as a container for the structure's information. It does not describe a specific geometry but is itself geometry. Abstraction makes it possible to depict the topology of a structure without giving any indication of the topographical conditions of a geometry. Nevertheless, conclusions can be drawn about the underlying nature, and by means of that it is possible to recognize different patterns, to compare and even to combine them. It allows for a discourse between different geometries, without neglecting its nature and origin.

5   Michel Serres, *Geometry: The Third Book of Foundations*, trans. by Randolph Burks (London: Bloomsbury Academic, an imprint of Bloomsbury Publishing Plc, 2017), 12.
6   de Bruijn, N. G.. 'Algebraic theory of Penrose's non-periodic tilings of the plane'. *I. Indagationes Mathematicae (Proceedings)*, 84, 1 (1981), 39–52.

This is not the case when the evaluation is based on the rendering, the specification of a nature. It is possible to abstract the topology from a geometry, but not vice versa.

> (...) mathematical language A is anterior to language B in the ordinary diachrony. It is almost always possible to translate A into B; conversely, we cannot go from B into A. Euclidean space can be translated into topological, metric, or vector language; conversely, in the Euclidean repertoire, no term corresponds to 'topological manifold'.[7]

In case of crystals, the topology describes the composition and order within the structure. There is no information about the embedded crystal's shape and geometry. Different crystals can be transferred into one another according to the rules of the topology, but they can still have different geometries. It is not sufficient, therefore, to characterize a crystal only by its topological composition, since even isomorphic graphs, networks which have an identical link pattern, can have different topologies. Just like the graph of the trefoil knot, which has the connection structure of a ring, cannot be topologically converted into a ring without breaking the structure.[8]

Topologically, nodes, as intersections of vectors, have no concrete location in space; they are abstract elements that can be placed anywhere, provided that their pattern scheme remains identical to all other nodes. The process of assigning specific coordinates of our common (Euclidean) three-dimensional space to abstract-mathematical nodes and edges depends on the translation of the code, which in the case of algebraic crystals acts as a geometrical renderer. The sequence of scalars is combined with the vectors and then translated into a particular coordinate system. This process of projection, of higher-dimensional information into a relative subspace, leads to structures of specific crystal lattices in Cartesian space.

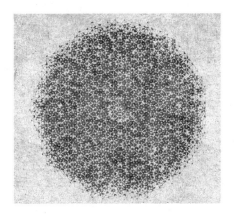

FIG I
shadow projection of a three-dimensional dodecahedral quasi-crystal cluster

7   Serres, *Geometry*, 19.
8   Frank Hoffmann, *Faszination Kristalle und Symmetrie: Einführung in die Kristallographie*, Studienbücher Chemie (Wiesbaden: Springer Spektrum, 2016).

But the projection is only successful at a specific angle. Otherwise it reveals nothing. There is a lot of noise between. The crystal keeps the information hidden and only by putting it under the sun does it reveal the encrypted information. The parallel projection unfolds the crystal code, which is not apparent through the central perspective, in the shadow of the artefact that can be read differently: It keeps the information under its noisy appearance.

As Serres observes, Thales's inversion of the gnomon, the casting shadow of the pyramid in relation to the shadow of a gnomon, gives information about the unmeasurable height of the Pharaonic tomb. By that Thales didn't measure the pyramid. Instead he invented an abstract space, where the shadows are relative and open up a space of comparability. It deals with the proportionality of relations of numbers. With the gnomon, it is possible to see something which is only reachable through the introduction of the sun as the third.

> Turning this entire process around, Thales poses and then resolves the inverse problem of the gnomon. Instead of letting the pyramid talk about the Sun, that is, the invariant say the scale of the variable, he asks the Sun to speak about the pyramid, that is to say, asks the changing to say something constantly about what remains.[9]

Even the distinction of crystals and quasicrystals is achieved by relating their shadows' symmetries. The casting of the shadow, however, reveals the quasicrystal's nature only at specific angles. Everything in between is a vivid state of indecisiveness: a flickering which jumps from state to state; a three-dimensional key that incorporates multiple two-dimensional projection patterns. The shadow of a regular crystal can also have various patterns at particular angles, but they only embody repetitive patterns and the transition between the states are more traceable. In principle, the projection does not reveal more information than the structure of the crystal itself. But every quasicrystal casts a different shadow. It is like a fingerprint encapsulated in a three-dimensional structure, where the code is only accessible through the third, the sun. The sun acts as a translator, with the parallel projection being the universal language and shadow on the plane is the translation. But like any translation, the reduction of dimensionality has a price. The projection acts as a renderer of the crystal and the various renderings do not give the insight of the overall structure behind it. Only the movement of the sun's trace in time, in combination with the projection of the shadow, defining the origin and reference of both, unfolds the higher-dimensional nature.

9   Serres, *Geometry*, 116.

And therefore, in order to know and comprehend, in order to see, we must be able to move according to the new dimension, following, in the course of the projection, precisely the direction accompanied by the rays of the sun. Space becomes a set of possible movements.[10]

In case of a three-dimensional quasicrystal, the artefact is already a reduction of a higher-dimensional crystal. For example, an icosahedral quasicrystal derives from a six-dimensional space, where the shadows are renderings of spectra.

EXPRESSION

In addition to the fact that different crystal arrangements vary geometrically and in their chemical constitution, their underlying code may even contain different information. By recognizing patterns in the code, regularities and recurring sequences can form single unit crystals, as in case of perfect crystals, or several differently shaped ones, in composed structures. In crystals, which do not possess simple periodicity, these sequences in code do not only describe the units of which the crystal consists, but also provide an insight into sections of larger crystal clusters. These recurring patterns can be perceived as an expression of a language, where the individual elements in the code are like single letters in the alphabet or indices of a finite set. They form single words and several words result in a series, which can form a sentence. But a repetitive arrangement of words does not consequentially inherent any literary expression.

The perfect crystal with a periodic structure can, therefore, be seen as a series of contiguous words. The simplicity in information, which in turn also reflects the stability and robustness of the structure, is the self-referencing composition. Each element describes the entire sequence without defining the beginning nor the end. The structure is unified and any fault in the series can be compensated by the element itself.

Crystals, which consist of several units and therefore have a more complex composition, form simple repeating sentences. This makes it possible to express a specific syntax that depends mainly on the elements. The overall recurring structure is the reflexivity of the cluster of elements, which originates from a circular motion. It is a manifestation through repetitive recitation, characterized by a particular order. The sequences of elements as a common denominator are no longer clearly discriminable, and they can only be defined by the relation among the elements, as the boundaries within the series can shift.

Structures of several units that do not have a repeating periodicity resemble a quasicrystal. Different sections of quasicrystals

10   Ibid., 118.

epitomize varying crystal clusters, which contain, as a whole, specific information. They depict a system that encodes information into an aperiodic sequence.

In his book, *What is life?* published in 1945, the Austrian physicist Erwin Schrödinger postulated that in order for a molecular system to carry information, it must be regular, but also aperiodic. According to him, irregular amorphous materials are too chaotic to have the practical ability as information carriers, but total regularity diminishes the ability to encrypt complex information. Schrödinger believed that the hereditary material is a molecule that, unlike a regular crystal, does not repeat itself. Its non-periodic nature allows it to encode an almost infinite number of possibilities with a small finite number of atoms. He already talks about an aperiodic crystal, even before the discovery of real quasicrystals:

> In physics we have dealt hitherto only with periodic crystals. To a humble physicist's mind, these are very interesting and complicated objects; they constitute one of the most fascinating and complex material structures by which inanimate nature puzzles his wits. Yet, compared with the aperiodic crystal, they are rather plain and dull. (...)
>
> That is the case of the more and more complicated organic molecule in which every atom, and every group of atoms, plays an individual role, not entirely equivalent to that of many others (as is the case in a periodic structure). We might quite properly call that an aperiodic crystal or solid and express our hypothesis by saying: We believe a gene—or perhaps the whole chromosome fiber—to be an aperiodic solid.[11]

Although the discovery of deoxyribonucleic acid (DNA) as a carrier of hereditary information followed later and the underlying structure is not of a crystalline kind, it has properties predicted by Schrödinger. It is a regular but aperiodic molecule. In case of DNA, Schrödinger's prediction for encoding information as an aperiodic crystal was crucial for the discovery of the DNA's nature. Just as sequences of the four different nucleotides (A, T, G, C) express the DNA information of cells, code sequences in crystals represent the instruction for crystalline growth and development. The DNA helix structure can be understood as a one-dimensional quasicrystal, since the non-periodicness of sequence in code, in the case of DNA with its four bases, resembles that in quasicrystals and never repeats periodically.[12]

11   Erwin Schrödinger, *What Is Life?: The Physical Aspect of the Living Cell with Mind and Matter et Autobiographical Sketches* (Cambridge: Cambridge University Press, 2012 [1944]), 2012, 5, 60.
12   Jacques Monod, *Chance and Necessity; an Essay on the Natural Philosophy of Modern Biology*, trans. A. Wainhouse (New York: Vintage Books, 1972 [1971]).

The aperiodic structure acts as a language and a code. What they both have in common is the meaningfulness in organization. It is as if they deal with permutation and combination of a small finite set of basic units in order to create systems of communication. On the contrary to a written text, however, the sequence of the DNA itself does not inherit any meaning. The DNA is much like a programming language, through which the computation of the code gains in significance.

In the world of quasicrystals, specific sections of the code describe aperiodic crystal clusters. Simple periodic order or complex aperiodicity is embedded in the code and certain segments describe respective properties. The development of this specificity is equivalent to the structure of a narrative: It is a language that makes it possible to articulate and differentiate in crystalline structures. The crystal code can be interpreted differently, and the translation can show various renderings. The way abstract language is translated into geometry varies with the projection. This act of differentiation of geometry allows a universal abstract system to be understood in different bodies.

SHIFT

There is not one crystal space, but the articulation and interrelation of multiple ones: combinations of multiple crystals, where their co-existence and juxtaposition are articulated. The non-locality, which describes the nature of quasicrystals, is coupled with a contingent appearance. Quasicrystal structures are neither stochastic nor deterministic. It is never about being able to define and thereby to freeze a certain quasicrystal state. The implication is to appreciate it as a spectrum of multiple configurations. Through instantiation, the constant flux of shifts become graspable and can serve as a statue of communication.

The crystal as an algebraic language never makes a statement, but only translates and communicates. It acts as a communication channel, a placeholder of information, where there is a table of many crystals. But like any language the single letters are just ciphers, like the many single crystals, and the expression and potential are rendered through the process of crystallization—an abstract analogy that represents the crystallization as an articulation of information. Communicating does not mean to agree with each other, but is a discourse like the gnomon in Thales. It sets up a space of homothesis. Communication is not the linkage of two fixed states or positions, but the interlinking of possibilities.[13]

13   Ludger Hovestadt and Vera Bühlmann, *Domesticating Symbols: Metalithikum II* (Basel: Birkhäuser, 2014), 112–177.

· **NONPERIODIC (PATTERN)**

The absence of a periodic property in a pattern. In a non-periodic arrangement, it is not possible to generate the pattern only by the translation movement of a periodic patch. It is simply one that is not determined by some non-trivial translation. For example, irrational numbers in the decimal system have an aperiodic decimal fraction evolution, just like in the circle number pi. The order of decimal numbers never repeats and goes to infinity.

· **NULL VECTOR**

The null vector is in mathematics a special vector of a vector space, namely the uniquely determined neutral element to the vector addition. In a scalar product space, the null vector is orthogonal to all vectors of space.

· **ORIENTATIONAL ORDER**

It means that groups of atoms or molecules lie in the same direction or on the same plane of reference. The distances between these patterns need not be regular.

· **PERIODIC (PATTERN)**

A pattern is considered periodic if a section or cut out of the pattern recurs at regular intervals. It is the principle for defining the basic structure of crystals.

· **QUASIPERIODIC OR APERIODIC (PATTERN)**

Is a special form of non-periodicity. It is based on the aperiodicity found in quasicrystals, in which the specific forbidden noncrystallographic symmetries are apparent. A tiling is quasiperiodic if a section of any size can be repeated without the pattern as a whole being periodic.

· **SCALAR**

In linear algebra, scalar denotes an element of the body of a vector space that is characterized solely by the specification of a numerical value. The multiplication of a vector with a scalar is called scalar multiplication or scaling and results in the scalar multiple of the vector.

· **TRANSLATION (MOVEMENT)**

It is a movement in which all points of a physical system or fixed bodies, (e.g. periodic pattern) experience the same shift. Any physical body has in space three degrees of freedom of translation and three degrees of freedom of rotation.

· **UNIT VECTOR**
A unit vector in analytic geometry is a vector of length one.

· **VECTOR PROJECTION**
In geometry, a vector projection is the mapping of a point to a line or plane so that the connecting line between the point and its image is in the direction of the given vector. In linear algebra, this concept is extended to higher-dimensional vector spaces. The orthogonal projection (the vector is in the normal direction of the plane) is then the projection of a vector onto a sub-vector space such that the difference vector of the image and the output vector lies in its orthogonal complement.

ARCHITECTURE OF THE DIAPHANOUS
RICCARDO M. VILLA

XIV

RICCARDO M. VILLA is assistant researcher for the Department for Architecture Theory and Philosophy of Technics since September 2017. He holds a master's degree in architecture from the Polytechnic University of Milan, where he graduated with honours with a dissertation about the contemporary mutations of the architectural profession. He is currently pursuing a PhD at the department, and his recent interests revolve around architecture in its production, under a spectrum of investigation that spans from aesthetics and semiotics to biopolitics. His professional background includes collaborations with several practices around Europe, from small ateliers to large architectural companies. Since 2009 he is a member and part of the editorial board of GIZMO, a Milan-based architectural research collective, and a platform for publications, events and exhibitions. He has contributed to magazines and to other publications dealing with architectural history and criticism.

The following notes are an attempt to investigate and open up the 'device of transparency' as something which must be understood as being forged in and that is strictly tied to the Modern Era, and to which the Modern is tied in return. The label of *modernity*, mostly pertaining to historiographical concerns, easily escapes any sort of 'exact' attribution. Of its many beginnings, often traced back to early Renaissance, 1851 can perhaps be considered one. This is the inauguration year of the Great Exhibition of London, which finds housing under the iron and glass-made vaults of one of the largest greenhouses ever built: The Crystal Palace. Here, a never-before-seen richness of goods is gathered in exhibition stands that are not enshrined but rather displayed through an architecture of transparent arcades that echoes the smaller *passages* of cities like Paris and London. Perhaps for the first time, the whole world is 'collected' and 'stocked' under the same roof. The modernity staged here is the one described by Walter Benjamin, the one of an accumulation of goods and of total loss of any 'auratic distance' of artefacts, in favour of an *immediate* (as non-mediated) fruition of the commodities and of their exhibition value. The goods displayed in the crystalline galleries of the Great Exhibition are transfigured in the eyes of the visitor, who is taken by what Benjamin himself defines as a '*phantasmagoria*'.[1] Moreover, the total limpidity of Paxton's halls almost dissolves any difference between interior and exterior, placing one as a display of the other and vice versa, setting the conditions for the 'disparition' of its architecture and offering itself as a foundation for the 'myth' of the 'immaterial'.

The architecture of the Crystal Palace and the event of the Great Exhibition are one amongst many expressions of the Modern Era. If, on the one hand, it seems a quite difficult task to define what modernity *is*, a rather easier task is to say what it *is not*. In this sense, the Middle Ages can be hardly associated with modernity and have instead been used since the Enlightenment as a sort of 'backdrop' onto which it was possible to delineate (and *emancipate*) the singularity of the latter, by developing it into a line of *progress* that weaves together Renaissance, Enlightenment, and eventually the industrial revolutions. Yet, it is perhaps in this truly pre-modern time *in-between* times that a pre-specific explanation to the 'question' of modernity can be found. From the

---

1   "We define the aura [...] as the unique phenomenon of a distance, however close it may be." (Walter Benjamin, 'The Work of Art in the Age of Mechanical Reproduction', in *Illuminations*, ed. by Hannah Arendt (New York: Schocken Books, 1986), 211–44); "World exhibitions glorify the exchange value of the commodity. They create a framework in which its use value becomes secondary. They are a school in which the masses, forcibly excluded from consumption, are imbued with the exchange value of commodities to the point of identifying with it: 'Do not touch the items on display.' World exhibitions thus provide access to a phantasmagoria which a person enters in order to be distracted." Walter Benjamin, *The Arcades Project* (Cambridge, Mass: Belknap Press, 1999), 7.

completely diaphanous facets of the Crystal Palace we move then back to the coloured glassworks of the Basilica of St. Denis: the substantial *transparence* of both these architectures being perhaps an indication of an 'invisible' connection. The same light that glares upon the goods, unstopped by the panes of Paxton's gigantic greenhouse, shines through the decorated windows of the early gothic cathedral, and—even before lighting the space of the church—it illuminates the *image* impressed on the window itself, making it visible to the eyes and *intelligible* to the mind.[2] This subtle difference, that seems now to be confined to a mere issue of architecture history, if not physics of light, can be accounted for instead as a symptom of a much wider question, the core of which is perhaps the confutation and the refusal by some key Christian theologians—and, to a certain extent, of the West itself—of the notion of a 'separate intellect'.

Introduced by Muslim physician and theologist Ibn Rushd (better known as Averroes) in a 'long commentary' to Aristotle's writings on the soul, the formulation of a 'separate mind' tries to answer the question of the 'unity of the intellect', that is to say how one man can think the same way and the same ideas of others, yet have different, particular thoughts and therefore be an *individual*. To solve such *magna quaestio*, Averroes postulates a unique, separate intellect to which all individual minds are connected through their own 'images'. This unique and transcendental mind, split in a purely potential 'material intellect' and into an only-operative 'agent intellect' is described by the philosopher through an interesting analogy:

> Just as light is the actuality of a transparent medium, so the agent intellect is the actuality of the material intellect. Just as the transparent medium is not moved by colour and does not receive it except when there it is lit upon, so too that intellect does not receive the thoughts which are here except insofar as it is actualized through the agent intellect and illuminated by it. As light turns colour in potency to actual colour, so that it can act upon the transparent medium, so the agent intellect turns the thoughts in potency to actual thoughts in such a way that the material intellect can receive them.[3]

2   The Basilica of St. Denis is considered to be one of the earliest (if not the first) example of a Gothic church. Its Romanesque fabric was entirely 'reformed' in 1127 by the powerful Abbot Suger, whose readings of Pseudo-Dionysus supported the analogy between heavenly hierarchies and the transmission of light; see: *Abbot Suger on the Abbey Church of St.-Denis and Its Art Treasures*, ed. by Erwin Panofsky, 2. ed (Princeton, N.J: Princeton University Press, 1979).

3   Averroes (Ibn Rushd) of Cordoba, *Long Commentary on the De Anima of Aristotle*, Book III (Yale University Press, 2009), 328. The translation has been here edited by the author, in accordance with the Latin text (Averroes, *Commentarium Magnum in Aristotelis De Anima*, edited by F.S. Crawford. Cambridge: Cambridge University Press, 1953).

It is not light, but *transparency* to be posited as *something*; without transparency no light is possible, one could paraphrase. By affirming transparency as pure, formless potentiality, yet as a *substance*—the one of a 'material' intellect—against an intuitive notion by which light hits objects without the need of any mediation, Averroes highlighted the position of an 'excluded third'. His material intellect, configured as a 'transparent medium', is a substantial element without which no communication nor knowledge can be possible.

As Emanuele Coccia remarked, the 'absolute medium' of the material intellect cannot simply be a collection of the totality of all actual thoughts and ideas;[4] it cannot be associated with an overload of 'sensible data,' so to speak. It is rather when all men stop thinking—in the total *absence* of any actual thought—that the possibility of a material intellect can be contemplated. In its other qualification of 'possible' intellect, such a 'mind' resembles an untouched clay tablet, waiting to be written upon. Its 'materiality' must not be misunderstood as 'matter' that can be 'transformed' in any idea, nor as the presupposition of forms by the combination and transformation of which new thoughts can be 'produced'. The material intellect is a substance subject not to transformation nor to production, but only to *information*: Its only 'power' is to be affected by forms—to literally be 'informed'.[5] The distinguishing mark of the separate intellect resides then not in the fact that it contains and stores *all* present, past, or future information, but in its absolute 'disposition' to welcome it *in potentia*. Potency is then the 'measure' of such disposition, or the capacity of being affected by forms (to be informed). Yet, the challenge of Averroes is to think of this separate intellect not just in the 'virtuality' of an absolute potency, but as a *potency* that is nevertheless *substance*, leading thus to "the paradox of a substance that *is* the less it is form."[6] The material intellect is the 'subject' (the Aristotelian *hypokeimenon*) of its own receptivity, the *locus* in which such receptivity becomes substance.[7]

It is in fact the figure of a 'locality', as Coccia notes, the one that seems to suit best the notion of the intellect as a transparent medium—not an *extensio* but an 'emplacement', a place besides the existence of things, "what exists besides and beyond the bodies without

---

4   The present essay is in this matter largely indebted with his outstanding work, and
    all the discussion over Averroes' *material intellect* is fully derived from it. Emanuele
    Coccia, *La trasparenza delle immagini: Averroè e l'averroismo*, (Milan: B. Mondadori,
    2005). Not being unfortunately translated in English at the time of publication, all
    translations of the excerpts are mine.
5   Coccia, *La trasparenza delle immagini*, 84. Concerning the 'materiality' of the intellect, Coccia refers to it as "the thinnest of all matters" (p. 115), evoking a sort of *inframateriality* which is perhaps close to the one which Michel Serres' *'logiciel'* works upon.
6   Ibid.
7   Ibid., 106.

GHOSTS OF TRANSPARENCY

participating to their extension."[8] Such a transcendental *locus* can be conceived once again through an 'optical' analogy: the one of *reflection*. Any object reflected in a mirror loses its materiality of being a thing to be present only in its pure form—in its pure *intelligibility*. In the mirror, an object can be perceived in its pure 'species', and its form can exist *outside* its own (real) place; it can be grasped in a (sovereign) *ausnahmezustand*.[9] Just as we can perceive the form of an object in a mirror through our vision, in the same way we can 'look' in the space of the separate mind through our 'speculative' intellect. This latter, which does not belong to the material intellect but—exactly like hearing, taste, touch and vision—rather to the 'sensitivity' of each individual, is what allows us to look into the images of the separate intellect, to 'speculate' (from Latin *specio*, 'to look') its invisible 'spectrality'. The connection between separate intellect and individual mind happens then by the means of *images*—'*intentiones*' as Averroes calls them, or 'phantasms'—that do not belong to each individual but are 'actualized' by the agent intellect itself. Such 'spectrality' of images becomes then the bridge by which every man and the unique mind are connected.

It is important here to remark that Averroes's 'intentions' are not *universals*, nor can the separate intellect be assimilated to Plato's *hyperuranion*. Despite being compared as a space which our mind looks at as our senses do with sensible reality, the certainty of 'truth' is here insured not by a trustworthy external reality, but rather by the images themselves, as a sort of *co-incidence* between individual minds and separate intellect. This does not mean that truth is fictitious or 'artificial', but that such a position also takes distance from any 'existentialist' standpoint, to express it with an anachronism. Averroes's material intellect is neither the *locus* in which truth can be 'found' (the Greek *heurisko*) nor 'created' *ex-nihilo*, but where it is *in-formed* or, in a way, *invented*. It is in this sense perhaps that its images are not so much 'copies' of an original (as the term *imago* would suggest) but *in-tentions*, something 'tending' to a matching point whose 'emplacement' stands *outside* any sensible or empirical reference. From this perspective,

8   Coccia, *La trasparenza delle immagini.*, 117–118. Such 'emplacement' could perhaps be thought in analogy to the 'locational' understanding of the *parasite* by Serres.

9   "Sovereign is the one who decides over the exception [*Ausnahmezustand*]". Carl Schmitt, *Politische Theologie. Vier Kapitel zur Lehre von der Souveränität* (Berlin: Duncker & Humblot, 2015 [1922]). And further on, concerning the *exoticness* of such an 'absolute' emplacement: "The *bios theoretikos* places the living being outside the city; it is not a coincidence that Aristoteles compared the speculative life with the one of the stranger, to that *bios xenicos* that the law is not able to grasp nor to articulate, as absolutely exterior to the *nomos*." (Coccia, *La trasparenza delle immagini*, 192). This exteriority to the *nomos* remarks how such an 'emplacement' cannot be considered a 'state', unless perhaps in a 'vanishing' way; in this sense, no 'state of exception' can ever properly exist: it stops being 'exceptional' in the very moment it is considered (or *actualised*) as a 'state'.

Averroes's 'anatomical dissection' of the intellect bears amongst its potential consequences an equal 'disassembly' of the notion of truth.[10]

The architecture of the Renaissance is perhaps the one to inherit and make use of such an original form of 'invention'. It is by looking through a *mirror* that Filippo Brunelleschi succeeds in reproducing a 'veritable' image of the Baptistery of Florence, 'inventing' drawing as *perspective*. By the means of a reflective (*speculative*) surface, the Florentine architect becomes capable of looking at things in their pure form, in their 'speciality'. As the closest thing to a 'space of absolute potency', the surface of the mirror seems to wipe out any pre-conception or disposition that the presentation of the image might be affected by, leaving nothing else but the sole point of observation, which is then posited as the 'scientific' gaze of the artist as a 'subject'.[11] The reality of the drawing, its 'truth' (or, to use a modern term, its 'high-*fidelity*'), stops relying on the preciousness of its materiality (like in a Byzantine icon), or in the correctness of its measurements (like in an axonometric drawing), and finds instead its truthfulness in that matching point of the lines that stands outside of its representation, and outside sensible experience *par excellence*—therefore 'vanishing'. Stepping in the focal point opened by such speculations earns Brunelleschi the glory of one of the first 'creative geniuses' of Renaissance, if not its invention. In a way, his famous cupola that covers the gothic cathedral of Santa Maria del Fiore closes the open *fabrica* of medieval knowledge one century after the start of the averroistic quarrel. The *Last Judgement* depicted on its vaults comes now to obstruct and replace the unlimited sight of the open sky.

If not for the condemnation of Averroes's theories by Christian philosophers, the *episteme* that its *Commentary* had outlined would have left a permanent mark for the centuries to come. Benjamin's *phantasmagoria* can perhaps be seen as a first sign of uneasiness caused by the oblivion to which the 'third intellect' was condemned, as it evoked a sort of multitude of fetish-images (the phantasms) that could be summoned in the conversion of all goods in their exchange value. It is in fact money, seen as general equivalent, that is the operator allowing material goods to be *transfigured* in their phantasmagorical dimension. In this sense, money operates precisely as an *agent intellect*, being capable of indexing—or *actualizing*—an absolute field of potentiality (the material intellect), abstracting from any

---

10   "The phantom does not generate a new form in thought, nor a new act of thought: it rather lays in us the foundation of a relation (*habitudo*) or of a certain disposition (*aptitudo*), which allows us to be connected with the unique intellect" (Coccia, *La trasparenza delle immagini.*, 157).

11   Cfr. Brian Rotman, *Signifying Nothing. The Semiotics of Zero* (Stanford: Stanford University Press, 1987).

specificity, and remaining totally indifferent to the *object* of its opera-tion. If Benjamin's notes, despite their extraordinary acuteness, seem to be still too narrowed down to a socio-economical field of concerns, it is perhaps Martin Heidegger who is the first to record the issue and to frame it under a more comprehensive standpoint. In the essay *Die Zeit des Weltbildes*, the German philosopher poses the question of the 'exactness' of modern science as an interrogation that finds its truth only in the form that has itself pre-casted, stressing how modern knowledge can only be attained in the form of a 'picture', but it does so in the illusion of a direct, 'objective' speculation, on the presupposi-tion that what it 'sees' is the 'real,' and not its *medium*.[12] Man looks at the form of things in their reflection, but forgets about the optics (the *perspective*) of the mirror.

The conflation of such space of transparency into an 'imme-diate' coincidence between what *we* see and what *is* seen—into an 'objectivity' of things—presupposes (and is presupposed) by a paral-lel rise of the 'subject' as we know it. As Coccia brilliantly notes, the space that Averroes's *Commentary* highlights is not only the one of a transparent medium, but one between the *human* and the *rational*: Such a coincidence—of man as a *rational subject* of knowledge—is then 'sealed' in the very idea of *consciousness*,[13] a notion that will span through all of modernity, from Descartes to Freud. Subject and consciousness reveal themselves in their prime nature of *juridical* (and therefore *political*) categories. The urgency by which Thomas of Aquinas and Albert the Great condemned Ibn Rushd's readings of Aristotle—an urgency fully supported and even pushed by the politi-cal power of the time—is explained as the need to refer thoughts (and the actions derived from them) to an individual human soul, to *impute* them to a *subject*. The doubting of such coincidence entails not only the opening up of a space of *anomy*, but would put into question *free-will* itself, a notion of essential value for Christianity and for western thought; in order to be held 'accountable' for his *own* actions, the indi-vidual must be 'free' to commit them.[14]

This two-way entanglement between the emancipation of a free will and the foregrounding of a 'bearing subject' is perhaps one of the distinctive traits of the Modern: "The 'Enlightenment', which

12 "We first arrive at science as research when and only when truth has been transformed into the certainty of representation." Heidegger, Martin, 'The Age of the World Picture', in Julian Young, and Kenneth Haynes, *Heidegger, Off the Beaten Track* (Cambridge: Cambridge University Press, 2002), 127.
13 Coccia, *La trasparenza delle immagini.*, 58.
14 Ibid., 191, 196.

discovered the liberties, also invented the disciplines."[15] The transparency (as immediacy) of the modern subject finds one of its most evident manifestations in the prison as a 'mechanism of control': here, the 'panorama' of the Heideggerian world-picture reverts into a *panopticon*. As Michel Foucault famously described, in such architecture man is both subject and object, observing and observed. The immediacy of the gaze is the sole principle upon which such a 'mechanism' works.[16] What man is looking at in the mirror is now only but himself: Subject and object appear divided just as for the effect of an 'optical illusion'.

The division and affirmation of an 'objective' reality, the objectiveness of which relies in the fact that it can be only experienced by *anyone* as long as this 'anyone' can be categorized as a 'subject', is constitutive for modern knowledge at large and in such a 'key of encryption' lays the foundation of its order. The understanding of 'science' as the product of *research* (Heidegger) or as what is 'proven' via *examination* (Foucault) highlights the 'submission' of such a modern form of knowledge to the principles of *law*: If the notion of 'subject' comes to support the modern scientific understanding, the one of 'person' rises in parallel as a figure of the modern political order. As Coccia points out, the modern notion of 'person' finds its roots in Roman law, according to which a *persona* was not necessarily a person, and a person was not necessarily a *persona*,[17] but was rather a legal entity by which contracts could be stipulated and judgement in court made.

The forgetfulness over such a 'categorical' nature of the subject—i.e. its relation to a legal and juridical discourse—can then perhaps be seen under the same need for order, advocated by the rising political powers of the West from feudal times on, to 'codify' the unordered and incoherent collection of laws they inherited from the past—a will that would eventually culminate with the French Revolution and the

---

15 Michel Foucault, *Discipline and Punish: The Birth of the Prison* (New York: Vintage Books, 1995), 222. In the same regard, Heidegger: "What is decisive is not that man frees himself to himself from previous obligations, but that the very essence of man itself changes, in that man becomes subject. We must understand this word *subiectum*, however, as the translation of the Greek *hypokeimenon*. The word names that-which-lies-before, which, as ground, gathers everything onto itself. [...] However, when man becomes the primary and only real *subiectum*, that means: Man becomes that being upon which all that is, is grounded as regards the manner of its Being and its truth. Man becomes the relational centre of that which is as such." (Heidegger, 'The Age of the World Picture', 128).

16 Foucault, *Discipline and Punish*. In this sense we can refer to the panopticon as a "machinery designed to exclude" that 'third' (here the transparent medium) which is proper of the "will to truth" (Michel Foucault, 'The Order of Discourse', in *Untying the Text: A Post-Structuralist Reader*, ed. by Robert Young (Boston: Routledge & Kegan Paul, 1981), 48–78). More at large, Foucault is undoubtedly the one to have more accurately graphed the 'seismic waves' of such an 'epistemic shockwave' as the one started by the Christian refusal of Averroes's readings; in this sense *The Order of Things* can be read as the most complete and articulated response so far to this *magna quaestio*.

17 Coccia, *La trasparenza delle immagini.*, 211.

GHOSTS OF TRANSPARENCY

systematization of laws into a comprehensive 'legal code'. If the *subject* can be seen as the *co-incidence* of the person as a *persona*, then the legal code can be understood as an effort to equally 'cover' in a comprehensive and exhaustive manner the 'field of reality' with a set of laws conceived as a *system*. At the same time, the push by the Enlightenment to emancipate law from divine right gave birth to the first constitutions; right was not conceived to be coming from a transcendent, invisible ruler, but from the actuality (the so-called "naturality") of law itself, the truth of which was residing not in the skies above, but in the "contract" stipulated by its *subjects*.[18]

Such a wave of modernization that resulted in the conversion of absolute powers of feudal origin into constitutional monarchies and in the birth of the first modern republics found a singular exception in the Papal State, the sole European 'divine monarchy' that could survive the Revolution. Inside its boundaries, the 'memory' of a peculiar form of right was (and still is) preserved by the 'device' of the *jus canonicum*, a law that finds it source not in a social contract, but primarily in the interpretation (exegesis) of the divine message contained in the scriptures—that is to say in the Revelation. The 'canon' is here not only a rule, but a 'device of translation' between a transcendent law and a human one. In this sense, its notion precedes the Catholic state form and expands beyond the field of law, finding its first diffusion in the domains of art (literature, architecture, music, etc.). Generally speaking, a canon is a stick (from Greek *kanon*) that serves as measure, similar to a ruler. Different from a ruler, a canon is not 'prepared' with any pre-assigned 'units' nor follows any 'external' system of measurement other than the one dictated by its own form. The reason why a canon is fundamental in artistic practices is that it allows for the reproduction of an original order or, in other words, for the *equivalence* between two (or more) artefacts. What such equivalence entails is nevertheless a *reduction* (or an *expenditure*) *at the cost* of the artwork itself: The thing that is reproduced (or put in equivalence) is made so only by the terms and by the measure of the canon itself (by its 'picture').[19] What

---

18 Jean-Jacques Rousseau's *Social Contract* and Thomas Hobbes' *Leviathan* stand, still with their differences, as the most clear example of this new attitude. It is nevertheless important to remark that British *common law* seem to be an exception to the continental codification effort.

19 This equivalence is precisely what is at work in the stipulation of the social contract, a juridical and political device for which all men are *equal* as long as their essence is 'reduced' to the 'figure' of the person; it is not a case that *persona* also bears in its etymology the meaning of a theatrical 'mask': *per-sonare* is 'to sound through'. The incommensurable reduction that the canon operates finds an even more powerful manifestation when applied to the communication of sacred texts, as it turns into a real 'ontological difference' between the divine *logos* and its human, 'Babelic' translation; see: Franz Overbeck, *Zur Geschichte Des Kanons. Zwei Abhandlungen* (Chemnitz: Ernst Schmeitzner, 1880).

the canon does is then to *encode* its objects by abstracting an image of them. Canon and code, initially appearing as distant from each other, find here a mutual relation.

As ruler, the canon cannot be used on the 'sea'—a compass, despite being an instrument that could be easily associated with a ruler, cannot be considered as such—a canon is an 'earthly' (a *geo-metric*) instrument, and as such it builds and cultivates; it separates only in order to harvest, lays the foundations for a *tradition*. Foundation and tradition save in their etymology the encoding or, better, *encrypting* power of the canon: If the Latin *condere* means 'to found', but also (as the Greek *krypto*) 'to conceal', the word 'tradition' shares its etymology with the one of 'betrayal', as an allusion to the fact that, in order to be preserved as the same, something must be first betrayed.[20] The constitution of a canon can then perhaps be seen as a peculiar form of forgetting and abstraction, of 'cleaning' the 'clay tablet' (the *codex*) while preserving in it a certain 'disposition' that *prepares* it to receive new information.

The Modern founds itself on and in opposition to an 'antiquity' that modernity itself declares as such, a 'classical' time whose *canon* is constituted only after its age has *passed*. It is then this in-between time of the Middle Ages, this sort of 'non-empty fracture' between antiquity and modernity, transcendence and immediacy, that seems to have known how to fabricate the 'secret key' of its encryption.

But what now? Since Lyotard's essay of 1979,[21] present time seems to have left modernity behind. The time in which we live is less and less attributed with such a label—except perhaps for colloquial terms—and is rather identified simply as 'contemporary' or 'postmodern'. The first definition seems to be entrapped in the loop of a self-referential equation: Every time is in a way 'contemporary' to itself. At the same time, 'con-temporary' may also suggest a time in which *everything is present* or rather in which everything is *actual*—a time that seems therefore to exclude that space of 'absolute potentiality', like Averroes's separate intellect, that so much troubled the 13th century. The second definition, the one of a 'post-modern condition' is equally interesting, as it evokes a similar kind of 'discomfort' of naming an age by avoiding to re-discuss the fundamental dichotomy of *antiquity* and *modernity* to which the Middle Ages were also subjected.[22]

Contemporary myths such as the ones of the 'creative genius' and of 'total transparency' (as the dream of an *immediate* information)

---

20 It is the same 'mechanism' at work in the *sacrifice*; see: René Girard, *Violence and the Sacred* (Baltimore: Johns Hopkins University Press, 1977).

21 Jean-François Lyotard, *La Condition Postmoderne: Rapport Sur Le Savoir* (Paris: Éditions de Minuit, 1979).

22 An alternative denomination of the Middle-Ages is in fact the one of a "Post-Classical History."

can therefore be seen as the heritage that the unmastered reception of the modern condition left us with. The Crystal Palace seems to have entrapped us all in its phantasmagorical circulation of goods that follows no other 'intelligence' than the primacy of exchange value and trade economy. How can we escape from such a total system? How can we focus on and see its 'invisible' gears? How can we 'bury' modernity as tradition, when its ghosts keep on haunting us? How can we feel at home in the place of *any otherness* (of general equivalence)? A position that is not able to see such a 'third intelligence' except by evoking it as a *persona*—may it be human or fictitious: demons, God, Hobbes' *Leviathan*, the Hegelian Ghost, Rousseau's general will, Marx's general intellect, Freud's *Es*, sociology, progress and production, etc.—and by seeing itself as its *subject* will be condemned to its 'universal plan', and doomed to a deterministic and an *apocalyptic* worldview.[23] Looking at the separate intellect as if its 'disposition' was not the one of an absolute potency (the one of an absolute receptivity) but as if it was conceived as already informed and 'flooded' with data would be like staring directly at the sun from outer space: The eyes would burn without seeing any light at all. It is, in a way, the description of a *universal judgement*, a supreme intellect that summons to its tribunal all the souls of the universe—it *actualizes every potency*, bringing it in an 'absolute contemporaneity'—and 'burns' them with its own splendour. What Averroes's intellect seems to suggest then is that the only way to look at the sun is in the 'lunar' translucency of the *diaphanous*, of the transparent medium.[24]

Very few houses can reach the same fame and be equally described as '*the* modern house' as Mies van der Rohe's Farnsworth House. Built between 1945 and 1950—just a decade before the period which Lyotard pointed to as the 'beginning' of the post-modern condition—Mies's iconic villa is undoubtedly the archetype of the glasshouse *par excellence* (even if 'robbed' of the label by its post-modern yet anterior copy designed by Philip Johnson). Despite its clear essence of house, this architecture seems all but cosy and 'homey'. It is a house with no walls, where any 'individual privacy' relies on nothing but a white curtain that slides behind its transparent screens. Most of its photos show it as completely empty, almost as if the presence of someone would corrupt its image. If Averroes forces us to ask ourselves whether there is thought when no man thinks, it is as if Mies asked himself how a house can be such when no one dwells. Yet, the less it

---

23 "The real system of science consists in a solidarity of procedure and attitude with respect to the objectification of whatever is—a solidarity that is brought about appropriately at any given time on the basis of planning." M. Heidegger, 'The Age of the World Picture', 126.

24 This is, to my understanding, the very legacy of Europe's "negative thought": not the one of a dialectical opposition, but rather one of a triadic disposition, that 'hosts' the unconceivable without 'positivising' nor negating it.

appears as inhabitable and inhabited, the more it emerges as an absolute icon of modern 'houseness': Its figure ripples like a wave, reproduced by a countless number of projects and circulated in magazines, movies, books, websites; its image transcends the 'real extension' of the house and finds its place in the symbolic space of the collective imagination of an age. Contrary to most of Mies's projects, the house has no plinth nor precinct, but 'floats' on its steel columns, 'abstracting' itself from the ground. Farnsworth House is then perhaps an 'ark', ready to survive the 'end' of the modern time of which its architecture is a product. Invested by the 'deluge' of the post-modern condition (the 'liquid modernity', as Bauman would call it), Mies's house lets it 'wash away' its own age and settles down in the *tabula rasa* that comes after it. By the intelligence of its own abstraction, it ensures its 'heritage' not through a rush to a total accumulation, but in the 'fertility' provided by its design as a dwelling space of absolute potency.

THE DESIGNS OF THE NATURAL

MARTYN DADE-ROBERTSON

XV

MARTYN DADE-ROBERTSON is the reader in Design Computation at Newcastle University. He specializes in emerging technologies in design and has masters and PhD degrees in design and computation from Cambridge University and an M.Sc. Degree in synthetic biology. His most recent work has focused on bio design, developing biotechnology for the built environment with a particular emphasis on the development of engineered living materials (ELMs) using microbial synthetic biology. To this end he has set up a Bio Design Lab at Newcastle University with more than one million pounds in research funding. He has published over 50 peer reviewed publications including the book The Architecture of Information (Routledge 2011) and is the editor for the forthcoming Routledge series on Bio Design.

If digital technology dominated many of our discussions of architecture and design at the end of the twentieth century, it is sometimes suggested that the twenty-first century will be dominated by biological technologies.[1] This new technological revolution will, Joi Ito suggests, lead to "the end of the artificial":

> Unlike the past where there was a clearer separation between those things that represented the artificial and those that represented the organic, the cultural and the natural, it appears that nature and the artificial are merging.[2]

This entanglement between the natural and the artificial seems to reach its limit through the emergence of fields such as synthetic biology. Synthetic biology enables the 'design' of living organisms through genetic modification and conceptualizes biological systems in engineering terms. However, this blurring of the artificial and the natural is about more than the material reality of the technology. The terms we use play a significant role in defining the practices and outcomes of fields like synthetic biology.

At the heart of the discourse on biotechnologies, a distinction between the natural and artificial are important and have implications on how we design using biological media.

INTERFACES BETWEEN NATURAL AND ARTIFICIAL THINGS

The title of this essay makes deliberate reference to Herbert A. Simon's *The Sciences of the Artificial*.[3] Simon's text is now considered a classic and one of the founding texts of the field of Design Science.[4] *The Sciences of the Artificial* brings together computer science, economics, political science and psychology (and more besides) through a wide-ranging discussion of the design of artificial systems. Simon distinguishes between existing notions of science concerned with analysis and an engineering that is concern with synthesis. The designer is "concerned with how things ought to be."[5] Design, he argues, "distinguishes the professions from the sciences."[6] Simon's thesis emerges in response to a post-war culture in American universities seeking greater academic credibility through degree programs in natural sciences and by closing professional programs considered as "intellectually soft, intuitive, informal and cookbooky."[7]

1   R. Armstrong, *Living Architecture: How Synthetic Biology Can Remake Our Cities and Reshape Our Lives* (New York: TED, 2012).
2   Joichi Ito, 'Design and Science: Can Design Advance Science, and Can Science Advance Design?', *Journal of Design and Science*, 2017.
3   Herbert A. Simon, *The Sciences of the Artificial* (Cambridge Mass.: MIT Press, 1996).
4   D. J. Huppatz, 'Revisiting Herbert Simon's "Science of Design"', *Design Issues*, 31.2 (2015), 29 <https://doi.org/10.1162/DESI>.
5   Ibid., 4.
6   Ibid., 111.
7   Huppatz, 'Revisiting Herbert Simon's "Science of Design"', 114.

Simon's thesis answers this problem by proposing programmes of research and teaching concerned with making design theory 'explicit and precise' through rational framework for professional decision-making. In other words, establishing scientific rigour in the design of human systems. Since the publication of the first edition in 1969, *The Sciences of the Artificial* has been widely criticized by, for example, Rittel and Schon.[8] These critiques are widely rehearsed and I will not revisit them here. However, I do want to cast Simon's text in a different light.

Through the lens of (part of) Simon's thesis, what happens when we make the simple exchange of terms by swapping out 'sciences' for 'designs' (a word which, as a verb, is rarely used in the plural) and 'artificial' with 'natural'?

This is more than wordplay. Simon's text makes distinctions between natural and artificial that have implications for his consideration of design. He suggests a number of 'boundaries' for the study of the artificial:

· Artificial things are synthesized (though not always or usually with full forethought) by human beings.
· Artificial things may imitate appearances in natural things while lacking in one or many respects the reality of the latter.
· Artificial things can be characterized in terms of functions, goals and adaptations.
· Artificial things are often discussed particularly when they are being designed, in terms of imperatives as well as descriptives.[9]

In the process of designing artificial things, Simon defines an outside environment, which acts as a mould that shapes artificial things. Artificial things are thus defined by a relationship between an 'inner' and 'outer' world. A sundial, for example, will only work when the sun is shining and through its orientation and the organization of its gnomon and dial plate. A clock to use at sea without the fixity required for a sundial requires a time piece whose mechanisms are balanced in order to counter the motions of the waves. The natural is thus described in terms of the elemental forces of the sea and sun and the artificial is clearly declared as the internal human-made mechanisms of the clock. Design is concerned with an interface between this inner and outer world in terms of either isolation or degrees of connectivity between natural forces and artificially-produced machines.

NATURE'S MACHINES

Simonian thinking has found a new home in the emerging field of synthetic biology. Before the molecular revolution in the field, initiated in the

---

8   Jean-Pierre Protzen and David J. Harris, *The Universe of Design: Horst Rittel's Theories of Design and Planning* (London: Routledge, 2010); Donald A. Schon, *The Reflective Practitioner* (London: Basic Books, 1984).
9   Simon, *The Sciences of the Artificial*, 5.

1940s, biological science was seeking rigour provided by the reductionism of physics or chemistry, starting with scientific breeding programmes.[10]

The latest efforts in synthetic biology, suggests Campos, are far from revolutionary and are based on a tradition that has been around since the early part of the twentieth century.[11] This modern synthetic biology tradition is based on three guiding principles:

- to control nature, making living organisms in relation to human needs and goals;
- to frame their work as creating life through the "dissolution of the distinction between artificial and natural creations,"[12] and
- through researchers such as Jacques Loeb reimagining biology as a discipline concerned with synthesis rather than analysis.[13]

From this historical backdrop, an idea of synthetic biology is coalescing around the definition of a discipline "to design and engineer biologically based parts, novel devices and systems as well as redesigning existing, natural biological systems."[14] Within this definition are concepts that would have been familiar to Simon—notably a focus on abstraction and hierarchical assembly, implied, hierarchy of parts, devices and systems. In fact, Synthetic Biology could have been founded on Simonian principles that are "neatly packaged" and "that pivot around broad and abstract engineering design principles"[15] and in its aspiration to move beyond the 'artisan craft' of genetic engineering.[16] Throughout these endeavours to control and ultimately construct life has persisted a machine metaphor. Seeing nature through the lens of the artificial world has its origins in creationism and God as an intelligent engineer.[17]

There is certainly nothing in *The Sciences of the Artificial* which precludes synthetic biology. Although Simon makes little mention of, for example, molecular biology, his definition of the artificial can be applied to biology as much as any other system. In Simon's logic, a biological system

10   Lily E. Kay, 'Life as Technology: Representing, Intervening and Molecularizing' in Sahotra Sarkar (ed.), *The Philosophy and History of Molecular Biology: New Perspectives* (London: Kluwer, 1996), 87–100.

11   Luis Campos, 'That Was the Synthetic Biology That Was', 2009, 20–26 <https://doi.org/10.1007/978-1-62703-625-2>.

12   Sharon E Kingsland, 'The Battling Botanist: Daniel Trembly MacDougal, Mutation Theory, and the Rise of Experimental Evolutionary Biology in America, 1900–1912', Isis, 82.3 (1991), 479–509 <https://doi.org/10.2307/233227>.

13   Philip J. Pauly, *Controlling Life: Jacques Loeb and the Engineering Ideal in Biology* (Oxford: Oxford University Press, 1987).

14   Christopher Voigt, Synthetic Biology Scope, Applications and Implications (London: Royal Academy of Engineering, 20 January 2012), 6 <https://doi.org/10.1021/sb300001c>.

15   Adrian Mackenzie, 'Design in Synthetic Biology', *Biosocieties*, 5.2 (2010), 180–98 (182) <https://doi.org/10.1057/biosoc.2010.4>.

16   Jane Calvert, 'Engineering Biology and Society: Reflections on Synthetic Biology', Science Technology & Society, 18.3 (2013), 405–20 <https://doi.org/10.1177/0971721813498501>.

17   Maarten Boudry and Massimo Pigliucci, 'The Mismeasure of Machine: Synthetic Biology and the Trouble with Engineering Metaphors', *Studies in History and Philosophy of Science Part C: Studies in History and Philosophy of Biological and Biomedical Sciences*, 44.4 (2013), 660–68 <https://doi.org/10.1016/j.shpsc.2013.05.013>.

can be treated as an artificial system simply by reframing our understanding of it—not in terms of its substance, but in terms of human-defined goals. This reframing of biology is an essential ingredient of synthetic biology and extends to include ways of modelling and representing biological systems that are oriented towards these defined goals. To this end, synthetic biology is rooted in an imperfect but pervasive machine metaphor.[18]

If synthetic biology is described in terms that Simon would have recognized, however, the machine metaphor and the design approaches this implies is contested. The consideration of biology as an extension of our designed artificial systems is provocative and, for some, controversial. The challenges facing synthetic biologists have been well-articulated from within the scientific press.[19] There is a sense of discomfort about simplifications made to, for example, our understating of living cells with Lazebnik suggesting, for example:

> Engineering approaches are not applicable to cells because these little wonders are fundamentally different from objects studied by engineers (...) What is so special about cells is not usually specified, but it is implied that real biologists feel the difference.[20]

This discomfort with synthetic biology, approached through the lens of the artificial, goes beyond the biological science community. A general distrust of all things 'genetically modified' for example inevitably leads to press headlines of playing 'God' or Frankenstein.[21]

This distrust is amplified by distaste. The attempt to modularize and simplify biology can be seen as an unhealthy attempt to commodify and control life.[22] Furthermore, fields such as synthetic biology lead to the creation of what has been termed 'deep technologies,' which will ultimately transform "the natural to become the artefactual" through a "deeper level" of material manipulation than has been possible before.[23]

THE ARTIFICIAL AS A PRODUCT OF INTENTION

Seen in the context of synthetic biology, Simon's distinction between the natural and the artificial offers a number of challenges. In defining

---

18 Ibid.
19 Roberta Kwok, 'Five Hard Truths for Synthetic Biology.', *Nature*, 463.7279 (2010), 288–90 <https://doi.org/10.1038/463288a>.
20 Y. Lazebnik, 'Can a Biologist Fix a Radio? – Or What I Learned While Studying Apoptosis', *Biochemistry*, 69.12 (2004), 1403–8 (1405–6).
21 Henk van den Belt, 'Playing God in Frankenstein's Footsteps: Synthetic Biology and the Meaning of Life', *NanoEthics*, 3.3 (2009), 257–68 <https://doi.org/10.1007/s11569-009-0079-6>.
22 Jane Calvert, 'The Commodification of Emergence: Systems Biology, Synthetic Biology and Intellectual Property', *BioSocieties*, 3.4 (2008), 383–98 <https://doi.org/10.1017/S1745855208006303>.
23 K Lee, *The Natural and the Artefactual: The Implications of Deep Science and Deep Technology for Environmental Philosophy* (Oxford: Lexington Books, 1999).

the artificial, Simon sets it in contrast to a notion of 'natural' for which he offers no definition. For example: "Artificial things may imitate appearances in natural things while lacking, in one or many respects, the reality of the latter."[24] The 'reality' of natural things is, however, never described by Simon. It is, at best, an intuitive category. Where intuition will suffice in distinguishing between, for example, a clock and the rolling ocean, how might we distinguish between wild type bacteria and genetically modified bacteria? The genetic modification may mean that the new engineered bacteria lacks "in one or more respect the reality of the latter" but does this mean that the engineered bacteria has lost its nature. Surely, it more than resembles a natural thing. By growing, subdividing and metabolizing in ways that are unrelated to its human designed functions, it retains all but a small part of its nature.

There is also a question of synthesis. Artificial things are synthesized by human beings. A clock is clearly a product of human synthesis; but could genetically modified bacteria be said to be a product of human synthesis? We may have provided the environment for the bacteria to grow, deleted or added a gene to its genome, but the putting together of its parts is done in vivo—it is largely self-synthesizing. It may be clearer with an example such as Gibson and colleague's work to chemically synthesize a Mycoplasma genitalium genome.[25] The chemical synthesis of the first cell genome was printed using a process of artificial gene synthesis. However, thereafter, the cells divided and (aside from a few DNA 'watermarks') the measure of the project's success was the ability to transplant the synthesized genome into an already synthesized cell membrane and to have the cell reboot and behave exactly like the wild type cell by metabolizing and dividing.[26] The scientific achievement was, nevertheless, contested, since the team had "not created life, only mimicked it."[27] Arguably, based on Simon's definition of the 'synthetic', Mycoplasma genitalium resembles all the reality of a natural thing. It also falls short of being natural since it is described in terms of human goals and functions. The Gibson-lead team was using the organism to prove that such a feat of biological engineering was possible. The goal of publishing a paper in *Nature* and inspiring provocative newspaper headlines cannot necessarily be ascribed to the organism.

24 Simon, *The Sciences of the Artificial*, 5.
25 Daniel G Gibson, Gwynedd a Benders, and others, 'Complete Chemical Synthesis, Assembly, and Cloning of a Mycoplasma Genitalium Genome.', Science (New York, N.Y.), 319.5867 (2008), 1215–20 <https://doi.org/10.1126/science.1151721>.
26 Daniel G Gibson, John I Glass, and others, 'Creation of a Bacterial Cell Controlled by a Chemically Synthesized Genome.', *Science* (New York, N.Y.), 329.5987 (2010), 52–56 <https://doi.org/10.1126/science.1190719>.
27 Nicholas Wade, 'Researchers Say They Created a "Synthetic Cell"', *The New York Times*, 2010 <http://www.nytimes.com/2010/05/21/science/21cell.html?_r=0> [accessed 4 December 2017].

GHOSTS OF TRANSPARENCY

It is clear that terms like natural, artificial and design become contestable in Synthetic Biology, because intention and outcome are not always perfectly matched. Catts and Zurr, for example, point to what they describe as the "single engineering paradigm" in which control of life is led by an "intolerance to uncertainty."[28]

Calvert also describes synthetic biologists in terms of heterogeneous engineers incorporating "social, political, economic and human factors into their technical work."[29] O'Malley claims that: "While engineering certainly contributes to the practices of synthetic biology, my claim is that it is doing this in more complicated ways than might be envisioned in the 'pure' engineering ideal."[30] He cites the principle of limited sloppiness in scientific research, which enables novel insights and accidents, translated in engineering terms into 'kludging' (finding solutions which are klumsy dumb but good enough).

THE NATURAL AND THE ARTIFICIAL

One distinguishing feature of the definitions of both 'natural' and 'artificial', suggests Bensaude-Vincent and Newman, is the "absence of any clear and unambiguous terminology for distinguishing artificial and natural products in the English language."[31] In patent law, it is possible to describe a modified living organism as an invention. Since many artificial things are products of nature (indeed all artificial things start with natural materials since we cannot synthesize fundamental elements), the division between the natural and the artificial becomes about the extent and type of transformation. Bensaude-Vincent and Newman cite the example of cooking. Boiling and roasting, for example, take foodstuffs, which themselves are clearly products of nature. The transformative process of cooking mimics natural processes of heating. Cooked food therefore is natural. By a similar logic, however, glass is also a product of nature. Glass is created from a naturally found substance and transformed by "nature's own agencies."[32]

This strange position is manifest in our treatment of biology. Few, for example, would argue that a cow is an artificial object. Yet it is the result of hundreds of years of selective breeding. A genetically engineered crop, however, might be considered a patentable invention and, for a protester of genetic modification, an artificial aberration of nature. The

---

28 O Catts and I Zurr, 'Countering the Engineering Mindset: The Conflict of Art and Synthetic Biology', in *Synthetic Aesthetics: Investigating Synthetic Biology's Designs on Nature*, ed. by A Ginsberg and others (Cambridge Mass.: MIT Press, 2014), 27–38 (28).
29 Calvert, 'Engineering Biology and Society: Reflections on Synthetic Biology'.
30 M. O'Malley, 'Making Knowledge in Synthetic Biology: Design Meets Kludge', *Biological Theory*, 4.4 (2009), 378–89 <https://doi.org/10.1162/BIOT_a_00006>.
31 Bernadette Bensaude-Vincent and William. R Newman, 'Introduction: The Artificial and the Natural: State of the Problem', in *The Artificial and the Natural An Evolving Polarity*, ed. by Bernadette Bensaude-Vincent and William. R Newman (Cambridge Mass.: MIT Press, 2007), 1–19 (4).
32 Ibid., 6.

distinction is that natural selection is using 'nature's own agencies' as opposed to the synthetic process of genetic manipulations conducted in the highly unnatural controlled confines of a lab. Art violates nature, claim Bensaude-Vincent and Newman, by means of "forcible constraints."[33]

CONCLUSION

I began this essay with Joi Ito's contention that 'nature and the artificial are merging'. This, I suggested, is posited as a contemporary issue which is caused, in part, by fields such as synthetic biology which, through the design of biological systems, blur distinctions between natural and artificial. Held up against the rigid categorizations of Simon in *The Sciences of the Artificial*, the Designs of the Natural problematizes the strict interface between inside (artificial) and outside (natural) systems. When engineering (a discipline most associated with the designs of the artificial) is applied to biological systems, there are shortcomings on the methods we adopt and the metaphors (notably the biology as machine metaphor) we use to describe biological processes. Designing the Natural suggests a greater tolerance to uncertainty and engineered biological systems. However, I have also suggested that this blurred distinction between natural and artificial is not new. Definitions of the natural and the artificial have been attempted since Aristotle and, although not conclusive, lead us to recognize that the artificial can be seen more properly as a degree of control over the natural, whether this be by forcible control (cutting a piece of timber) or through the application of 'nature's own agencies', for instance, cross-breeding and selection. These examples are already part of the discourse in synthetic biology with, for example, the explicit criticism of playing 'God' or creating 'Frankenstein', implying that genetic modification is a forcible constraint when compared to nature's own agencies in selective breeding.

This is far from a conclusion, of course, but I do want to make the following claim. The biological, as framed by synthetic biology, sits at an important intersection between natural and artificial and our definition of those terms has important implications for our design practices and products when we modify systems that were once considered natural. Considered as simply an extension of our artificial and engineered worlds, synthetic biology applies design paradigms, which were applicable to traditional engineering, to systems which are complex, unpredictable and can only be guided and never fully designed. Alternatively, an uncritical and romanticized view of nature, as distinct from the artificial, ignores the deep relationship between human and natural worlds and ignores the distinctions between intentions and outcomes and the agencies of change.

33   Ibid., 10.

MYTHIC NOISE: ARCHITECTURES OF GEOLOGICAL COMMUNICATION
ADAM NOCEK

XVI

ADAM NOCEK is assistant professor in the philosophy of technology and science and technology studies in the School of Arts, Media, and Engineering at Arizona State University. He is the founding director of the Center for Philosophical Technologies and author of numerous articles and edited collections on technoscience, process philosophy, design and media theory, and the history of science. Nocek's forthcoming book is titled, *Molecular Capture: Animation, Governance, and Design.*

Geocommunication technology—this is likely to call to mind geoinformational tools capable of aggregating, synthesizing and communicating complex geological, atmospheric, and infrastructural data to a variety of stakeholders concerned with planetary systems at a variety of scales.[1] Such a notion might also encompass satellite technologies—geostationary and low earth orbit (LEO) satellites, for instance—that have had important applications in weather forecasting, planetary telecommunications, defence and intelligence systems.[2] One might also be inclined to think more broadly about geocommunication in terms of the multiple layers of planetary-scale computing that exist simultaneously, as well as the new systems of planetary governance that have emerged in their wake.[3] Whatever the case, geocommunication tends to call up notions of highly sophisticated computational systems that gather, store, and process data about earth systems at multiple spatial and temporal scales.

What we usually do not associate with geocommunication technologies, however, are low-tech and/or analogue methods for information transfer. And we certainly do not associate systems of oral communication that flourished in prehistoric and pre-modern eras with a modern technics of geocommunication. But that is exactly what I claim here, or rather, I demonstrate that myths about geological transformations and natural disasters are a part of the intellectual genealogy of modern geocommunicational media. In many ways, this is new territory for the humanities. While media studies have become ever more attentive to the materiality of media by unearthing new connections to geological systems[4] and science studies has made room in its epistemologies for mythmaking and non-modern practices more generally,[5] the humanities and social sciences have yet to see mythmaking through the lens of geocommunicational media.

1   See for instance, Anuj, Karpatne, Imme Ebert-Uphoff, Sai Ravea, Hassan Ali Babaie, and Vipin Kumar, Machine Learning for the Geosciences: Challenges and Opportunities"; Hua-Dong Guo, Li Zhang, Lan-Wei Zhu, "Earth Observation Big Data for Climate Change Research"; NRC (National Research Council), *Earth Observations from Space: the First 50 Years of Scientific Achievements*; and *Communicating Environmental Geoscience – Special Publication no 305 (Geological Society Special Publication)*, edited by David Gordon Earl Liverman, C. G. Pereira, and Brian Marker (London: The Geological Society, 2008).

2   See for instance, Huadong Guo, Wenxue Fu, Xinwu Li, Pei Chen, Guang Liu, Zhen Li, et al., 'Research on Global Change Scientific Satellites', *Science China Earth Sciences*, 57.2 (2014), 204–15 <https://doi.org/10.1007/s11430-013-4748-5> and Huadong Guo, Lizhe Wang, Fang Chen, and Dong Liang, 'Scientific Big Data and Digital Earth', *Chinese Science Bulletin*, 59.35 (2014), 5066–73 <https://doi.org/10.1007/s11434-014-0645-3>

3   Benjamin H. Bratton, *The Stack: On Software and Sovereignty* (Cambridge, MA: MIT Press, 2016).

4   See Sean Cubitt, *Finite Media: Environmental Implications of Digital Technologies* (Durham: Duke University Press, 2016); and Jussi Parikka, *A Geology of Media* (Minneapolis: University of Minnesota Press, 2015).

5   See Isabelle Stengers, 'Introductory Notes on an Ecology of Practices', *Cultural Studies Review*, Vol. 11, no. 1, 2005; and Latour, Bruno, 'Facing Gaia', *Eight Lectures on the New Climactic Regime* (Cambridge, UK: Polity, 2017).

In what follows, I flesh this connection out by showing how a very specific information architecture underwrites the practices of the rapidly growing field of geomythology in the earth sciences, an architecture that in many ways guarantees its participation in the long lineage of geocommunication technologies. What I go on to demonstrate, however, with the help of Afrofuturist film, the work by François Laruelle, Isabelle Stengers, and others, is that this lineage also presupposes a deeply colonialist conception of noise that primes us to ask whether there are other communicative, or perhaps post-communicative, architectures for geomythic media. In the concluding sections of this chapter, I propose one such architecture that is liable to open up new post-communicative genealogies for myth.

MYTH: A NOISY CHANNEL

The field of geomythology has emerged in recent years as a hotbed of research activity, especially as the earth sciences scramble to piece together histories of the planet that predate modern scientific thought.[6] Although geomythological methods of scientific inquiry have been around for centuries (Robert Hooke, for instance, used myths about land formations from Plato, Virgil, and others to buttress his theory about geological transformations; and the father of palaeontology, Georges Cuvier, drew on Native American legends about petrified bones to support his research into fossilization[7]), the geologist, Dorothy Vitaliano, was the first to identify it as a legitimate scientific field in 1968.[8] And in the past ten years, geomythology has begun to capture the imagination of many earth and atmospheric scientists as they endeavour to cobble together a comprehensive theory of the earth's transformations over time.[9]

In its most basic formulation, the science of geomythology seeks to extract verifiable facts about the earth's prehistoric and pre-modern history from out of the explanations dreamed up by civilizations that did not have the benefit of modern scientific methods. So for instance, Plato's *Timaeus* and *Critias* include the earliest references to the myth of Atlantis, and scientists have determined that this story accurately depicts changes in landmasses and coastlines. Similarly, Noah's flood in the Book of Genesis actually describes, "postglacial melting elevated sea levels to the extent

6   See for instance, L. Piccardi, and W.B. Masse (eds.). *Myth and Geology: Geological Society Special Publication 273.* (London: The Geological Society, 2007)

7   See Adrienne Mayor, 'Geomythology', In *Encyclopedia of Geology*, eds. Richard Selley, Robin Cocks, and Ian Palmer (San Diego: Elsevier Science Publishing Co Inc., 2004).

8   See Dorthy Vitaliano, 'Geomythology: Geological Origins of Myths and Legends', In Piccardi, L and W.B. Masse (eds.). *Myth and Geology: Geological Society Special Publication 273* and Dorthy Vitaliano, *Legends of the Earth: The Geologic Origins* (Bloomington: Indiana University Press, 1973).

9   In a forthcoming article, 'Geology, Myth, Media', I offer a more thorough investigation of the methods and aims of this field, especially as they relate to modern scientific epistemology. See Adam Nocek, 'Geology, Myth, Media', *SubStance* 146, Vol. 47, no. 2, (2018).

that the Mediterranean broke through into the Black Sea depression, drowning out so many settlements that a universal flood legend resulted."[10] Countless other geomyths are now the subject of serious scientific scrutiny that aims to track down "the actual geologic origins of natural phenomena which were long explained in terms of myth and folklore."[11]

There is much more that could be said about the methods and aims of this relatively young science.[12] But in what follows I want to identify two fundamental assumptions regarding the design of geomythic communication that guarantee myth's relevance for modern scientific epistemology. In each assumption, we witness the emergence of a communication architecture capable of divesting the mythic statement of what distinguishes it from the scientific statement.

FIG I
The Last Angel of History, dir. John Akomfrah (1996)

1. *Geomythologists presume the truth of a classical information theory.* According to the editors of the 2007 Special Publication of the Geological Society titled, *Geology and Myth*, scientists aim to decode the "encoded memories of past geological events" as a part of a general strategy to collate scattered and fragmented planetary memories in ways that are legible to scientific thought.[13] What this means,

10   See Vitaliano, "Geomythology," 4.
11   According to Vitaliano, there are really two kinds of geological myths. The myth is either a story about "some geologic feature or the occurrence of some geologic phenomena has inspired a folklore explanation" or it is a "garbled explanation of some actual geologic event, usually a natural catastrophe" (Piccardi, L. 'Preface', *Myth and Geology: Geological Society Special Publication 273*, (London: The Geological Society, 2007) vii; see also Vitaliano, "Geomythology").
12   See Piccardi, and Masse *Myth and Geology* for a careful and comprehensive assessment of the methods and stakes of geomythology.
13   See Piccardi, "Preface," vii.

according to W. Bruce Masse and his colleagues, is that "mythology is the function of oral transmission of linguistically encoded data"; and thus "myths are not just silly 'cultural fiction,' they are carriers of information ..." even though "[r]ecovering that information is not always easy or even possible."[14] The debt to classical information theory should be clear: Just as Claude Shannon demonstrates in his seminal paper from 1948, *A Mathematical Theory of Communication*, how a sender encodes a message into a signal so that it can be transmitted across a channel and decoded by a receiver, and in doing so attempts to resolve how to "reproduc[e] at one point, either exactly or approximately, a message selected at another point,"[15] likewise, pre-modern myths are thought to encode (original) messages about planetary events that can be now decoded by contemporary scientists.

This is precisely why geologists and archaeologists claim that only scientists, instead of literary and cultural theorists, can appreciate the efficacy of myths. These stories carry valuable information from another epoch; they are not *mere* historically and culturally situated fictions.[16] Where humanities scholars fixate on the situated and fictional aspects of myth, scientists, by contrast, pay special attention to how they are transhistorical couriers of information. Geological myths are like time capsules designed to communicate with future geoarcheologists. This is not unlike the communicative scenario that John Akomfrah imagines in his seminal docufiction, *The Last Angel of History* (1996). Where the drum is depicted as a mythological Afrofuturist technology that communicates across distant times and spaces (the drum "sound covered the distance between the old and the new world"), and provides acoustic messages from premodern Africa to a technoscientific future, likewise the geological myth is a communication technology, a mythic media device, for connecting the ancient past to the present and future.[17] What the scientists' wager, then, is that this mythic communication device is designed in order to permit ancient messages to be decoded by modern scientists.

14   W. B. Masse, Elizabeth Wayland Barber, Luigi Piccardi, and Paul T. Barber, 'Exploring the Nature of Myth and Its Role in Science', in Piccardi, L and W.B. Masse (eds.), *Myth and Geology: Geological Society Special Publication 273* (London: The Geological Society, 2007), 18.

15   Shannon, Claude E., 'A Mathematical Theory of Communication', Bell Labs Innovations. Repr. with corrections from *Bell System Technical Journal* 27 (1948). Available at: http://affect-reason-utility.com/1301/4/shannon1948.pdf. (Accessed on December 2017), 1.

16   See Masse et al., 'Exploring the Nature of Myth and Its Role in Science', 9. After discussing the history of myth and its many theories (from antiquity to hermeneutics and post-structuralism), they conclude that "these [theories] have one fundamental shared characteristic—none is seemingly willing to suggest that a real observed natural process or event may lie at the core of myth storylines" (ibid., 13). See my discussion of this in 'Geology, Myth, Media'.

17   See Francesca Royster, *Sounding Like a No-No: Queer Sounds and Eccentric Acts in the Post-Soul Era* (Ann Arbor: University of Michigan Press 2013), 169.

FIG 2
*Stringing telephone
wire on a tree
in Enewetak Atoll,*
Marshall Islands,
c. 1944.

2. *Myths are noise.* This assertion may come as a surprise given
that geological myths are also communication devices carrying
messages from distant pasts. And yet a myth is only valuable to
geoarcheologists and other scientists insofar as those elements
in the narrative that bear the mark of situated and poetic figurations of the earth's processes are muted or otherwise controlled
so that a scientifically verifiable message can be extracted from it.
In the Shannon communication model, noise refers to any physical disturbance to the transmission of information. This disturbance is not
outside of the overall communication model, however; rather, it is a part
of communication system as such.[18] Though Shannon's paper identifies

18   In reference to Shannon's communication model Jussi Parikka rightly notes that "even
though noise is seen as coming from the outside and invading the mediating powers of
a communicative act, it is still is diagrammed in the same image, as an integral part of
the system. Hence it is accorded a position within the diagrammatic framework instead
as residing as pure noise outside of the communication act" (Parikka, Jussi. *A Geology
of Media.* Of course the image Parikka is referring to is the classic diagram of a general
communication system that Shannon develops in his seminal paper, 'A Mathematical
Theory of Communication' (Figure 1).

various kinds of "noiseless systems"—even offering a theorem for a "noiseless channel"[19]—communication is generally seen to be a noisy process, and so the noise in any given communication system has to be measured and managed. To this end, Shannon's "noisy channel coding theory" was able to show how every channel has a maximum capacity to transmit error-free messages.[20] This is even true for channels with low-bandwidth, or channels that are determined to be excessively noisy. In these instances, error-free communication of discrete data is achievable provided that the maximum capacity has not been exceeded. What's more, Shannon also describes how the error detection and correction techniques, first developed by Richard W. Hamming, and later synthesized in his paper, *Error Detecting and Correcting Codes* (1950), may be applied to the communication system to retrieve the original message that may have been contaminated.[21]

My hypothesis is that what we see happening in the field of geomythology is the deployment of error detection and correction techniques to retrieve messages that have been corrupted. Mythical stories are noisy channels for geological messages. Scientists endeavour to detect and restore what has been "garbled" (*sic*) through mythical communication.[22] What's at stake here is washing the message clean of those elements that would prevent it from being verified by scientists, or in other words, those culturally situated modes of making sense of geologic and atmospheric phenomena. In short, the wager is that the message can be cleansed of its 'superstition'. This epistemological stance is precisely what motivates Masse and his colleagues' telling assertion that, "myths are not just silly 'cultural fiction,' they are carriers of information..." (cited above); or Vitaliano's claim that geological myths often contain "the garbled explanation of some actual geologic event, usually a natural catastrophe."[23] Scientists are betting on the fact that the noisy interferences of situated knowledge can be detected and controlled so

---

19 See Shannon, 'A Mathematical Theory of Communication', 9.
20 Also known as Shannon's Theorem or the Shannon-Hartley Theorem that was based on the work of Ralph Hartley. See Ralph Hartley, 'Transmission of Information 1', Bell System Technical Journal, 7.3 (1928), 535–63 <https://doi.org/10.1002/j.1538-7305.1928.tb01236.x>
21 See Shannon, 'A Mathematical Theory of Communication', 27. Also see Richard W. Hamming, 'Error Detecting and Correcting Codes', *The Bell System Technical Journal. Journal*, vol. 29, no. 2, (1950); and Thomas M. Thompson, *From Error-Correcting Codes through Sphere Packings to Simple Groups, Vol. 21*. (Washington, D.C.: The Mathematical Association of America, 1983).
22 As Luigi Piccardi insists, the "interpretation of geological folklore, to be correctly and exhaustively carried out, requires the integration of knowledge in the fields of geology, archeology, history, comparative mythology, and anthropology" (Piccardi, 'Preface', vii). For this reason, "the process of extracting from myth such records of natural events and processes in most cases will not be easy" (Masse et al., 'Exploring the Nature of Myth and Its Role in Science', 25).
23 Ibid., vii.

that error-free communication can be forged between the past and present. The wager is that geological myths can be placed in very same lineage as other forms of modern geocommunication, with the caveat that a great deal of error detection and correction will have to be carried out, and this will likely happen at the intersection of multiple disciplines.[24]

In the ideal scenario, myths that are cleansed of their subjective and cultural mediation can bring the geological and atmospheric past into full view for scientists. These are messages capable of standing up to the careful and rigorous scrutiny of scientists because they have proven themselves to be thought independent. They index a planetary past that is fully independent of the historically and culturally situated subjects who produced them.[25] The situated, felt, and poetic modes of sense making, or in other words, all those things that distinguish mythic statements from scientific ones, are noisy interferences that disrupt the communication of verifiable information about the earth's prehistoric and premodern history.

So if there is indeed some resonance between the mythic time capsule dreamed up by geomythologists and the mythic drum depicted in Akomfrah's film, then we cannot confuse or conflate their political projects. Where there is an all but explicit "ethnic cleansing" of the message in the communicative architecture presupposed by geomythologists,[26] the percussive communication technologies fabricated in *The Last Angel of History* build a continuity between the past and future of the African diasporic condition. Such communicative technics emerge out the need to piece together the fragments of *alien*(ated) black experience rather than out of the desire to build an objective modern history. And so what amounts to noisy interference for geomythologists, namely, stories about the experience of situated subjects, is precisely what is brought into sharp focus through the new sonic mythology that Akomfrah fabricates.

POST-COMMUNICATIVE MYTHIC MEDIA

I want to start this section with a question: Might there be another way to think about the efficacy of geological myths outside of, or perhaps adjacent to, a genealogy of geocommunicative media? While this

---

24 Ibid.; see note 22.
25 There are interesting resonances between what Quentin Meillassoux's claims in *After Finitude* (London: Bloomsbury, 2010), especially his attempt to think a Real independent of, or decorrelated from, all thought, and the work of geomythologists, or at least the latter's commitment to a mythical statement that can index a geological time and space independent of the thought that produced it.
26 In his essay, 'Fragment from The Message Is Murder', Social Text, 34.3 128 (2016), 137–52, Johnathan Beller explains that Shannon's communication model produces the "structural exclusion of social difference," and "the weighted bias against nonnormative, which is to say nonhegemonic, signification..." (Johnathan Beller, 'Fragment from *The Message Is Murder*', *Social Text*, September 2016; 34.3 128 (2016), 151).

lineage uncovers the mytho-technics of geomythology, this technics is also inseparable from the colonial violence of Western science and technology.[27] In short, classical communication theory is inadequate for addressing the situated practices of geomythic storytelling: It performs an "ethnic cleansing of the message." To unpack what an alternative to this communicative framework might mean, I want to entertain the following hypothesis: that communication might not be an adequate model for addressing the value of geological myths—in any era. Why, for instance, do we assume that geological myths must communicate something in order for them to be important to our thinking about the earth's processes? Clearly, the deeper issue here has to do with what we take to be Reality and whether it is inherently communicable.

François Laruelle writes about the philosophical presumption of "sufficient communication" in his 1987 (translated 2010) essay, *The Truth According to Hermes: Theorems on the Secret and Communication*. He begins this short and provocative piece by noting that, "[t]he unitary or dominant way of thinking is that of a generalized hermeneutics, a hermetology. The economy of hermetology and its most general structure are both those of a 'difference'. Hermetological Difference is the indissoluble correlation, the undecidable coupling of truth and its communication."[28] Laruelle goes onto demonstrate the deep and abiding correlation between communication and truth in philosophical thought, and then proposes that,

> [n]early all philosophers were the mailmen of truth, and they diverted the truth for reasons less to do with the secret that with authoritarian censure. Meaning, always more meaning! Information, always more information! Such is the mantra of hermeto-logical difference, which mixes together truth and communication, the real and information. The most extreme version of this hermeto-logical ambiguity is the Hegelian and Nietzschean principle: The real is communicational, the communicational is real. It is in the omnipresent effectivity of communication that hermetology itself deteriorates.[29]

For Laruelle, the crucial point is not only does philosophy assume that everything is philosophizable according to the Principle of Sufficient

27 On colonization and science, see Kavita Philip's groundbreaking, *Civilizing Natures: Race, Resources, and Modernity in Colonial South India* (New Brunswick: Rutgers University Press, 2003); and Susantha Goonitilake's insightful, *Global Science: Mining Civlizational Knowledge*, (Bloomington, IN: Indiana U Press, 1998).

28 Laruelle, François, 'The Truth According to Hermes: Theorems on the Secret and Communication', trans. Alexander Galloway. *Parrhesia* (2010), 19.

29 Ibid., 22.

Philosophy,[30] but that it is also communicable via a communicational decision; and in some ways, writes Eugene Thacker, the latter "is even more insidious than the philosophical decision."[31] Laruelle's own non-philosophical stance, as it plays out across his works and in his very particular vocabulary, is unmistakeably committed to radical immanence, as there is no transcendent 'Real', since it is everywhere and all pervasive. Hence, Laruelle is in many ways a part of the same French intellectual genealogy as Henri Bergson, Gilles Deleuze, Michel Henry, and other thinkers of immanence.[32] However, and this is one of the crucial differences, the Real or the One is completely inaccessible for Laruelle; it does not manifest itself, it is not given to thought or experience, and is therefore withdrawn, and equally so for all thought and practice.[33]

There is no thought *of* the One in Laruelle, only *from* the One, or as "Vision-in-One."[34] The Real is 'unilateral'; it is unaffected by any thought or representations of it, although they nevertheless all proceed *from* it. In this context, Deleuze, the philosopher of immanence *par excellence*, still instates the sufficiency of philosophy for Laruelle: In Deleuze (and Deleuze and Guattari) immanence is not radical enough, which is to say, *given without givenness*. Immanence is *given* to itself through philosophical intellection: The evolving duality of philosophical concepts—virtual and actual, molar and molecular, and so on—is what produces the plane of immanence that it must nevertheless presuppose for its existence.[35] For Laruelle, in contrast, the Real is radically immanent, it is already given, but is not philosophizable and cannot be communicated to thought.

30   According to Laruelle, "philosophy is regulated in accordance with a principle higher than that of Reason: *the Principle of sufficient philosophy.* The latter expresses philosophy's absolute autonomy, its essence as self-positing/donating/naming/deciding/grounding, etc. It guarantees philosophy's command of the regional disciplines and sciences. Ultimately, it articulates the idealist pretension of philosophy as that which is able to at least co-determine that Real, which is most radical (Laruelle, François, 'A Summary of Non-Philosophy', trans. Ray Brassier, in *Pli: The Warwick Journal of Philosophy 8* (1999) 138–139).

31   Eugene Thacker, 'Dark Media', in *Excommunication: Three Inquiries into Media and Mediation* (Chicago: University of Chicago Press, 2014), 124.

32   See John Mullarkey, especially *Post-Continental Philosophy: An Outline* (London: Continuum, 2007), as well as *All Thoughts are Equal: Laruelle and Nonhuman Philosophy* (Minneapolis: University of Minnesota Press, 2015).

33   See Laruelle, 'The Truth According to Hermes', 22; and François Laruelle, *Philosophy and Non-Philosophy*, trans. Taylor Adkins (Minneapolis: Univocal, 2013).

34   See Laruelle, *Philosophy and Non-Philosophy*, 33–78.

35   In *What is Philosophy?* trans. Hugh Tomlinson and Graham Burchell (New York: Columbia University Press, 1994), Deleuze and Guattari explain that immanence is both the ground of the philosophical concept and constructed by the concept. Hence, immanence is presupposed by the concept but it does not preexist it, which is to say that the plane of immanence is constructed *as* the presupposed ground of philosophical thought. See *What is Philosophy?*, 78.

Laruelle's work has profound implications for media and communication theory. And as I have written about elsewhere,[36] it is in an effort to disentangle the Real and its communication that Alexander Galloway, Eugene Thacker, and McKenzie Wark co-author *Excommunication: Three Inquires in Media and Mediation*. Drawing on Laruelle, both together and separately, they explain that any and all communication is always already an excommunication (or xenocommunication[37]) of some sort. Where media theory (and philosophy more generally) tends to presume the sufficiency of communication as a model for media, they want to draw attention to broader practices of mediation (where media devices are only one species of media) and how this challenges the fundamental assumption, at least in the West, that "communication is possible and even desirable ... that 'there will have always been communication,' even before a single word has been uttered? A common language, a common ground, an agreed-upon topic and rules of engagement ... so much has already taken place prior to the first words being uttered or the first message being sent."[38]

To suspend the sufficiency of communication, and to put forward a model of excommunication, "does not simply destroy communication, but evokes the *impossibility* of communication, the *insufficiency* of communication as a model. In this way, excommunication is prior to the very possibility of communication."[39] This does not mean that nothing is communicated, and that we are living in vacuum-sealed capsules with no information exchange whatsoever, rather, and far more provocatively, it means that any and all communication also harbours the annihilation of its own communication. "Every communication," they go onto insist, "evokes a possible excommunication that would instantly annul it. Every communication harbours the dim awareness of an excommunication that is prior to it, that conditions it and makes it all the more natural. Excommunication—before a single word has been said." [40]

In the short space that remains, I won't take us any further down the rabbit hole of Laruellian thought, and the possible media theory that follows from it; I leave it to others to be our guides through these murky waters.[41] I would, however, like to pay special attention to how the insufficiency of communication might function as a proposition for us

36 In 'Geology, Myth, Media', I generate a more elaborate framework for thinking about the relation between geomythic fabrication in a non/excommunicative framework, as well as how it relates to Isabelle Stengers' work on Gaia (see below).

37 See McKenzie Wark, 'Furious Media: A Queer History of Heresy', in *Excommunication: Three Inquiries into Media and Mediation* (Chicago: University of Chicago Press, 2014).

38 Alexander Galloway, Eugene Thacker, and McKenzie Wark, 'Introduction: Execrable Media', in *Excommunication: Three Inquiries into Media and Mediation* (Chicago: University of Chicago Press, 2014), 10.

39 Ibid., 16.

40 Ibid., 10–11.

41 See Alexander Galloway, *Laruelle: Against the Digital* (Minneapolis: University of Minnesota Press, 2014).

instead of true statement about the communicative act. A proposition, writes Alfred North Whitehead, is neither true nor false in itself, but it is rather a lure for feeling the world differently, and its efficacy is determined by what it does, by what it makes possible to feel and think.[42] And it is in this spirit that I want to entertain how the insufficiency of communication, the fact that all communication also harbours its own impossibility, might function as an opportunity to think about the efficacy of geological myths today outside of a communicative framework.

To see what might be at stake here, it's worth looking to Isabelle Stengers' most recent work that centres on the problem of climate change and more specifically on how to fabricate responses to the threat the earth poses to human and nonhuman life.[43] Like many other theorists, she bemoans the faith that so many of us place in mathematical models and information technologies to answer questions that we pose to them about the history and transformation of the earth's surface environments. The threat that these technologies announce "has no face," Stengers writes; rather, scientists propose "a complex interrelated set of models and data" that are incapable of addressing themselves to the lives, experiences, and situated practices of those who are so dramatically affected by the changes on the earth's surface.[44] And yet Stengers insists that there can be no aggregation of perspectives, no collating or synthesizing of data points—from science and elsewhere—in order to forge a coherent, if always evolving, perspective on the whole.[45] And it is precisely insofar as geomytholgy—*qua* scientific discipline—finds itself embedded in this discursive and epistemic space of aggregation that it is captured by the very same abstractive operations as mathematical modelling.

What Stengers drives home for us is that the earth is *mute* concerning our requests for it to be understood, to our desperate pleas for it to manifest itself, to give itself over to comprehension, however partial and incomplete that givenness may be.[46] This is why she insists that the earth—named, Gaia—intrudes in our lives but it is indifferent to us and our requests, it does not offer an explanation for itself, nor does it prescribe

42 Alfred North Whitehead, *Process and Reality: Corrected Edition*, edited by D. R. Griffin and D. W. Sherburne (New York: Free Press, 1978 [1927–28]), 178.

43 See Isabelle Stengers, *In Catastrophic Times: Resisting the Coming Barbarism*, trans. by Andrew Goffey. (Open Humanities Press, 2015); and Isabelle Stengers, 'Gaia: The Urgency to Think (and Feel)'. Delivered in Rio de Janeiro, September 2014. Available at: https://osmilnomesdegaia.files.wordpress.com/2014/11/isabelle-stengers.pdf (Accessed December 2017).

44 See Stengers, 'Gaia: The Urgency to Think (and Feel)', 2.

45 See Stengers, *In Catastrophic Times* and Adam Nocek, 'On the Risk of Gaia for an Ecology of Practices', in *SubStance: A Review of Theory and Literary Criticism 146*. Vol. 47, no. 2 (2018).

46 Stengers: "their Gaia [the scientists'] is definitively mute for what concerns the answer to be given to the question she imposes on us. She has no unifying power other than to authorize sounding the alarm" (Stengers, 'Gaia: The Urgency to Think (and Feel)', 3).

a course of action or adequate response.[47] The earth is *given without given-ness,* as Laruelle would say. What is at stake in this hypothesis is that there actually is no possibility for sufficient communication with the earth's surface environments, every geocommunicative act always already harbours its own insufficiency, which is to say that the communicative act is haunted by the fact that no common ground has actually been forged, which is the very presumption of communicative acts as such.

What's so striking then about the geological myths featured in the field of geomythology is that anything that deters the narrative from communicating verifiable information about the earth's history is deemed to be a noisy interference. But what I want to suggest here, and in conversation with both Laruelle and Stengers, no matter how dissimilar their intellectual projects appear to be, is that the inverse of this is actually true: The efficacy of geological myths might actually lie in their capacity to bring their own situatedness and therefore insufficiency for communicating planetary processes into sharp focus. Those elements deemed to be *noisy* interferences to the science of geomythology, and therefore to modern science more generally, are actually the ingredients that resist providing a global or totalizing perspective on planetary phenomena. Mythic *noise* is what is most relevant.

In this view, geomythic communication always harbours its own insufficiency for communicating global climate transformations, the timescale of geological epochs, the emergence and fate of the 'Anthropocene', and so on. These myths are from somewhere, rooted in a specific historical and cultural milieu, and addressed to someone, instead of from nowhere and therefore capable of speaking on behalf of a planetary whole. Thus, any attempt to frame planetary events in mythic form is already an insufficient communication of the earth's processes.[48] They are stories catalysed *by* the earth, expressions and enactments of sense making that are produced out of humans engaging with and being shaped by the earth's transformations, but they are incapable of speaking on behalf *of* the earth. Perhaps then geomyths perform a non- or even post-communicative mediation of planetary phenomena? Finding the right media-mythic vocabulary will require much more fine-tuning, but the hope is that it would be able to flesh out how the post-communicative architectures of mythic media are capable of impacting us today.

---

47 Stengers writes that *Gaia is* "blind to the damage she causes" (Stengers, *In Catastrophic Times,* 43). Indeed, she is "indifferent to our reasons and our projects" (47), and she is "herself is not threatened unlike the considerable number of living species who will be swept away with unprecedented speed by the change in their milieu that is on the horizon" (46).

48 Please see *Dust and Shadow,* a design-research collaboration among FoAM (Earth), the Laboratory for Critical Technics (Arizona State University) and the Global Institute of Sustainability (Arizona State University), for an attempt to design mythic propositions for engaging the unacknowledged dimensions of urban desertification in the American southwest: https://fo.am/dust-and-shadow/

I want to end this chapter with a final thought concerning Stengers' own invocation of the Gaia myth. We might speculate that Stengers is already helping us to think through what geomyths might mean for us today as a part of genealogy of geocommunicative media. Stengers' Gaia is a myth explicitly fabricated in the midst of a historical and cultural milieu—it is constructed *par le milieu* in Gilles Deleuze's sense[49]—that no longer has the privilege of forgetting about the threat the earth poses to life and that has been thoroughly cleansed of the efficacy of myth for addressing this threat.[50] Her myth has no quasi-scientific pretension that aims to communicate verifiable facts about the interconnectedness of the earth's surface environments as James Lovelock's or Lynn Margulis' Gaia seems to.[51] Stengers' Gaia is a geofiction that is not beholden to the same communicative project. Rather, her wager, I'm almost tempted to suggest, is that this fiction is capable of communicating the impossibility of communication with the earth, and on this basis, ask whether and to what extent this provides the ground for a very different relation to the earth's surface environments, one that is attuned to what a mythic practice does, to what its effects are, instead of whether it has an appropriate signal-to-noise ratio.

My final provocation then is this: that Stengers, along with Laruelle, provide the ingredients for a *mytho-praxis* of geomythology. Such a mytho-praxis would determine the relevancy of a myth based on what it does, what it makes possible, how it transforms our sensibilities—it is a *doing*—and not whether it is conformal to a pre-existent model. Not only does such a mytho-praxis align with what Whitehead says about the proposition (that its relevancy is determined by what it does), and so leaves open the possibility that myths are *propositional media*, but it also opens up a very different genealogy for geomythology: one that places geomyth in an increasingly important lineage of practices (such as those imagined in *The Last Angel of History*) that are noisy interferences to the technics of geocommunication.

---

49 See Isabelle Stengers, 'Introductory Notes on an Ecology of Practices', in *Cultural Studies Review*, Vol. 11, no. 1 (2005).
50 See Stengers, *In Catastrophic Times*, 49.
51 Ibid., 47.

PHOTONIC COMMUNICATIONS
PHILIPPE MOREL

XVII

PHILIPPE MOREL is an architect and theorist, cofounder of EZCT Architecture and Design Research (2000) and more recently of the Large-scale 3D printing corporation XtreeE (2015, initiator and founding CEO). He is currently an Associate Professor at the ENSA Paris-Malaquais and the head of the Digital Knowledge department (http://dk-digital-knowledge.com/; cofounded with Pr. Christian Girard). He was in the past both an invited Research Cluster and MArch Diploma Unit Master at UCL Bartlett. Prior to the Bartlett he has taught at the Berlage Institute (Seminar and Studio) and at the AA (HTS Seminar and AADRL Studio). His long-lasting interest in the elaboration of a Theory of Computational Architecture is well expressed in his numerous essays, projects and lectures.

Photonics is the physical science of light (photon) generation, detection, and manipulation through emission, transmission, modulation, signal processing, switching, amplification, and detection/sensing. Though covering all light's technical applications over the whole spectrum, most photonic applications are in the range of visible and near-infrared light. The term photonics developed as an outgrowth of the first practical semiconductor light emitters invented in the early 1960s and optical fibres developed in the 1970s. [...] Photonics also relates to the emerging science of quantum information and quantum optics, in those cases where it employs photonic methods.[1]

Let me, first of all, clarify the title of this short essay which, beyond the obvious reference to a still relatively new field of scientific and technical research, refers to John McHale's famous diagram (fig. 1) published by R. Buckminster Fuller in 'World Design Science Decade: 1' (1963). This diagram accompanies Buckminster Fuller's recurring remark that all the great advances since the First World War have occurred in non-visible and non-audible frequency domains.[2] Although the Wikipedia definition states that "most photonic applications are in the visible range [of the light spectrum] and near-infrared light," what counts today is even more than for Buckminster Fuller, invisible and/or inaudible to our unenhanced senses, be it the Internet, wireless communications (WiFi etc.), war electronics and electromagnetic jamming devices, DNA or quantum computers.[3] We have entered the age of abstraction—in fact since the end of the nineteenth century—and beyond the few declarations of principle architecture has given it only minimal attention. The widespread use of scripting and the deployment of Parametricism (as a style and global ideology of contemporary architecture) have in fact led us to grasp some of the abstraction of our new reality but they do not make it possible to cover all manifestations of 'the invisible which governs the world' or, to use Buckminster Fuller's words, the invisible which governs (human) *technical affairs*.

1   https://en.wikipedia.org/wiki/Photonics. Last accessed on October 15, 2018.
2   "All major advances since World War I have been in the infra and the ultra-sensitive frequencies of the electromagnetic spectrum. All the important technical affairs of humanity today are invisible." From R. Buckminster Fuller, *Design in a Dynamic Technology*, Lecture held on 7–9 November 1967 at the State University of New York.
3   We can indeed say that "everything is invisible" in the sense that it is not the light as such that matters, and therefore its visibility in the phenomenological sense, related to the fact that only certain wavelengths are visible by humans, but light as a *vector of information*—a light incidentally taken here as a paradigm because we could as well choose non-audible sound waves, etc. But nobody "sees" the information in the strict sense, it can only be measured indirectly with the help of specific devices. It is therefore in this informational sense that we must understand here the general hypothesis of communication as invisibility and phenomenological transparency which, we will discuss further, will lead to a project of "semantic transparency" which aims, in fact, within the very "communicative transparency", to "find the visible" or at least the comprehensible.

Being itself a logical-mathematical and symbolic approach to design operations that goes far beyond the narrow confines of architecture, scripting represented a first step towards a concrete apprehension of the *algorithmic* nature of the world, therefore, in fact, of its *effective and calculable* part. Beyond a purely utilitarian use of algorithms that concerns us little here, the artists, architects, engineers, designers and various theorists have, through their multiple algorithmic approaches to design, most often returned, in a traditional manner, to the terms mentioned in the presentation of this book by Selena Savić, Michael Doyle and Vera Bühlmann, namely: *code, protocol, channels, data* and *information*. What has hitherto been called 'scripting' in architectural design corresponds to the interweaving of algorithms which are, by definition, deterministic, and whose strange results are in fact only the consequence of *our* sensory and computational limitations, which beyond a certain degree of complexity prevent *us* from predicting or foreseeing. When we succeed in predicting the result, for example when we use topological optimization algorithms for form, we foresee a *global result*, in part only and not in all the details, based on our knowledge (for example in the geometry of structures) and our acquired experience (for example having already been confronted with many topological optimization results with similar input parameters). The relative strangeness of the results is thus accompanied by a relative predictability of these same results, and the couple formed by these two elements (strangeness/predictability) exists against a phenomenological background; this without the knowledge that allows us to predict being limited to a phenomenological knowledge: An abstract and highly mathematized knowledge of the mechanics of structures is, for example, quite possible. So that which escapes our *unenhanced* senses or our natural calculation abilities is strange, to the extent that an *enhanced* human being would find the results provided by most current architectural design approaches perfectly predictable and 'traditional'. Examples of this situation are provided to us very regularly. All that is required is to look at the reactions of a novice faced with the formalism of contemporary architecture, a formalism which seems *to him* to be *extraordinarily strange*, and to compare these reactions with those of blasé designers to the morphologies referred to by his algorithms. Without dealing here with the romanticism that one could possibly associate with the search for the strange or the bizarre—an association which some do make and which leads them to honour again, but above all at little cost and with even less effort, a neo-rationalist formalism—to overcome the relative lack of strangeness that can be said to be intrinsic to the deterministic and calculable nature of classical algorithmics, many architects and designers have resorted to 'less deterministic' models that introduce randomness (real or not) into the actual calculation steps (for example evolutionary algorithms), or leave room for the emergence of an 'intelligence' resulting from the collaboration of a multitude of individuals who initially lack it (e.g. Particle Swarm Optimization), or both. In the first two cases, we are facing both sides of the same coin—and with the third case we are facing the three faces of the same die ... On the one hand, it is a question of *extending the domain of the* algorithmic' to natural phenomena that are difficult to compute (even with computing capacities far greater than those present) or simply impossible to compute (for example if they involve purely random physical phenomena), to bring them into the domain of the simulable: It is a usual phase of formalisation-mathematisation of nature. On the other hand, it is a question of naturalizing the algorithmic by showing that it is ultimately not so far removed from that which occurs spontaneously in nature. All with the following objectives: 1) to give the strangeness of nature and astonishment that it does not cease to produce the possibility of a sufficiently faithful replication in the artificial world, 2) to allow access from the algorithmic to complexity and vice versa, and 3) to also provide this algorithmic with a complementary *jus naturalis* dimension that removes it from the recurrent reproach of artificiality. In the first two cases (the third one is bordering on morality, it is not dealt with here) the results are *phenomenologically both emergent and predictable*. They are emergent because of the complexity of the phenomena dealt with and/or because of the introduction of randomness, which is real or not[4], and largely predictable when implementing knowledge which has been long understood, whose applications have been apprehended many times, and which, in any case, are implemented in a probabilistic framework that reduces the unpredictability of isolated elements to a relative overall predictability.

PARAMETRICISM

In terms of Parametricism, things are not fundamentally different. Technically, it makes use of what we have just mentioned and all the algorithms available. If, considering agents as social actors, it pushes the semiotisation of forms further than naturalistic approaches do, it is even limited by this to a coarser granularity, superior in several orders

---

4   Strictly speaking, randomness does not exist in a computer, it is only approached thanks to various algorithms of generations of (pseudo) random numbers. As for the emergence, which remains limited to the domain of deterministic chaos, it results above all from the extraordinary capacity of computers to calculate consequences on billions of billions of steps of computation (and time) of slightly changing initial conditions. If on a conceptual level the millions of possible pseudo-hazards do not form a pure randomness, on the phenomenological level they can reasonably be considered as an introduction of pure randomness.

of magnitude to those one can find in 'naturalistic' approaches referring to the different scales of natural phenomena (an ant, the microstructure of a bone, the mesh of a crystalline element, a molecule, an atom, etc.), and also superior in several orders of magnitude to pure approaches for which the algorithmic granularity potentially reaches each step of a computation. From the phenomenological and communicative point of view that it calls for itself, Parametricism aims at what I would call a '*homogenization of complexity*'. With it, complexity is not reduced to the mathematical universality of calculation *then* made visible in its 'raw' form (for example by the discretism of voxelization), nor is it limited to the structural or even 'structuralist' approach to naturalism. In fact, Parametricism brings all phenomena back to their informational and communicative nature, phenomena for which it seeks a *unique and unitary* form of expression. Nature is perceived as what it is, namely intrinsically multi-scale, but *in fine* it is always applied and '*smoothed' on the scale of human phenomena*, thus making Parametricism an *expressionist humanism*, also assumed by its creator.[5] Yet it is precisely this withdrawal of all forms of information and communication to a single *expressive* and even overtly *expressionist* communication which prevents it from expressing the non-expressive part of communication, an openly *post-human, massive, invisible* part, largely made possible by advances in photonics. In fact, this communication—more precisely this *communication of information*—is as invisible to our non-enhanced senses as are photons carrying information compared to the light we perceive naturally. The only *human communication* simply does not describe *communication*, the first is only an ever-smaller part of the second and even the mere *effect* of the second.

NOISE BEYOND COMPUTABILITY

Whether the algorithmic design is accompanied by a parametric or non-parametric 'overlay' aiming at filling the semantic/humanistic void of a Shannon approach to information/communication, its reductionist penchant remains present in nearly all practices. If the latter try to grasp the *totality* of the '*architectonics of communication*', they actually only capture part of it: The communications of which we know the context and for which we are capable of establishing a distribution law. By promoting certain forms of strangeness produced by various algorithmic practices, designers favour the *uncertain*, obviously containing more information than the known and/or predictable. *These designers*

---

5   We refer readers to the various conferences by Patrick Schumacher as well as the main works *The Autopoiesis of Architecture, Volume I: A Conceptual Framework for Architecture* (Chichester: John Wiley & Sons, 2011) and *The Autopoiesis of Architecture, Volume II: A New Agenda for Architecture* (Chicester: John Wiley & Sons, 2012).

assume that the quantity of information—therefore the amount of thought—communicated is directly proportional to the degree of strangeness reached.[6] Nevertheless, this approach has its limits: 1) By producing information massively and at the same time (valid in isolation), we give rise to a background noise that no human can interpret as a *carrier of information*. This is the problem of the strangeness of so-called 'subversive' art in a globalized world as much as Parametricism is used as 'protest formalism.'[7] The multiple subversions are indeed only *big data* for which the original meaning has long disappeared ... 2) By favouring the uncertain in the sense of 'a little strange' but not 'radical strangeness', the contemporary designers limit, for understandable reasons, their approaches to that which can be measured and computed, and thus to a form of *mathematical and semantic stability.* At an instant t of the progress of an algorithm (thus of a step-by-step calculation) or of a computer simulation, an element E represents, however, a Boolean variable, an agent, a beam, an abstract node of a graph or a physical assembly node of a structure, but at time $t+1$, this element E represents either *the same thing* (the most common case) or *another thing but of which we can predict the appearance.* Nobody imagines doing a simulation in which a variable would pass *perfectly unpredictably* from a numerical quantity to a human agent, or a beam, a doorknob, a shower curtain or whatever ... We could no longer really talk about 'variables' as the latter, not being definable, would simply not exist. The 'variable' would actually only be a simple random parameter ... *Radical strangeness* does not exist in a computer simulation for the simple reason that it only leads to the absurd. But in nature, for example with certain quantum phenomena, we encounter intrinsically random phenomena whose knowledge at an instant t tells us nothing of what it was at $t-1$, nor of what it will be at $t+1$. For all that, we are not only reluctant to qualify these phenomena as absurd, but we even try to understand them in order to deduce a meaning. In fact, a causality of the type 'if we have this at instant t it is because it occurred as a consequence of

6   This relationship between strangeness and information is reminiscent of the strategy theorized by Berthold Brecht under the term *Verfremdungseffekt* ("effect of strangeness") which aims, in his plays, to create a necessary distance at the critical reception between the work and the viewer. Nevertheless, although Brecht's modern theatre with its *"explanatory and interrogative realism"* was situated in a pre-information society, today we are evolving within an information society for which explanations no longer really exist ... To convince oneself of this, we need only look at the stream of unanalysed data that is created every second, or the effectiveness of artificial intelligence based on Deep Learning and for which there are no mathematical explanations or, at least, they come *after* the algorithmic deployment. Faced with the acceleration of the electronic media society, Marshall McLuhan said that *"if it works it's old-fashioned,"* we could say 50 years later that *"if we understand how—and why—it works, it's old-fashioned."* On B. Brecht, cf. *Notes on Mahagony, Writings on the Theatre,* 1930.

7   It is important to note that Patrik Schumacher avoids this pitfall and even this *contradiction* by claiming the "mainstream" dimension which must be that of parametricism.

GHOSTS OF TRANSPARENCY

t-1 according to a certain probability'. In doing so, we could quantify the phenomenon, transform it into positive knowledge and thus *exploit* it. In the words of David Hilbert and the famous epitaph of Göttingen, 'there is no ignorabimus', 'we must know, and we will know' (*Wir müssen wissen, Wir werden wissen*). This general desire to render computable what is non-computable or to quantify a mere manifestation to make it real information[8] illustrates in fact the positivism intrinsic[9] to all forms of contemporary design, including those that call at random for emergence, etc. In fact, each time it is necessary to find the causal links that will allow (all) the phenomena to enter a (large) '*architectonic of communication*' within which everything is reduced to a series of effective procedures (algorithmics).

This dream or at least this *project* is a sort of hunt for the '*phantom of transparency*' as expressed in the eponymous title of the book by Jean-Yves Girard[10] as in this publication. For J.-Y. Girard this 'hunt', under cover of objectivism and 'verismo' is only an ideology that he calls 'transparentism'. The latter "[...] is based on three subliminal slogans: We can answer everything, we can compare everything, we can predict everything."[11] But "the experience of knowledge teaches us that there is no Final Reality, that every train hides another. Evidence that it is not easy to accept, hence the idea of this ultimate train, the one that would hide nothing. Transparentism postulates the existence, beyond the immediate perception, of a world, a level of reading, completely intelligible, that is, explicit and immediate. Hence this belief in so-called 'X-rays of knowledge' that would unveil the other side of the universe." To understand, to master and in particular to instrumentalize at all times what we 'do not see'—in the phenomenological sense but also in the abstract sense—to 'make ourselves master and possessors of nature', no longer, as Francis Bacon invited us, to old hydraulic machines, or steam, etc., but thanks to the algorithms, it remains the only current large-scale project, whatever the approach: openly positivist, naturalist-biomimetic, symbiotic, etc. The world has become transparentist simply because of the massive use of algorithms, AI or big data, which no longer have meanings, strictly speaking, but only *correlations* that force (and forge) meanings. At the very moment

8   Knowing that such a life jacket is red would be of no use if we were not sure that five seconds later—just as certainly five seconds earlier—it will still be red, unless its colour is erased by sea water, etc. The stability of phenomena is simply what allows us to operate in the world.
9   About 12 years ago I called this positivism intrinsic to *all knowledge*, including that denouncing positivism, '*embedded positivism*'. Here I would therefore like to refer the reader to the original essay, *Embedded Positivism (or Everything is Theoretical)*, Haecceity Papers, Vol. 1 / issue 1 — "The End of Theory?", Fall 2005.
10 Jean-Yves Girard, *Le Fantôme de la transparence*, (Paris: Éditions Allia, 2016).
11 Ibid., 49.

when paradoxically—but apparently only—individuals constantly denounce ambient opacity (financial arrangements, the stock market, algorithms, deep learning, etc.) ... Indeed, to produce *mechanically*—i.e. *algorithmically*—from opacity, it was previously necessary to know and master a certain number of 'laws of nature' to concretely launch into the pursuit of the 'ghosts of transparency'. Asking society for more transparency is a paradox that is not really a paradox, since this same society is far more transparentist than the most radical dream of transparency ideologues ... It does not need a global project, a politician or theorist but only the accumulation of tens or hundreds of millions of individual scientific research, multiplied today by the phenomenal computing power as by the "unreasonable efficiency of artificial intelligence."[12] There is no longer any need for the moral imperative of D. Hilbert ('we must know') to affirm that 'we will know'. And even if we never know it, it will have no consequence on the nature of a society which will behave on every occasion *as if* it knew or as if it were going to know. If for almost all individuals of the pre-computational era the world was opaque as it was mostly unknown, for most inhabitants of the computational era the world is opaque because it is mainly *known*. At the same time, it is transparent *and* opaque: conceptually transparent and phenomenologically opaque, the exact opposite of what has always been until us.[13]

What can this imply from the design point of view? *Indirectly*, being aware of the double transparent/opaque nature of our future environments[14] will distance us as much from the 'desire for meaning'—the

12 I refer here, evidently, to the essay by physicist Eugene Wigner ('The Unreasonable Effectiveness of Mathematics in the Natural Sciences. Richard Courant Lecture in Mathematical Sciences Delivered at New York University, May 11, 1959', *Communications on Pure and Applied Mathematics*, 13.1 (1960), 1–14), which observes that the structural descriptions of mathematics apply to a number of physical phenomena that lie outside the framework for which these descriptions had been established, "*beyond any reasonable explanation.*" It seems to me that we can say the same about artificial intelligence especially when, unlike the mathematics mentioned by Wigner, we do not even fully understand "why it works."

13 The primitives see the "same" stars as us but do not see the same concept ... They do not see the same stars.

14 Without doubt these environments will be (they are already) those of multiple "logical (re)constructions of the world," environments produced by computer simulations which testify to the entry into the expansionist phase of the "science of computation"—that of the pancomputationalism—which follows its reductionist phase—from the origins to Turing and, on the philosophical plane to the logical positivism including that of Rudolf Carnap. Of all the scientists and thinkers who have directly taken part in the work that led to IT and computers as we know them today, it is Charles Babbage who has best understood the exceptional power that the "Science of calculation" would deliver in the future, in all fields of knowledge, theoretically and practically, and without exception. He understood, better than anyone, that the reductionism that would culminate in the *universal* Turing Machine could only logically be accompanied by an expansionist phase linked to the widespread and universal application of calculation *over the whole of the existing world.*

semantic, holistic, and transparentist research of Parametricism—as from the anti-scientific rejection of transparentism—this time because of scientism[15]. *Directly*, this consciousness invites us to introduce into the design an extended vision of information, not only as probable knowledge (by analogy with Shannon's information theory) but also as 'non-knowledge', as an irreducibility of real complexity (by analogy with the algorithmic theory of information). Then conceptual and formal horizons open up that go beyond most 'traditional' problems such as optimizations, whether or not they are bio-inspired or topological, now too little to express the nature of the world present or to enrich it.

15   J.-Y. Girard's critique of transparentism is based on the fact that this transparentism is intrinsically scientistic. It is therefore in no way an anti-scientific or anti-rationalist critique. Nevertheless, and unfortunately, it must be recognized that in most cases the critiques of scientism are in reality antirationalist critiques of science, and therefore scientistic critiques themselves.

SOFTNESS, HARDNESS: CONTEMPLATING ARCHITECTONIC CIRCUITS OF MEDIACY AND IMMEDIACY
MICHAEL R. DOYLE

XVIII

MICHAEL R. DOYLE is an assistant professor at the Université Laval School of Architecture since January 2019. He was previously a guest lecturer and research assistant at the Department for Architecture Theory and Philosophy of Technics (ATTP) at the TU Vienna. He holds a PhD in Architecture and the Sciences of the City from the École polytechnique fédérale de Lausanne (EPFL) and a master's (M.Arch.) and master's in science of architecture (M.Sc.Arch) from Université Laval. His research interests revolve around novel ways to think the milieu in architecture and urbanism, computational techniques of abstraction in the production of architectural artefacts and the articulations of mediacy and immediacy in perception and action in the built environment.

Limitless opportunities for applying the new control sophistication will appear, once we recognize as obsolescent the old economic pressures which reduce people to that average required by a rigid external environment—once hard architecture begins to be replaced by soft (Brodey 1967, *Soft Architecture*, p. 12).[1]

I believe that the 'softs' are an important vehicle to responsiveness, but they must be studied with great caution. In the same way that I refute computer graphics' proliferating Gaudiesque architecture, I worry about the obvious materials of 'responsive architecture' foisting a soft-Soleri, or globular, mushy architecture. Not everybody wants to live in a balloon (Negroponte 1975, *Soft Architecture Machines*, p. 147).[2]

Ironically, the development of man-environment studies, at least in their early days, led to an even greater neglect. The attempt to be 'scientific,' to apply positivistic approaches, led to a neglect of the fuzzy, 'soft' aspects of the environment such as meaning (Rapoport 1990, *The Meaning of the Built Environment*, p. 19).[3]

To keep things simple, we can describe opportunities for experience from two extremes. One extreme is the street with a 'soft edge' with shops lined up, transparent façades, large windows, many openings and goods on display. Here there is much to see and touch, providing many good reasons to slow down or even stop. The other extreme, the street with a 'hard edge,' is a diametrical contrast: the ground floors are closed and the pedestrian walks past long sections of façades of black glass, concrete or masonry. There are few or no doors and all in all little to experience or even reason to choose that particular street, short of necessity (Gehl, 2010, *Cities for People*, p. 79).[4]

[T]he terms soft and hard identify several tensions in the field of architecture: between indeterminate and determinate approaches; between the possibility for users to adapt space according to their needs and the designer determining use over time; between flexibility in the hands of the users and the provision of flexibility, only on the architect's terms; between designing in redundancy and slack space and tight-fit functionalism (Schneider 2011, *Discard an Axiom*, p. 100).[5]

1 Warren M. Brodey, 'The Design of Intelligent Environments: Soft Architecture', *Landscape*, 1967, 8–12.
2 Nicholas Negroponte, *Soft Architecture Machines* (Cambridge, Mass: The MIT Press, 1975).
3 Amos Rapoport, *The Meaning of the Built Environment: A Nonverbal Communication Approach* (Tucson: University of Arizona Press, 1990).
4 Jan Gehl, *Cities for People* (Washington, DC: Island Press, 2010).
5 Tatjana Schneider, 'Discard an Axiom', in *Transdisciplinary Knowledge Production in Architecture and Urbanism*, ed. by Isabelle Doucet and Nel Janssens (Dordrecht: Springer Netherlands, 2011), 97–115 <https://doi.org/10.1007/978-94-007-0104-5_7>.

Architecture and urbanism tend to employ the terms 'soft' and 'hard' in order to establish distinctions with regard to expressions of materiality, authority and autonomy. They tend to separate and classify gestures of 'joining', mapping them to binaries such as 'bottom up' and 'top down', 'indeterminacy' and 'determinacy', 'flexibility' and 'rigidity'. Explicitly or implicitly, the architectonics of the 'hard' finds itself subjected to "old economic pressures" and to a "rigid environment" (Brody), to "positivistic approaches" (Rapoport), to "determinacy" and to a "tight-fit functionalism" (Schneider). The 'soft' is associated with "new control sophistication" (Brody), "responsiveness" (Negroponte), to the meaningful (Rapoport), to that which can be directly experienced (Gehl) and concerns that which finds itself "in the hands of the users" (Schneider).

Such an opposition appears to mirror that of the sciences and the humanities and seems to fuel debates on the primacy of experience over reason, immediacy over mediacy, perception over understanding and everyday language over mathematics.[6] One could question whether characterizing the 'soft' and 'hard' in such a way only serves to perpetuate a prejudice pitting the real against the imaginary, for which theory and the metaphysical are perceived as imposing a veil in front of the real, forming a barrier to the authentic truth of experience.[7] In the end, forms of symbolization, like writing and mathematics, are regarded with suspicion or accused of exacerbating the distance between the individual and his or her sensory experience. In this essay, I contemplate this distinction as an architect and researcher socialized in this tradition. I will try to examine the soft-hard distinction in a fashion orthogonal to that of the dualisms mentioned above. It will specifically pick up on how they appear in the work of French philosopher Michel Serres, whose work is committed to breaking down the barriers between reason and experience.

MUTUAL IMPLICATIONS OF SOFTNESS AND HARDNESS

Serres' account of the 'soft' and the 'hard' addresses the two with regard to scales of energy and instruments of measurement. The 'soft' concerns any order that can be deciphered using a particular measuring device. The 'hard' is on the side of that which acts as background noise, or a channel upon which measuring devices, techniques of discretization, may act. The soft always implicates the hard and the hard always implicates the soft. The physical concept of mass is mathematical, enfolding both the soft (on the side of generic orders that hide within it) and the hard (the physical matter that natural processes have ordered and

6   C. Snow, *The Two Cultures*, Canto Classics (New York: Cambridge University Press, 2012); Michel Serres and Bruno Latour, *Eclaircissements: Cinq Entretiens Avec Bruno Latour* (Paris: F. Bourin, 1992).
7   Gilles Dowek, *Ces préjugés qui nous encombrent* (Paris: Le Pommier, 2009).

informed). The genetic code of living organisms is an example of the softness of life itself, which organizes a hard that is always already coded (having always a 'softness'), the imperfect deciphering and decoding of which leads to the mutations we can observe at various temporal scales.

The mutual implication of the soft and the hard suggests that one is always accompanied by the other. Before meaning is born, mass already has direction, has 'sense'. To reason the world is in part to code it, to generate information and to be plunged into the experience of this reasoning. Of course, the world about which one reasons is not a passive mass, a tabula rasa upon which reason imprints itself, towards which the 'soft' directs its 'hardness'. Rather, as Serres puts it, "there is meaning [sens] in space before the meaning [sens] that signifies."[8] There is a softness to the hard. In *Hominescence*, Serres seems to offer a fourfold setup for dealing with this mutual implication: the softness of the soft [*le doux du doux*], the softness of the hard [*le doux du dur*], the hardness of the soft [*le dur du doux*] and the hardness of the hard [*le dur du dur*].[9]

To say that there is a softness to the soft suggests that codes carry latent orders, that they can themselves be symbolized further. If Serres equates this with a certain angelic form of communication, it is because the softness of the soft is more like the prepositions in the French language, like fleeting messengers that are neither substance (nouns) nor actions (verbs).[10] The scale of energy they operate on is relatively low. The 'softness of the hard' recognizes that mass is mathematical, that there is something always already written on the tabula rasa. The genetic code is one way of looking at the softness of the hardness of the physical organism as this latter energetically acts to stay alive while reproducing itself—coding and decoding (processing and storing) while receiving and emitting.

As Léon Brillouin demonstrated mathematically, a message without noise would require an infinite amount of energy.[11] This hardness of the soft suggests that orders are always articulated with regard to a background noise or material upon which symbolization can be foregrounded by an instrument of observation. The call for the purity of the soft feigns an innocence that forgets the energetic nature of the message in transit. To establish social orders, to set up devices of discretization (policies of 'sorting'), is never innocent and operates energetically on various levels. Raising one's voice against these mechanisms of ordering is not passive, but channels energy, gives that energy a sense/direction, sets up the possibility of engendering meanings that challenge the codes and their mechanics of operation.

8   Michel Serres, *Rome: The First Book of Foundations*, trans. R. Burks (London: Bloomsbury Academic, 2015 [1974]).
9   Michel Serres, *Hominescence* (Paris: Pommier, 2001).
10 Michel Serres, *La légende des anges* (Paris: Flammarion, 2009).
11 Léon Brillouin, *Science and Information Theory*, (Mineola, NY: Dover Publications 2013 [1962]).

Even if the hard always implicates the soft, its hardness comprises a potency for the production of channels upon which new symbols can ride. If the breath necessary for language becomes vowel and consonant through bodily articulations, this latter must respond energetically to that which the breath's hardness is capable (often combining complimentary bodily movements to economically use the energy necessary to keep the breath flowing). The hardness of the hard is this potency: an energetic potential.

Serres undoubtedly sees a promise in a prominence of 'softness' that can be observed today in information technology and in the proliferation of techniques of symbolization.[12] Unlike the technologies inherited from the Industrial Revolution, for which the movement of messages operates on large energetic scales (of steam engines and fossil fuels), in the context of the 'digital revolution', messages travel at faster speeds and at lower energetic scales—not only thanks to semiconductor technology but also to the growth and penetration of the Internet and satellite technology, of what Serres has referred to as 'world objects' [des objets-monde].[13] Logical systems, founded upon tradition or convention, lose their hold in a world where people can code themselves, saturate their identity with varying degrees of affiliation different from those based on geographical proximity or kinship and family. Individuals can learn to cultivate their identity through techniques of differentiation ('I am not like the others') and dedifferentiation ('I share something with the others').[14]

BIFURCATION, BIAS:
THE SOFTNESS AND HARDNESS OF DATA THAT IS 'MASSIVE'

This conception of the soft and hard inspires me to organize my thoughts around 'data' and 'information', which are important terms for both those who are technically-inclined and technically-averse among my peers. Like the physical concept of mass (in French, 'big data' is even sometimes translated as 'données massives'), data has a softness and a hardness. The distinction between data and information is not perfectly immediate but mediated by a cipher—a mathematical formalization—and a dexterity—an application of that formalization to a 'given' that is, itself, also dually hidden.[15] If we were to settle for the idea that data constitutes 'the hard' while information is 'the soft', we

---

12   Michel Serres, *Darwin, Bonaparte et le Samaritain: une philosophie de l'histoire* (Paris: Pommier, 2016).

13   Michel Serres, *Le contrat naturel* (Paris: Flammarion, 2009).

14   For a development on differentiation and de-differentiation, on the human body, see Michel Serres, *Genèse* (Paris: B. Grasset, 1982); Michel Serres, *Variations Sur Le Corps* (Paris: Pommier-Fayard, 1999); in nature, see Michel Serres, *L'incandescent* (Paris: Editions le Pommier: Diffusion Harmonia Mundi, 2003).

15   Michel Serres, *La Naissance de La Physique Dans Le Texte de Lucrèce: Fleuves et Turbulences*, Collection Critique (Paris: Éditions de Minuit, 1977).

would lose the fourfold setup. All data has informational content; it has been 'informed' by the double articulation of a code, a 'softness', and its application to prior data, to 'previously given givens', a 'hardness'. Data is thereby both explicit and implicit, constative and performative.[16]

Some are quick to cry out that data is biased. If we want, however, to distance ourselves from the accusatory nature of such a statement, to be 'biased' means to be inclined or at an angle. It means to have a direction—there is softness to hardness. This is true of any data like it is true of any information decipherable from it. To order, to negate entropy (to render it negentropic, or informational) requires differentiating, inclining, giving angularity to noise. It is an act of differentiating figures from grounds. Without 'bias', such differentiation would not be possible. There would be nothing discrete in the continuous.

What is at stake today seems to be related less to these statements about data and information than to the nature of the processes by which softness and hardness are mutually implicated. And this is of course of importance, because these processes channel different intensities of energy, which have 'material' consequences. Communicational circuits parasitize data, decoding and recoding. In a linear conception of time, one can think of this parasitizing as bifurcating the data, addressing it as continuous and then discretizing it sequentially—like the act of speech, to pick up an earlier example. The mouth modulates a continuous breath (the air itself as data) of varying intensities that it discretizes with the lips and teeth, forming the consonants. What the sender receives must be decoded by listening, excluding the noise (the breath itself as well as modulations that are slightly 'angled' such as in regional accents) and extracting only the linguistic elements in the patterns of their occurrence. Such linguistic elements are received in the frequency domain, in a time that is cyclical. These two domains are orthogonal to each other—they cannot be brought into perfect correlation.[17] This is why it is difficult to affirm the very possibility of a perfect transmission between sender and receiver. The receiver does not merely record word-for-word what is received, but translates the datum received in time to an informational network of connections. The coding of the received information in this way takes the datum out of time into a frequency domain in which one can quasi-objectively interpret or make sense of that which is deemed as informational.[18]

16 Jean-Yves Girard, *Le Fantôme de La Transparence* (Paris: Éditions Allia, 2016).
17 The Fourier transformation translates between the time and frequency domain, for more on this in computer science, see Vahid Moosavi, 'Pre-Specific Modeling: Computational Machines in a Coexistence with Concrete Universals and Data Streams', in *Metalithikum IV, Coding as Literacy*, ed. by Vera Bühlmann, Ludger Hovestadt, and Vahid Moosavi (Basel: Birkhäuser, 2015), 132–66.
18 On the quasi-object and its relationship to parasitism, see Michel Serres, *Le Parasite* (Paris: B. Grasset, 1980).

GHOSTS OF TRANSPARENCY

The architectural project also deals with articulating 'softness' and 'hardness' as it encounters and produces data and information. The challenge, as I see it, is that we often begin with 'a lot' and must learn to reason this 'lot' without being able to properly experience it, as we are faced not only with the materiality of the site, of the potential building materials, but also building codes, actual or potential clients and users, larger problematics like sustainability or urban sprawl and the relevant or intriguing things that we pull in from other disciplines or our own intellectual interests.

What I observe as I reflect upon the design project in architectural education is the result of this dichotomous, mutually exclusive treatment of the soft and the hard. It is as if the project is to begin with the 'soft' and then turn to the 'hard'—we can decide what to do in the most economical way only after we have gathered as much 'relevant' information as possible from the 'available' data. The disciplinary side of architectural education offers (if not imposes) various analytical methods, from site and precedent analysis (in their social or material aspects) to the study of the interests of stakeholders, sometimes even bringing these latter in as part of the production of the design brief. These methods are strategies of discretization, but ones that operate with predefined classifications and systematizations, often within the normative (methodological) constraints of the social or natural sciences from which they are borrowed. They imply logical systems or semantic ontologies, often grounded in convention and tradition and some of which are disciplines in their own right (typology, morphology, ecology, sociology, anthropology, etc.).

The performativity of these methods makes them attractive, because they seem to guarantee an objective overview from which one can best identify what is to be done. If the 'hard' is treated as the material reality of the project (as the citation from Jan Gehl seems to suggest), then these methods promise to lift the veil behind which meaning is hidden. To argue for a close proximity to meaning and to the soft (against 'positivistic approaches' as Rapoport seems to suggest) is to look warily upon the type of mediacy offered by mathematics, theory and technology, by the symbolisms that make abstract reasoning possible, but that tend to precisely move us away from the immediacy of the meaningful.[19] I think we can also read in a similar manner the wariness

---

19   As Gilles Dowek puts it, 'les théories et les formules font écran entre le sujet et le réel: ils ne voient plus le réel, ils ne voient plus que la formule qui le représente, mais qui, en le représentant, le trahit' Dowek, 36.

of architects for digital techniques of conception that produce forms that appear disconnected from anything known or experienced, that seem to come more from theoretical or mathematical abstractions than from 'meaning' (Negroponte: 'not everyone wants to live in a balloon'). It is perhaps this wariness that also drives us to ask of our digital tools the same explicitness as analytical methods. If the semantic ontologies of the social sciences promise openness and transparency, does the turn towards Building Information Management ('BIM') or parametric set-ups based on systems theory feign a similar 'honesty' that sheds all veils between the 'soft' and the 'hard'?

The fourfold setup I read in Serres' thinking on the soft and hard offers a way to address the soft and hard as mutually implicated and in terms of 'softness' and 'hardness', always in mixtures and never in a pure form. The logical system is thereby not the best figure for thinking architecture as an art of joining, for in such a semantic ontology, the elements and their relationships are already given. If joining is an art, an *ars*, then it is also a craft whose implicit practices of joining are precluded by logic. A more appropriate figure is the circuit or semiconductor where electrical currents pass, where the soft and hard flow in mutual implication (energetically and informationally). These circuits are not mechanical or thermodynamic systems, because they are informational and can incorporate any code and accommodate various energetic intensities.

What is our own agency in such a circuit? Who are we as architects if we are to be someone other than what a logical system would tell us to be? When picking up a method of analysis as objective and transparent can we do anything other than serve its authority, or speak, criticize and administrate in its name? When employing a method (or perhaps, more abstractly, an algorithm) and challenging its authority with our own, doping it with softness and hardness in a circuitous fashion, with sophistication and cunning, how can we learn to speak as a political individual who cannot claim a natural right to be heard? I would like to think that we are to act less like an administrator or a royal figure than as a joker or a harlequin whose position is not attributed by a logical system but negotiated within circuits of mediacy and immediacy.

SOFTNESS AND HARDNESS: DOPING IN AN ART OF JOINING

Architecture as an 'art of joining' is more than design, more than problem-solving[20]: It is an inventive act of placing into communication that which otherwise would not resonate, not have a logical common ground.

---

20   Anne Meyer, *The Art of Joining: Designing the Universal Connector.*, ed. by Stiftung Bauhaus Dessau (Leipzig: Spector Books, 2019).

It is about articulations of softness and hardness and of the instruments by which such articulations can be inventive. Through doping, by adding 'more', such articulations pick up contingency, require cunning. This understanding of the mutual implication of the soft and the hard sheds new light on that which the 'soft' and 'hard' tend to stand for and permits us to read differently, and at a higher level of abstraction, the quotations selected from architecture and urban theory presented at the beginning of this chapter. Their statements pick up implicitly or explicitly narratives of alienation and emancipation: The 'soft' has been neglected in favour of the 'hard', but there is a way out that has implications for planning and architecture. 'Soft architecture' is more flexible, more easily adaptable, responsive (Brody), which risks (according to Negroponte) in becoming literally 'soft' to the eye (formalistically) or the body (materially). To argue for the 'soft' is to call for a return to 'the meaningful' (Rapoport), to 'the indeterminate' to 'the user' (Schneider) or to 'fuzzy boundaries' (Gehl).

If we take the hard and the soft out of the ontological fixity that such oppositions imply, addressing them instead as mutually implicated and as ciphered (rather than logically determined), the stakes for architecture and urbanism do not look the same. I would like to think that it allows us to see the architectonic artefact as the result of a projection from an arbitrary (but 'designed') set of elements whose joining is an inventive craftiness (an art; an *ars*) of an architect. The mutual implication of the softness and hardness implies a certain statuesque autonomy of the artefact while at the same time being authored by a human intelligence. The artefact cannot transparently speak of its origin, but neither can its author. The artefact has a softness and a hardness and part of their implication remains veiled and ciphered. Its meaning must be continually generated, translated: a circuit where the softness of its hardness is made soft again while maintaining a hardness.

From this perspective, what seems to be at stake in stories of alienation and emancipation is the potential exclusion of the human intellect from the performances that give birth to and keep 'meaning' alive. The risk that one 'bias' will become implicitly adopted or explicitly codified and that all energy (human or otherwise) will be devoted to ensuring that everything is clear, understandable, irrefutable and accessible to all. The elements and the alphabets would have to be settled, banks of words limited, sets of vocabulary closed.[21] The only freedom would become combinatorial and eventually the relationships between the elements would become codified for the sake of efficiency, optimization or consensus. Certain 'readings' would be able to be claimed to be wrong because authority would have been granted to one logical system (whether from

21 Ivan Illich, *ABC: The Alphabetization of the Popular Mind*, trans. by Barry Sanders (San Francisco: North Point Press, 1988).

the 'bottom' or the 'top'). To maintain the stability of such an authority would require the softness to have a hardness, mobilizing the levels of energy necessary to prevent unwanted deviations, to precisely avoid the type of importations that would change the accepted meanings.

The paradox here is that embracing a 'softness' that operates on a planetary scale today means the ability to distance oneself from the mundane—and precisely the opposite of what the proponents of a triumphal return to the soft would be arguing for. To address the softness and hardness within a circuit of mediacy and immediacy calls for contemplation in higher levels of abstraction. To be able to artfully join the disparate and the dissimilar means inventing a space in which none of the elements are native, in which none has a greater (and certainly not a logical) claim: A space that, like a semiconductor, is 'doped' such that the relations between the elements can be redefined. Where 'softness' and 'hardness' are kept in play. A space where the elements begin to lose their distinctions; a space that dedifferentiates. Where an individual becomes a person (a political *persona*), who can stand up and say something that has never been heard before about the very things that seem to have been taken for granted. I wonder what it would look like to learn to reason around this circuit of softness and hardness, to dope the proximate with the distant, immediacy with mediacy, transparency with opacity.

EXCERPTS FROM CHRONICLES OF THE DIGITAL

XIX

GILLES DOWEK

TRANSLATED BY SELENA SAVIĆ AND MICHAEL DOYLE

GILLES DOWEK is a researcher at INRIA (Institut National de Recherche en Informatique et en Automatique) and a professor of computer science at the ENS Paris-Saclay. He is interested in the formalization of mathematics, in proof processing systems, in physics of computation, in the safety of aerospace systems, and in the epistemology and ethics of informatics. He is also interested in education, insisting on the importance of introducing computer science in K-12. He has held the position of Deputy Scientific Director of Inria in charge of the domain Algorithmic, Programming, Software and Architectures. He had also been a consultant for the National Institute of Aerospace, a lab of the NASA Langley research center. He received the Grand prix d'Alembert des Lycéens from the French Mathematics Society in 2000. The Académie française has awarded him the Grand Prix de Philosophie in 2007, for his book *Les métamorphoses du calcul, une étonnante histoire de mathématiques*. He tries to popularize science with books, videos, a monthly column in Pour la Science.

The following are a selection of short texts composed by Gilles Dowek for the French magazine Pour la science, *several of which have since been published in* Vivre, aimer, voter en ligne: et autres chroniques du numérique *(Le Pommier, 2017). They are reproduced here for the first time in English.*

IDENTITIES AND IDENTIFIERS: CIVIL STATUS WITHOUT THE STATE[1]

In order to use an online service—an email, a social network, a store—we need an 'identifier', which distinguishes us from other users of the service. Often, we choose this name ourselves, from those that are not already taken.

But we do not have the same freedom when we choose, for example, an electronic mail address, because there is no central database containing all the addresses already in use. Providers of email services use a more complex technique, which skilfully articulates centralization and decentralization: Each country chooses first an identifier, for example 'fr' for France, under the control of a global authority that makes sure there is no duplication; in each country, each provider then chooses an identifier— 'pourlascience', 'orange', etc.—under the control of a national authority; finally, each user chooses their identifier under the control of the service provider. Each user is thus distinguished by the triplet: user@provider.country.

The technique is not new: Telephone numbers have always been attributed using a similar method. Even if we sometimes want to use different names on different services, certain services like messaging ask us to reuse an identifier such as our telephone number, which we already use as our user name elsewhere. Thus, these identifiers go beyond the scope of a particular service. They truly become 'names'. The techniques of identifier attribution thereby belong to a long tradition of anthroponomy, which permits groups of people to designate a different name to each of their members. In the Middle Ages, for example, each village attributed a name—Jeanne, Arthur, etc.—to a person at birth, without concern for whether there was already another 'Arthur' in the neighbouring village, with which they had little contact. But as the size of the groups grew, it became necessary to add a surname to this name in order to avoid homonymies. The surname, at the end of the Middle Ages, became hereditary: a 'family name'. This technique, which is only one of the numerous techniques used around the world, did not guarantee the absence of homonymy: Distant relatives, who had the same last name, could receive the same first name at birth. We have since invented

1   Originally appeared as Gilles Dowek, 'Internaute, Quel Est Ton Nom?', *Pour La Science*, 20 December 2017 <https://www.pourlascience.fr/sd/informatique/internaute-quel-est-ton-nom-10005.php#> [accessed 19 October 2018].

other techniques that are less prone to homonymy: for example, the registration number in the directory of the INSEE [the French National Institute of Statistics and Economic Studies]. In theory, seven-letter words would be sufficient to distinguish between all humans. But, in the global village, no single one of these techniques functions: Pairs of last and first names are too numerous, numbers from the INSEE directory are only used in France; adjoining the date and place of birth to the first and last name creates names that are too long; assigning a name of seven letters to each newborn requires a central authority, etc. Electronic addresses and telephone numbers are thus the only names that guarantee the absence of homonymy. Because of this, they tend to become, little by little, our civil status. These 'names' bring several novelties: We often choose them ourselves; we can have more than one; we can change them a number of times during our lifetime; they do not outlive us and the State plays no role in their attribution. Thus, administrations, insufficiently computerized and internationalized, seem to no longer go to the trouble of giving us names.

LIVING ON THE NETWORK: BEYOND LOCAL AND GLOBAL[2]

The photons circulating through fibre optic cables and carrying our ideas, our opinions, and so forth, do not stop at borders to present their documents. Even if the Internet is global, however, our values and laws are local. What is allowed in one country is not necessarily allowed elsewhere.

Even when the values are the same in two different countries, their relative importance is often perceived differently. In France as well as in the United States, freedom of expression is cherished and crimes against humanity are despised. But when these values clash, the dilemma is resolved differently: in favour of the condemnation of the advocacy of crimes against humanity in France, in favour of freedom of expression in the United States. Wearing a Nazi uniform is thereby condemned by the French penalty law but protected by the First Amendment of the American Constitution.

When such an event happens on the Web, which is not situated in any particular country, it is not easy to know which law to apply. In the early 2000s, a lawsuit set the International League against Racism and Antisemitism against the web site Yahoo! on which Nazi objects were being sold. The suit started in France in 2000 and came to a close in the United States in 2004. It led to a decision by an American court recognizing that France had the right to forbid the sales of an object on its territory and that Yahoo!, being active in that country, needed to respect French laws.

2   Originally appeared as Gilles Dowek, 'Cohabiter Sur Le Réseau: Un Défi', *Pour La Science*, 31 January 2018 <https://www.pourlascience.fr/sd/informatique/cohabiter-sur-le-reseau-un-defi-10067.php#> [accessed 19 October 2018].

Beyond this particular case, it is a fact that the network puts us in contact with persons whose culture, values and laws are different. How can we organize ways to live together?

One way would be to rely on the fact that, as people are getting closer by means of the network, their values will also become closer. Thus, the abolition of the death penalty or the respect of the rights of minorities are values promoted by global movements, which ignore regional particularities. The emergence of these common values may encourage us to write them into universal laws and to imagine international tribunals in charge of respecting them. Numerous intergovernmental structures dedicated, for example, to health, work, or atomic energy, already function in this way.

However, even if such institutions emerged, cultural differences would most likely persist, and, like in Molière's Tartuffe, seeing Dorine's breast will continue to bring to mind shameful thoughts to some and to others not. One other way to organize this life together is for everyone to take one step in the direction of the other. This would mean, for Dorine, to cover a part of her breast and for Tartuffe, to suffer the view of the other that is not covered, because they both know that this semi-effort is the condition for their peaceful cohabitation.

Either way, we have to learn to judge an action not in a system of values that are considered absolute, but simultaneously in several systems, searching not to reach a perfect judgement but an acceptable compromise.

Thinking differently is not impossible: Take the example of the geometers from the 19th century who learned to reason simultaneously in Euclidean and Non-Euclidean geometries. The possibility that, because of the network, we might adopt such an attitude is without doubt moral progress—something we should all be happy about.

SHANNON VS. TURING: THE PROPORTIONAL CONSEQUENCES OF ERROR[3]

Among the first *Homo sapiens informaticus*, certain figures, such as Norbert Wiener, Claude Shannon and Alan Turing, have built conceptual frameworks in which we still think computer science today. But even though they were contemporaries, these theoreticians have based their reflections on very different ideas: that of control—which gave the word 'cybernetic'—for Wiener, that of communication for Shannon, and that of a calculating machine for Turing. This diversity makes the intellectual history of this period hard to comprehend.

If, some decades later, Turing's mode of thought imposed itself on our computerized world, the ideas of Wiener and Shannon are still

---

3   Originally appeared as Gilles Dowek, 'L'erreur selon Shannon et Turing', in *Vivre, aimer, voter en ligne: et autres chroniques numériques* (Paris: Le Pommier, 2017), 172–75.

present in certain branches of computer science such as those dealing with networks or robotics.

The difference between the approaches of Shannon and Turing can be illustrated by the status of the notion of error in their work. One essential contribution of Shannon concerns the transmission of a message over a channel, such as a telephone line. These messages are discrete: finite successions of symbols chosen from a finite alphabet. But, for Shannon, the discrete character of these messages does not protect them from deformations in their transmission. These errors are inevitable, but they can be statistically corrected, and they are not catastrophic, as long as they are limited. We tolerate small errors in numerous everyday situations. For example, while making a tiramisu, if we do not put 100 but 120 grams of sugar, it might be too sweet but still a tiramisu. There is very little risk that this error will transform it into a panna cotta. It is therefore not surprising that Shannon used the theory of probability to define methods for error-correction. It is not surprising either that those who pursued his work on correction and compression of messages have devised algorithms of compression 'with loss', which introduced small errors into messages—for example a few pixels in an image, invisible to the naked eye—in order to compress more. Following Shannon, specialists of Big Data analysis teach us today that some errors in the data set, provided that they are few, have a statistically limited impact.

Turing's view is very different because, for him, the fact that machines treat discrete information makes errors avoidable. But, if it is not avoided, a small error can have enormous consequences. Statistics and probabilities are in such a case of very little help. Again, we know that a small error can have disproportionate consequences in numerous everyday situations. For example, if someone is giving us directions for the way to go from one city to another — 'take the highway towards the north, drive 100 km, get off the highway, etc.'—a small error in these directions, for example the substitution of the word 'north' by 'south' can take us very far from our destination. Likewise, on the 15th of January 1990, half of the subscribers of an American telephone provider were deprived of long-distance calls, because of a unique bug in one line of the programme.

In our computerized world, discontinuity—small causes, big effects—has become the rule.

PENTIMENTO IN WRITING[4]

When, at a time long before the 21st century, I started to use word processing software, I learned that, in order to write a word in italic, one

---

4   Originally appeared as Gilles Dowek, 'Écrire et se repentir', in *Vivre, aimer, voter en ligne: et autres chroniques numériques* (Paris: Le Pommier, 2017), 64–67.

should first change the mode by clicking on the 'italic' button, type the word in question, and then come back to the initial mode, by clicking on the button once again.

I believe, nevertheless, that I have never proceeded like that: I have, like everybody else, first written the word in Roman characters, selected it and then clicked on the 'italic' button to change the typeface. This possibility to alter, to modify *a posteriori*, distinguishes painting from sculpture, musical composition from improvisation, and writing in a word processor from writing by hand.

The old method—to change the entry mode—which exists still in the majority of word processing software, is a relic from the time when alteration was not possible, when in order to write a word in red instead of black one had to change the pen before writing this word, and not after.

Writing by hand was generative. It required skill in producing a perfect text from the first draught, or at least limiting the number of draughts. For this, the most important was to know how to make an outline, to organize precisely enough a text that had yet no materiality. Writing by hand required the coincidence of the temporalities of writing with those of the text. For example, the introduction would have to be written first, because it would arrive first. Lastly, one had to have a certain dexterity for spotting repetition before it happened and avoiding it by choosing synonymous words before it was too late.

Writing with word processing tools is generative and transformational. It requires totally different skills. More useful than knowing how to devise a perfect outline from the start is knowing how to restructure a text after we have decided to change its outline. If, for example, we decide to swap two parts, we often have to rethink the transitions and imagine being the reader who reads first that which we have written second. If we decide to merge two parts, which turn out to be redundant, we have to know how to recover the central idea in each of them, to give them a common structure and to reorganize the text.

The work on sentence level is also different: It is no longer necessary to know how to place an adverb right away, but rather to sense when it opposes the rhythm of the text and then move it. Likewise, it is no longer necessary to write directly in good style, but to know how to change one's style retrospectively by replacing an informal expression with a more serious one, or by transforming a conditional proposition with an independent clause.

Even more interesting, we have to know how to change the perspective of a text. In order to discuss one specific question, we began by telling an anecdote and then decided, with the development of the text, to enlarge its aim and to blend the anecdote in a larger narrative. One must therefore know how to re-examine one's account or one's argumentation in order to summarize it in relation to the rest of the text.

GHOSTS OF TRANSPARENCY

When teaching schoolchildren to write, we should probably teach them that, when they write with a word processor, like when they write a programme, the outline of the text, its register, its perspective, do not need to be decided in advance and then projected onto the sheet like onto the wall of a cave: They often emerge through a patient work of writing and altering.

This makes writing more creative, because, as Pablo Picasso used to say, himself an avid user of pentimento: "the painting is not thought and fixed in advance; it follows the mobility of thought while one is making it."

SUPERVISED OR UNSUPERVISED:
FROM COMPUTATION TO THE CLASSROOM[5]

Machine learning algorithms are methods that enable computers to acquire knowledge and, as always, it is enlightening to compare methods used by computers to those that we, humans, use for the same purpose.

Machine learning algorithms are divided into two big families, based on whether they learn by themselves or from another person. For example, by analysing the data that describes mice and elephants, an algorithm can classify these animals into groups: big ones and small ones, without anyone having to indicate which quality corresponds to which animal. Likewise, no one had to teach us to make a difference between a bicycle and a car. We learned on our own to classify vehicles onto different categories.

The learning algorithms that involve the intervention of a person, called 'the trainer' of an algorithm, can be divided in two categories: those that we call supervised and those that function by reinforcement, according to whether the person intervenes early or late in the process.

For example, in order to learn to recognize the letters of the alphabet, a supervised learning algorithm uses numerous images, previously tagged, which means that the trainer had indicated which image corresponds to which letter. Given a new image, the algorithm associates it with the tag that corresponds to the most similar images.

On the other hand, in an algorithm that learns by reinforcement, the trainer intervenes later. He leaves it to the algorithm to attribute a letter to an image randomly at first, exploring in this way mainly incorrect hypotheses. For example, it associates letter 'j' to images of the letter 'a'. But, if by chance, the algorithm would associate them to the letter 'a', the trainer would indicate that this is a correct answer. The algorithm would henceforth associate this letter to all similar images.

---

5   Originally appeared as Gilles Dowek, 'La bonne stratégie pour apprendre', in *Vivre, aimer, voter en ligne: et autres chroniques numériques* (Paris, Le Pommier, 2017), 160–63.

The distinction between these techniques recalls the difference between pedagogical methods, where the teacher either transmits knowledge to the learners, or leaves them to engage with it, intervening only to correct their mistakes. This difference also echoes two ways in which sciences build theories. According to the English philosopher Francis Bacon, observations and experiences give us access to facts. Theory emerges through a generalization process: induction. For Bacon, the construction of theories is therefore a process of supervised learning. Three centuries later, Karl Popper proposed another scenario: scientists construct, by will of their imagination, the most diverse theories, and then eliminate those that are disproved by observations and experiences. The construction of theories appears to be a process of learning by reinforcement.

Do these recent experiments in machine learning allow to solve this ancient controversy between Bacon and Popper? Yes: They teach us that both methods are useful, in different situations. Supervised learning gives very good results for form recognition. But when a robot discovers its environment, reinforced learning proves better.

And, far from being in opposition, these methods can be used in combination: The recent success of computers playing the game of Go is the result of a clever combination of supervised learning—by analysing a large number of rounds of the game—and reinforcement learning—letting the computer advance by playing against itself.

TRAVELLING ON PLANETS OF RESONATING CONCEPTS. IDENTIFICATION AND DIRECTIONALITY BETWEEN COMPUTATIONAL AND ARCHITECTONIC

SELENA SAVIĆ

XX

SELENA SAVIĆ is an architect interested in the way information technologies and communication techniques shape and transform architectural thinking, and vice versa. She holds a joint PhD from École polytechnique fédérale de Lausanne (EPFL) and Instituto Superior Técnico (IST), Lisbon, with a thesis entitled *Space. People. Networks: Exploring the relationship between built structures and seamless wireless communication infrastructures* (2015). She graduated with a degree in architecture (Dipl. Ing. Arch) from the Faculty of Architecture, Belgrade University in 2006, and in media design (MDes) from the Piet Zwart Institute, Rotterdam in 2010. She writes about the digital and architecture and exhibits works that address technics, communication and organization in space. She was previously a guest lecturer and postdoc fellow at the Department for Architecture Theory and Philosophy of Technics (ATTP) at the TU Vienna. She is currently a postdoc researcher at the Institute for Experimental Design and Media, FHNW Basel.

At any given moment of the day, the breeze plays on your cheek,
and since it carries codes from everywhere,
it's telling you about the state of the body of the world.
　　　　　　　　　　　—Michel Serres, *Angels. A Modern Myth*

When the night train departs from Zurich main station, the conductor
in the sleeping wagon collects the passengers' tickets and keeps them
for the night. He holds on to what used to be a unique copy of one's en-
titlement to travel, allowing him to keep track of people on board, both
to make sure they do not overstay and to wake the passengers up before
their station. Tickets are digital today, and can be printed in as many copies as we wish, but a stamped ticket is still a proof of travel. It is the key
to the trip, something with which we can track somebody's movement.

Unlike the movement of passengers between two places, which
requires energy to move the body and is usually intentional, concepts
turn up in distant disciplinary discourses without much effort and without a plan. Between domains of thinking, concepts appear to move and
propel novel articulations, new ways of thinking. But ways of thinking are always augmented if we really are thinking, because thinking
is inventing, observed the French philosopher Michel Serres.[1] When
concepts 'travel' between discourses, for example between computer
science and architecture, they store information on directionality that
propels this movement. Instead of tracing particular travels of concepts,
for which a ticket and a unique identity is needed, I propose to look
at concepts as message-bearers, which let messages propagate almost
transparently, almost without effort. This text articulates a proposal
for a sort of travel agency on a planet of resonating concepts. On this
planet, concept-passports open up communication between different
arguments and positions. The agency proposes itineraries by indexes
of similarity, such that one can experience the excitement of an intellectual adventure or the pleasure of familiarity with provincial ideas;
the joy of engaging with the local or the comfort of travelling globally.

How could we demonstrate, and reflect upon the indexes of important concepts and phrases that store information on their different
meanings? Disciplinary discourses tend to concentrate and homogenize,

---

[1]　Serres makes his argument about thinking (inventing) and information (rarity) by putting these two notions in a relation: "What is thinking, if not at least carrying out these
four operations: receiving, emitting, storing and processing information like all existing
things? [...] This information circulates in the world of things and between living things
as well as between us—humans—and it constitutes the bedrock of thinking. [...] thinking means inventing: getting hold of rarity, discovering the secret of that which has the
huge and contingent chance to exist or to be born tomorrow—*natura*, nature, means
that which will be born" Michel Serres, 'Information and Thinking', in *Philosophy After
Nature*, ed. Rosi Braidotti and Rick Dolphijn, trans. Joeri Visser (London; New York:
Rowman & Littlefield International, 2017), 14.

　　　　　　　　　　　　　　　GHOSTS OF TRANSPARENCY

inclined towards increasing precision of technical terminology at the cost of having a systemic overview. Treating concepts as vessels made up of the 'stuff' through which they navigate could potentially open this jargon and homogeneity of discourses to self-organized vectors of meaning. Engaging with secluded disciplinary discourses can be confusing or downright dangerous at times—it means confronting contradictory arguments, challenging those that one holds unchallengeable. Concept-passports could serve as a way to identify the terminology, document the conditions for coming in and going out, and establish this space as an organized and public space. The vectors lend themselves to be navigated by a sort of a travel agency—an agency that could make one care for concepts, to be interested in articulating thought precisely.

IDENTIFICATION AND PASSAGE OF CONCEPTS
IN HUMANITIES AND NATURAL SCIENCES

In a disciplinary discourse, concepts act as vectors that give direction and facilitate identification of meaning. We could observe intentionality in the movement of individual concepts if we were to focus on the intentions of authors who used them, or imported them from different discourses. For example, Johnathan Culler traced the movement of the concept of *performative* between philosophy and literature.[2] He documented prominent use of the concept, starting with J. L. Austin's *How to Do Things with Words*, in which he claims that language not only reports, but performs. Culler then explains the 'mutations' the concept of performative went through when picked up by literary critics who discussed literature *as* performative; by Derrida and de Man who focus on the iterability of language; and finally by feminist theory and cultural studies, where the question of gender is addressed through the notion of performativity. This interest in gender, coupled with the attention given to semiotic materiality, propels an articulation of an onto-epistemology in new materialist tradition, a way of looking at meaning as always/already coming from somewhere.[3] For Culler, the travel of the concept of performative is a series of generalizations of specific aspects—that of utterance or iterability—which result in sometimes contradictory interpretations of Austin's treatment of *speech act*. We can take notice then of how Culler chooses to emphasize the difference in what is at stake for Austin and Butler, or for Austin and Derrida. He observes and makes us see the disparities. Although he claims not to look for the 'right' use, his gesture is diagnostic, analytical, looking for anomalies and

---

2   J. Culler, 'Philosophy and Literature: The Fortunes of the Performative', *Poetics Today* 21, no. 3 (1 September 2000): 503–19, https://doi.org/10.1215/03335372-21-3-503.
3   Iris van der Tuin, 'Diffraction as a Methodology for Feminist Onto-Epistemology: On Encountering Chantal Chawaf and Posthuman Interpellation', *Parallax* 20, no. 3 (3 July 2014): 231–44, https://doi.org/10.1080/13534645.2014.927631.

misunderstandings. Culler's analysis treats travel as 'rare' while in fact, the movement of concepts, just as speech is abundant.

Mieke Bal promises us no such journey. In her book *Travelling Concepts*, she tries to capture the movement of concepts on a more abstract plane: She proposes a kind of a "rough guide" for specific interdisciplinary endeavours.[4] Bal's chapter, *Performance and Performativity*, is a discussion on productive confusion, starting from the common root of the two words and the fact that they rarely appear together. Performance is prominent in art history, which never speaks of performativity; when performativity is discussed in humanities, performance is not mentioned. Bal proposes a look at artworks as theoretical objects that foreground the performativity of performance. Bal focuses on *intention* confirmed in the separation of the two concepts, and the way *performativity* breaks the dogma of intentionalism in cultural studies. Bal approaches anti-intentionalism from the context of authorship ('to mean something'), challenging the position of authority that comes with it. She specifically addresses her criticism towards the treatment of artworks in art history, which focuses on authors' intentions to give the meaning to objects. Bal's approach treats artworks as theoretical objects, replacing intentionalism with a different voice of subjectivity.[5] We cannot own knowledge, Bal insists: Truth is in the many meanings of the cultural object. Operating within and addressing the problems of cultural analysis, she uses concepts in cultural analysis as a way to understand the object on the object's own terms.[6] Bals' continued attention to the object's participation in the production of meaning points in the direction of Serres' objective knowledge, the impersonal agency of thinking seeking instructions from its object[7], but her ambition to analyse culture parts ways with the possibility to treat contingencies objectively.

Concepts, Bal insists, need to be explicit, clear and defined so that they can do what they do—they mean something and facilitate invention—while at the same time needing to be flexible, so that they can move. *Travel* suggests that these qualities—being explicit, clear and defined and at the same time flexible—are the basis for an intellectual adventure. Bal's gesture produces a map of this trip. Her *Travelling Concepts* therefore operates topologically, it maps the territory travelled by concepts.

We can sense in the work of Culler and Bal the interest in movement as something that opens more interesting perspectives than scrutiny of individual words or concepts as methods. Informed by, but not continuing these efforts, the interest of this text is to consider ways

---

4   Mieke Bal, *Travelling Concepts in the Humanities: A Rough Guide*, Green College Lectures (Toronto: University of Toronto Press, 2002).
5   Ibid., 181.
6   Ibid., 8.
7   Vera Bühlmann, *Mathematics and Information in the Philosophy of Michel Serres*, Michel Serres and Material Futures (London: Bloomsbury Academic, 2019).

to work with concepts, which is outside of tracing their use in specific contexts (such as literature studies, cultural analysis, philosophy, or computer science and architecture). It is about a spectrality of sense, about letting concepts radiate the abundance of information that they collect by being present in different discourses.

Mieke Bal's take on the movement of concepts between science and culture relates to Stengers' gesture of probing travelling concepts in natural sciences. Stengers observes a certain disinterest, Bal tells us, propelled by the realization of the loss of neutrality in scientific discourse. She thus proposes in her book *d'une science à l'autre,* to think of concepts as issues of debate. Bal discusses how the normative epistemology of natural sciences gets imported and incorporated in humanistic inquiries. She presents the way these two nevertheless share a concern with concept *propagation—diffusion* or *contamination*, depending on the seriousness and interest in the concept's application. Bal asserts: A good concept is capable of founding a scientific discipline or field.

In her treatment of language, Mieke Bal emphasizes the distinction between words and concepts—concepts are theoretical tools and words are ordinary, we use them every day.[8] But this distinction blurs the most important claim about the way concepts appear in discourses: Their directionality is generic, undecided. Instead of carefully tracing how concepts travel in specific instances throughout literature and scientific writing, I propose to use concepts to transport ourselves to a planet of arguments. A travel guide organizes stories around places where they happened. A travel agency, on the other hand, proposes places to enjoy based on indexes of liking.

Michel Serres makes a different gesture with the apparently similar movement. The similarity is in the attempt to articulate the movement between the two domains of intellectual inquiry. Both Serres and Bal talk about the communication between natural sciences and humanities. Bal takes an analytical approach, proposing two types of propagation: one that is productive of meaning and the other which is somehow destructive of it. Serres, on the other hand, places no judgement as to how this movement is supposed to happen. Using the shipping passage in northern Canada connecting the Atlantic and the Pacific as a metaphor, he shows how unstable the passageway between the natural sciences and the humanities is: The Northwest Passage changes every year with freezing water and melting ice.[9] Providing maps does not help. There can be no general map or method that secures the passage; one has to find a way each time, whenever one wants

---

8 Bal, *Travelling Concepts in the Humanities,* 23.
9 Michel Serres, *Le Passage Du Nord-Ouest,* Collection 'Critique' 5 (Paris: Editions de Minuit, 1980).

to travel these dangerous waters. The passage opens with communication. Communication, though possible and vital, is always difficult and unique.[10] Translation is what bridges and connects the opposing sides.

Unlike Bal, who is concerned with demonstrating concepts as a methodological basis in cultural analysis and humanities in general[11], Michel Serres seeks specifically to address concepts that travel between the humanities and natural sciences. Serres is not concerned with characterizing propagation in terms of productiveness (what Bal characterizes as diffusion and contamination in the way concepts propagate) but in letting them be undecided, to be decided upon each use. The passage requires thinking, and this implies reflection rather than original brilliance. Let us now have a look at the passage between the domains of architecture and computation, and how terminology here informs and brands thinking.

THE PASSAGE BETWEEN ARCHITECTURE AND COMPUTATION

The connection between the domains of architecture and computer science is apparently more stable. Import and export are traced with relative ease. We can observe two dominant ways in which computational terminology has been used to propel new ways of thinking in architecture. On one side, theorists examine how computer software affects the practice of architecture, mainly in terms of generative morphology. They document how computational concepts change (or not) the thinking about geometry and morphology[12], form and structure[13] in the practice of architecture. This fascination with structure points towards an assumption that there is an underlying logic or order, one that can give form to a building or arrange nodes of a network. Architecture as a formal structure lends itself to such interpretation in terms of grammar and style. The connection between computation and architecture, in this theoretical tradition is made in terms of structure. The fascination with non-standard, perceived irregularity appears as the key indicator of objects and projects of interest. The role of the computer here is pragmatic—it is able to compute and represent complex geometries efficiently and clearly. One more thing typical of this thinking is that its considerations are past-oriented, looking at practice in an interpretative way. It projects as a mainstream future vision that which is already happening in marginal practices—the gesture is to extrapolate and then spread, distribute.

10 Michel Serres, *Hermes. Literature, Science, Philosophy*, ed. Josué V. Harari and David F. Bell (Baltimore: Johns Hopkins University Press, 1982). (See the introduction, *Journal a plusieurs voies* by editors Josué V. Harari and David F. Bell.)
11 See Bal, *Travelling Concepts in the Humanities*, 5.
12 Frédéric Migayrou, ed., *Architectures Non Standard: Exposition Présentée Au Centre Pompidou, Galerie Sud, 10 Décembre 2003 – 1er Mars 2004* (Paris: Centre Pompidou, 2003).
13 Rivka Oxman and Robert Oxman, eds., *Theories of the Digital in Architecture* (London; New York: Routledge, Taylor & Francis Group, 2014).

On the other side, some authors contemplate the connection between algorithms and architectural design in terms of similarity, rather than causality. This promotes the use of metaphors of computational processes to describe contemporary reconfigurations of structural, organizational and spatial experiences. These descriptions, informed by culture studies and media theory, take up a topic from the professional domain of architecture—such as urban design, or building form—and map its contemporary practice to computational processes. Keller Easterling's active form (a way to address algorithms that orchestrate urban design)[14] and Benjamin Bratton's layer in the 'Stack' (discussing the way global and pervasive computation inhabits and (re)organizes space)[15] are vivid examples of this approach. Spatial experience is thus a consequence of the operation of these concepts, a passive, given material upon which they act, or is an abstraction that organizes its activity.

In both these ways, the treatment of computational concepts and processes discussed stays on a highly instrumental level, where technical terminology is simply appropriated and pragmatically put to use. There is a lack of deeper engagement with concepts. The dislike of concepts amongst some popular architects can be likened to Stengers' disinterest and loss of seriousness. Computational concepts, such as algorithms and software stacks are left to *diffuse* in their propagation, precisely because they serve to rebrand the thinking about form-giving processes, but not inform them.

We cannot know what will happen when concepts appear in places where they are unfamiliar, what the concept of algorithm will bring to the table for discussing urban policy. Simply propelling novel ways of thinking with strange concepts does not necessarily make thoughts more precise or productive. How could we think about computability architectonically? How could we think about architecture computationally?

The distinction between architecture as a way to organize matter from architecture as a way to organize information is blurring in recent years. Architecture seems to be the paramount concept to address buildings as well as the organization of computer software and hardware components, information structures and arrangement of cells—cytoarchitecture. The use of the term 'architecture' in these different contexts propels, if nothing else, many new job descriptions.[16] And while we could apply the approach

---

14   Keller Easterling, *Extrastatecraft: The Power of Infrastructure Space* (Brooklyn: Verso, 2014).
15   Benjamin Bratton, *The Stack: On Software and Sovereignty*, Software Studies (Cambridge, Massachusetts: MIT Press, 2015).
16   See, for example, the job descriptions for Information Architect job description: https://www.jobhero.com/information-architect-job-description/ [Accessed 01. 04. 2019] and Architectural Designer https://www.jobhero.com/architectural-designer-job-description/ [Accessed 01. 04. 2019]. The JobHero page contains many other 'architect' job title overviews, namely Infrastructure Architect, Software Architect, Application Architect, Architectural Drafter, Cloud Architect, Data Architect, Database Architect, Design Architect, IT Architect, Network Architect, Project Architect, Solution Architect, etc.

proposed here with the planet of concepts to any discourse, it is specifically in the frame of the interest in thinking about computation architectonically (or the other way around) that such an effort should be understood. Architecture seems to have more in common with coding and information than with what is articulated as computer-aided design software: the use of computers to conceptualize an architectural project.[17] Architectural thinking could give access to materiality of code, and formality of computation.[18] The planet of concepts is an architectonic articulation of abundant information on directionality of words. Conversely, treating this information with algorithms of self-organization is a way to think about architecture computationally. How might we generalize these sometimes secluded domains of thinking without destroying meaning, but caring for concepts?

IDENTIFYING AND CHARACTERISING CONCEPTS, TOURISM BASED ON INDEXES OF SIMILARITY

In the 1950s, John Rupert Firth suggested that a word can be known by the company it keeps, demonstrating, with his distributional hypothesis, a way to communicate the information words keep about their context.[19] Differing from formal linguistics and the Chomsky tradition, the distributional hypothesis was fundamental for the development of distributional semantic model or word embeddings—a computational way to work with words as vectors whose relative similarities correlate with semantic similarity. These techniques are used by researchers to produce continuous vector spaces, where words that share common context are located in close proximity to one another.[20] Thus, there is no need to distinguish *a priori* between concepts (theoretical tools) and (ordinary) words, as Mieke Bal does explicitly. With computational power we have at our disposal today, we can let the discourse inform us on the words that comprise it.

---

17 See the work of Nikola Marinčić: thesis dissertation 'Towards Communication in CAAD: Spectral Characterisation and Modelling with Conjugate Symbolic Domains' (ETH Zurich, 2017), https://doi.org/10.3929/ethz-b-000216502.2017 and his text in this volume, in which he discusses and models of natural communication from the perspective of architectonics and the architectural ability to abstract in order to integrate on a higher level. See also Ludger Hovestadt, 'Elements of Digital Architecture', in *Coding as Literacy: Metalithikum IV*, ed. Vera Bühlmann, Ludger Hovestadt, and Vahid Moosavi, Applied Virtuality Book Series (Basel: Birkhäuser, 2015), 28–116; and Ludger Hovestadt, 'Cultivating the Generic: A Mathematically Inspired Pathway For Architects', in *EigenArchitecture*, ed. Ludger Hovestadt and Vera Bühlmann, Applied Virtuality Book Series (Basel: Birkhäuser, 2014), 7–67.
18 Vera Bühlmann, 'Vicarious Architectonics, Strange Objects. Chance-Bound: Michel Serres' Exodus from Methodical Reason', in *Architectural Materialisms: Nonhuman Creativity*, ed. Maria Voyatzaki (Edinburgh University Press, 2018), 267–92, http://www.jstor.org/stable/10.3366/j.ctv7n093b.
19 J. R. Firth, 'A Synopsis of Linguistic Theory 1930–55.' 1952–59 (1957): 1–32.
20 Tomas Mikolov et al., 'Efficient Estimation of Word Representations in Vector Space', *CoRR* abs/1301.3781 (2013), http://arxiv.org/abs/1301.3781.

The planet of concepts is a whole lot of words. I open up a socket, and let in all the speech I am interested in. The words store information on lots of opinions. The more company, the better we will know those many words. We can then treat this speech—the coded text—with an algorithm of self-organization, which clusters concepts by similarity. This forms a sphere, a continuous travelling space. A planet. The planet of concepts forms a continuous, self-organized vector space.[21] It can always be travelled again, and differently. Movement here is not determined by necessity, but by the contingency of opinions.

CODA: ALWAYS COMING FROM SOMEWHERE

In *Angels: A Modern Myth*, Michel Serres presents planes and passengers as angel-messengers.[22] This *Modern Myth* is a setup with two poles: the contradiction between the *myth*, which relates to an origin; and the *modern*, which is contemporary. It begins with death and ends with birth at the airport. It is an encounter of a fixed (doctor) and a moving (inspector) figure, a double articulation of movement, passing. The inspector is down-to-earth in the way he speaks, the doctor is 'in the clouds' in how she speaks, yet it is he (the inspector) who is always in the clouds physically and she (the doctor) who is on earth. Between them, a conversation takes place. In a single day at the Charles de Gaulle Airport in Paris, Serres demonstrates through the conversation of Pia and Pantope, the directionality of messengers: They are everywhere and yet, they have situated encounters wherever they converse. Informedness implies porterage—the holding up of unmoving forms. But informedness is more than that: It is the transformation resulting in information: communication, interference, transmissions and messengers. Halfway through *Angels*, Pia says: 'You'll soon end up talking like me'. Their inversion, the down-to-earth-ness in speech and in presence makes the full circle of the story.

With *Angels*, Serres talks about quasi-objects that create relationships between living and inert things in this circulation that is expected to always happen in transparent mediation. Quasi-objects are not merely passive, they create relationships between living and inert things. They are at the same time quasi-subjects: We take objects that write and think and make others that can think for us.

---

21 For more on how to deal with a lot, see Roman's dissertation *Play Among Books. A Symposium on Architecture and Information Spelled in Atom-Letters* as well as his chapter in this volume. Working with online discourse on architecture, its different weathers and atmospheres, Roman suggests, in a similar gesture to the way I envision the travel agency, using taste as a digital filter to enjoy the different flavours of information.
22 Michel Serres, *Angels. A Modern Myth*, trans. Francis Cowper (Paris: Flammarion, 1995).

This in-between-ness, between first beginnings (architectonic) and contemporaneity (computational) is the space to travel with concepts. The interest in such a material-discursive setup proposes concepts as matter of the planet. In *The Story of Semiconductors*, John W. Orton discusses inventive ways of working with and processing matter.[23] Control of materials means mixing them—creating alloys, or doping such as to increase the conductivity of semiconductors. Conditions in the material change with heat, which creates conditions for charge to move through the material in an organized and directional flow (conduction). With semiconductors, this flow can be controlled—an invention central to all kinds of applications of information and communication technologies.[24] Information is transmitted quantum-physically. Serres identifies this as the soft age—ours is the age in which we finally understand that everything emits, receives, stores and processes information; this circulation is the bedrock of our thinking.[25] With softness, Serres refers to energy scales in terms of information rather than mechanics—all communication uses energy, it has a price.

Angels hide themselves in things that are transparent, from an epistemological point of view that reasons. There is no message without resistance, no message without noise. Noise is that which is not communicated. Information, on the other hand, is negentropy—rarity[26] "If a transmitter does his job properly, he disappears."[27] Information constructs the universe, by means of networks. Message-bearing systems encompass the world and the world in turn is constructed by them. Wind, water, climate, networks. The constant breeze.

...

On a planet of concepts, movement is abundant. Concepts facilitate travel through areas of argumentation with which they have affinity, to which they are similar. One can move between areas they know well and those they do not. One can have multiple passports. The travel agency recommends itineraries one might like, areas where one might experience adventures, or simply enjoy the familiar. Travelling in the night without a ticket.

The night brings favourable conditions for thinking. Serres picks up Jules Verne's portrayal of the cave from his *Star of the South* to develop a metaphor for thinking: a dark vault with a thousand objects that reflect light. Usually, we consider light to be the model for knowledge (as in Enlightenment). But the sun as a single source of light is totalitarian: It stands for only one possible truth, Serres argues, while the night can

23 John W Orton, *Semiconductors and the Information Revolution: Magic Crystals That Made IT Happen* (Amsterdam: Elsevier, 2009), http://international.scholarvox.com/book/88812047.
24 Bühlmann, *Mathematics and Information in the Philosophy of Michel Serres.*
25 Serres, 'Information and Thinking'.
26 Ibid.
27 Serres, *Angels. A Modern Myth.*

GHOSTS OF TRANSPARENCY

concurrently host many: "where every star shines like a diamond, where every galaxy flows like a river of pearls, where every planet, like a mirror, reflects the light it receives."[28] Truth-stars stand out against black background of non-knowledge. Night is a better model for knowledge, which is multiple, precise and ever-evolving, Serres asserts. In the beginning, I introduced an interest in identification through grounding directionality, not as a gesture of *policing* speech—telling right from wrong about the way concepts are used or telling one where to go—but facilitating tourism, so we can travel into different customs of speaking without being an offence. Mieke Bal characterized tourism as both destructive and productive: Scholars doing cultural analysis are tourists—superficial visitors who destroy the culture they admire; their position is embarrassing and it is in this embarrassment that they can be potentially effective.[29] She stays cautious of affirming tourism, as she later describes it as a form of gaining knowledge-as-possession[30], which is conclusive, pertains to ownership, tyrannical in the way of Serres' Sun-Ego. On a planet of resonating concepts, concepts do not orient but they transport us, they facilitate a kind of tourism on a planet where arguments cast shadows. A travel guide would provide orientation, but an agency promises adventure and entertainment.

When travelling, our identities need to be confirmed in all clarity and uniqueness whenever we cross borders or physical environments (e.g. board a plane). Having an identity enables us to travel. Concepts, however, resonate with meaning. They need no prior identification; they *are* the passports. The two stand for the two sides of communication: the subjective, where we need identity, and the objective, which turns into the concept planet. Concepts move with the breeze, like angel-messengers.

While interested and invested in architecture and computation to begin with, the proposed treatment signals a gesture for working with concepts as always coming from somewhere. It is a gesture that is situated (in the discourse?) and generic (across discourses?) at the same time. Without trying to judge them as good or bad, appropriate or strange, whether they bring something or not. We do not make the concepts travel. We travel with them. The tourism on a planet of concepts offers a way to afford being interested in concepts we are not familiar with; it produces novel vernaculars. It offers a way of being 'friendly' with discourses, without taking part in a community.

Discourses import words, concepts, expressions, they are like the common land with political regimes, built on mythical origin. Existential import and export—concepts always come from somewhere. Like the wind.

28 Serres, 'Information and Thinking', 17.
29 Bal, *Travelling Concepts in the Humanities*, 247.
30 Ibid., 327.

AN ESSAY ON THE GLOSSOMATIC PROCESS OF COMMUNICATING COMMUNICATIONS AND OTHER WORDS

XXI

JESSICA FOLEY

JESSICA FOLEY works as a writer and creative transdisciplinary researcher. She is currently an Irish Research Council Postdoctoral Fellow at Maynooth University (MUSSI) 2018–2020 where she is developing research exploring the functions of fiction in parsing 'Smart Cities' and 'Internet of Things'. She is also a co-founding member of the *Orthogonal Methods Group* at CONNECT, the Science Foundation Ireland Centre for Future Networks and Communications. The Orthogonal Methods Group are unique in this context, bringing creative arts practices, critical pedagogy, feminist STS and new materialisms, new media scholarship and anthropology into critical conversation with science and technology research and industry.
During her PhD research at CTVR/CONNECT, Trinity College Dublin, Jessica pioneered a research-creation method called *Engineering Fictions* with engineering researchers and artists. Since 2013 *Engineering Fictions*, along with its twin *Stranger Fictions* (2018), has become a methodology that embraces the power of fiction and writing to foster and exercise creativity, honesty, diversity and ethical courage in Science and Technology research and industry.
Working contingently with people and contexts, materials and texts from across the worlds of contemporary art and design, education and engineering, Jessica's work focuses on opening up possibilities for embodied criticality and creative thinking and practices in ways that can support processes of change, healthy relations of difference and the enlargement of generosity and community.
Jessica's transdisciplinary practice is informed by her education in Graphic Design (B.Des. LSAD), Art and Design Education (H.Dip. LSAD), Contemporary Art (MA Art in the Contemporary World, NCAD) and Telecommunications Engineering (PhD. CTVR/TCD).

Writing in the first person, my voice strains, sore and tight. For such a long time, I have aped the voice and academic writing style of Engineering, cloaking myself amongst the procedural trappings of the third person technical writer, the voice of the 'modest witness'.[1] During my doctoral research, I sought to inhabit a challenge facing a telecommunications research centre, that of engendering critical and self-reflective communication in engineering research. My doctoral research was complicated.

Working in between scientific and artistic epistemologies, I was motivated by the idea that it was possible to create conditions for generous and generative communication in between disciplines like Engineering, Architecture and Contemporary Art. I wanted to gain insights on what communication could be in relation to this task, taking into consideration things like embodiment, sociality, academic conventions and the occupational politics of engineering as a profession. I called this process 'inreach', a critical and creative counterpoint to education and outreach practises in science and technology research. Inreach meant thinking with words, ideas, materials and histories of communication and then choreographing conversational experiments to generate critique within the context of engineering research, specifically, the Centre for Telecommunications Value-Chain Research (CTVR) at Trinity College Dublin.[2]

In the process of 'writing-up' these conversational experiments, I surreptitiously lost my voice to the third person; the examination system insisted that I inhabit the passive voice of technical writing. If you look at the table of contents in my doctoral thesis, it has the appearance (organizationally) of an engineering thesis; every chapter broken down, as if procedurally, into numbered sections and subsections. And if you read the text, you will hardly hear my voice at all, except maybe in the footnotes, or muffled behind the third-person narrator of the research. As a result, I have not really used my voice in years. The thesis was written and defended… Pardon me, I mean to say: I wrote my thesis, I defended it, and I graduated with a Ph.D. in December 2016. The following spring, I went to Vienna, to consult with labyrinths and statues and architectural philosophers at the ATTP. I went to Vienna to echo against European epistemologies and to listen to myself thinking out loud.

INTRODUCTION

Language is a central theme of the research discussed in this report, in particular the power of words to shape and orient research practises,

---

1 Steven Shapin and Simon Schaffer, *Leviathan and the Air-Pump: Hobbes, Boyle and the Experimental Life.* (Princeton and Surrey: Princeton University Press, 1985); Carolyn R. Miller, 'A Humanistic Rationale for Technical Writing', *College English*, 40. 6 (1979), 610–617; Donna Haraway, 'Situated Knowledges: The Science Question in Feminism and the Privilege of Partial Perspectives', *Feminist Studies*, 14.3 (1988), 575–599.
2 https://ctvr.ie/ [Accessed 31.10.18]

attitudes and cultures in science and technology contexts. In our time, this theme surfaces urgently out of masses of alphanumerical data generated by pervasive networked radio-computing technologies. From city dashboards to everyday search queries on internet web browsers, in a digital world words have become instruments of political and economic power. Pip Thornton's work highlights this in her multifaceted and poetic critique of Google AdWords as a mode of linguistic capitalism: " … in an age of digital capitalism and big tech monopolies, words have become commodities that gain economic value the more and the faster they circulate through digital spaces."[3] The AdWords platform monetizes the words that browsers search via Google, generating the bulk of the company's wealth.[4] Thornton argues that Google's AdWords platform effectively "strip[s] narrative context from the words we use while loading them with dissonant capital … The text of e-mails, blogs, news, search queries, and literature is all in some way generating capital for one private, opaque, and ultimately unchallengeable company."[5]

The decontextualisation and subsequent commodification of words are foreshadowed in the work of Uwe Poerksen, whose critique of *Plastic Words* in the 1980s expounded on transformations in vernacular language and the consequences of such changes, at a time when society was becoming increasingly 'scientized' and 'technologized,' or as we might say today, 'datafied' and 'digitized'. Plastic Words, Poerksen argues, are 'connotative stereotypes' that emerge out of an everyday mingling of science and technology language in society.[6] Such words, Poerksen argues "tend to form sentences, even without verbs," for example: "Information is communication. Communication is exchange. Exchange is a relationship. A relationship is a process. Process means development. Development is a basic need. Basic needs are resources. Resources are a problem. Problems require service delivery. Service delivery systems are role systems. Role systems are partnership systems. Partnership systems require communication. Communication is a kind of energy exchange."[7] J.M. van der Laan stresses the loss of ethical meaning in plastic language, arguing: "There is no link between an actual speaking human being and the words that are used."[8] Thus, the

3   Pip Thornton, 'A Critique of Linguistic Capitalism: Provocation/Intervention', *GeoHumanities*, 2018, 1–21 <https://doi.org/10.1080/2373566X.2018.1486724>.
4   Frederic Kaplan, 'Linguistic Capitalism and Algorithmic Mediation', *Representations*, 127.1 (2014), 57–63 <https://doi.org/10.1525/rep.2014.127.1.57>; Thornton, 'A Critique of Linguistic Capitalism'.
5   Thornton, A Critique of Linguistic Capitalism: Provocation/Intervention'.
6   Uwe Poerksen, *Plastic Words: The Tyranny of a Modular Language*. (Philadelphia: Pennsylvania State University Press, 2004).
7   J. M. van der Laan, 'Plastic Words: Words Without Meaning', *Bulletin of Science, Technology & Society*, 21.5 (2001), 349–53 <https://doi.org/10.1177/027046760102100503>.
8   Poerksen, *Plastic Words*, 62; van der Laan, 'Plastic Words: Words Without Meaning', 351.

increasing prevalence of plastic words and the commodification of language more generally combine as a de-personalizing force in society.

These broad concerns resonate with and reflect many contemporary initiatives to create glossaries that specify and narrate the meaning of particular words and phrases, re-contextualizing them in a provisional and in relation to time, place and use. It is more and more common for researchers, artists and practitioners to provide glossaries as appendices to the materials and research they are working with and narrating for readers. One recent European initiative has been the New Materialisms Glossary developed as part of the COST Action IS1307.[9] Closer to hand, in my doctoral thesis I supplied a glossary in order to contextualize the specific ways in which I used words like 'occupation,' 'foiling' and 'communication' in the context of engineering research.[10] This glossary has since become one of the research-creation methods of the Orthogonal Methods Group[11] at CONNECT, Trinity College Dublin.

Plastic words create tautological, self-referential or redundant effects that orchestrate impressions of narrative or, at least, orientation. The decontextualized quality of such words means they are deceptively functional and meaningful. But as Pip Thornton and others have argued, decontextualized and commoditized words have real effects on the way people live and experience the world.[12] And so too, the plastic words declaimed by Poerksen, van der Laan and many others before them (George Orwell for example) have a very real and powerful presence in the world.[13] Arguably, the tendency towards such plastic, decontextualized and commoditized language generated the conditions that led to my work with the Centre for Telecommunications Value-Chain Research (CTVR).[14]

9 The website featuring the New Materialisms Almanac was inaccessible at the time of writing. The address: www.newmaterialism.eu has been suspended. Details of the New Materialisms COST Action IS1307 can be found: https://www.cost.eu/actions/IS1307/#tabs|Name:overview [Accessed 20th October 2018].

10 Jessica Foley, 'Inreach: A Choreographic Process of Transversality' (unpublished PhD in Engineering, Trinity College Dublin, 2016).

11 The Orthogonal Methods Group is an interdisciplinary group of researchers based at CONNECT (formerly CTVR) interested in communications engineering, technology and society. Founded in 2015, the group emerged out of the collaborative research practice developed between myself and Prof. Linda Doyle during my doctoral research. Since then, the members have developed publications, exhibitions, public events and research residencies exploring the politics and ethics of technology in society. For further information visit: https://connectcentre.ie/omg [Accessed 20th October 2018]

12 Franco Berardi, The Uprising: On Poetry and Finance, Semiotext(e) Intervention Series, 14 (Los Angeles: Semiotext(e), 2012); Arjun Appadurai, Banking on Words: The Failure of Language in the Age of Derivative Finance (Chicago: The University of Chicago Press, 2016); Thornton, 'A Critique of Linguistic Capitalism'.

13 George Orwell, Politics and the English Language (London: Horizon, 1946); Poerksen.

14 This research centre has since expanded to become CONNECT www.connectcentre.ie www.ctvr.ie [Accessed 20th Oct 2018]

The narrative and art-based doctoral research I developed through this CTVR took the plastic language of telecommunications engineering as a point-of-departure. From the everyday mingling of the language of art and telecommunications, I began improvising ways to creatively and to subtly critique the conditions and aspirations of technological research with engineering researchers. By inhabiting CTVR's question 'How do we Communicate Communications?', I created a writing workshop methodology called *Engineering Fictions* that structured a space and time for engineering researchers, artists and others to experience and reflect upon cultures and imaginaries of technological research.

This report offers a revised glossary of a number of words and phrases drawn from my narrative and practice-based research with CTVR. To this end, the objectives of this report are to contribute a working glossary of terms, stemming from my doctoral research practice, *Inreach*, that can contribute to this aim. In March 2017, while on a Short Term Scientific Mission with the ATTP, as part of the New Materialisms COST Action IS1307, I opened up a selection of words, phrases and practices from my doctoral research with the ATTP. Less the presentation of a glossary (i.e. a foreign, obscure or obsolete word which needs explanation), this approach reflects a *glossomatic* turn, a self-aware, social process of spontaneous thinking and emoting (drawing on the etymology of the suffix -*matos*, 'thinking, animated').

In that process, my glossomatics became subject to a process of *enstrangement* (discussed below), with the effect that my own apperception of them became enlarged and critically sharpened. In conversation with the ATTP, the poetry of my research came to the fore as meaningful to the formation of a more capacious literacy of communication(s).

METHODS

I travelled to Vienna from Dublin in early March 2017, to undertake a Short Term Scientific Mission as part of the New Materialisms COST Action IS1307. My intention was to explore the glossomatic method I had developed during my doctoral research in a different context and with a different research community. My hope was that the ATTP would act as a foil to my practice, helping to *enstrange* the conversational experiments and concepts I had been working with, i.e., *Communicating Communications, inreach* and *Engineering Fictions*. The concept of enstrangement (остранение, ostranenie) had been important throughout my doctoral research, helping me to theorize 'inreach' practice as an artistic device. 'Making strange' has always, in some way or other, been part of the way I experience and express curiosity, model ethics and enact politics. Victor Shklovsky's theory of enstrangement (1919) created a space in my research to think the embodiment of in-betweenness, where ambiguity, uncertainty and humour mingle with the facts, fictions and conventions of engineering as an epistemic and technical discipline. My interest in Shklovky's concept lies in its attention to techniques of renewing perception by enlarging our ways of noticing, such as those employed by the writer Tolstoy in his ability to "reach our conscience" not by "calling a thing or event by its name but by describing it as if seen for the first time, as if happening for the first time."[15] In his essay, *Art, as Device*, Shklovsky argues that the work of enstrangement activates perceptions of non-identity and affinity coming into relation in the same image or, in the case of my research, poetic communicational space. This approach infuses the glossomatic process, which seeks to generate conditions whereby words reveal their excess materiality and agency in the world, thereby enstranging words in order to stimulate perceptions and "reach our conscience" anew. Shklovsky's understanding of Art as "the means to live through the making of a thing" speaks to the ways art-based and creative research methods can structure and make space for reflection and apperception, and for the production of insight, imagination and knowledge, and for lives "that can be seen, felt, lived tangibly."[16]

On the 10th of March, 2017, I presented a selection of what I called '*Invarious Vignettes*' from my ongoing research to the ATTP. I used a Power Point slideshow, a script and my voice as rhetorical devices. My choice of the word 'invarious' was not accidental but indicated a glossomatic process in action. From my conversations with Prof. Bühlmann I understood this was a concept that stimulated mutual interest, though it was clear our understanding was asymmetrical (Prof. Bühlmann has written extensively on this concept[17], I had merely overheard it and was intrigued by its poetic and philosophical affordances). By working this word into my presentation title, I was indicating this mutual interest but also signalling the possibility for productive mis-understanding (a glossomatic process is nothing if not risk-taking). The word 'invarious' was selected as a choreographic object to arouse attention, curiosity and critique within the conversational space and duration of the presentation and subsequent discussion. Ultimately, the aim of this narrated *Power Point* presentation was to invite the ATTP to act as a foil to my research vignettes, thus opening up an atmosphere of enstrangement to elicit interpretation and critique.

RESULTS

My engagement with the ATTP encouraged me to claim my artistic research practice as both glossomatic and poetic. By presenting 'Invarious Vignettes' on my research to a room of ATTP researchers (approximately

---

15   Viktor Shklovsky, 'Art, as Device', trans. by Alexandra Berlina, *Poetics Today*, 36.3 (2015), 151–74 https://doi.org/10.1215/03335372-3160709. 163.
16   Ibid., 154.
17   Braidotti and Hlavajova, *Posthuman Glossary*, (London: Bloomsbury Academic, 2018), 212–216

twenty people were gathered to listen and respond), I was afforded an opportunity to model and explore my glossomatic process in a different epistemic and technical context. The (previously unpublished) script of my presentation and the transcription of the discussion which followed illustrate the insights and critique generated through this encounter. Therefore, I have edited excerpts of these together (a kind of textual montage) to form a new script. For additional context, I have also included some references from my doctoral thesis.[18] These excerpts are then organized around three phrases that go towards making a revised glossary of the glossomatic method developed during my doctoral research with CTVR. The excerpts also work as a provisional critique and discussion of glossomatic processes, situating them in a wider philosophical and technical context for further elaboration.

COMMUNICATING COMMUNICATIONS

FOLEY: She wanted to know how to Communicate Communications—she was pretty confident that the Eameses had nailed it. "Surely," she seemed to say to me, "we can reverse engineer the Eameses film?" I didn't know any better. I said, why not? I've nothing to lose.

In 1953, Ray and Charles Eames released *A Communications Primer*. It was informed by Claude Shannon's 1948 paper on information theory, the one, it is often said, that changed the game of telecommunications. She was charmed and inspired by this film and it was this film that brought me into touch with telecommunications research. When I met Prof. Linda Doyle, the Director of CTVR, she wanted to know how Information and Communications Engineers could do engineering through the lens of Architecture. She felt strongly that everyone would benefit.

Inversely, the very reason that Ray and Charles Eames made *A Communications Primer* was because they believed that architects stood to benefit from knowing about Information Theory (The beginnings of the Smart City). As Charles Eames said: "I had the feeling that in the world of architecture they were going to get nowhere unless the process of information was going to come and enter city planning in general. You could not really anticipate a strategy that would solve the increase in population or the social changes which were going on unless you had some way of handling this information... so we made a film called A Communications Primer, essentially for architects."[19]

18   Jessica Foley, 'Inreach: A Choreographic Process of Transversality'
19   Paul Schrader, 'Poetry of Ideas: The Films of Charles Eames,' *Film Quarterly*, 23.3 (1970), 2–19 https://doi.org/10.2307/1210376 9.

While trying to learn how to single-handedly reverse engineer
the Eameses work, I got deeply distracted by their earliest film,
Blacktop, made in 1952. Finding this film more compelling than
the former, I began to 'reverse engineer' or read this film in detail,
trying to gain insight on how the Eameses approached filmmak-
ing. It was by reading this film, counting the seconds and register-
ing the movements and flow of each shot, making an account of it,
that the theory of phronesis became relevant. According to David
H. Fisher, phronesis "disrupts familiar ways of seeing: it disrupts
the narcissism of liquid life, inviting a different kind of movement
than the restless search for the new, the gratifying, the linked. A
conversational movement between figure and ground—figure and
the immediate focus of perception, ground as tradition (Gadamer),
ground as the polysemic voices of the other (Ricoeur)—becomes a
basis for expanded possibilities of judgement and action in the present, responding to the claims of the other."[20] The Eames's baroque
films became choreographic objects for me to work with—objects
that 'urged participation' of a different texture within CTVR...
reading their works in this context began to open up the idea of
communication and what this could mean for telecommunications
research in a place like Dunlop Oriel House (CTVR's building at
Trinity College Dublin). This is how CTVR began to work more
architectonically, by bringing excessive or surplus-to-requirement
things/ideas/artefacts into relation. Through the Eameses and
telecommunications research, I was learning how to work intimately and impotently[21] within this context... and it was in this
way that a choreographic process of communicating communications was set in motion through CTVR.

ATTP (VERA BÜHLMANN): What I'm wondering is your... the notion of
sterility, the impotence... you said several times that your position in this research group was an impotent one?

FOLEY: So this is something I just snuck in, in the past couple of days,
and it's something I'm curious about. Because I'm in Vienna I

---

20 *Gadamer and Ricoeur: Critical Horizons for Contemporary Hermeneutics*, ed. by
Francis J. Mootz and George H. Taylor, Continuum Studies in Continental Philosophy
(New York: Continuum, 2011). 158

21 This word was used as another 'choreographic object', much in the same way 'invarious'
was used. It prompted an interesting discussion around the logic of potential, high-
lighting this an important vector of critique for an Architectonics of Communication.
The choice of the word 'impotent' was prompted from listening to the language and
reading the texts of the ATTP in the first week I was with them, and linking this with
an essay I was concurrently reading by Beatriz Colomina on the architect Adolf Loos.
Beatriz Colomina, 'Intimacy and Spectacle: The Interiors of Adolf Loos', *AA Files*, 20,
(Autumn 1990), 5–15. Using the word 'impotency' in relation to Adolf Loos', architectural style was part of a glossomatic process of placing myself while opening up a
critique of architectonic method with ATTP.

was looking at Adolf Loos ... so this [using the word impotency] is just me thinking out loud ... the use of the word impotent and intimacy ... it has to do with comfort. Beatriz Colomina talks about Adolf Loos's architecture, his [interior] spaces, as a combination of intimacy and control. Intimacy and Control equal comfort.[22] [I was thinking about] the opposite of control—impotent was one of the words that came up–powerlessness—so I'm just playing with that. When I began it was a very asymmetrical group—me and the engineers. I think it's important to acknowledge those power relations and structures.

ATTP (VERA BÜHLMANN): I think it's also interesting because everyone wants potentiality now, potential, potential, potency ... so, we don't want possibilities anymore, we want a kind of material and potential ... and then to say, okay, I'm going to void this, that is to symbolize it in a way, to actually say it's impotency, that's also a very interesting move ...

FOLEY: A lot of the time I don't know what the language is doing, but it just seems like it's the right thing, and then it takes forever to try and translate it. And I think in order to translate these things you can't do it on your own, which is also one of the reasons why I'm here. I want to know, if I give you these terms, what do they translate as?

ATTP (LUDGER HOVESTADT): But I think impotency and potency ... you are playing the same game ... I think ... I don't know English language enough ... the same with, it's very sensible and beautiful how you use language, but to get it I really have to check it, look it up ... but impotency, I think you have to get out of the ... I appreciate the vector you are trying but you have to get out of the potency ...

CHOREOGRAPHIC OBJECTS

ATTP (OLIVER SCHÜRER): What is the Choreographic Object in your work? Could you tell us more about this and its relation to the classical understanding of choreography?

FOLEY: The research I was doing was very opportunistic. It was always about finding things that could help me work in that place (CTVR). The idea of the Choreographic Object came from the choreographer William Forsythe. What I understand by it is that he might use a balloon in a room and he would invite people into the room, and the balloon becomes a choreographic object, it begins to attract people to it or if there are many balloons ... so it's about power and how objects move people. And it's not that

22 Colomina, 'Intimacy and Spectacle'. 5.

the object is necessarily telling you what to do, it's more how ... what's the relationship between the object and the person as they encounter each other? He's conscious of the fact that placing things in space set about certain movements. I think that's what he means by choreography. It's not necessarily prescribed; it's not like a programme or even an algorithm. It's more a possibility. So that's what I liked about it. I used the concept after the fact. I'd be doing the research and then trying to find 'oh, I need language to describe what I'm doing'. Erin Manning's interpretations of Forsythe's concept of the choreographic object describe them as objects that "activate an environment for movement experimentation. The idea is to create an atmosphere that slightly tweaks the time of everyday movement, inviting it to tend toward the time of the event."[23] For Forsythe, a choreographic object is "an alternative site for the understanding of potential instigation and organization of action" which "would draw an attentive, diverse readership that would eventually understand and, hopefully, champion the innumerable manifestations, old and new, of choreographic thinking."[24] I perceived a relationship between CTVR's desire to Communicate Communications and the principle of thinking choreographically.

ATTP (OLIVER): This comes close to Social Engineering?

FOLEY: It's a bit unnerving when you put it that way. Well, there's a kind of doubleness in the process, because there's—and this is one of the things about language and trying to figure out how to be more precise with words—because, you feel a little bit like a Demon or a Saint. And it's really terrifying, being always in that feeling. That's how I've been for, you know, seven years. Social Engineering ... I don't think I would ever like to say I'm doing Social Engineering ... that's not the point. It's an ongoing struggle, finding a language that can describe this. Which is why I'm interested in what you (ATTP) are doing. You seem to be using language in a really specific way ...

ATTP (VERA BÜHLMANN): The way that you have described the choreographic object to me sounds so familiar to the quasi-object of (Michel) Serres actually ... this dance you are describing, you feel like a Demon, you evoke some kind of presence in the social space, you do, but you don't cause it. And that's how he describes the communication process ... with Serres, instead of thinking about Communication as from a Sender to a Receiver, it's always

23   Erin Manning, Always More than One: Individuation's Dance (Durham: Duke University Press, 2013), 93.
24   https://www.williamforsythe.com/essay.html [Accessed 31.10.18]

GHOSTS OF TRANSPARENCY

the point of view of the interpreter, so that sendings and receivings are going on—this is the nature of it—and whenever you communicate you are the interceptor, always. And then by intercepting you share your secret ... And then this strange idea of being a kind of medium in this demonic way becomes no more mysterious than when you dig in the ground and water comes out. And also, the way that you use the two-word poems, I didn't understand that before, that's powerful, I think. This is great!

TWO-WORD POEM

FOLEY: This is an ongoing poetic experiment in my research practice, to make two-word poems that have agency in the world. This is a two-word poem:
Engineering Fictions
It felt like the statement of a problem. When I composed it, I was getting intimate with the research centre and its inhabitants. With my questions about communication, I made people feel at once at ease and uncomfortable. I made myself uncomfortable. I perceived telecommunications engineering as a way of writing the world. I felt, without understanding, it's vast power. But the engineers I worked alongside did not seem to feel as I did: that their work was powerful. For many, it was tedious. Dull. Making the internet go faster. The occupation of 'Engineer' seemed to follow a cliché, as if Engineers were only either the Heroes or Handmaidens to power (the Nation State, the Multinational Corporation, the Private Affluent Person). So, I expanded my two-word poem into a living support structure to begin a sideways investigation—I imagined this poem as a kind of stent that could help increase the flow of thoughtful, playful and critical conversation and literacy within the research centre. And this two-word poem became Engineering Fictions, the writing workshop as a cultural stent ...

ATTP (VERA): So you need the poem in order to have Engineering Fictions, and then it works, you see! Because then you have, either from the Engineering or the Fiction, you have a metrum (a measure), but the metrum is not about measuring precisely, it's about giving some kind of structure where some kind of presence can appear through the words.

FOLEY: And the coining and subsequent improvisation of *Engineering Fictions* (as a writing workshop), its architectonics if you will, was provoked by three choreographic objects picked up through my hanging around CTVR: The Eamesian concept of 'fictions of reality'; an excerpt from Ludwig von Bertalanffy's General System Theory on the 'verbal model'; and also my own process of learning to write fiction through a workshop with the Irish author Pat McCabe. What this two-word poem, this poetry of naming, afforded me was the possibility for a critical and playful 'poetry of ideas' to flow within CTVR. For example, by working with the idea of fiction we begin to think about our assumptions of fact; by thinking about the power of verbal models, we begin to think about the power of mathematical models and we how we come to know the world; by learning to write fiction, becoming attentive to the idea that certain things cannot be taught or cannot be packaged into so-called 'transferable knowledge', we begin to imagine that some knowledges might only be inhabited and experienced, or that certain kinds of knowledges can only emerge over time, like wisdom.

ATTP (OLIVER): The poem aspect would interest me more, what makes these 'Engineering Fictions' into a poem ... and would something like 'Scandalous Scaffolding', for example, also be a poem? What makes one poetic and the other not?

FOLEY: Well, scandalous scaffolding would mean more to you than to me ... I'm creating patterns of meaning, that's what I'm doing ...

ATTP (VERA): To speak to your question, Oliver, about what makes it poetry ... so you could say, it's declaration, what makes it poetry. So you could say it's a title. Or you could say it's a label. But then you tell another story. So the point, I guess, as I understand your work, and that's the subtlety I see in it, is that words alone don't say it ... but they are themselves like a choreographic object. And then they are familiar enough to engage people, so it's not some esoteric secrecy language. But it doesn't try to be neutral, it doesn't try to claim a presence on its own. And I think this is very much the heart of poetry, to look at words like that. Because you don't really have an author, for example. So the poet is not the author of his poetry, he is giving form to a kind of inspiration, that's still, that's why poetry and lyrics are so important to give form to a soul, and soul is not a literal thing. As long as it takes on some kind of communicative presence. So this is the context of poetry since antiquity. It's older than drama and all of that. So it's, yes, by declaration I would say. And that's what's interesting, also, because in (computer) programming we have these two paradigms, these two main paradigms: declarative programming and instructional programming.

DISCUSSION

I began this essay by acknowledging a strain in my voice, a difficulty in moving beyond the style of the 'modest witness' espoused for so long (albeit attenuating) by scientific and technical disciplines like engineering.

GHOSTS OF TRANSPARENCY

To write in the first person, with the critical and enlarged 'I' of methods like participant observation and autofiction, remains a challenge. Arguably, this is a challenge facing all those whose modes of inquiry slip and move in between formal and established disciplines and seek to at once embody and express creative intellectual endeavour. Underlying such endeavours repeals the adage espoused by arts educator Corita Kent and conceptual artist John Cage: "You cannot create and analyse at the same time. They are different processes."[25] Glossomatic processes are those that accept this adage and yet continue to push and pull against its constraints. Such inquisitive and critical processes, as outlined above, are doomed to strangulation if they refuse (or are rendered unable) to accept that voice, word and movement are key devices in its method.

The very idea of a 'glossomatic' process was unavailable to me prior to writing this essay. This in itself is an indication of a glossomatic process at work, where voice and word intercept a context, opening up another channel for communication and theory to emerge as part of a larger pattern. Prof. Bühlmann contextualizes such processes in relation to Michel Serres work on the 'quasi-object' when she says, "whenever you communicate you are the interceptor, always. And then by intercepting you share your secret...." Continuing with Prof. Bühlmann's thinking, a glossomatic process is such that offers, "some kind of structure where some kind of presence can appear through the words." These reflections are instantiations of the generous act of foiling that comes with glossomatic processes, whereby an ethics is summoned through the declaration of specific words in context with other listening bodies. This is what the poet Séamas Heaney highlights as part of poetry's power as a method of "offering consciousness a chance to recognize its predicaments, foreknow its capacities and rehearse its comebacks in all kinds of venturesome ways."[26] Such poetic effects are tangible in the transcripts from my conversation with the ATTP, in our discussion of what constitutes a poem and in the opening up of a critique around the logic of potential. Where and when such critiques move next remains unprescribed.

25 For an overview of this adage visit https://www.brainpickings.org/2012/08/10/10-rules-for-students-and-teachers-john-cage-corita-kent/ [Accessed 31.10.18]
26 Séamas Heaney, *The Redress of Poetry: Oxford Lectures* (London and Boston: Faber and Faber, 1995), 2.

WHEN OTHERS PASSING BY BEHOLD: MEDIA STUDIES AND ARCHIVES ACROSS CULTURES
MATT COHEN

XXII

MATT COHEN is a professor in the Department of English at the University of Nebraska-Lincoln and a Faculty Fellow at the Center for Digital Research in the Humanities there. He is the author or editor of five books, including *The Networked Wilderness: Communicating in Early New England* (University of Minnesota Press, 2010) and, most recently, *Whitman's Drift: Imagining Literary Distribution* (University of Iowa Press, 2017). He is a contributing editor at the *Walt Whitman Archive* (http://www.whitmanarchive.org) and a co-editor of the *Charles Chesnutt Digital Archive* (https://chesnuttarchive.org/). Cohen is currently at work on a new book on intercultural theory and method in early American studies, tentatively titled *The Silence of the Miskito Prince: Imagining Across Cultures in Early America*.

In the month of May, in 1633, the Wampanoag people in the area near now-famous Plymouth Plantation made a prediction, duly recorded by William Bradford:

> [A]ll the month of May, [there] was such a quantity of a great sorte of flies, like (for bigness) to wasps, or bumble-bees, which came out of holes in the ground, and replenished all the woods, and ate the green-things, and made such a constant yelling noise, as made all the woods ring of them, and ready to deafen the hearers. They have not by the English been heard or seen before or since. But the Indians told them that sickness would follow, and so it did in June, July, August, and the chief heat of summer.[1]

Bradford's *Of Plymouth Plantation* tells us enough to guess that these 'flies' were of the species *magicicada septendecim*, or seventeen-year cicadas. The insects make several kinds of calls, one of which sounds like yelling, especially when there are a lot of them. This was before much of eastern Massachusetts got paved, so the chorus was likely astonishing, especially to the uninitiated, as Bradford confesses his fellow religious emigrés to be.

Many readers today might see in this event and its recording a dark ecological warning: The ignorance about the powers of the earth of the newly arrived developers of America; English wonderment at indigenous knowledge even as *Of Plymouth Plantation* records the violent displacement of Native people; and the deadliness of the "chief heat of summer." It's a romantic vision, but for all that, perhaps a salutary one. But if for the Wampanoags the cicadas were spiritual heralds, the swarm was also an epidemiological and historical marker. The holes they made upon emerging formed a predictive pattern, delineated a submerged archive. The last time those cicadas had appeared, after all, must have been during the massive epidemics suffered by the Natives on the eve of English settlement, in 1616–17—though Bradford seems not to have inquired far enough to discover that connection. The patient waiting of the cicadas as they grew and their seeming re-birth after such a length of time, no less than the terrors they induced in the English, may point to other, less romantic, symbolisms in the long view—perhaps to what N. Scott Momaday has called the Native community's "long outwaiting" of colonial settlement.[2]

Bradford's inclusion of the detail about the cicadas coming out of "holes in the ground," and his narrative's tendency to cordon off or obscure indigenous archival knowledge, start us on a trail of links and resonances that knit together media, history, culture, and how we study

1   William Bradford, *History of Plymouth Plantation, 1606–1646*, William T. Davis, ed. (New York: Charles Scribner's Sons, 1908), 514.
2   N. Scott Momaday, *House Made of Dawn* (New York: Harper Perennial Modern Classics, 2010), 53.

all of these things. The tension between how American Indian communities built or apprehended archives and the construction of Bradford's account cues this essay's contemplation about how we might build digital archives today. My focus is less on media, per se, than on the movement from media to archive as it has been conditioned by colonialism. Even so precise an observer of the world as James Gibson, in 1986 and amidst a self-reflexive revolution in anthropological method, could reiterate the time-worn equation: "images, pictures, and writing, insofar as the substances shaped and the surfaces treated are permanent, permit the storage of information and the accumulation of information in storehouses, in short, *civilization*."[3] No permanent information storage, no civilization.

For centuries, indigenous American media worlds and their confrontation with European systems and modes of communication have been an evidentiary site for debates about the role of media technologies, formats, and protocols in human history and consciousness.[4] Here I continue that conversation but leave behind some of the concerns and assumptions that have most clearly made the debate itself a sometimes unwitting partner in colonization. Instead I emphasize what I would claim as the conjunctive intercultural importance of the forms that archives take, offering a methodological reflection on the architecture, broadly understood, of digital cultural archives today. I focus on early colonial American media contests—and how Native American archival practices have been contained by subsequent representations of them—to highlight the Western liberal practices and desires that subtly shape the building, maintenance, and promotion of electronic archives today. Disagreements today about networked archives are often continuations of contests over information design and access with colonial origins and objectives. But such disagreements are also opportunities to change the way archives function, both in the imagination and in the legal architectures of states, tribes, and other collectives, by considering forces beyond any of those architectural epistemes as we build the digital archives that will represent the things of the North American past for the future.

3   James J. Gibson, *The Ecological Approach to Visual Perception* (Hillsdale, New Jersey: Lawrence Erlbaum Associates, 1986), 11 (emphasis added).
4   See Jorge Cañizares-Esguerra, *How to Write the History of the New World: Histories, Epistemologies, and Identities in the Eighteenth-Century Atlantic World* (Stanford: Stanford University Press, 2002); José Rabasa, *Writing Violence on the Northern Frontier: The Historiography of Sixteenth-Century New Mexico and Florida and the Legacy of Conquest* (Durham, NC: Duke University Press, 2000); Michel de Certeau, *Heterologies: Discourse on the Other* trans. B. Massumi (Minneapolis: University of Minnesota Press, 1986); Jacques Derrida, *Of Grammatology*, trans. G. C. Spivak (Baltimore: Johns Hopkins University Press, 1976).

D. F. McKenzie suggested in the 1980s in his study of the Treaty of Waitangi with the Maori in New Zealand, and scholars like Walter Mignolo and José Rabasa have argued in the context of Spanish colonialism, that close study of the materiality and genres of indigenous media reveals a less utopian story than the triumphalist myth of alphabetic literacy leading to human freedom would claim. The same goes for how we archive and give access to media of the past.

Consider the criticism embodied in the National Museum of the American Indian's Bibles and guns exhibit. The exhibit, designed in part by Comanche cultural critic and art historian Paul Chaat Smith, displays over one hundred Bibles translated into American Indian languages on one side of a curved display wall, and a swarm of guns, all pointing the same direction, representing the evolution of firearms used both by and against Natives on the other side. Though it's quieter than Bradford's cicada invasion, the visual-spatial effect is similar. The installation is located on the top floor of the museum, a use of the space that enhances the sense of being channelled and constrained that is instilled by the gallery's winding layout.[5] If the Bible functions metonymically for the mediums of writing and the book, the display counterposes two different technologies that, from one perspective, might be regarded as at odds. But then, it suggests to the contrary, these two kinds of objects have worked towards the same ends. One more turn of the screw: The exhibit's signage stresses the way in which these technologies were also adapted and mastered by American Indians.[6] For media scholars, such a display in a museum on the National Mall of the United States, with its national rhetoric of equality and democratic access to education, might provoke a series of questions, from the historical to the affective: At what cost have books, in this case, moved across the boundaries of race—and a racialism which rose coevally with, and perhaps out of, colonial expansion? Are indigenous media now, as has been the case for some Native communities in the past, in certain cases designed expressly *not* to cross boundaries, to remain off the grid? If the social practices, rules and manners associated with media are as important as the medium, as many critics argue, do media in fact ever really 'cross' cultures? The display seems designed in part to make a settler colonial museum visitor *feel* the constraints of colonialism's media culture in the

5   This display, curated by Jolene Rickard, Ann McMullen, and Paul Chaat Smith, was part of the exhibition *Our Peoples: Giving Voice to Our Histories*, National Museum of the American Indian, Smithsonian Institution, Washington, D.C.
6   For discussions of this and other aspects of the NMAI, see Amy Lonetree and Amanda J. Cobb, ed., *The National Museum of the American Indian: Critical Conversations* (Lincoln: University of Nebraska Press, 2008).

          GHOSTS OF TRANSPARENCY

way an American Indian might. A largely Native-designed museum, the NMAI in this exhibit and in others puts visitors' senses of media, authority, and history into uncomfortable relations, beholding the archive even as they are held by it.

Thinking about media and early American colonization throws into relief the way a phrase like 'new media' implicitly positions itself as transcending cultural differences, even as it paradoxically obscures the historical meanings attached to media development under colonization.[7] To Natives at first contact, alphabetic writing and print were new media; books, pamphlets, broadsides, and the like were new formats. Controversies among indigenous intellectuals, politicians, and artists from early encounter times to today have kept a focus on the politics of entanglement these media and formats offer. An early colonial narrative claim—that Indians regarded these technologies as gifts from the gods—was important to some Europeans in justifying dispossession and enslavement. But the incomplete qualities of that claim were clear to any colonizer confronting indigenous rebellion or, more importantly, the rapid pace at which indigenous people began to use such forms and formats. Europeans debated with themselves which American forms and formats were new, but the generally agreed-upon story has been that championing print and alphabetic literacy was key to a colonial ideology based on the linked concepts of civilization, progress, and Christianity.[8] No one doubted that indigenous people possessed information media and formats, both familiar, such as painting, architecture, pottery, and spoken language, and less familiar, such as knotted strings, tattooing, and piles of sticks. But the rhetoric of superiority, as Eric Wolf has argued, was built around the question of whether or not these could these be *archived*—could history be made and transmitted beyond memory?[9]

The relationship between media and historicism is an important hinge in the articulation of a concept of 'media' to the colonialist legacy that shapes discourses of technology and media today (and does so strikingly in the United States). The outlines of that relationship are visible in Thomas Harriot's 1588 account of Virginia and an observation by the Pilgrim Edward Winslow forty years later in New England. *A Briefe and True Relation of the New Found Land of Virginia* became one of the most

7   See Lisa Gitelman, *Always Already New: Media, History, and the Data of Culture* (Cambridge: MIT University Press, 2006); and Brian Hochman, *Savage Preservation: The Ethnographic Origins of Modern Media Technology* (Minneapolis: University of Minnesota Press, 2014).

8   See Phillip Round, *Removable Type: Histories of the Book in Indian Country, 1663–1880* (Chapel Hill: University of North Carolina Press, 2010); Hilary Wyss, *Writing Indians: Literacy, Christianity, and Native Community in Early America* (Amherst: University of Massachusetts Press, 2000); Matt Cohen and Jeffrey Glover, eds., *Colonial Mediascapes: Sensory Worlds of the Early Americas* (Lincoln: University of Nebraska Press, 2014).

9   See Eric Wolf, *Europe and the People Without History* (Berkeley: University of California Press, 1982).

popular accounts of America, and, with the other twelve volumes in a series called *America*, one of the most enduring sources for what today we would call ethnographic information about American Indians. Harriot, a mathematician who recorded an account of the 1585 journey to Virginia backed by Sir Walter Raleigh, offered this description of Native reactions to English technologies:

> Most thinges they sawe with us, as Mathematicall instruments, sea compassess ...gunnes, bookes, writing and reading ...and manie other thinges that wee had, were so straunge unto them, and so farre exceeded their capacities to comprehend the reason and meanes how they should be made and done, that they thought they were rather the works of gods then of men, or at the leastwise they had bin giuen and taught us of the gods.[10]

Harriot's account, together with a set of engravings by Theodor de Bry based on watercolour sketches John White made on-site, make clear that the Virginians not only have inscriptive technologies such as the tattoo, but use them as an integral part of social organization (fig. 1). As the caption to "The Marckes of sundrye of the Cheif mene of Virginia" reads, "The inhabitats of all the cuntrie for the most parte haue marks rased on their backs, wherby yt may be knowen what Princes subiects they bee, or of what place they haue their originall."

FIG I
Theodor de Bry,
"The Marckes of
sundrye of the Cheif
mene of Virginia,"
engraving from
*A Briefe and True
Report* (1590).
John Carter Brown
Library.

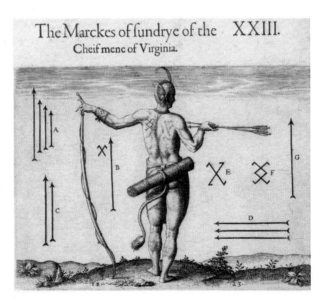

The Marckes of fundrye of the XXIII.
Cheif mene of Virginia.

10   Thomas Harriot, *A Briefe and True Report of the New Found Land of Virginia* (London: 1590), 27.

Elsewhere in his account, Harriot likens the Virginians to the Picts, his English readers' ancestors; the parallel humanizes the Natives, even as it distances them by exemplifying the European ability to compare and to master history that inscription practises such as writing and engraving seem to enable by leveraging time and space. "When viewers of the *Report* gazed at its images of American Indians," Michael Gaudio has argued, "they were declaring their difference from the savage by doing precisely that which the savage cannot do—by achieving a perspective on the world."[11]

The leaders of the Separatists who settled Plymouth colony, such as Bradford, had almost certainly read Harriot's account, along with many others available by that time. While events such as the 1622 massacre by Powhatans of settlers in Virginia had tarnished the utility of the trope of writing as a gift of the gods, Bradford's account of the cicadas still attempts to position European knowledge as superior by exemplifying how collecting, storing, and narrating information in written form can improve a community. But it was not the only account.

The fact that it was almost certainly Wampanoags that told the Pilgrims about those "greate ...flies" that emerged from holes in the ground reveals a perhaps not completely coincidental congruence: The Wampanoags were known to use holes in the ground to record human events.[12] Bradford's fellow Pilgrim and negotiator Edward Winslow, one of the more sympathetic and attentive observers of indigenous ways, published a description of the holes and the protocols associated with them:

> Instead of Records and Chronicles, they take this course, where any remarkable act is done, in memory of it, either in the place, or by some path-way near adjoining, they make a round hole in the ground about a foot deep, and as much over, which when others passing by behold, they enquire the cause and occasion of the same, which being once known, they are careful to acquaint all men, as occasion serveth therewith. And lest such holes should be filled, or grown up by any accident, as men pass by they will oft renew the same: By which means many things of great Antiquity are fresh in memory. So that as a man travelleth, if he can understand his guide, his journey will be the less tedious, by reason of the many historical Discourses will be related unto him.[13]

This passage revises, in a complex way, Harriot's claim that the Americans had "no letters nor other such meanes as we to keepe recordes of the

11 Michael Gaudio, *Engraving the Savage: The New World and Techniques of Civilization* (Minneapolis: University of Minnesota Press, 2008), xix.

12 See Neal Salisbury, *Manitou and Providence: Indians, Europeans, and the Making of New England, 1500–1643* (New York: Oxford University Press, 1982).

13 *Good News from New England by Edward Winslow: A Scholarly Edition*, Kelly Wisecup, ed. (Amherst: University of Massachusetts Press, 2014), 111.

particularities of times past."[14] It is significant that Winslow does not proceed by analogy. Rather than claim a relation—inferior, universal, or otherwise—to Western practices, his description breaks down the archiving of "historical discourses" into components: a material inscription, a method of transmission, a conservation strategy. Memory and social practice are regarded as key, just as in the interpretation of any kind of inscription, since the holes cannot interpret themselves.

The choice of location, 'in the place' or nearby, is also significant, as the interaction with archival information proceeds within the richly informative space of the event recorded. Information access is mostly, but not completely, open: A passer-by can request the information, which triggers a 'careful' reproduction of the information from the archive, but with the minor, significant qualification that the telling is 'as occasion serveth therewith' and only if you can understand your guide. The final protocol, of rounding out the hole after telling the story to keep it distinctive, blends pragmatism, a lesson about the decay that nature brings on all attempts at remembering, and a symbolic representation of the social nature of information—of the participatory potential of memorial institutions. Almost everyone is an archivist here; in the logic of this preservation system, to hear or to tell the 'many historical discourses' of the Algonquian forests is to take some responsibility for perpetuating them.

That Winslow, unlike Bradford or Harriot, foregrounded not just the media that eastern Algonquians used but also their protocols for storing and retrieving information about the past, suggests the complex differences among English reactions to the new transmissive technologies and formats they were witnessing and into which they were being folded. Negotiators like Winslow and his contemporary Roger Williams had to pay close attention to how Algonquians stored and retrieved information, even when they had a decent working grasp of the difficult grammar of Algonquian dialects. Winslow's account and Williams's *A Key into the Language of America* (1643) are among the most important sources today for ethnohistorical information about seventeenth-century indigenous information practises in the region. But the study of them is difficult, because their depictions of American Indians are framed by religious, commercial, political, and other influential concerns of their writers and the audiences for these texts.[15]

The difficulty of that movement between the accounts of the past and the ones that we offer today can hold true even, sometimes

14 Ibid., 26.
15 See Patricia Rubertone, *Grave Undertakings: An Archaeology of Roger Williams and the Narragansett Indians* (Washington, DC: Smithsonian Institution Press, 2001); Matt Cohen, *The Networked Wilderness: Communicating in Early New England* (Minneapolis: University of Minnesota Press, 2010); Andrew Newman, *On Records: Delaware Indians, Colonists, and the Media of History and Memory* (Lincoln: University of Nebraska Press, 2012); Nicole Gray, 'Aurality in Print: Revisiting Roger Williams's A Key into the Language of America', PMLA 131.2 (2016): 64–83.

especially, when careful attention is being paid to the material histories of inscription practises. A recent scholarly analysis of the importance of media history in analysing the colonial past serves as a cautionary example. In *Engraving the Savage*, Michael Gaudio points to the fundamental importance of the techniques of engraving in creating the Western idea of the 'savage'. Alongside and in conjunction with the art of printing, copperplate engraving exemplified technological progress even as it represented people who supposedly could not imagine it, creating the fulcrum of the savage-civilized distinction. Gaudio points to the multivalent presence of a copper plate, uninscribed, around the neck of one of De Bry's chiefs, in an engraving in Harriot's *Report*. The image of the neck plate is a nexus, where the savage within and the potential of the savage to become civilized rotate around an axis of both authenticity (*this is an engraving of an Indian, who is therefore real*) and fantasy (*this is an engraving, which Indians can't make—or can they?*).

A cheiff Lorde of Roanoac. VII.

FIG 2
Theodor de Bry, "A cheiff Lorde of Roanoac," engraving from Harriot, *A Briefe and True Report* (1590). John Carter Brown Library.

Gaudio stops short of articulating the real implication of his argument. The copper plate that Harriot describes as indicating the chief's 'authority' is a reminder that you don't have to engrave an object yourself in order to use it to create authority: "engraving," Gaudio says, "begins to look a lot like the matter with which the savage signifies his own authority."[16] This is to say, by extension, that 'civilisation' is a function of a capacity for representation, rather than the acquisition of particular

16   Gaudio, *Engraving the Savage*, xxi.

skills or tools. Knowing that the meaning of 'civilization' was under-mined by the very technologies that represented it helps us under-stand, in part, why that unstable culture was so effective at convincing itself to dominate American indigenous people. But, in the end, it does not move us past that paradigm of domination, because the scholarly act does not enfold an awareness of, nor does it enact, alternative repre-sentational epistemes. Whether the chief's other markings constitute an engraving technology, or the blank plate signifies a future potential for it (and I think both of those readings were certainly available and likely), the risk of putting illustration and engraving at the evidentiary heart of our analytics is that these might impede us from perceiving other ways that humans have organized and recorded their worlds. The intense scholarly interest in, almost fetishization (perhaps required by the historical-scientific method) of the materiality of inscription prac-tices sits in uneasy relationship to the awareness that engraving, in this case, has in the big picture been a blinding act that has had vio-lent effects on real people. To understand European technologies in this case is to do so using a logic derived from Western philosophy and the technologies that propagated it. Gaudio rightly observes that too often, "the material body of the signifying mark becomes a secondary or accidental quality subordinated to its emblematic value."[17] But if the tendency of previous analyses of images of the New World has been to look too quickly past the medium to the signs (with a few notable ex-ceptions), the tendency of textual studies and art history hasn't often been to collaborate with indigenous people or consider colonial media technologies in the same frame as on-the-ground slavery, murder, and dispossession.[18]

The electronic archive seems to offer an occasion for just such collaboration and reconsideration. Yet I think that the digital archive, considered as an illustrative technique, carries the same risks that en-graving brought with it. What we find in an electronic archive—surro-gates of texts, objects, and images, and metadata about them—tends to be presented in a unifying visual frame, removed from the sociality and the three-dimensional space of the brick-and-mortar archive. Derrida would remind us that the sociality of the archive, who gets in and who does not, who can visit and who cannot, who is funded and resident and who is not, and so on, constitute the same kind of authority as engrav-ing as well.[19] But this is something we tend to believe doesn't happen

17 Ibid., 7.
18 See Gordon Brotherston, *Book of the Fourth World: Reading the Native Americas through Their Literature* (New York: Cambridge University Press, 1992); and Walter Mignolo, *The Darker Side of the Renaissance: Literacy, Territoriality, and Colonization* (Ann Arbor, MI: University of Michigan Press, 1995).
19 See Jacques Derrida, *Archive Fever: A Freudian Impression*, trans. E. Prenowitz (Chicago: University of Chicago Press, 1996).

GHOSTS OF TRANSPARENCY

with electronic archives if they are publicly available. In other words, archive-builders, even if they are not on a civilizing mission, when they represent indigenous materials are entangled in the same history of power and of ideas of cultural difference that the European engravers of Native peoples in the sixteenth century were.

OTHERS, PASSING BY

New media in the early English New World functioned at the cutting edge of colonial exploitation and expropriation. The archives that were created over the course of the colonial expansion of North America were media records, to be sure, but they were also tools of colonial mastery. This is equally true of the compendium of letters, political documents, and historical narrative that make up Bradford's *Of Plymouth Plantation* and of the collections and publications of historical societies like the American Antiquarian Society, which was founded in 1812 at a moment when the Puritan and Native American past were being claimed as the basis of the United States' exceptionalism.[20] What lessons, then, does the colonial era hold for us today, given that our access to it is profoundly conditioned by the histories of these institutions and narratives? Should we not open and simplify the protocols, both for accessing and for including objects within the archives, and transcend the colonial dynamics of selection, historicization, and dispossession that characterized the information management regimes of the past?

If what Lisa Lowe calls the "intimacies of four continents" are to be uncovered by research that looks beyond ethnic or national boundaries and links hitherto obscured archives together, then the networked electronic infosphere would seem to offer quick passage to the revelation of North America's enmeshed histories.[21] In early American studies, in particular, the study of indigenous materials has been aided by the World Wide Web's multimedia capacities both in content and to the degree that they transform users' expectations of how media interrelate to create meaning. "Semiotic functions," writes Galen Brokaw of indigenous media, "are distributed across a number of different media, most, if not all, of which also employ to one degree or another multiple types of semiotic conventions."[22] While Brokaw argues that this is true in any culture, a particular attention to other-than-textual and interdependent modes of communication has taken hold in early American studies as a way of analysing encounter and colonization that moves across both

20 See Abram Van Engen, *The Meaning of America: How the United States Became the City on a Hill* (New Haven, CT: Yale University Press, forthcoming).
21 Lisa Lowe, *The Intimacies of Four Continents* (Durham: Duke University Press, 2015).
22 Galen Brokaw, 'Indigenous American Polygraphy and the Dialogic Model of Media'. *Ethnohistory* 57.1 (Winter 2010), 120.

the European-indigenous divide and contemporary disciplinary ones.[23] Being able to collocate a range of different media in an online space has certainly made this argument more forceful, and promises important revelations that will alter the field in profound ways. But these capabilities have not yet revolutionized the teaching of early America in a widespread way. The utopian language of freedom and interconnection that often permeates discussions of new media and digitization has been well critiqued. But even the now equally familiar indictments of the shallowness of humanities big data analysis or the corporatizing complicity of neoliberal digital humanism take a form that envisions technology creating, if not a unified society, one with deeper and better shared meaningfulness and ethos. Even if this isn't an individualistic stance, it is still a Western one, not particularly focused on the sacred and implicitly governed by a progressivist historical sensibility. Knowing that an enormous computational and infrastructural effort is required to make Internet-based computer work appear fluid and democratic, and that such an appearance can be exploited by sinister forces both major and minor, leaves us with the question of what might be beyond the narrative of progress and its dependence upon the concept of openness.[24]

It seems as if Western openness, in the cases of blogs, Facebook, and Twitter, for example, is both aiding liberation worldwide and cultivating disastrous new forms of fascism. This lesson about technology, and the fondest wishes for it to concretize progress, is learned time and again; the unveiling of its double-edgedness has become a familiar ritual. The network giveth, and the network taketh away. Geolocation technologies offer a good example. Once I worked with a group of computational linguists on a project to improve the machine recognition of place names in text-based sources. I wanted, when teaching an early travel narrative, to generate a map of all of the toponyms in it quickly and reliably—but place names are notoriously difficult to disambiguate. My part of the project used literary texts to test our algorithms, while another group used the Twitter feed. They were perfecting an algorithm

23 See also Hilary Wyss and Kristina Bross, eds., *Early Native Literacies in New England: A Documentary and Critical Anthology* (Amherst: University of Massachusetts Press, 2008); Sandra Gustafson, *Eloquence Is Power: Oratory and Performance in Early America* (Chapel Hill, NC: University of North Carolina Press, 2000); Susan Stabile, *Memory's Daughters: The Material Culture of Remembrance in Eighteenth-Century America* (Ithaca, NY: Cornell University Press, 2004); and Robert Blair St. George, *Conversing by Signs: Becoming Colonial in Early America* (Ithaca, NY: Cornell University Press, 2000).

24 See Mark Poster, *What's the Matter with the Internet?* (Minneapolis: University of Minnesota Press, 2001); Matthew Kirschenbaum, *Mechanisms: New Media and the Forensic Imagination* (Cambridge, MA: MIT Press, 2008); and most recently see Daniel Allington, Sarah Brouillette, David Golumbia, 'Neoliberal Tools (and Archives): A Political History of Digital Humanities', *Los Angeles Review of Books* (1 May 2016) < https://lareviewofbooks.org/article/neoliberal-tools-archives-political-history-digital-humanities/#! > and the subsequent controversy over it.

that guesses the location of a given tweet based on comparing its content to the overall feed and other contemporary textual sources.[25] Using Twitter feeds to locate people geographically, in addition to sounding cool, is an exciting test for computational linguistics and certainly helps us build better models for disambiguating toponyms in other textual sources. It is not difficult, however, to imagine how such an ability might be exploited in order to do violence. The frontier always moves, and it doesn't always move forward.

Let us return to Winslow's memory hole and dig it out a bit more, to think about digitally based Native archiving today. Western standards of preservation and access, from libraries to the online Open Access movement, seem self-evidently beneficial, and are often backed by a claim to promoting democracy. But the Wampanoag insistence on the dimensions of sociality, repetition, and the responsibility for curation held by each visitor to the archive implies different standards than the ones we tend to associate with digital archives. Indigenous communities' protocols for information access, while as elaborate as those of traditional Western archives (some places undergrads can look at manuscripts; some places you have to have a doctoral degree to do so, and so on), sometimes clash with the ideology of open or meritocratic access to information. A number of scholars, archivists, and librarians are working on the question of how to take up a more partial, but perhaps more ethical, approach to building archives online.

For many indigenous people, the stakes of controlling access to cultural information are high, even as the need to present a public face for purposes of achieving or maintaining sovereignty calls for a modicum of self-exposure. While the United States' Native American Graves Protection and Repatriation Act provides guidance for archivists in the physical realm, allowing for the return of mortal remains and artefacts to tribes from anthropological collections and other holdings, its domain is limited and the question of its applicability to the digital world is still open. Controlling access to information about cultural heritage is a problem that anthropologists of aboriginal Australia, among others, have been grappling with for years, using database technologies and interface design. Cultural anthropologist Kimberly Christen's projects are designed to privilege the cultural restrictions of information sharing in indigenous contexts. Her *Mukurtu Wumpurrarni-kari Archive* used Warumungu cultural protocols to restrict database access based on users' information: by family, gender, status in the tribal community, and country of origin. Within the archive, content is also organized

25   Benjamin Wing and Jason Baldridge, 'Simple Supervised Document Geolocation with Geodesic Grids', *Proceedings of the 49th Annual Meeting of the Association for Computational Linguistics*, Portland, OR (June 19–24, 2011) 955–964.

according to Warumungu cultural categories. The archive was created in an ongoing collaboration with Warumungu community members.[26] The *Mukurtu Archive* takes advantages of operating systems' ability to set user-based permissions and the complex contingent relations among tables available in databases to create a digital model of the social structure of information access in an aboriginal community and, by extension, to present its values through transmissive activity. As in the case of Winslow's 'passer by', then, a casual visitor to the archive may not be able to hear or see much at all without a tribal member sharing.[27]

The principles that informed the architecture of the *Mukurtu Archive* were used by Christen's group to create a more general content management system, *Mukurtu CMS*. The platform has been used by a number of different groups and institutions, and facilitates not just community archiving and access control, but in some instances the collaboration of anthropologists, librarians and curators, and tribal members in cultural preservation efforts that bridge group boundaries—an approach Christen calls "reciprocal curation."[28] But the success of the platform generally will be a function not just of its technological affordances and the broader sustainability of web-based cultural preservation. Not all tribes are federally recognized, which means that both policy domains and access to resources for cultural preservation can vary substantially. Like all groups, tribes are fluctuating entities, and their members' attitudes towards cultural heritage are heterogeneous, shifting, and contested. Any archivist enters ongoing internal debates when initiating a preservation project with a tribe, and tribal technologists are often pulled in multiple directions by competing community needs. All of these complexities take place within a landscape of archival possibility that is increasingly shaped by the presence of a small number of tribes with large reservation gaming incomes and, as a result, uncharacteristic latitude in how they can approach cultural archiving.

These complexities, together with the success of recent indigenous digital archive initiatives, raise questions that return us to the early colonial era and how we tell its stories, by way of broad problematics in the social lives of archives. What implications does the 'reciprocal curation' approach have *beyond* the indigenous context, for building cultural heritage archives? What constitutes a group, for the purposes

---

26 See the discussion of Mukurtu, other indigenous cultural heritage preservation sites, and the tradeoffs of leading content management platforms at http://www.mukurtu-archive.org/.

27 Kimberly Christen and Chris Cooney, 'Digital Dynamics across Cultures', *Vectors Journal* (2008) <http://www.vectorsjournal.org/projects/index.php?project=67&thread=ProjectCredits>. For another example of a digital archive-building project with decolonial potential, see the Colored Conventions project, http://coloredconventions.org.

28 Kimberly Christen, 'Opening Archives: Respectful Repatriation'. *The American Archivist* 74 (2011), 196.

of pursuing this sort of database ethics? A tribe is a political entity (among other things), with boundaries (however controversial) and a specific colonial history in relation to a state government. But what about a religious group like the Amish in the United States? Or cases in which religious separatism and Native American history cross—should scholarly standards encourage editors of works like William Bradford's or Edward Winslow's to collaborate with indigenous communities? Cherokee scholar Betty Booth Donohue, in a monograph on Bradford and *Of Plymouth Plantation*, argues that Bradford's is an "Indian book," and one might extrapolate from this to argue that its curation, if curation is imagined as an act of cultural heritage-making, ought best to be made an inter-cultural collaborative activity.[29]

What rethinkings of archive-building will be required, if an emphasis on collaboration and mutual responsibility is to be foundational? The rise of 'post-custodial curation' has occasioned thinking among museums, libraries, and archives about the kinds of training and institutional resource allocation required to build—or un-build—archives across cultures in this way. For a number of years, the American Libraries Association debated a proposition about how libraries should handle 'Traditional Cultural Expressions'—a proposal that in its first draught form put pressure on libraries to maintain close ties with Native communities and to give them considerable control over access policies.[30] If a version of this proposition passes and becomes a recommendation, it will mean major changes in the ways in which libraries relate to Native communities, and much more time and energy devoted to decisions about how or whether to offer access to library-held resources of indigenous materials. Curation models in which original objects stay with cultural groups, while umbrella organizations host them digitally, are beginning to spread as well: The Human Rights Documentation Initiative at the University of Texas at Austin uses this model, and in at least one African case even has mirrored web and local storage, providing a computer and database locally to a museum because of the unpredictability of local Internet access.[31]

---

29 Betty Booth Donohue, *William Bradford's Indian Book: Being the True Roote and Rise of American Letters As Revealed by the Native Text Embedded in Of Plimoth Plantation* (Gainesville: University Press of Florida, 2011).

30 See for example the posts at the American Libraries Association web site on TCEs, including the 'TCE Task Force Final Report', <http://wo.ala.org/tce/2011/01/28/tce-task-force-final-report/>. Librarians have also been actively involved in both the creation and the critique of various international standards and recommendations for handling Traditional Cultural Expressions, including the World Intellectual Property Organization's.

31 The Human Rights Documentation Initiative, University of Texas Libraries, < http://www.lib.utexas.edu/hrdi/ >. See in particular the discussion of the politics and mechanics of 'digital return' in Hannah Alpert-Abrams, 'Unreadable Books: Early Colonial Mexican Documents in Circulation', PhD diss, University of Texas at Austin (2017).

There are many web-based projects that emphasize how the history and structure of communities of interest might serve as the structural guide for archive building and interface design. Some operate in the academic domain, such as the Great Lakes Research Alliance for the Study of Aboriginal Arts and Cultures, a collective of indigenous researchers, archivists, and scholars, which uses "information technology to digitally reunite Great Lakes heritage that is currently scattered across museums and archives in North America and Europe with Aboriginal community knowledge, memory and perspectives."[32] The *He Pātaka Kupu Ture* (*Legal Māori Archive*) focuses on legal matters between states and specific groups in New Zealand. *He Pātaka Kupu Ture* is explicit in restricting the documents it offers to those "designed to be circulated and read by many."[33] And, of course, indigenous people are, like almost everyone else, using the web to create collections, both in mass applications like Flickr and Facebook and in more specialised, explicitly pro-Native venues such as *IsumaTV*. *IsumaTV*, created by the Inuit makers of the *Fast Runner* film series, is a multimedia publication platform that allows for broadcast, user-generated content hosting, and interactivity, organized by channels. The interface, simple and clean, seems to convey a corporate feel, and its one-framework-fits-all logic—put your multimedia here—seems Google-inspired. Yet the site looks more like the Wampanoag hole as one digs deeper: It lays claim to, and argues, the common political and representational situation of all indigenous people. "Our politics emphasize oral Inuktitut uploads rather than syllabic texts," the *About Us* page declares. While the site focuses on Inuit concerns and materials, its creators have explicitly opened the platform to other indigenous users. "Unfortunately, most indigenous communities do not have sufficient Internet bandwidth access, to view and upload multimedia, at full quality and speed," the site observes, "The IsumaTV Mediaplayer is designed to allow remote communities to participate equally in a world driven by media, in their own language and in the immediacy of our times."[34]

Signs of emergence, those holes in the ground were a technology of preservation for both insects and Native Americans in early colonial North America—cultivated, deliberately maintained excavations. The bugs Bradford heard earned their Latin name, *magicicada*, from their seemingly supernatural ability to derive life from self-burial. "The emerging media of today," Sandra Gustafson has written, "can help us

32 Great Lakes Research Alliance for the Study of Aboriginal Arts and Cultures, https://grasac.org/gks/gks_about.php. See also Tim Powell, 'Digitizing Cherokee Culture: Building Bridges between Libraries, Students, and the Reservation', *MELUS* 30.2 (2005), 79–98.
33 He Pātaka Kupu Ture / Legal Māori Archive, University of Wellington, http://www.nzetc.org/tm/scholarly/tei-corpus-legalMaori.html .
34 Isuma.TV, http://www.isuma.tv/en/about-us .

to better understand and preserve the emerging media of early America, making visible the range of textual forms from wampum belts to staged readings."[35] In effect, Gustafson argues that we will be able to do history better, to see more with new technologies. No doubt this is true in part. But the pathway of questioning might go both ways in time. Bradford, Harriot, and Winslow offer us a sense of the disagreements about indigenous media archiving in the early colonial era; today's contests about networked archives, information design, and access often have both colonial origins and persistently colonialist objectives. But such disagreements are also opportunities to change the way archives function, both in the imagination and in the legal architectures of states, tribes, and other collectives. Even as we make knowledge of the newly widespread contents of databases of previously obscure or rare or ancient material, we must interrogate the very constitution and maintenance of those databases and their relationship to the colonial past and still-colonial present. We are passersby, becoming diggers of holes.[36]

35 Sandra M. Gustafson, 'The Emerging Media of Early America', *Proceedings of the American Antiquarian Society* 115.2 (2005), 249.
36 "The text is delivered to the user," Hans Zeller has written, "not for permanent ownership, but rather as a task in which to participate." Zeller, 'Record and Interpretation: Analysis and Documentation as Goal and Method of Editing', *Contemporary German Editorial Theory*, George Bornstein et al., eds. (Ann Arbor, MI: University of Michigan Press, 1995), 50.

FLUID SPACES, ENCHANTED FORESTS

YASMINE ABBAS

XXIII

YASMINE ABBAS is an assistant teaching professor at the Stuckeman School of Architecture and Landscape Architecture at the Pennsylvania State University. A French architect and strategic designer, her research explores mobility, digital culture, and augmented place-making, with current focus on fabricating atmospheres, generative mapping, cartography, and the computational design of ambiance. She received an SMArchS from the Massachusetts Institute of Technology (2001) and a Doctor of Design from Harvard University (2006) for her work investigating neo-nomads, researching strategies for the design of living environments across contemporary conditions of expanded physical, digital and mental mobilities. She is the author of *Le néo-nomadisme: Mobilités. Partage. Transformations identitaires et urbaines* (2011) and co-editor of *Digital Technologies of the Self* (Abbas, Y. & Dervin, F., 2009). She is co-founder of the Agbogbloshie Makerspace Platform, an open architecture project that has been exhibited at the 2017 Seoul Biennale for Architecture and Urbanism, 2018 Dak'Art Biennale and "Digital Imaginaries" exhibition at ZKM | Center for Art and Media in Karlsruhe, Germany.

Observe a river. Water meanders downstream, moulds the form of stones and gravels ... Much like what happens to us in the spaces we inhabit, molecules in a liquid take the shape of their vessel. For a short moment, together they become one—i.e. *font corps*, to become one body. But the stream is capricious, depends on the inflow of (melt/storm)water as well as on intermittent obstacles and geographical accidents. As the fluid progresses, stones clatter, banks erode, sediments are carried away, the river bed morphs, water follows. Soon enough, an interstice in the embankment, caused by a root stretching to the water, gives way to a side stream that grows over time ... The shape of a fluid (and its properties) is uncertain. It adjusts across space and time to the milieu with which it comes into contact.

Liquids, or materials of flow, are signs of contemporary societies—they indicate our 'liquid modernity' and our 'liquid life'[1] and the 'space of flows' where information technologies have contributed to fluidize relations, productions and economies.[2] Within volatile life circumstances, the figure of the global and 'cultural hybrid' emerges and is, according to Bauman, ideologically 'extraterritorialized.' While increasing numbers of displaced populations face a great number of threats and long for safe return to their homeland, "'Cultural hybrids' want to feel everywhere *chez soi*—in order to be vaccinated against the vicious bacteria of domesticity."[3] Our 'liquid life', as described by Bauman, implies a spatial crisis where inhabiting—taking the time to root—becomes irrelevant or ... vaporizes. Seeking to circumvent the consequences of uncertainty, neo-nomads—people who are simultaneously, and to varying degrees, physically, digitally and mentally mobile—take steps to create a 'sense of place' and anchor in fluid contexts.[4] The mobile space of 'Home', much like water, changes states, from liquid to solid and gas.

Many architects have acclimatized to our 'liquid modernity' by designing *for* the various shades of mobility: temporary—often disposable—flexible, modular, portable, packable, and light, kinetic, adaptive and interactive, exploring the 'oblique function' (Architecture Principe, Claude Parent and Paul Virilio) to induce disequilibrium, engaging bodies with surfaces and smooth spaces, parametrically generated, inviting even more roaming. Technologies, pervasive and infra-visible, are imbuing environments with magical attributes, fluidizing and charging them with emotional stimulants. Fluid spaces or enchanted forests are sentient, have the property to perceive and communicate—and surveil. They are also mental transportation vehicles. Within this realm, architecture behaves as an

1   Zygmunt Bauman, *Liquid Modernity* (Cambridge Malden, MA: Polity Press Blackwell, 2000).
2   Manuel Castells, *The Rise of The Network Society*, The Information Age: Economy, Society and Culture, Second (Malden, MA: Blackwell Publishing, 2000).
3   Bauman, *Liquid Modernity*, 29.
4   Yasmine Abbas, *Le Néo-Nomadisme: Mobilités, Partage, Transformations Identitaires et Urbaines*, Présence. Essai (Limoges: Fyp, 2011).

'epidermis', writes Toyo Ito, becoming the interface between augmented environments, 'media forests' and our connected bodies.[5] Yet, within Ito's 'media forest', 'Tarzans', humans and non-humans, creatures of all sorts, glide ... pass by each other and sometimes, temporarily, coalesce, creating a memorable situation located both in space and time.[6] Designing spaces that accommodate these magical moments, when place precipitates, when it permeates with significance and enables 'wayfounding', i.e. orienting, connecting and anchoring ourselves within, finding our place in the world becomes an ever greater challenge.[7] While 'wayfinding' relates to the mechanics of locating oneself in an (urban) milieu, 'wayfounding' subsumes into serendipity, and the electrochemistry of chance encounters. It calls for atmospheric spaces—forests of enchantment.

The 1950s-60s Lettrists and Situationists imagined the aesthetic practice of the *dérive* (drift) to spring *"déquotidianisation,"*[8] that is, inhibit routines and the boredom they cause. Responding to the dull and frozen expression of our becoming liquid modernity, the "functionalization, moralization, militarization and commodification of urban spaces"[9] and going with the flow—not the one imposed by the power in place—the Situationists then designed 'influential cartographies,'[10] mapped, collected and collaged what they called '*unités d'ambiances*,' 'islands' or 'atmospheric capsules' as writes Bégout.[11] They envisioned reproducing these phenomenal situations to reprogramme cities, infusing them with the emotions they lacked.[12] Likewise, to enable 'wayfounding', architects are inviting movement not to serve the space of flows but, by making use of the property of fluids to change state, to create atmospheres—something that blurs the materiality of spaces, creating the condition for our emotional connection to our environment.

'Atmospheric capsules' or '*unités d'ambiance*' have nonetheless, borrowing the expression of anthropologist Eduardo Kohn, a "fluid efficient form."[13] The patterns of formation of components—humans and non-humans—of fluid efficient forms have synergy. For example, as Kohn writes, the fractal pattern of the waterways that form in the Amazonian

5   Toyo Itō, 'Tarzans in the Media Forest', *Architecture Words*, 8 (London: Architectural Association, 2011).
6   Yasmine Abbas, 'The Cartography of Ambiance', in *Ambiances, Tomorrow. Proceedings of 3rd International Congress on Ambiances. Septembre 2016, Volos, Greece*, ed. by Nicolas Rémy (dir.); Nicolas Tixier (dir.) (Volos, Greece: International Network Ambiances, 2016), i, 253–258 <https://hal.archives-ouvertes.fr/hal-01409727>.
7   Abbas, i.
8   Bruce Bégout, *Dériville: Les Situationnistes et La Question Urbaine* (Paris: Inculte-barnum, 2017), 25.
9   Ibid., 24, my translation.
10 In French: *Cartographie influencielle*.
11 Bégout, *Dériville*, 39-40.
12 Patrick Marcolini, *Le Mouvement Situationniste: Une Histoire Intellectuelle* (Montreuil: L'Échappée, 2012); Bégout, *Dériville*.
13 Eduardo Kohn, *Comment pensent les forêts: vers une anthropologie au-delà de l'humain*, trans. by Grégory Delaplace (Brussels: Zones Sensibles, 2017), chap. 5: 'La fluide efficacité de la forme', 205–248.

forest, meets and interrelates with the distribution of the rubber trees in the landscape (their distribution is, furthermore, a consequence of the presence of *Mycrocyclus ulei*, a fungal parasite) and corresponds with the pattern of the spread of shamanism as well as that of the rubber colonial exploitation.[14] Each element of the landscape or situation is born from constraints (a type of information) that influence its shape or state of mind, and each has its own agency. Together they create a form suffused with meaning.

When bodies and forest converge, humans 'grow into' their milieu, go through a 'mechanism of camouflage' whereby they modulate their identity with regards to what surrounds them.[15] The 'sensuous correspondence' operates, not only visually, by the way of, for example, 'mimesis,' 'becoming,' 'sympathetic magic,' 'narcissism,' 'belonging,' or 'sacrifice', as Leach explores, but also via all our other senses. Designing for 'wayfounding' therefore implies recognizing the parameters that generate both: the 'fluid efficient form' and the 'sensuous correspondence' that these forms enable. The Janes and Tarzans navigating media forests are in need of meaningful and anchoring encounters. They are longing for the conditions to be in this world, to belong, to be able to camouflage and to 'attune' to spaces in memorable and transformative ways.[16] Spaces that afford such richness of experience, making themselves memorable, can be considered atmospheric.

Architects who seek to build atmospheres are, in many ways, spatial tricksters. They are the masters of artifice—from the Latin word *artificium*, rooted in the words *ars* (skill) and *facere* (to do or to make). They are experts at the art of making effects, ingenious in developing processes and techniques to design and fabricate 'virtual' or 'mental' spaces to "trick the senses."[17] The materiality of 'meteorological architecture'[18] can become that of the ensemble of atmospheric devices used to produce atmospheric effects: from László Moholy-Nagy's 1930 *Light Prop for an Electric Stage*[19] and François Dallegret's illustration of a "baroque ensemble of domestic gadgetry"[20] to the 35,000 high-pressure nozzles[21] of Diller and Scofidio's *Blur Building* or the different "artificial cooling devices [/] apparatus working on meteorological phenomena" of the *Jade Meteo Park*.[22] Peter Zumthor, in comparison, relies less on technology than materiality and tectonics. He incorporates the sensory qualities of space, such as their 'sound' and

14 Ibid.
15 Neil Leach, *Camouflage*, Architecture/Design (Cambridge, MA.: MIT Press, 2006).
16 Alberto Pérez-Gómez, *Attunement: Architectural Meaning after the Crisis of Modern Science* (London: MIT Press, 2016).
17 Jean Baudrillard and Jean Nouvel, *The Singular Objects of Architecture*, trans. by Robert Bononno (Minneapolis: University of Minnesota Press, 2002), 8.
18 Philippe Rahm, *Architecture météorologique* (Paris: Archibooks, 2009).
19 *Human – Space – Machine. Stage Experiments at the Bauhaus*, ed. by Torsten Blume, Christian Hiller, and Stiftung Bauhaus Dessau, Edition Bauhaus, 38 (Leipzig: Spector Books, 2014).
20 Reyner Banham, 'A Home Is Not a House', *Art in America*, 53 (1965), 70–79 (71).
21 https://dsrny.com/project/blur-building (Last accessed April 16, 2018)
22 Philippe Rahm, 'Form and Function Follow Climate', *AA Files*, 55 (2010), 2–11.

GHOSTS OF TRANSPARENCY

'temperature'[23] in the initial stages of his design process through model-making.[24] He, literally, has a hand in the production of spatial effects, sometimes creating models using the projected building material.[25] Spatial tricks are not simulacra; they are not meant to deceive. Rather, they aim at provoking emotional fireworks,[26] melting the frozen faces of spaces, proposing alternatives to the dullness of contemporary living or to its hyperactivity.

Within the realm of computational design or data-driven architecture—also thought as liquid—architectural designers compose with data, choosing a variety of parameters to guide the fluid arrangement of forms. In order to design for atmospheres, such a process of computation begins with optimizing spaces for sensory effect: to create 'an optimal sound map' for the *Elbphilharmonie* (Herzog & de Meuron, 2016) in Hamburg[27] or an immersive space of visual delight under the canopy of the *Louvres Abu Dhabi* (Ateliers Jean Nouvel, 2017). Apart from their entanglement in the space of flows and their contribution to the society of the spectacle, the projects mentioned above successfully utilize the computing capabilities of machines to generate forms that stimulate the senses, that produce particular intended effects, a sonic or visual condition forever perfect, controlled. Where the sea meets the museum, the interplay of light and shade with air moisture, material reflection and the taste of salt in the air modulate the intended atmosphere and by that contribute to its lasting impression.

Enchanted forests are atmospheric. More flesh than skin, they form conditions with which humans and non-humans communicate, biologically and (electro)chemically, and, in the process, change the properties of the overall milieu in both expected and unexpected ways. Together, they form a climatic architecture that climaxes: an atmospheric architecture whose program and materiality co-depend on the trajectories of its constituents and their confluence—an architecture made for weathering.

The paradigm of fluidity calls for electro-chemical and spatial encounters, an atmospheric architecture—'unités d'ambiances', 'atmospheric capsules' or 'islands'—for epidermal reactions—enchanted forests that neither dictate a way to feel nor cast us adrift, but that rather acclimatize, help keep our bearings by creating a space to moor, momentarily and experientially.

23 Peter Zumthor, *Atmospheres: Architectural Environments—Surrounding Objects* (Basel: Birkhäuser, 2006).
24 Mathieu Berteloot and Véronique Patteeuw, 'Form / Formless. Peter Zumthor's Models', *Building Atmorphere*, OASE.91, 83–92.
25 Sigrid Hauser, *Peter Zumthor—Therme Vals*, ed. by Peter Zumthor (Zürich: Scheidegger & Spiess, 2007).
26 In French an "artificier" is a firework technician, a person who fabricates, sells or launches fireworks (via http://www.cnrtl.fr/definition/artificier, last accessed April 11, 2018).
27 E. Stinson, 'What happens When Algorithms Design a Concert Hall? The Stunning Elbphilarmonie' in *Wired*, (2017) online: https://www.wired.com/2017/01/happens-algorithms-design-concert-hall-stunning-elbphilharmonie/ Last accessed 2017/12/12.

SPACE AS AFFECTIVE SENSE-MAKING CAPACITY
DARÍO NEGUERUELA DEL CASTILLO

XXIV

DARÍO NEGUERUELA DEL CASTILLO. Docteur ès sciences/PhD. EPFL. An architect and researcher from Madrid and currently established in Switzerland, Darío was Head of Research at ALICE lab (École polytechnique fédérale de Lausanne, Switzerland), until March 2019. Currently, he is the Academic Coordinator of the new Zurich Centre for Digital Visual Studies, UZH-MPG (start Sept. 2019). In 2017, Darío completed his PhD thesis entitled *The City of Extended Emotions*, addressing the mutually constitutive dynamics between space and collective agency. More precisely, the research looks into the way urban space enacts collective agency (social movements) through affect and emotion and how, in turn, these agencies modify and produce new space. His academic parcours includes a Diploma of Advanced Studies (DEA) from Madrid School of Architecture (ETSAM, Universidad Politécnica de Madrid), an MSc. in Architecture and Urban Design from TU Delft, the Netherlands, and a Bachelor of Architecture and Urban Design from the University of Westminster London, U.K.

In this essay I argue that the interactive, spatio-relational and necessarily socio-participatory nature commonly thought of for any communicative process must be extended and applied to cognitive processes in urban settings. To what degree can we consider the interactive, cumulative and interrelated patterns of bodily movements, displacements and other essentially socio-spatial practices as the substrate upon which social collective spatial meaning is built? New paradigms in cognitive sciences postulate that the physical modes of interaction constitute not just the limit of a given communicative process, but the very structure that determines the way in which we come to construct and fix meaning. In a converging manner, understanding space as 'a capacity' from the entry point of action and practice, we come to the conclusion that the spatial dimension strongly influences the interaction process through which sense-making is enacted. This very idea carries relevant consequences for our shared reflection on the architectonics of communication. For instance, distinctions between cognizing and feeling need to be revised in the context of embodied sense-making. This is of accrued relevance for reformulating urban cognition and the emergence of new forms of space making sociality. Finally, I consider whether this line of reflection and research may allow us to link and relate particular epistemological frameworks and paradigms previously thought to be mutually exclusive.

INTRODUCTION:
SPACE AS THE AGENTIAL SUBSTRATE OF SOCIAL INTERACTION

How do we enact, derive or build meaning of and in our cities? In this brief essay, I want to elaborate on a path, which, delving into various different theoretical origins, points towards a constructive and emergent stance on urban cognition. My intention here is to argue for the consideration of the constitutive and intertwined role of the affective and spatial dimensions in any cognitive process of the city (and, perhaps, the urban condition). To that aim, I depart from an understanding of space consisting of mere definitions of space as either physical metric distance or as location, and seek to reconstruct its agential capacities. This, I argue, can prove operational for further involving the concourse of affect in how we mobilize and enact architectures of sociality in the contemporary city.

Our material, bodily and situated perspective opens the door to this particular narrative. Social interaction, if considered as one of the bases for the constitution of any social sphere, certainly requires minimum doses of mutual understanding. While much emphasis has been placed on the different forms of verbal communication and their articulation into varied forms of social dialogue, my attention turns here to the spatial and bodily dimensions of social interactions as a

GHOSTS OF TRANSPARENCY

basis for the cognitive. Physical co-presence can amount to more than the simple possibility of non-verbal interpersonal communication in the form of visually remarking behaviour of others. Indeed, the ways in which bodies resonate with other bodies are varied. Bodies register, assess, interpret, vibrate and feel. Space has long been a suspect in all things social and it has been speculated that it plays a protagonist role in those environments, like our cities, where most social, economic and cultural innovations tend to occur. Authors from a diversity of backgrounds and approaches have recognized that the very spatial dimension of cities structures, in fact, our social interactions[1]. From the lively but yet distant conversations in a street market to the moments of intimacy in a restaurant, the regimes of engaging with the world emerge from their non-trivial bodily substrate. And those interactions are the substance of our regimes of sociality. Recurrent and still relevant concepts like *Gemeinschaft* and *Gesellschaft*[2] elaborate on the consequences of such modalities of encounter, favoured or constrained by the dense and artificial environments where we spend most of our lives.

Alternatively, the heterogeneity that is assumed or desired as the quintessential urban quality is key in opening up the horizon of future possibilities. Alterity and heterogeneity in our environment seem intimately related to the plurality we need in our societies in order to avoid the dangers of post-political demagogy. In this respect, I consider the presence of the Other as the crucial substrate of any societal endeavour.

INTERPRETATIONAL DRIVE AND AFFECTIVE ENACTMENT OF MEANING

What can, then, be the role of affect in all of this? I propose two key elements for the lucubration on the role of affect in what previously has been considered the reconstruction and ultimate understanding of these communicative situations by means of reasoning or 'cold' cognitive abilities. First, the unavoidable presence of the affective dimension as constitutive of any appraisal, any perception, any enactment of a

---

1   See, for instance, sources as varied as: Vinicius M. Netto, *The Social Fabric of Cities* (Abingdon: Routledge, 2016); Jacques Levy, 'Penser la ville: un imperatif sous toutes les latitudes', *Cahiers d'études sur la Méditerranée orientale et le monde turco-iranien*, 1997 <https://cemoti.revues.org/1458> [accessed 17 August 2017]; Jane Jacobs, *The Death and Life of Great American Cities* (New York: Vintage Books, 1961); Martina Löw and Donald Goodwin, *The Sociology of Space: Materiality, Social Structures, and Action*, Cultural Sociology (New York: Palgrave Macmillan, 2016).
2   Concepts reflecting different social structure through their basis on either affiliation of kind and resemblance or on complementary interest, or mechanical and organic solidarity as Durkheim would put it. Émile Durkheim, *The Elementary Forms of the Religious Life*, ed. by Mark Sydney Cladis, trans. by Carol Cosman, Originally published in 1912 (Oxford: Oxford University Press, 2001).

worldview[3]. Second, the less explored idea of emotions as interpretative evaluations that may come to complement and extend appraisal and enactive theories of emotion.

Within current emotion research, a wide array of appraisal theories posit that affective phenomena are, in essence, the result of the shortcut evaluation of a perceived stimulus, sometimes complementing and sometimes contradicting our higher cognitive reasoning. In this stream of emotion theory and research, this assumption performs a timely overturn, allowing us to scrap the pejorative tarnish of sentimentality, hysteria and weakness that has often accompanied emotions in our cultural and scientific models.

The postulations of affect as evaluative judgements proper speak of the synthetic interpretative performativity of emotion and affect[4]. They emerge from the most immediate confrontation with our situation in the world and, as such, constitute the most direct appraisal of 'apparent reality'.[5] The essential power of emotions as synthetic interpretative evaluations of such apparent reality is evident in the fact that they are elicited by composites that pertain to different degrees of complexity. While the interpretative work involved might vary greatly between, say, the perception of a spider and the perception of the collapse of a financial system, emotions always perform meaning.[6] In a social context like the city, such apparent reality is configured not only by the appraisal of what environmental events are in themselves, but most importantly of what the actions and expressions of others might mean for our well-being.

Communication is made possible through substitutions, allowing for an endless process of recoding and articulation. If we are to believe that emotional and affective behaviour and expression constitute a basic and non-substitutable channel of communication among individuals (as many scholars argue that emotions are actually and foremost intended at social communication[7]), does this need to rearticulate, to

3   As postulated by and further developed by enactive approaches to affectivity (e.g. Giovanna Colombetti and Evan Thompson, 'The Feeling Body: Toward an Enactive Approach to Emotion', in *Developmental Perspectives on Embodiment and Consciousness* (New York: Lawrence Erlbaum, 2008), 45–68; Giovanna Colombetti and Joel Krueger, 'Scaffoldings of the Affective Mind', *Philosophical Psychology*, 28.8 (2014), 1157–76 <https://doi.org/10.10 80/09515089.2014.976334>; Daniel D. Hutto, 'Truly Enactive Emotion', Emotion Review, 4.2 (2012), 176–81 <https://doi.org/10.1177/1754073911430134>.

4   Martha C. Nussbaum, 'Emotions as Judgments of Value and Importance', in *Thinking About Feeling: Contemporary Philosophers on Emotions*, ed. by Robert C. Solomon (Oxford: Oxford University Press, 2004).

5   Nico H. Frijda, *The Emotions* (Cambridge: Cambridge University Press, 1986).

6   To an extent to which the epistemology of emotions claims they are meanings in themselves.

7   See for instance, the argumentation about the rethorical nature of emotion in in Daniel M. Gross, 'Introduction Being-Moved: The Pathos of Heidegger's Rhetorical Ontology', in *Heidegger and Rhetoric*, ed. by Daniel M. Gross and Ansgar Kemmann (Albany: State University of New York Press, 2005) <http://www.sunypress.edu/pdf/61167.pdf> [accessed 22 February 2017].

interpret also happen with emotion? Do we need to interpret a set of symbolic cues that signal an appraisal of something which is no longer there, which is absent? If so, social interaction, as based upon all possible forms of communication, needs to be regarded as an act of constant emotional interpretation (in both meanings of performance and decoding) of our eventful contexts.

This implies that our situatedness in a populated heterogeneous and plural world demands a work of constant interpretation, which seems to be more the working grounds of a reflexive approach than one concerned merely with impersonal and purely technical decoding. Moreover, it might imply a constant generation of new meanings, new interpretations. The reunion of the active and enactive dimensions of affect with such unavoidable interpretational dimension perhaps leads us to reconsider such practice of emotions as essentially a rhetorical art in the sense implied by Daniel M. Gross and close to original Aristotelian postulates.[8] The importance of this appraisal/interpretation resides in its essentially agential nature. The very capacities of an agent, meaning her horizon of possibilities, are sketched by her enacted construction of a worldview, which in turn, give a measure of its constitutive situatedness.

These views are, of course, not new nor strictly mine. The original sketch of agency laid out by Maturana and Varela[9] in their theory of autopoiesis, anchors agency in the interactive situatedness of the organism, which by means of its emergence through organizational closure also make sense of its environment and its changing conditions. As such, the concept of agency put forward by autopoiesis is not, thus, grounded in a pre-existing *élan vital*[10], but simply emerges out of the interaction with materially bounded elements. Moreover, this lays the first stone upon which the enactive approach proper would develop its ideas, bridging the divide between previously distinctively theorized areas of perception and cognition (appraisal). Varela, Thompson, and Rosch, defined this novel approach in the following manner: "the enactive approach consists of two points: (1) perception consists in perceptually guided action and (2) cognitive structures emerge from the recurrent sensorimotor patterns that enable action to be perceptually guided."[11]

8   Ibid.
9   F.G. Varela, H.R. Maturana, and R. Uribe, 'Autopoiesis: The Organization of Living Systems, Its Characterization and a Model', *Biosystems*, 5.4 (1974), 187–96 <https://doi.org/10.1016/0303-2647(74)90031-8>; Humberto R. Maturana and F. J. Varela, *Autopoiesis and Cognition: The Realization of the Living* (New York: Springer, 1980).
10   Henri Bergson, *L'Évolution Créatrice* (Paris: Félix Alcan, 1907).
11   Varela, Thompson, & Rosch, *The Embodied Mind: Cognitive Science and Human Experience*. (Cambridge, MA: MIT Press, 1991), 173

THE COGNITION OF THE CITY.
INTERPRETING HETEROGENEITY, AGENCY AND UNCERTAINTY.

In order to figure out how this might be helpful in our endeavour, let us now return to the city and the problem of making sense of it all. The consideration of the question of cognition has, since the beginning of the modern social thought, been postulated around one of the foundational problems of sociology and the social sciences. Agency and structure[12], best exemplified by Simmel's reflection on the loss of individual agency as the main problem of city life, in the initial passages of his *Mental life and the Metropolis*.[13] I propose, moreover, that it is crucial to reconsider the role of space in the relation between all those expressions of emotion that are in fact absent and the process of interpretation.

The problem is manifold, but it certainly involves the regulation and filtering of modes of co-presence, and perhaps more importantly of coexistence of diversity. Such is the case when urban form is actively regulating modes of human interaction that have relevant outcomes. For instance, in many urban protests, the urban space regulates the probabilities that those claims will be witnessed by local populations, those living in that particular neighbourhood, or by those actually passing by on their way to their job or school or simply visiting, or, rather, by a mixture of those. This regulation of different modes of co-presence can help the actions of a group reach a particular potential of exposure to otherness, and extimacy.[14] The spatialized interaction between those diverse and different, yet proximal, realities is what engenders the richness and multiplicity of meanings from which different agencies are born. Thus, the urban would seem to have a say in the constitution of a shared framing of our experience. This observation belongs to the line of reflection that grants cities qualities well above and beyond the mere container for our actions, ranging from the aggregated effect, as cities often "represent the possibility of weaving our actions into complex associations"[15] to the capacity of cit-

---

12 On the one hand, the opposition between humans' capacity to act and change their environment and fate, based on an understanding of free will. On the other, the constraints that our environment, be it through physical material dimension or through values, beliefs, norms and rules arising from social institutions, exert upon humans, conditioning their capacities and delimiting their freedom to think, to choose, to act.

13 "The deepest problems of modern life flow from the attempt of the individual to maintain the independence and individuality of his existence against the sovereign powers of society, against historical heritage's weight and the external culture and technique of life. This antagonism represents the most modern form of the conflict which primitive man must carry on with nature for his own bodily existence," Georg Simmel, *Mental Life and the Metropolis*, trans. Kurt Wolff (New York: Free Press, 1950 [1902]).

14 David Pavón-Cuéllar, 'Extimacy', in *Encyclopedia of Critical Psychology* (New York: Springer, 2014), 661–664 <http://link.springer.com/10.1007/978-1-4614-5583-7_106> [accessed 23 January 2017].

15 Netto, *The Social Fabric of Cities*.

GHOSTS OF TRANSPARENCY

ies, as elaborate artefacts, to qualitatively change the communication performed by our social interactions.[16]

In addition, situated engagement can be said to "encourage noisy and unruly engagement in situated, material, discursive and conceptual places."[17] It therefore requires a particular ethical opening up, in coherence with the Levinasian notion of 'situated availability'[18], as well as a decanted projective capacity.[19] Accordingly, this view of agency grants importance to socio-spatial modalities of interaction, and sees them inscribed in a non-trivial time dimension. In other words, it seeks to actualize agency as a temporally embedded process of social and spatial engagement that engenders a 'reciprocity of perspectives'.[20] In practical terms, it means that the spatial configuration can be seen now as constitutive of human individual and collective agency, and not as mere crystallization of institutional 'structural' constraints.

COLOPHON: SPACE AS AFFECTIVE (AGENTIAL) CAPACITY.

If we follow the line of reasoning proposed here above, we come to recognize that we build our worlds not only through an appraisal of a fixed and flat state, but rather through a tentative affective interpretation of what our surrounding material interactions might mean. This is the case as our surroundings do not just cause us pain or happiness for their intrinsic qualities or content, only assess our environment, including the events that give it shape and duration in time. For instance, one's feeling of frustration and perhaps even anger when trapped in rush hour, has not only to do with the fact of being stuck in the car or in an overcrowded metro wagon, but most importantly with the consequences we infer this condition has for our following material interactions, even for a whole lifestyle and thus, for our well-being and those around us. Or, in other words, via the enactment of multiple futures. We navigate this field of uncertainty through contingent and emergent meaning, requiring the concourse of all. The implications of this are multiple, but perhaps the

16   Juval Portugali, *Complexity, Cognition and the City* (New York: Springer Science & Business Media, 2011).

17   Deborah Bird Rose, 'Indigenous Ecologies and an Ethic of Connection', in *Global Ethics and Environment*, ed. by Nicholas Low (London: Taylor & Francis, 2002), 13 <https://doi.org/10.4324/9780203015254-17>.

18   Ibid.

19   "Such approach informed by the past (in its 'iterational' or habitual aspect) but also oriented toward(s) the future (as a 'projective' capacity to imagine alternative possibilities) and toward(s) the present (as a 'practical- evaluative' capacity to contextualize past habits and future projects within the contingencies of the moment)" Mustafa Emirbayer and Ann Mische, 'What Is Agency?', *American Journal of Sociology*, 103.4 (1998), 962–1023 <https://doi.org/10.1086/231294>.

20   Alfred Schutz and Thomas Luckmann, *The Structures of the Life-World*, Northwestern University Studies in Phenomenology & Existential Philosophy (Evanston, IL: Northwestern University Press, 1973), 60–68.

most important, in my opinion, is the radical call for an inherent welcoming of the collective contingency of meaning through co-presence, should we still believe that the urban holds an emancipatory promise.[21]

It is important to stress that the notion of space as interpretative passion that I intend to put forward understands space as something produced through its practice[22], and not as a pre-given datum. What emerges is a view of (urban) space as enacted and invested by the endless becoming of human material interactions. A view that sees space engendered by myriad exchanges that give birth to and result from our contingent trajectories and which, also produce new relational dimensions insofar as they are felt, interpreted and cognized. And such becoming is translated in the agential capacities of matter, epitomized by higher complexity living forms, like ourselves. To put it differently, I propose space to be read in relation to what Solomon[23], echoing ancient wisdom, has captured by his enunciation of the 'passions' (that which makes us do, what drives our lives). In this respect, space pertains to a complex nature. It does not only influence the results of our interpretative emotional appraisal, it is enacted through our very emoting, which raises, in intellectual terms, the question of whether the city can indeed set us free.

21 Netto, *The Social Fabric of Cities*
22 Alberto Corsín Jiménez, 'On Space as a Capacity', *Jroyaanthinst The Journal of the Royal Anthropological Institute*, 9.1 (2003), 137–53; Mathis Stock, 'Spatial practices, theoretical implications', *Revue électronique des sciences humaines et sociales*, (2015). <http://www.espacestemps.net/articles/spatial-practices-theoretical-implications/> [accessed 14 March 2016].
23 Robert C. Solomon, *The Passions: Emotions and the Meaning of Life* (Indianapolis: Hackett Pub. Co, 1993).

GHOSTS OF TRANSPARENCY

A FEW PROTOCOL SENTENCES ON: NON-SYNTHESIS, THE VOLUMINOUS FORM OF IDEAS, TEMPORALITIES OF CREATION, HYPER-COMPATIBILITY

XXV

ANNE-FRANÇOISE SCHMID

ANNE-FRANÇOISE SCHMID is an honorary professor of the INSA Lyon, an associated researcher at the Chair of Theory and Methods for Innovative Design (TMCI), MinesParisTech and at the Poincaré Archives (UMR of the CNRS 7117, University of Lorraine). Specialist of Poincaré, editor of Russell and Couturat, she has developed a generic epistemology, depending upon no discipline in particular, and is working on a new style of philosophy, working with existing philosophies rather than in any one particular philosophy.

§ 1
Science without disciplines is a silence.

§ 2
How to invent a generic writing?

§ 3
Generic space is dynamic and energetic; it accommodates the *forms* of ideas under consideration of how time has the property of *thickness (voluminous and energetic)*.

§ 4
We need an object-centeredness for thinking such temporalization, not a theory-centeredness.

§ 5
The objects that temper such temporalization energize the generic space.

§ 6
We need three factors to think such generic objectivity:

> Operators: *Fiction* as extension (point of exteriority), *the virtual* as the possibility of a change of scale, *future* as a cut in the present.
> Collective Intimacy: modification of the place of negation.
> Shared Memory: The present is a *Dynamic Hole* that puts past and future into relationship. The future as a cut that drops in the present. The past as a middle platform for known events

§ 7
The present as a dynamic hole is a domain of superpositions that build Chimera: Visions of futurity that enlighten the present and the past.

§ 8
The objects produced by the present as a dynamic hole are non-synthetic: For them, there is no correlation between experience and theory.

§ 9
There is intention at work in their production, but it is shared and dispersible.

§ 10
There is rigorous reasoning at work in their production; this reasoning is generic and dynamic.

GHOSTS OF TRANSPARENCY

§ 11

From an epistemological point of view, generic and dynamic reasoning regards the present as a dynamic whole:

For philosophy: To see the Eternity and Multiplicity of philosophies without placing them in competition.

For science: Interdisciplinarity with modelling, simulation and rigour without disciplines.

For the arts: Integrative objects and asymmetrical openness without concepts.

Products: Phantoms who create the current characters.

§ 12

From an epistemological point of view, generic and dynamic reasoning regards the past as a middle platform:

For philosophy: Philosophical tradition as a unifying platform for rising philosophies.

For science: Disciplinary or specialized fields, history of sciences.

For arts: History of archaeology, subjective models of re-appropriation of the past.

Products: Avatars, who can have a new life, as phantoms and chimera.

§ 13

From an epistemological point of view, generic and dynamic reasoning regards the future as an operator:

For philosophy: Unknown counterpoint between unexpected concepts and empirical stubbornness.

For science: New and unknown scientific objects, hyper-integrative objects, invention of regimes of creation.

For arts: Cuts between opacity and light, space and figures, non-Art as extension.

Products: Chimeras as superposition of all fields in one.

§ 14

Music of time and flows in invention are as fiction and knowledge extensions of counterpoint (= superposition of voices).

§ 15

If it is possible to translate scientific invention into music, then these are a few proposals and names by which we can learn more about them:

There is an ecosystem of the sciences with a regime of creation (Dinu Lipatti).

There is a measure between disciplines and fragments (Maurizio Pollini)

There is a music between disciplines, where each fragment is a separate parameter and a moment of superposition (Glenn Gould).

There is an interdisciplinary laboratory: invention of passages in a generic space without exclusion (Pierre Boulez, Michaël Levinas, Lucas Debargue).

REFERENCES

BOOKS

· Legay, Jean Marie and Anne-Françoise Schmid, *Philosophie de l'interdisciplinarité: Correspondance, 1999–2004, Sur La Recherche Scientifique, La Modélisation, et Les Objets Complexes, Transphilosophiques* (Paris: Petra, 2004)
· Mathieu, Nicole, and Anne-Françoise Schmid, *Modélisation et interdisciplinarité. Six disciplines en quête d'interdisciplinarité.* (Versailles: Editions Quae, 2014)
· Schmid, Anne-Françoise, and Academos (Research team), eds., *Épistémologie Des Frontières*, Collection 'Transphilosophiques' (Paris: Éditions Pétra, 2012)

PAPERS AND BOOK CHAPTERS

· Coutellec, Léo, and Anne-Françoise Schmid, 'Modélisation, simulation, expérience de pensée: la création d'un espace épistémologique. Regards à partir des œuvres de Vernadsky et de Poincaré', in *Modéliser & simuler: épistémologies et pratiques de la modélisation et de la simulation.*, ed. by Franck Varenne and Marc Silberstein (Paris: Éditions matériologiques, 2013), ii
· Hubert, Bernard, and Nicole Mathieu, 'Convoquer Les Disciplines Au Banquet Des Interdisciplines. De l'"intime Collectif" à l'intimité Collective Comme Dimension de l'épistémologie Générique', in *Interdisciplinarités Entre Natures et Sociétés Colloque de Cerisy* (Brussels: P.I.E-Peter Lang S.A., Éditions Scientifiques Internationales, 2016), pp. 143–66 [accessed 11 March 2019]
· Schmid, Anne-Françoise, and Armand Hatchuel, 'On Generic Epistemology', *Angelaki*, 19 (2014), 131–44
· Schmid, Anne-Françoise, and Muriel Mambrini-Doudet, 'L'identité Scientifique En Régime Interdisciplinaire (Losev et Laruelle)' (presented at the Congrès pour le 120e anniversaire de la naissance de Alexei Federovitch Losev, Moscow: Éditions de la Maison Losev, 2013), ii, 265–81
· Schmid, Anne-Françoise, Muriel Mambrini-Doudet, and Armand Hatchuel, 'Une nouvelle logique de l'interdisciplinarité', *Nouvelles perspectives en sciences sociales*, 7 (2011), 105

WORKSHOPS AND COURSES

- Anne-Françoise Schmid & Tony Yanick: *Mystical pragmatism: Philo-fiction and Invention*, invited conference, Lisbon, Centre for Philosophy of Science, University of Lisbon, Lisbon, Portugal, by Catarina Pombo Nabais, November 10th, 2017.
- Anne-Françoise Schmid & Alice Lucy Rekab, course "Integrative objects in philosophy and in arts", New Center of Reseach and Practice, 2017.

A PAPER ON GENERIC EPISTEMOLOGY

- Chrysos, Paris, 'Autour Des Travaux d'Anne-Françoise Schmid: Le Potentiel Scientifique d'un Courant Épistémologique', Natures Sciences Sociétés, 24 (2016), 251–60

SHORT FILM

- "Letre" by Benoît Maire, production: Benoît Maire et Raphael Pfeiffer, cast: François Laruelle and Anne-Françoise Schmid, MK2, Paris, Palais de Tokyo, 2015.
  https://vimeo.com/124386817, mot de passe: letre 2015

THE DIGITAL, A CONTINENT? ANARCHIC CITIZENSHIP WITHIN THE OBJECT-SPACE OF CUNNING REASON

XXVI

VERA BÜHLMANN

VERA BÜHLMANN is a Swiss writer, and since 2016 professor for architecture theory at the Vienna University of Technology TU where she directs the Research Unit Architecture Theory and Philosophy of Technics ATTP at the Faculty for Architecture and Spatial Planning. Together with Ludger Hovestadt she co-directs the laboratory for applied virtuality at ETH Zurich, and is co-editor of the Applied Virtuality Book Series (Birkhäuser, since 2012). She studied English Language and Literature, Philosophy, and Media Science at the Swiss Universities in Zurich and Basel, from where she obtained her Master (2002) and her PHD (2009). At the core of her research is the interest in a notion of literacy and semiotics that extends to computation, coding, and information, as much as to language and mathematics. Her most recent publication is *Mathematics and Information in the Philosophy of Michel Serres* (Bloomsbury, London 2019 (forthcoming)).

This article is based on a keynote lecture delivered with the same title at the conference "Towards a Quantum Literacy," organized by the Department for Architecture Theory and Philosophy of Technics ATTP at Vienna University of Technology in April 2017, in the context of the EU Horizon 2020 Project Ethics of Coding, A Report on the Algorithmic Condition. It has originally been published by Azimuth. Philosophical Coordinates in Modern and Contemporary Age, *Issue X, 2017: "Intersections: At the Technophysics of Space", edited by Georgios Tsagdis and Susanna Lindberg.*

"What any country expects first from migrants, namely that they learn to speak and write the language of their guest country, this we should perhaps also accept as being expected, in analogue fashion, from all of us, with regard to that digital continent to which we find ourselves, whether we want to or not, forced to immigrate."[1] I want to depart from this formulation, which, in my opinion, is as unsettling as it is timely, and unpack a particular implication that presents the question of nativity within a new light: What is so peculiar of this novel Continent, the Digital, if it can be called so, is foremost perhaps that no one is native to this strange, insubstantial kind of quasi-territory.

So, what kind of a mother-tongue might be at stake here? What kind of language is there to be learnt? We cannot approach this question by asking about regulations regarding something like an Immigration Status—because, *whom* should we be asking for this? Who, indeed, might be in a position to give us paternal protection with regard to the developments underway? Picking up a term that has recently been introduced by Homi K. Bhaba, Judith Butler, and others, I want to approach the issue by asking about the peculiar kind of citizenship that pertains to the locus in question *as the subjects of a Spectral Sovereignty.*[2] In my approach, the citizenship at stake is that of a *civic* citizenship—citizenship which obliges everyone who is to be a political subject to compulsory schooling. Let's remember where this comes from: Civic modern nation states grant rights to its citizens insofar as they subject to a manner of service to the public, accept their duties in order to be granted rights—and among those duties is the famous *Dare to know!* Have the courage to use your own understanding (*Sapere aude*). This entails that

1   https://www.architektur-aktuell.at/termine/veranstaltungen-vortraege/towards-a-quantum-literacy-vortraege-und-seminar-an-der-tu-wien

2   This term, spectral sovereignty, has been introduced by Homi K. Bhaba in order to address issues of collective identity in relation to vernacular cosmopolitanism and cosmopolitan memory, and picked up by Judith Butler and others in relation to an increasing tendency of suspending the rule of law out, with regard to issues of globalization that need to bridge concerns for International Law (whose subjects are Nation States, not individual persons) and National Laws. Cf. Paulo Lemos Horta and Kwame Anthony Appiah, *Cosmopolitanisms* (New York: New York University Press, 2017); as well as Judith Butler, *Precarious Life: the Powers of Mourning and Violence,* (New York: Verso, 2004).

citizens must affirm to be educated, and this puts 'education' in an odd middle-ground between 'emancipation' and 'oppression'—as becomes strikingly clear, in its conflictual setup, if we listen to Kant's formulation: "Enlightenment is man's emergence from his self-imposed nonage," as he put it. "Nonage is the inability to use one's own understanding without another's guidance." And a bit later he continues:

> Laziness and cowardice are the reasons why such a large part of mankind gladly remain minors all their lives, long after nature has freed them from external guidance. They are the reasons why it is so easy for others to set themselves up as guardians. It is so comfortable to be a minor. If I have a book that thinks for me, a pastor who acts as my conscience, a physician who prescribes my diet, and so on—then I have no need to exert myself. I have no need to think, if only I can pay; others will take care of that disagreeable business for me.[3]

I want to think, in short, about the relevance and actuality of this famous motto for our own time. I want to think of the language spoken in the Digital Continent as the language of coding, and I want to address this language, as I hope to explain a little with regard to why, as the language of a *Quantum Literacy*.[4]

But first, and in terms of spatial metaphorics, how *can* it possibly be adequate to speak of a 'Continent' with regard to the Digital at all? Isn't this allusion rather misleading, as a continent promises stability and static reference, in the midst of waters, sure, but still as the very opposite to the fluidity of the seas? Doesn't this digital world feel much more like something that *dripples in* and *swells*, like a threatening rising flood of pre-emptive inklings, inklings that reach us from a strange, a total amount of what is considered possible? Are we not drowning

---

3   Immanuel Kant, *What is Enlightenment*, 1784. Here following the translation by Mary C. Smith (http://www.columbia.edu/acis/ets/CCREAD/etscc/kant.html#note1). In the original German version the passage reads: "Aufklärung ist der Ausgang des Menschen aus seiner selbst verschuldeten Unmündigkeit. Unmündigkeit ist das Unvermögen, sich seines Verstandes ohne Leitung eines anderen zu bedienen. Selbstverschuldet ist diese Unmündigkeit, wenn die Ursache derselben nicht am Mangel des Verstandes, sondern der Entschließung und des Mutes liegt, sich seiner ohne Leitung eines anderen zu bedienen. *Sapere aude!* Habe Mut dich deines eigenen Verstandes zu bedienen! ist also der Wahlspruch der Aufklärung. Faulheit und Feigheit sind die Ursachen, warum ein so großer Teil der Menschen, nachdem sie die Natur längst von fremder Leitung frei gesprochen (*naturaliter maiorennes*), dennoch gerne zeitlebens unmündig bleiben; und warum es Anderen so leicht wird, sich zu deren Vormündern aufzuwerfen. Es ist so bequem, unmündig zu sein. Habe ich ein Buch, das für mich Verstand hat, einen Seelsorger, der für mich Gewissen hat, einen Arzt, der für mich die Diät beurteilt, u.s.w., so brauche ich mich ja nicht selbst zu bemühen. Ich habe nicht nötig zu denken, wenn ich nur bezahlen kann; andere werden das verdrießliche Geschäft schon für mich übernehmen." Immanuel Kant: *Beantwortung der Frage: Was ist Aufklärung?* In: *Berlinische Monatsschrift* 4 (1784), 481–494.

4   Cf. Vera Bühlmann, Felicity Colman, Iris van der Tuin, 'Introduction to New Materialist Genealogies. New Materialisms, Novel Mentalities, Quantum Literacy' in *The Minnesota Review: New Materialist Genealogies,* Volume 2017, Number 88, 2017.

in contingency, and *therefore* forced to affirm the status of a nomadic subject? Isn't the digital *percolating* from a kind of future that already seems to inhabit the here, now, a future that keeps informing us about ever more possibilities whenever we try to decide, to delimit, to make a decision, to reason critically?

If we can be Civic Citizens of this Digital Continent, then there must be a lawfulness to it. And indeed, how could there *not* be one, since everything digital is engendered by calculation, by mathematics, by algebra? And yet, this lawfulness at stake seems to be precisely what is swelling with an abundant plenty of instructions and decrees, it presents itself—indeed like mathematics does—as *the corpus* of a *cornucopia.* And it is a *frightening* horn of plenty. One that, rather than being generous and helpful whenever we feel prepared for it, presents itself obtrusively, even oppressively, as we often feel. It tends to *erode and take away* our confidence in reason, critical judgement, and responsible self-determinacy. The most outrageous aspect of it is perhaps that the *erosion* it triggers is not a consequence of this lawfulness's principle unpredictability and irrationality, but quite the opposite! The erosion is driven by this lawfulness *because it is* so very rational and predictable—indeed *super-rational,* since *computational,* and functioning best if left to *automatic* self-organization.

The more we try to reason the status of lawfulness in computation, the more we fuel its abundant 'gifts'.

THE GREAT GREEK RUSE

Are we then, indeed, captured within a *vicious circularity* that is—as Martin Heidegger tried to explain to us[5]—the very ground (reason) of the Modern age's *essential* character, that of post-metaphysical science with its striving for innovation in research? The notion of the *vicious circle in reasoning* was given the general sense of 'a situation in which action and reaction intensify one another', according to the etymological dictionary. Any kind of critical agency that is caught up within such a space of vicious circularity would inevitably be a dangerous agency, a corrupting one, a pretentious one, even one that, demonically, *mocks* any idea of equilibrium—from which moral notions of justness, righteousness, balanced valency and so on surely are being derived. For Heidegger, modern science is *exact* science that installs the conditions of measuring according to its essential value, that of *exactitude.* And just because of this, Heidegger maintained, it is also a science which does not truly *think.* By this science, reasoning is driven to greater and greater speed. It is hasting towards its own corruption.

---

5   Martin Heidegger, "The Age of World Picture," *The Question Concerning Technology and Other Essays,* translated by William Lovitt (New York: Harper and Row, 1977), 115–54.

And indeed, how else to understand the status of Law, not mathematical now but Common or Civic Law[6], when every plane we manage to expose as integrative, when every explanation that accommodates a variety of circumstances within one *plane of reference,* immediately produces novel circumstances that don't fit, and that are not yet accounted for by this explanation? How to *break out of* this intensification of action and reaction, how to lead, as Hannah Arendt famously put it, an active and free life?

My aim is to propose a different approach to circularity. If we want to think of the language spoken in the Digital Continent as the 'language' of 'coding', we cannot maintain a clear distinction between numbers and linguistic signs. What information technology confronts us with is exactly such a confusion: we are dealing with 'information' as a mathematical quantity (Shannon and Weaver), but it is a quantity notion that introduces a notion of 'order' that is, nevertheless, to be considered also as a *qualitative* order.[7] This is why I want to address this 'language' of 'coding' as the language of a *Quantum Literacy.*

In short: I want to propose thereby a different approach to thinking about circularity. But not by discrediting the important distinction Heidegger foregrounded, namely the one between rigour and exactitude, between rational reasoning and geometrical measuring. Where Heidegger opted for subjecting the former (rigour) to the latter (measurement), in a cascade that is headed by History, with its essential witnessing and testimonial mode that he calls *caring,* a quantum literacy approach, in relation to digital citizenship, sets the modes of historical accounts relative to a respective 'modelling' space within which the passing of time can be witnessed. For now, let's switch back to our context of this language at stake (that spoken in the digital continent), and formulate suggestively: If Heidegger attributes the circle the scope of an axiomatized space of time, then I want to speak of a circularity that attributes the circle a 'civic' scope in a space of discretion ('politeness', manners and forms of conduct) and cunning. We can think of such a space as that of the rotational scope of a circle based on *algebraic* geometry, that is within a geometric space that needs to take into account both the bracketing discreteness of

---

6   It is important for following the discussions of "Civic Citizenship" in this paper to be informed about the philosophical underpinnings of the two dominant traditions in thinking about the status of law, that of Common Law (uncodified, largely followed by the Anglo-American World) and that of Civic Law (codified, prevalent in European Countries as well as in Russia and most Asian and African countries). For a short overview cf. the article provided by the Robbins Collection, School of Law, University of California at Berkley: https://www.law.berkeley.edu/library/robbins/ CommonLawCivilLawTraditions.html; Cf. also Joseph Dainow, 'The Civil Law and the Common Law: Some Points of Comparison', *The American Journal of Comparative Law,* 15.3 (1966), 419–35 <https://doi.org/10.2307/838275>

7   I refer thereby to Leon Brillouin's landmark text *Science and Information Theory,* (New York: Dover, 2013 [1956]). Cf. Vera Bühlmann, 'Negentropy', in *Posthuman Glossary,* ed. by Rosi Braidotti and Maria Hlavajova, Theory (London: Bloomsbury Academic, 2018), 273–77

code as well as the continuity of consequentiality: the mechanical scope of an encompassing line that is 'restless' between the points it connects.[8]

I must expect that this is diametrically at odds with Heideggerian philosophy. But it seems that an encounter can take place, that there is a crossroad in the very space where Heidegger faces what I consider to be his core dilemma: Thought, principled by reason, tends to accelerate to light speed. Reasonable thinking thus appears bound to culminate in totalitarian, apocalyptic, or eschatological modes of discourse.[9] His own commitment then *to* the modern legacy of Critical Reason *is a reverted one*—he asks to counter-weigh this trend towards acceleration by finding a non-mathematical kind of thinking in *Art,* as an *anti-dope* to the viciously circular consequentiality that mathematics, in his understanding, inevitably installs and by which it is bound to render Reason bankrupt.

To think of the scope of a circle as the scope of a restless, encompassing line that takes into account discretion just as much as continuity is inspired by Michel Serres who, in his book *Les Origines de la Géométrie* (1989) calls the Principle of Reason *"The Great Greek Ruse."* I cite:

> Hierarchy remains inside reason, but since height, power or king are no longer spoken of, it becomes transparent inside reason, so invisible that no one has seen it, that no one thwarts this intelligent Greek ruse.[10]

While for Heidegger, mathematics is *the source of the vicious circle's viciousness,* Serres looks at mathematics as someone who knows it well, not as Sovereign Principality but as the very condition of possibility for clarifying ideas by active, leaping and daring, thought. We can now look at what to Heidegger is *the World-as-Picture* from the point of view of *Reason as a Ruse* as an *Architectonic Model of the World.* What we gain thereby is something like an architectural approach to Heidegger's concern with the *'Geviert'.* A model so understood (as an architectonic model) is to be accommodated not within the space of mimetical representation and mathematical demonstration, but within the abundant space of mechanical reason and civic cunning.

So how does it work, this ruse? Serres writes:

> As soon as hierarchy is translated as reference one can finally prove as reason and show as theoretical vision to every reasonable animal that it is reasonable to transfer the autonomy that they owe to the hazards of their existence to the element of reference, like the world to its earth or to its sun, like a variety

---

8 Michel Serres' discussion of the Gnomon, the Sun Clock, as an observatory, elaborates on the kind of space I am thinking of here. Cf. especially Michel Serres, "Gnomon" in: *A History of Scientific Thought: Elements of a History of Science,* Blackwell 1992, 73–123.

9 Cf. the study by Wolfgang M. Schröder, *Politik Des Schonens: Heideggers Geviert-Konzept, Politisch Ausgelegt,* Phainomena, 13 (Tübingen: Attempto, 2004).

10 Michel Serres, *Geometry: The Third Book of Foundations,* trans. by Randolph Burks (London: Bloomsbury Academic, 2017), position 1905.

GHOSTS OF TRANSPARENCY

of homogeneous space to its pole or any site in a system to its legislative centre. So, we naturalize the one who holds power, ineradicable from his place like the earth or the sun, unavoidable because without roots and endlessly stable. [11]

Let us pause and ask: *where* is the stance, from which Serres can be talking like this? In a Civic Space, we said. But is he himself speaking as a juridical persona, a defender or a prosecutor, or a judge even, when he—with a strange sense of admiration and respect—speaks of *the Greek Ruse*? Serres concludes the cited passage with the words: "better yet we theorize him [the one who holds power]." [12]

Now, how can this be an option—isn't this what Heidegger is warning us against? Theorizing theoretical depictions leads to further acceleration of reason*ing,* and reason*able,* 'thinking'.

But does it really?

The kind of theorizing that *algebraic geometry* proclaims is one that does not acknowledge the eradication of roots claimed by the centrality of Principled Reason. It is a *projective* geometry whose every metrics is rooted in a plane of reference. The Romantic intuition, that reason is rooted in—even actively roots!—tragedy, may well be true and adequate. But the *conditions of possibility* of reasoning as a praxis, method, and technique, consist in *mechanisms,* the Algebraic Geometer insists—those mathematical procedures where *cause equals to effects* (Newton, 3rd Law of Motion), or at least *where effects correspond to causes,* as Galileo had it when he said that nature was written in the characters of mathematics. [13]

Through involving many planes of reference within one algebraic scope, mechanical usage of metrics has never been, strictly speaking, *reasonable*! How did we forget about this? How did it happen that the unbound, free—Serres speaks of *anarchic*—reason[14] of the artistic mechanic came to stand for its very opposite, namely strict determination and foreclosure of events?

---

11 Ibid., position 1907.

12 Ibid., position 1910.

13 For Galileo, it was mathematics rather than Scholastic logics that affords a philosophy of Nature: "Philosophy is written in that great book which ever lies before our eyes — I mean the universe — but we cannot understand it if we do not first learn the language and grasp the symbols, in which it is written. This book is written in the mathematical language, and the symbols are triangles, circles and other geometrical figures, without whose help it is impossible to comprehend a single word of it; without which one wanders in vain through a dark labyrinth." Galileo Galilei, *The Assayer* (1623), as translated by Thomas Salusbury (1661), 178, as quoted in Edwin A. Burtt, *The Metaphysical Foundations of Modern Science* (Mineola, NY: Dover Publications, 2003 [1925]), 75.

14 Michel Serres, *Geometry,* position 1866. Serres writes: "The beginning expressed by the term 'archaism' is found again in the command of the word 'hierarchy'. Can, conversely and in general, an anarchical system be conceived, without reference or border, deprived of privileged place or referential, and yet rational? Yes, assuredly: it suffices to trace back to the multiple variations of beginning in Anaximander's indefinite. Things begin when the arche precisely goes absent, and command appears when they claim to begin."

Let's again hear Serres:

Legendary, the cleverness, the shrewdness of the Greeks impelled them to invent a ruse of reason, the ruse-mathematics. They give us systems and schemas to see that are so distinguished from each other that, taking their word for it, we align them along a linear evolution, whether interrupted or continuous.[15]

In his book *The Origins of Geometry* Serres explains how the postulation of Reason as a Principle was to *conceal* that all metrics is indeed *rooted* in planes of reference[16] that are, in fact, 'templums'—in the architectonic language, *Projective Dispositional Plans,* empty but planned and disposed for something indefinite to happen.[17] There may well be a kinship between Reason and Tragedy, but there is also one between Mechanics and Comedy. Again Serres:

Aristophanes or some other stage director must be bursting with laughter in their graves from seeing us trying to understand [a linear evolution of math]! They take a bowl and a jar out from of their horn of plenty, let us see then, like poor farmers, pots, then they put these objects back into the horn, and lastly suddenly take the same ones out again so that, from our place, we see a column and a sphere.[18]

Let's state our point clearly, for this is a serious issue: Reason, to Serres, is the *Great Greek Ruse* in that it sets mechanics equal to mathematical demonstration—without problematizing the manner in which such

15 Ibid., position 1937.
16 Ibid., position 1939.
17 In his book on Leibniz, Serres addresses the generalization of such plans as 'un géo-métral'. Cf. Michel Serres, *Le système de Leibniz et ses modèles mathématiques* (Paris: Presses Universitaires de France, 2015 [1968]). In the Introduction entitled 'Scénographie, Ichnographie', Serres writes with regard to "un embarras qui subsiste" in Leibniz, namely that it appears impossible to embrace Leibniz's overall organization *as* a system, and still understand it consistently and exhaustively *in* systematic terms—there remains an obscurity. But this, for Serres, needs no excuse but is, quite inversely, the crucial point with regard to his appreciation of Leibniz *as* a systematical thinker. As Serres puts it: "le sentiment confus d'une ordonnance potentielle qui se laisse toujours entrevoir et qui sans cesse se refuse, l'idée vague d'une cohérence per-çue mille fois en vue cavalière et qui dérobe son géométral, la sensation de progresser dans un labyrinthe dont il tiendrait le fil sans en avoir la carte. Perspectives offertes, points de vue multipliés, possibilités infiniment itérées: il ne parait jamais qu'on puisse parvenir aux limites exhaustives d'un plan synoptique, étalé, complet, actuel." Kindle edition, position 163.
18 Michel Serres, *Geometry*, position 1976. Serres writes for example: "The distinction of the homogenous and the heterogenous, of the continuous and the discontinuous, dominate the descriptions of space and time in Mircea Eliade for example. Profane, space is isotropic; sacred, it isn't, he says. In addition, profane time flows continuously, but sacred time presents ruptures. As a result geometry, cut off from sacralization, posits an undifferentiated space. But this isn't tenable, for there are as many scientific spaces as you please, orientable or not, centred, or metric, chaotic or regular, only some of which are homogenous. To say the converse amounts to underestimating geometry, to forcing it into impoverished reductions. Thus formal thought knows the spaces said to be mythic or cultural."

'equivalence' is being 'positioned'.[19] He calls this a ruse because it thereby *conceals* that what every metrics is producing (as the very condition through which it affords metricity) is *projection*—an *architectonic transformative projection* that comes together with a *procedure* of how projections can be produced.

The question we want to take from this is: having recognized, with Serres, this Great Greek Ruse, how *not* to become misologists? How to hold on to reason in a manner that does not subject it to a definite central and transparent position of power, as Reason's Principle? Serres asks: "Is reason defined by indifference toward all difference?" And puts it even more drastically: "Reason demands that there be no reason."[20] We must make defined space to ceaselessly refer to the indefinite, he holds and suggests that we should call universe "that which holds by this principle without principality."[21] With such a way to think of the circular, let us now come back to the issue of a 'Digital Continent'. The proposal I would like us to consider is to think of the Digital Continent in just this manner: as a Universe which *holds by this very principle without principality.*

THE MECHANIC'S ANARCHIC CUNNING

What I want to suggest, with raising the idea of a *quantum literacy* of a Digital Citizen in relation to the Mechanic's Anarchic Cunning, is to take from quantum science especially this one aspect: namely that 'form', in the domain of probabilistic amplitudes and their propagation, needs to be considered in the terms of *technical spectra* (each rendering regularity in terms of frequencies, due to the particle-wave character of each quantum). I want to suggest, hence, that it is a spectral kind of agency that is attributable to the Cunning Reason of the Mechanic as a Digital Citizen. It is a kind of projective spectrality that is perfectly reasonable, it is just *not principled*. It is anarchic. It is—so to speak—Reason *trespassing* the Reign of a Definite Rule of a Centre that puts itself up as Principle. The point thereby is that Mechanics as an Art can pick up its

---

19 In fact, Plato addresses this very point where he seeks to establish a difference between opinion and truth: there is an interesting, but seldom attended to, discussion about what Plato calls 'mobile' or 'run-away' statues (called 'daedalus', in the manner of the mythic persona's (Daedalus) mechanic art), as opposed to statements of knowledge to which he also refers to as 'statues', but statues that must be 'owned', statues that are in someone's 'possession'. Cf. Amélie Frost Benedikt, 'Runaway Statues: Platonic Lessons on the Limits of an Analogy', presented at the Twentieth World Congress of Philosophy, in Boston, Massachusetts from August 10–15, 1998, published online at *Paideia, Ancient Philosophy Archive*, Boston University: https://www.bu.edu/wcp/ Papers/Anci/AnciBene.htm.
20 Michel Serres, *Geometry.*, position 2078.
21 Ibid., position 2080.

ancient legacy that related it to a humanist ethics that does not accept fate without standing up against it, and challenging it.[22]

What do I mean thereby?

From a logical point of view, something is either at rest, or it is moving, but not both at the same time. Exactly this famous statement by Aristotle does not hold for the mechanic: how to describe for example, logically, a rotating spinning top which is at once at rest (its centre) while moving (its periphery)? Mechanics is an art and not a logical discipline in that it introduces a certain scope of deliberation which is objective, independent of a Cogito's belief or interpretation. The mechanic's descriptions are *mathematical*, but not logical. *Mechanical knowledge* is objective *and* ambiguous, undecided. There belongs a peculiar kind of agency and activity to the knowledge in which the mechanic is proficient that is not a subjective will or an arbitrary intention.

To make a long story very short: Both logical inference as well as mechanical constructions crucially depend upon geometry. The former depends on the axiomatic set up of theoretical geometry in the manner of Euclid. With the latter the relation is not so straightforward. The whole point of logics, we can say, is to yield *definitions*—to treat things within the scope of their finitude and delimitations. Thereby, axiomatic deduction follows one principle above all others: It shall not be possible to derive *contradictory statements from the same set of axioms*. The middle ground of an undecided, restless third state is what logical rigour seeks to exclude. Until the modern era, people thought of mechanics as an art, and as an ethics—indeed, as the twin other to logics, aligned with sophistication rather than truth immediately—because in mechanics too, one is concerned with treating things in their finitude, that is without need for belief of any sort that could not be objectively tested. This is why I suggest to address the space of cunning reasoning as an object-space, the space of objects among objects. Because at the same time, every mechanical construction lives exactly *from* such a third, middle, milieu, where opposites co-exist undecidedly. This is what makes mechanics architectonic. One could even say that the art

---

22 The Greek noun "Mechane" or "Mechanema" meant "cunning" as well as "means to an end, a supportive device", and often appears in classical texts in relation to situations of distress, accounts of emergencies, and how to get out of them. Cf. replace with: Wolfgang König, ed., *Propyläen-Technikgeschichte*, vol. 1 (Berlin: Propyläen-Verl 2000), 181ff.: a short note perhaps at this occasion also with regard to the notion of cunning in Hegel: whereas Serres is interested in exactly this link between mathematics and cunning, Hegel's interest appears to have been in severing this link, and in contrasting cunning as the mark of phenomenological reason as against merely mechanical, deterministic and automatic rationality. Such an attempted "hygienic separation" remains untenable for Serres, in antiquity (cf. footnote 14) and also today—this is the crucial message when he addresses the origins of geometry in the plural.

of mechanics is to *modulate* and *articulate* this transitory milieu of indefinite decidedness.[23]

The question remains, however: *Where*, in what kind of space is the Cunning Reasoning of the Mechanic to be situated? We can think of this space as an architectonic space that consists of projective transformations. The ruse of which Serres speaks is that of concealing that "The Greek's production is projection. And the optimization of a projecting site: the fly-over from on high or from outside the world."[24] The anarchic reasoning of the mechanic is like Atlas, whose power results from a projective point of reference, daringly placed in an outside.

Citizens of the Digital, as Public Personas, are Social Servants too, but in that they are not Heroes of Alternative Identities, or of Minority Cultures. They are Atlases. All of them. The space of Cunning Reason is the space indexed by all those projective points of reference, *out there*. We can think of it as the immanence of a space of translation, of encryption and deciphering.

Let me try to explain.

HORS-LÀ

In his book *Atlas* (1994), Serres is very fond of citing a short story by Guy de Maupassant entitled *Le Horla* (1886). Maupassant therein invents a character called Horla, which the protagonist in his short story keeps encountering in a peculiar kind of shadow. Horla is a phantom that is transparent (passive, lets shine through) but not without an irreducible lucidity of its own. It sits in front of the mirror and catches the images the mirror is about to reflect, before the mirror can actually do so. Serres writes about this peculiar character:

> What a strange shadow: it is and is not, present and absent, here and elsewhere, the middle which ought to be excluded but cannot, hence contradictory. This is why he [Maupassant] calls him Horla.[25]

Horla is, to Michel Serres, the fictitious character of a quantum-physical kind of spectrality that actively sums up all projections that could possibly be reflected, in a manner of summation whose total is indefinite and, not despite but because of that, determinable. To Serres, this story is a *realist* story—even though its main character is entirely invented. It is a realist story because it allows us to address philosophically the

---

23 Cf. a very interesting article on the notion of "stasis" in rhetorics: Otto Alvin Loeb Dieter, 'Stasis', *Speech Monographs*, 17.4 (1950), 345–69 <https://doi.org/10.1080/03637755009375016>

24 Michel Serres, *Geometry.*, position 1945.

25 My own translation based on the German version by Michael Bischof: Michel Serres, *Atlas*, trans. by Michael Bischoff (Berlin: Merve, 2005), 59.

particular kind of 'spectrality' at work in communication media: The space of Horla allows us to address the rendering of appearances that technical spectra afford (in all quantum physics-based science like chemistry or electro engineering).[26]

Now, within epistemological registers, the predominant question with regard to quantum physics is that of location, and the point of view of the observer. This famously poses a dilemma, puts reason in crisis. But remembering the algebraic legacy of the Mechanic's Cunning, with regard to circularity (circuitry, indeed), at once relaxes the situation *and* poses novel challenges: We can no longer think of objective reasoning as having an absolute reference. The space where Cunning Reason is localizable is a space of communication that is not, strictly speaking, logical, but also rhetorical and poetic as well: The mechanic has always known how to bring opposites into balanceable constellations by inventing a third, a mediate space to think in, a statuary structure that doesn't properly 'add up' to a consistent, non-contradictory domain—the space of Cunning Reason is an *architectonic*, and an *inventive* locus. The space of Horla helps us with addressing the active role of measurement in those spectra, i.e. their active rendering of appearances in a manner that is, even though it has *trespassed the domain of Reason's Principle*, not a single bit less objectively reasonable.

The space of Horla is the space where phenomena are rendered apparent that are *engendered by mediation*, by resorting to a middle ground *that from a logical point of view ought to, but cannot be excluded.* Of just such strange 'nature' is the quasi-physical domain that communication channels have been establishing for real, and for nearly a century now. How is it that this still sounds so spooky, so ghostly and untrustworthy to our ears?[27]

Technically speaking, the channels of electronic information/ communication technology are literally technical spectra: They render apparent a certain generic order which can be observed only before a 'plentiful background' of noise (entropy), rather than one of an empty tabula rasa. Serres illustrates this idea of a plentiful background with the colour spectrum, where white light stands for such a 'plenty' because it expresses any colour at all, and this in a material, physical manner: 'white light' is, ultimately, radiating nuclear activity of quantum-physical mass. Within such 'materiality', channels are established for 'surfing' on top of the singled-out frequencies, but nevertheless amidst

---

26 Cf. for an elaboration of this argument: Vera Bühlmann, 'Generic Mediality, Post-Alphabetical?', in *Philosophy after Nature*, ed. by Rosi Braidotti (Lanham: Rowman & Littlefield, 2017), 31–54.

27 Cf. for an elaborate discussion of this strange situation Wendy Hui Kyong Chun, *Programmed Visions: Software and Memory, Software Studies* (Cambridge, MA: MIT Press, 2011).

GHOSTS OF TRANSPARENCY

the massive agitation of what is, technically, called Brownian motion. The vicarious space of spectra is not empty in the sense of 'lack' as a substantive, but in that of 'lacking' as a kind of *frequentative preposition*: the zero-neutrality of white light *lacks* in that it *leaks*, and in the same sense as technical spectra *lack* in that they *leak*.

What if we thought of the digital as a percolating universe, an active container, a container that leaks reason, reason that accumulates into continental plates, here and there, always with its reference to the principle without principality, *hors là*. Out there, here. Speculative, but *anarchic* and *civic* rather than *utopic* and *innocent*. Might this perhaps be what it means to be Quantum Literate, as Citizens of Digital Continentality?

IMAGE REFERENCES

All websites were last accessed on 17 July 2019. We have taken great care to identify all rights owners. In the unlikely event that someone has been overlooked, we would kindly ask that person to contact the editors.

I   CRYPTO ARCHITECTURE: NOTES ON MACHINE LEARNING AND DESIGN
BY ROBERTO BOTTAZZI

FIG 1: Chuanren Lin, Lei Wang, Qiuyang Zhang, Xi Meng. *Fluff*. Studies for a tower based on wind data. Master in Urban Design, The Bartlett, UCL, 2016. Tutors: Roberto Bottazzi, Kostas Grigoriadis. © Roberto Bottazzi · **FIG 2**: Anna Kampani, Apostolopoulos Apostolos, Caitling Brock. *Perceptive Datascapes*. Diagrams showing formal transformations-based Machine Learning algorithms evaluating visual permeability. Master in Urban Design, The Bartlett, UCL, 2018. Tutors: Roberto Bottazzi, Tasos Varoudis. © Roberto Bottazzi · **FIG 3**: Chuanren Lin, Lei Wang, Qiuyang Zhang, Xi Meng. *Fluff*. Studies for a tower based on wind data. Master in Urban Design, The Bartlett, UCL, 2016. © Roberto Bottazzi.

II   AN INSTRUMENT FOR COMMUNICATION: SELF-ORGANIZING MODEL
BY NIKOLA MARINČIĆ

FIG 1: Kohonen's illustration of a system which implements an ordered mapping. Image source: Teuvo Kohonen, 'Self-Organized Formation of Topologically Correct Feature Maps', Biological Cybernetics, 43.1 (1982), 59–69 (60) · **FIG 2**: A typical representation of a self-organizing map as a visualization method based on Wikipedia featured article data. Image source: Denoir, 'Self-organizing map cartography', in *Wikipedia: The Free Encyclopedia*. <https://en.wikipedia.org/wiki/Self-organizing_map#/media/File:Self_oraganizing_map_cartography.jpg> · **FIG 3**: Example of Ultsch's U*Matrix of the 'Glio' data set. Image source: Ultsch, Alfred. 'U*-Matrix: A Tool to Visualize Clusters in High Dimensional Data', University of Marburg (2003), 7, accessible at: <https://pdfs.semanticscholar.org/1d9d/ba44f2d237ee9d8f0388299afbcc0e581621.pdf> · **FIG 4**: SOM algorithm represented in a form of Zafiris's motivic key. © Nikola Marinčić · **FIG 5**: Coexistence key of the self-organizing model. © Nikola Marinčić · **FIG 6**: Interpretation of Hjelmslev's notion of a concept within a partition spectrum. © Nikola Marinčić · **FIG 7**: The final data set after the pre-processing stage. Original images from *typologie+: Innovativer Wohnungsbau*, ed. by Peter Ebner et al., (Basel: Birkhäuser, 2009). © Nikola Marinčić · **FIG 8**: 23,393 floor plan parts on a single image. © Nikola Marinčić · **FIG 9**: 10,000 randomly chosen floor plan parts extracted from the initial data set and clustered into 100 sets of actual distinctions. © Nikola Marinčić

IV   VOIDS, BRANDS, CHARACTERS, AND HOW TO DEAL WITH LOTS
BY MIRO ROMAN

FIG 1: branding, mediating, curating, measuring, communicating, coding. © Miro Roman · **FIG 2**: A Specific Noise: Architecture. © Miro Roman · **FIG 3**: Poem for ArchDaily. © Miro Roman · **FIG 4**: Informational Encoding of Dezeen. © Miro Roman · **FIG 5**: A Cloud of Architecture. © Miro Roman · **FIG 6**: Textured Objects. © Miro Roman · **FIG 7**: Lonely Solids. © Miro Roman · **FIG 8**: New Chic. © Miro Roman · **FIG 9**: Patterns. © Miro Roman · **FIG 10**: Distilled Crystals. © Miro Roman · **FIG 11**: Green Garnish. © Miro Roman · **FIG 12**: Blend of the Day. © Miro Roman

VIII   ARCHITECTURE, AN ARTIFICIAL INTELLIGENCE
BY KRISTIAN FASCHINGEDER

FIG 1: The philosopher Aristippos goes ashore on the island of Rhodes and deduces the presence of people from the geometric Figures drawn in the sand. Image source: Michael Burghers: frontispiece in Ενκλειδον τα σωζομενα. *Euclidis quæ supersunt omnia ...*, trans. David Gregory (Oxford, 1703). Reproduction courtesy of the British Library (shelf mark: 678.k.6))

XI   PENTECOST — A MODEL OF COMMUNICATION FOR 21ST CENTURY ARCHITECTURE
BY JORGE OROZCO

FIG 1: Monads and The World. Gilles Deleuze, 1993. Image source: Gilles Deleuze, *The Fold: Leibniz and the Baroque*, trans. by T. Conley (London: The Athlone Press, 1993), 26 · **FIG 2**: Entropy in the case of two possibilities with probabilities p and $1-p$. Claude Shannon, 1948. Image source: C. E. Shannon, 'A Mathematical Theory of Communication', *Bell Systems Technical Journal*, 27.3 (1948), 379–423 (394) · **FIG 3**: Sebastiano Ricci, *Mercury, Herse and Aglauros*, 1720–1734, oil on canvas, 88.5 x 58.8 cm, Manchester Art Gallery, UK < https://artuk.org/discover/artworks/mercury-herse-and-aglauros-205902> · **FIG 4**: El Greco, *Pentecost*, c. 1596, oil on canvas, 275 x 127 cm, Museo del Prado, Madrid, Spain <www.wikiart.org/en/el-greco/pentecost> · **FIG 5**: *The Economist*, cover, May 2017. Image source: <https://www.economist.com/sites/default/files/imagecache/400-width/print-covers/20170506_cuk400_0.jpg> · **FIG 6**: Dorothy Vallens played by Isabella Rossellini in the film *Blue Velvet*, dir. By David Lynch (De Laurentiis Entertainment Group, 1986) · **FIG 7**: Diagram of Church of the year 2000, *Church of the year 2000*, Peter Eisenman, 1996. Image source: ©Eisenman Architects, <https://eisenmanarchitects.com/Church-of-the-Year-2000-1996> · **FIG 8**: Transcribing reality to architecture. Bernard Tschumi, 1981. Image source: Tschumi, B., *The Manhattan Transcripts* (London: St. Martin's Press, 1981), 50 · **FIG 9**: One of the three machines from Three Lessons in Architecture—The machines installation. Studio Libeskind, 1985. Image source: ©Libeskind <https://libeskind.com/wp-content/uploads/memory-machine-638x650.jpg> · **FIG 10**: A sourced quote in German translated to English by Yandex Translate API. © Jorge Orozco · **FIG 11**: Bar chart showing the number of unique words for 431 offices. © Jorge Orozco · **FIG 12**: Vocabularies of swiss-architects and Elliot, respectively. © Jorge Orozco · **FIG 13**: Learned topics of swiss-architects and Elliot, respectively. © Jorge Orozco · **FIG 14**: Scatter plot of three different models: BoW, tf-idf and topics. Each one showing the 431 offices. © Jorge Orozco · **FIG 15**: Detail showing the same office: 'schwarz-schwarz', in three different neighbourhoods. © Jorge Orozco · **FIG 16**: Elliot Alderson and his four closest neighbouring offices. © Jorge Orozco

XIII CRYSTAL OF THINGS
BY POLTAK PANDJAITAN
FIG 1: shadow projection of a three-dimensional dodecahedral quasicrystal cluster. © Poltak Pandjaitan

XVI MYTHIC NOISE: ARCHITECTURES OF GEOLOGICAL COMMUNICATION
BY ADAM NOCEK
FIG 1: *The Last Angel of History*, dir. John Akomfrah (Black Audio Film Collective, 1996) · **FIG 2**: *Stringing telephone wire on a tree in Enewetak Atoll*, Marshall Islands, c. 1944. Image source: United States Department of Defense, c. 1944, in *Wikipedia: The Free Encyclopedia*, <https://en.wikipedia.org/wiki/File:Communications_men.jpg>

XXII WHEN OTHERS PASSING BY BEHOLD: MEDIA STUDIES AND ARCHIVES ACROSS CULTURES
BY MATT COHEN
FIG. 1: Theodor de Bry, 'The Marckes of sundrye of the Cheif mene of Virginia', engraving XXIII from *A Briefe and True Report of the New Found Land of Virginia* (Frankfurt, 1590). Courtesy of the John Carter Brown Library · **FIG. 2**: Theodor de Bry, 'A cheiff Lorde of Roanoac', engraving VII from *A Briefe and True Report of the New Found Land of Virginia* (Frankfurt, 1590). Courtesy of the John Carter Brown Library.